A Thousand Miles of Dreams

Asian Voices
A Subseries of Asian/Pacific/Perspectives
Series Editor: Mark Selden

A Thousand Miles of Dreams

The Journeys of Two Chinese Sisters

Sasha Su-Ling Welland

ROWMAN & LITTLEFIELD PUBLISHERS, INC.
Lanham • Boulder • New York • Toronto • Plymouth, UK

ROWMAN & LITTLEFIELD PUBLISHERS, INC.

Published in the United States of America
by Rowman & Littlefield Publishers, Inc.
A wholly owned subsidary of The Rowman & Littlefield Publishing Group, Inc.
4501 Forbes Boulevard, Suite 200, Lanham, Maryland 20706
www.rowmanlittlefield.com

Estover Road, Plymouth PL6 7PY, United Kingdom

British Library Cataloguing in Publication Information Available

The hardback edition of this book was previously catalogued by the Library of Congress
    as follows:
Welland, Sasha Su-ling, 1969–
    A thousand miles of dreams : the journeys of two Chinese sisters / Sasha Su-ling
Welland.
        p.   cm.—(Asian voices)
    Includes bibliographical references and index.
    1. Ling, Shuhao, 1904–2006. 2. Ling, Shuhua, 1900–1990. 3. Physicians—United
States—Biography.   4. Authors, Chinese—Biography.   5. Artists—China—
Biography.   6. Immigrants—United States—Biography.   7. Chinese Americans—
Biography.   8. Sisters—China—Biography.   9. San Francisco (Calif.)—Biography.
10. China—Biography.   I. Title.   II. Series.
CT275.L4695W45   2006
979.4′610049510092—dc22
[B]

                                                                    2006009637

ISBN-10: 0-7425-5313-2 (cloth : alk. paper)
ISBN-13: 978-0-7425-5313-2 (cloth : alk. paper)
ISBN-10: 0-7425-5314-0 (pbk. : alk. paper)
ISBN-13: 978-0-7425-5314-9 (pbk. : alk. paper)

Printed in the United States of America

⊗ ™ The paper used in this publication meets the minimum requirements of American
National Standard for Information Sciences—Permanence of Paper for Printed Library
Materials, ANSI/NISO Z39.48-1992.

To
Amy Shuhao Ling Chen
and
Ling Shuhua

Seeking a Mooring

A leaf floats in endless space.
A cold wind tears the clouds.
The water flows westward.
The tide pushes upstream.
Beyond the moonlit reeds,
In village after village, I hear
The sound of fullers' mallets
Beating the wet clothing
In preparation for winter.
Everywhere crickets cry
In the autumn frost.
A traveller's thoughts in the night
Wander in a thousand miles of dreams.
The sound of a bell cannot disperse
The sorrows that come
In the fifth hour of night.
What place will I remember
From all this journey?
Only still bands of desolate mist
And a single fishing boat.

Wang Wei (ca. 1600–ca. 1647)
Translated by Kenneth Rexroth and Ling Chung

Contents

Illustrations

Acknowledgments

$\mathcal{O}$ ver the many years it took to write this book, I received help from numerous people. I wrote an essay containing the story's first kernel in Michael Cowan's class. Tom Simmons and Tom McNeal convinced me to keep writing. Renato Rosaldo and Sylvia Yanagisako supported the project in its early phase. A Robert Golden Grant from Stanford University enabled initial research in China. Martha Huang guided me through my first days in Beijing. Li Ningning and her family opened their home to me for what has become more than a decade of friendship and lessons in language and culture. Virginia Domínguez pushed me to transform a thesis into a book. Nancy Chen and Gail Hershatter launched me on years more of research. Chen Xueyong, Fu Guangming, and Yukiyo Hoshino shared their research on Ling Shuhua. Guo Yuying, Pi Gongliang, and Zha Quanxing generously spoke with me about their memories of Wuhan University. Wenqing Kang found books for me without my even asking and served as Tianjin tour guide par excellence. Jennifer Choo, the Chinese Law Net discussion group, and Adine Varah helped me appreciate the cultural nuances of law. Shiho Satsuka assisted with Japanese translations. Shiho, Gabrielle Banks, Jennifer Feeley, Cynthia Gabriel, Mae Lee, Leah Mundell, and Scott Walker read drafts and sustained me with their insights. Wendy Call proved an indefatigable writing partner, to whom I remain grateful for friendship in words and spirit. Gail Hershatter, more than one could ever hope for in a mentor, opened the door for me to a rapidly expanding scholarship on women in China and gave invaluable feedback on matters large and small.

The assistance of librarians at Tate Britain's Hyman Kreitman Research Center and the University of Sussex Special Collections was vital to my research. I am also grateful to Stephen Crook and Philip Milito at New York Public Library's Berg Collection; Rosalind Moad and Patricia McGuire at King's College Library, Cambridge; and Mindy S. Gordon at the Rockefeller Archive Center. A list of permissions to print published and unpublished materials appears at the back of the book. I also thank Abraham Parrish of the Yale University Library for his mapmaking expertise.

Residencies and scholarships at the Blue Mountain Center, Bread Loaf Writers' Conference, Hedgebrook Retreat for Women Writers, Millay Colony for the Arts, and Helen Riaboff Whiteley Center provided the gift of time to focus on writing. A grant from the Artist Trust GAP Program helped defray costs for photographic reproductions. Rowman & Littlefield series editor Mark Seldon shepherded the project toward publication; I am thankful for his editorial wisdom and belief in the book. My editor Susan McEachern and her assistant Sarah Wood provided steadfast guidance and vision for crafting the manuscript into a book.

Most of all, my far-flung family remained unfailing in their support and patience. Ying and John Chinnery set many of the wheels in motion that made this project possible. I am deeply grateful to Chen Xiaoying (Ying Chinnery) for meals, materials, and her numerous efforts on my behalf, especially when my questions brought up difficult moments from the past. I have tried my utmost to do justice to her memories and the lives of her parents. Colin Chinnery and Liang Wei kept me going with their understanding. Chen Yonghua and his family welcomed me with warmth. Isabelle and James Tweedie Sr. nourished me with undiminished enthusiasm. Kara and Ruben Aya-Welland continually teach me what really matters. My deepest debts are to my grandmother, whose life fills these pages; my father, Grant Vincent Welland, for the love in his voice when he turned to me once after dinner with my grandmother and said, "I wish you had known my mother"; my mother, Mei Chen Welland, who strove to give me everything, especially the freedom to choose my own path; and James Tweedie, who traveled with me, in every way, through the entire journey of this book.

Note

The system of Chinese romanization used in this book is pinyin, in which words are pronounced roughly as written, with the following exceptions: *c* is pronounced *ts*, *q* is pronounced *ch*, *zh* is pronounced *j*, and *x* is pronounced *hs*. Following pinyin, Mao Tse-tung becomes Mao Zedong, and Peking and Canton become Beijing and Guangzhou. Beijing was temporarily renamed Beiping after the capital moved to Nanjing in 1927, but to aid clarity for the general reader, I use Beijing throughout. The only exceptions to pinyin that I use are the widely recognized names Chiang Kaishek and Sun Yatsen, which reflect southern dialect pronunciation. Chinese names within the text are given with the surname first. All quotations and references in the notes follow the form (pinyin or otherwise) used by the author cited. All translations, unless otherwise noted, are mine.

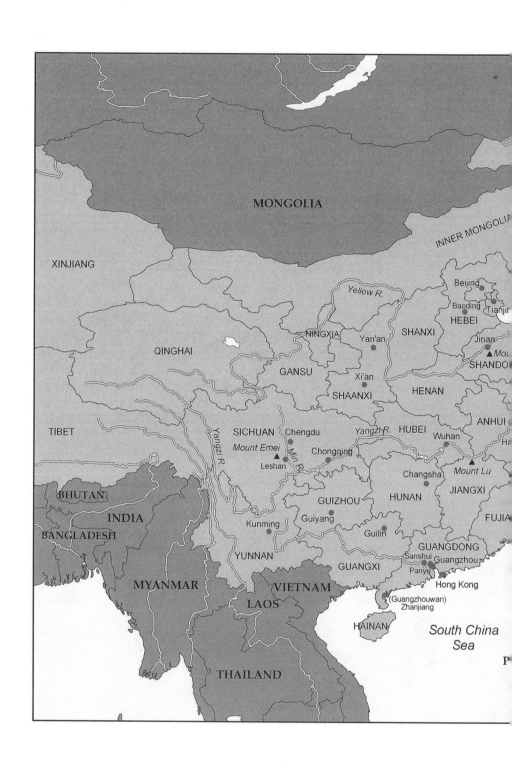

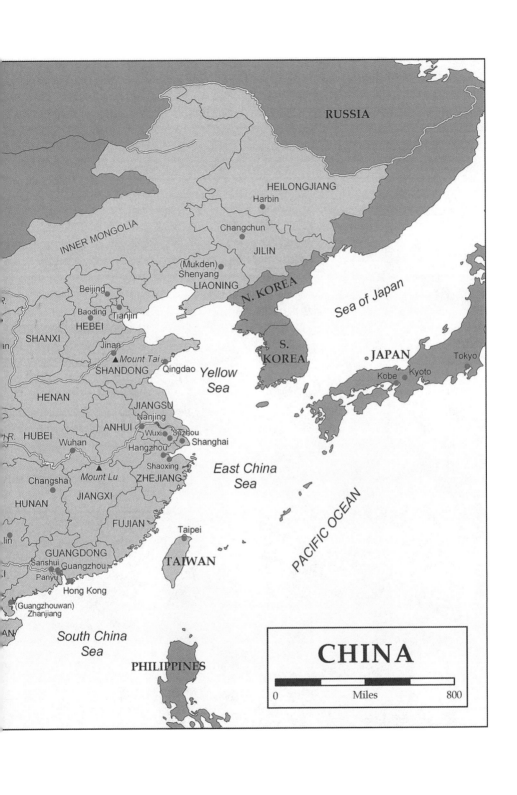

Prologue: Departure

$\mathcal{I}$ grew up a child of the American Midwest, at a time when Chinese meant chop suey on the sign of a gas station converted into a take-out shop. I understood little of what being Chinese meant to my grandmother. Still, I grew up eating dried lychees. Plants and trees, their fruits and flowers, and the many metaphors they blossom forth are usually rooted in native soil, but in my family they're preserved and packaged for travel. A cellophane bag of dried lychees meant we were visiting my mother's parents in San Francisco, where they spent summers and later retired after decades in Indiana. As we strolled down the sidewalks of Chinatown, away from the messy remains of a dim sum lunch and toward the parking garage under Portsmouth Square, my grandmother would pull me into a tiny grocery packed with smells that assaulted my untrained nose. From shelves of jars with labels I could not read and bags of dried spices and seafood products, she plucked familiar treats. On the rest of the walk to the car, I tripped happily behind the adults with a bag of lychees clutched in my hand. The sweet, musty flavor of dried lychee meat stuck in my teeth. Even more delightful was the perfectly smooth pit at the center of the bite-sized fruit. I rolled the pit in my mouth like a marble, while Chinatown receded through the rear window of my grandparents' car.

I didn't realize yet that a love of lychees connected my grandmother to the southern province of her infancy, where this fruit flourishes along rivers and near the seacoast. Only years later would I learn that families in Guangdong once vied to produce a superior variety. Prize fruit carried the clan name. Even from the distance of Beijing, where my grandmother's family moved shortly after her birth, her father maintained a lychee garden on the outskirts of Guangzhou. He hoped to retire to this grove of low, full trees. In the north, fed on family tales of the south, Amy grew up with a longing for lychees. Each summer, for a few short days in June or July, baskets of the jewel-like fruit, packed in layers of straw, appeared in Beijing. After their journey, the lychees smelled of extravagant ripeness. Swollen with sugary

1

juices that would soon ferment and spoil, they had to be consumed immediately.

The outer shell of a dried lychee is hard and prickly, thin and brittle. The shrunken fruit rattles around inside. I wouldn't know the taste of fresh lychees until I was a teenager, when my father and I went on a backpacking trip in British Columbia. It stunned us. We'd never before seen, let alone tasted, fresh lychees, which harvested straight from the tree come in a cluster like an oversized bunch of grapes. When you peel away the bumpy, pinkish brown shell, white opaque fruit appears directly under the surface. The taut skin pops between your teeth, flooding your mouth with a fragrant flavor, and the smooth chestnut-like pit at the center lands on your tongue, full stop. Dazed with our happy discovery of Canadian access to trans-Pacific fruit, we bought a huge bunch to bring home to my mother, but a customs official caught us at the airport. We quickly peeled and devoured the whole sweet bunch, until our mouths tingled with cloying discomfort.

In my family, lychees have become a taste of nostalgia. In the United States, they represent an almost unattainable moment of sweetness, always receding. But they are not to be overindulged in, for Chinese medicine indicates that immoderate consumption of lychees causes excessive internal heat, which can lead to fever or nosebleeds. A Tang dynasty story similarly cautions against folly committed out of partiality to lychees. Emperor Xuanzong indulged all the whims of his favorite concubine, most famously her passion for the most evanescent of southern fruits. At his order, envoys from southern China galloped on horseback thousands of miles to deliver fresh lychees to the capital in the northwest. They carelessly trampled the crops of poor farmers along the way.

Since at least the Tang dynasty, lychees have been a form of trade driven by remembrance of the tongue. Over a thousand years later, Xuanzong's imperial hubris had become the way of the world. Between 1903 and 1906, William N. Brewster, an American Methodist missionary stationed in China, shipped several specimens of the centuries-old "Chen Zi" or "Chen Purple" to Florida. American botanists renamed this lychee cultivar the "Brewster." Not long after, an American Presbyterian missionary in Beijing taught English to my grandmother Ling Shuhao and renamed her Amy Ling. Decades later, dried lychees bought in San Francisco took Amy back to her short infant days in a landscape of family origin.

When I ate my first dried lychee, I had yet to discover that for the sisters of this story taking leave was a way of life. My grandmother Amy and her sister Shuhua grew up in Beijing and the treaty port of Tianjin. The foreign legation quarter in the capital nestled against the southern wall of the imperial city; in Tianjin, concessions governed by Western countries that commanded influence in China ran through the city. The sisters spoke Cantonese at home, Mandarin outside, and later English and Japanese at school. At the beginning of the twentieth century, no single foreign power had colonized China outright, but each of the era's great powers staked claims throughout the ancient empire on the verge of collapse. Branches of thought from external sources were grafted onto an embattled tradition in the struggle to reinvigorate China.

The taste my grandmother and great-aunt had for the southern village of Panyu as their native place persisted throughout their lives. Yet, even with an anchor in the Pearl River Delta, Shuhua and Amy floated in the boundary waters between tradition and modernity. Born into a family clinging to conventions of a nearly bygone era, they sought a life radically different from that of their mother who, in certain whispered accounts, stepped off a "painted boat" of professional courtesans into her role in the Ling family as a concubine handpicked by their scholar-official father. The sisters emerged instead from the walls of a Beijing courtyard home to join the first wave of Chinese women who crowded into school dormitories. They were daughters of an official involved in nationalist politics during a time of national humiliation but attended colleges founded by Westerners, the first to admit women. The events surrounding May 4, 1919, when students gathered in Tiananmen Square to protest foreign imperialists and corrupt politicians, defined their youth. Leading intellectuals and reformers took up "science" and "democracy" as slogans, borrowed from the West, to vilify traditional Confucian values. Shuhua, Amy, and their classmates joined merchants in the streets to boycott Japanese goods. Striking factory laborers demanded better working conditions. May Fourth–era thinkers promoted women's emancipation as an important marker of China's progress toward modern nationhood, and the Ling sisters embraced this 1920s image of the modern girl, sauntering down the street with bobbed hair, knee-length dress, and a book tucked under her arm.[1]

While Panyu as place of origin remained reassuringly consistent, its temporal equivalent did not. Both sisters changed their dates of birth on multiple occasions. Shuhua, who became a writer, even once attempted a literary usurpation of Amy's position as the family's youngest child. This original uncertainty in time might seem an accident of life before birth certificates. However, as their stories compelled me to follow them further into the past, I recognized these manipulations of age as a strategy of control over the presentation of their lives. They became adept at this trick of flexibility, a deception laid before examiners, officials, and the altar of personal vanity, which sometimes enabled them an escape from time's fixity in order to make selfish sense of it.

Amy and Shuhua, as I learned over time, came from a large family. The number of children shifted in their different accounts but probably came close to twelve. They were the two youngest daughters, the ones most affected by the revolutionary change in early twentieth-century China. I know little about what happened to the rest of their siblings who lived into adulthood, which makes the bond between these two sisters even more striking. They competed with one another, bickered and fought, and told conflicting versions of family history. Yet, over lifetimes that spanned the entire twentieth century and three continents, they stayed in touch. Like the stunning first taste of fresh lychees, the puzzling intensity of their relationship drove my pursuit after it.

I have tried the timeline method of capturing and arranging events from the sisters' lives, a linear progression with cause and effect neatly plotted. But each time I capture a moment under glass, the specimen falls apart, refusing to be bound by my classification system. As I sort through the chronology of memory, I find its events ordered by emotional significance. A cat lay snoring by a pot-bellied stove, while currents of heat circulated the scent of orchids throughout the room. A girl sat among songbooks strewn across a bed, listening to her mother sing stories about mythical women competing in the imperial examinations. Her sister wobbled on the thin tires of a new bicycle through the streets of Beijing at dawn. She dressed like a boy. She pedaled toward the passing summer sweetness of lychees. These are the things that were too insignificant to lie about and too important to forget.

Ling Shuhua celebrated her ninetieth birthday on March 25, 1990, having recently changed her year of birth from 1904 to 1900. The party took place in the Shijingshan Hospital, a cement-block structure set back from a wide, wind-blown boulevard connecting old Beijing with this industrial suburb to the west. The sun shone through dusty windows, illuminating the pale green walls and her shrunken body under the covers. It glinted off the stiff icing of the birthday cake. Ling Shuhua's daughter, son-in-law, granddaughter, and grandson, joined by members of the hospital staff, gathered around the bed of the aged artist and writer to present her with a four-tiered cake. Having finally returned to China, she spurned their sugarcoated Western-style offering and ate a bowl of *longxu* dragon whisker noodles, for longevity.

She had returned to the city of her youth only a few months earlier, after forty-two years abroad—England, France, Singapore, Canada. She spent most of those years in England. Early in her time abroad, she sent a homesick letter to a fellow writer. Years later, Bing Xin could recall how the letter opened: "I don't want to be like those White Russians [in China] who sell carpet on the side of the road, I want to go home, how are you?"[2] She and

Bing Xin had once been at the cultural vanguard as "new women." They produced literary works in vernacular instead of classical Chinese and published in prominent journals. During that period of youthful flux, they wrote poems and stories about female characters not unlike themselves. While the later years of Shuhua's life in England provided a safe remove from the political upheavals of home, China never strayed far from mind. Finally, toward the end of 1989, an old woman with white hair cropped straight across the base of her neck and a back bent by the silent progress of cancer boarded a plane in London and returned to Beijing. *Luo ye gui gen.* 落叶归根. Fallen leaves return to their roots.

Amy Ling Chen celebrated her ninetieth birthday on September 10, 1994, in the carpeted recesses of a San Francisco Chinatown restaurant. The tuxedoed headwaiter she had known years before his hair turned white stood by the tropical fish tank to greet her. Her children, grandchildren, and great-grandchildren assembled noisily in a banquet room. The matriarch slowly walked in, one arm supported by my uncle, the other by my father, and took her seat at the head of the table: a small, hunched figure in a large brocade-covered chair. Curled, dyed black hair neatly capped her head. She wore a purple silk dress, which she claimed to have designed herself many years earlier. Toward the end of the evening, she exclaimed in time's face, "This is the best birthday party I've ever had. I want to live another ninety years."

She was once a young doctor, with the warmth of a newborn's wet head contained in the memory of her hands. She had lived in the United States for seventy years, ever since she disembarked from the SS *President Jackson* in Seattle. Only one of five women in 1925 to receive a Chinese national scholarship to study in the United States, she boarded a Cleveland-bound train with two steamer trunks and a dream of returning to China to open a women's clinic. She eventually worked as an obstetrician but gave up this position to assist with her husband's pharmacological research, raise a family, and become an avid follower of Wall Street. She returned to China only once, with her husband and American-born toddler son, to visit her aging mother in 1936. Her husband's ashes are buried in a St. Louis cemetery; her family lives in this country. She will not return again to China, so much changed since she left. *Luo di sheng gen.* 落地生根. Roots grow where the seed lands.

Ling Shuhua and Amy Ling Chen: this is one way of identifying the sisters. Ling is their surname, passed on by their father. When they commenced their studies, he gave them the names Shuhua 淑华 and Shuhao 淑浩. He assigned them, as children of the same generation, the same first character. There are two characters *shu* with the same written base. *Shu* 淑 with the three-drop water radical on the left means kind and gentle, maiden-like, the water connoting purity, fluidity, and femininity. *Shu* 叔

without the water radical literally means father's younger brother, suggesting more masculine qualities. Ling Shuhua published using the second *shu* 叔 in her name. Her *hua* 华 can be translated as brilliant or magnificent but also carries with it a reference to China, *Zhonghua* 中华. Ling Shuhao wrote her name using the *shu* 淑 with a water radical. Her *hao* 浩, which also has a water radical, is great, vast, and grand. Shuhua had the responsibility of blood and nation in her name. Shuhao had an unbridgeable ocean of water, later cast aside for Amy.

Amy Ling Chen, as she has called herself since her 1929 wedding in Baltimore, is my mother's mother. I have known her my entire life. Ling Shuhua is her older sister, my great-aunt. I was not able to meet her before she passed away in Shijingshan Hospital and have only learned about her through relatives and researchers, and her paintings and writings.

Like her age, my grandmother's account of the past continually shifted, yet I hesitate to accuse her of lying, because lies are stories. Her beloved childhood horse may change colors from white to black. Her father may treat her like a son or threaten to marry her off like her older sisters. She may or may not have a second brother who survived after the death of the first. These variations fuel the storyteller's cunning, and in her old age my grandmother claimed this as her vocation: teller of tales. From her perch atop a wooden chair with a blue tie-on cushion spotted with oil and soy sauce, she performed dinner-table poetry of stop-and-start stories in the San Francisco apartment that became her domain. With each passing year, she pared them down into increasingly simple and iconic fables. She fixated on ever more concrete details: her first bicycle, the steamer trunk that crossed the Pacific with her, a long-lost rock collection. She communicated through the sieve of a fiercely selective memory. Neither would admit it, but she and her sister shared this talent of artful editing.

In 1989, as a college student, I started listening to my grandmother's stories about her childhood in China and immigrant experience in the United States. What began as a way to spend time with her after my grandfather's death grew into my discovery of her past. My search after the history of this willful, independent Chinese woman suddenly expanded when I spent a year studying in Britain and met Shuhua's family. I had heard my grandmother praise this sister, the one who left China for England in 1947, as an accomplished painter in the Chinese tradition of landscapes, flowers, and birds. From Shuhua's daughter Xiaoying, however, I learned she was much more significantly a writer who had published three collections of short stories, numerous essays, and an autobiography in English.

Xiaoying gave me a copy of her mother's autobiography *Ancient Melo-*

dies. Published in 1953 by Leonard Woolf's Hogarth Press, the catalyst for the book could be traced to an earlier crossing of the Bloomsbury group and cosmopolitan Chinese intellectuals. Ling Shuhua met Julian Bell in 1935 during his stint as an English teacher in China. After his departure, she began a correspondence with his aunt, Virginia Woolf, who encouraged her, as Julian had, to write an autobiography in English. This suggestion impelled the presentation of her life for a Western audience.

As Xiaoying pressed a copy of *Ancient Melodies* into my hands, she said, "If I give you this book, you must never tell your grandmother. She would never let me know the end of it. She hated it. She didn't talk to my mother for years after it was published." What was revealed to me as I read, the divergence of the sisters' versions of the past, launched me on a long road of language learning, living in China, and contending with the partial truths of the stories I had inherited. It became my own journey of following after and reassembling the tale.

When I began visiting my grandmother with notebook and tape recorder in hand, she had just lost her husband, a companion of sixty years. I listened eagerly to her stories, which as she told them helped her remember and forget. Her animation and incredible endurance while telling the stories, often for several hours without a break, revealed her need for someone to listen.

My visits commenced with me waiting for the elevator. I stood impatiently in the lobby of her modern high-rise. I was inevitably late, guilty knowing that as I repeatedly jabbed the elevator button she sat by the phone, searching through the crossed-out entries of her address book for my most recent telephone number. After stepping into the empty car, I leaned against the plastic wood-grain paneling and hurtled through the building's dark core. What period of life would we unearth tonight? What new contradictions would her storytelling bravado pose to the literary voice of Shuhua, traveling as it did to me, not across the dinner table, but in measured prose from China and England?

Under a cold moon, where a runaway woman rests beneath luminous acacia blossoms and strokes the fur of a jade white rabbit crouched by her side, there was birth, ambition, love, and fighting; this, followed by lost relations, letters crossing continents, pebbles thrown into the pool of memory, and travel—above all travel—by horse, bicycle, train, ship, and airplane, until there was also stasis and death. I had been content to know nothing of the past until I heard the silence of my grandfather's grave. For weeks after his ashes were placed into a small frozen hole, I sat on the roof of my college dormitory at night, frustrated by unforthcoming sorrow, and stared at the inky sky, where a waxing moon reflected light from long ago. Then I found myself, at the age of twenty-one, lost in a welter of voices.

I have my grandmother's words, recorded on scratchy cassette tapes. I hear my fumbling with the buttons and her initial formal address to a machine; her patterns of language and words like "davenport" for sofa tell me when (the 1920s) and where (the Midwest) she polished her immigrant's English. I have always communicated with her in English, but it wasn't until I sat, headphones on, transcribing the tapes that I noticed the inflections of her accent. Because I also heard the strength and humor of her voice, I have decided, for the most part, to keep her words as she spoke them. To "fix" them completely would erase something, which she would probably want erased, but which helps me understand her.

I have the words of her sister, the "artist sister" as Amy called her, the writer sister, who—unaware to those of us in the United States—wrote books, in Chinese and in English, and who gained her taste for their possibility in the 1920s when a generation of writers made a revolutionary break from classical Chinese. I have these voices: some rambling on tape, some printed on paper, and some set in a time and language that I strain to understand. Now years and miles later, I've learned to follow these two voices, one of an immigrant talker and one of a writer whose language I must translate into my own.

Ok, my granddaughter wants me to record my stories. I came from China by boat to Seattle. I took the train to Cleveland and went directly to Western Reserve Medical College. The registrar looked at me and said, who are you, what are you to do? I want to go to American medical school to study medicine to be a doctor. I need a place to sleep and get up early to go to school. That's before I learned to watch the ticker tape. You know, Wall Street, pork bellies up or down.

Shuhua wakes to the sound of rain, London in winter. She lies in bed, her mind roaming, until she remembers the letter postmarked from San Francisco. Her younger sister has written from across the ocean about finding an apartment for her in America. We can live near each other again, do you need money, the little sister asks. Shuhua laughs at the prospect of living next to her *xiao meimei*, who thinks she is a "sudden rich" American. She inspects the scrawled characters of her handwriting and scoffs, she can't even write in Chinese anymore.

Well, young lady, now what do you want to know? In China, I did what I wanted because I dressed in boy's clothing. I rode a bicycle. I rode a horse. In Cleveland, I took the streetcar. I brought a bag of peanuts for the streetcar conductor who always told me where to get off. My mother sent me peanuts from China. She thought only China had peanuts. I ate them late at night while I studied. I memorized the names of all the small bones of the ankle, and then the hand. I like science, see, not like the artist sister. She's a painter. She always thought she was the smartest in the family. She always had *that notion.*

Shuhua presumes her sister doesn't know how sick she is, a captive of her London flat. To move to America would be ridiculous, especially because she yearns for China and childhood: the taste of sesame candy and a glimpse of their house's red door. The winter light, soft and feeble at the window, casts a pale rectangle across her bed. When afternoon fades to shadow, she scans the dark room, crammed with newspapers, paintings, bottles of ink, dirty dishes, clothes, and books. Over there, she thinks, in that pile, lie all of the books I have written, my stories in Chinese and English, too. Her eyes roam the crowded room, hungry for an empty space, a blank wall to draw upon with a little nub of charcoal.

I learned from peanuts that the grandmothers were smart; they knew how to get something. My father's grandmother grew peanuts. Very, very successful. That's why she could put her grandchildren everywhere she wanted them to study. She didn't put my father on the peanuts, but that's where she was successful. My father said I look just like her. I never met her, of course, because she was my father's grandmother. She invested in peanuts. I invest in stock.

Shuhua still paints in the classical style she learned as a child. She remembers Father telling her to never paint anything she didn't like. Paint everything, he said, for your own sake. She feels at home with a brush in hand, gently releasing ink from its pointed tip. She paints Chinese landscapes, even though the fog and the sailboat are English. She longs to sit by an ink-wash lake. She writes: "I sit on a rock and drop pebbles into the lake, watching the circles in the water ripple outward until they vanish."

Where is she? I've been waiting since five-thirty. These young people are always late. They leave you waiting. I should call her. She told me she would come today, didn't she?

Shuhua has lain in bed all day. She hears the cook from the Chinese embassy next door slide a tray of foil-covered food to the floor in front of her door. She talks to herself: "Get up and eat dinner. Either that or go home."

The elevator slowed with a pneumatic whoosh and then a hesitation. The doors slid open.

Amy told me about her family—a father and mother, three older sisters and the vague memory of a brother who died young—a picture that fit the familiar frame of an American nuclear family. She described Shuhua as the artist sister: "She writes and paints all the time. Ever since she was five years old. She never played. She didn't get along. She was just so quiet." In 1990, when Shuhua's daughter handed me the book proving her mother had not been so quiet after all, I gulped down what my grandmother hadn't talked about. The "Note" at the front of *Ancient Melodies* provided a jarring surprise. Shuhua's family tree begins with Father and ends with Sixth Mother. Shuhua and Amy are the two youngest daughters of Fourth Mother. Striving for narrative innocence, Shuhua made herself the family's youngest child even though she was several years older than my grandmother.

I felt deceived; someone was not telling the truth. I went to China hoping to disentangle life from fiction. I have since spent more than four years in China, slowly sinking into the quicksand of competing sources. During my first trip in 1990, I could barely decipher a map of Beijing, let alone my reactions to a city so changed from the one described by my grandmother. In that one-month visit, I traveled from the site of the old Ling house in Beijing to the new tomb of Ling Shuhua's husband, where her ashes were also buried, at the edge of Lake Tai near his hometown of Wuxi. The second time I stayed for two years, 1992 to 1994, and taught English in Beijing. From 2000

FAMILY GENEALOGY I

As described by Amy.

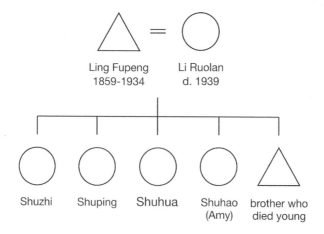

FAMILY GENEALOGY II

As presented in the "Note" at the front of Ling Shuhua's *Ancient Melodies*. Shuhua identifies herself as the youngest, Little Tenth, and gives Amy the name Mai. She does not number Amy, perhaps an ambiguous concession to the fact that Amy is really the youngest child. She also fails to number Elder Brother and skips from Sixth to Eighth Sister with no mention of a Seventh Sister.

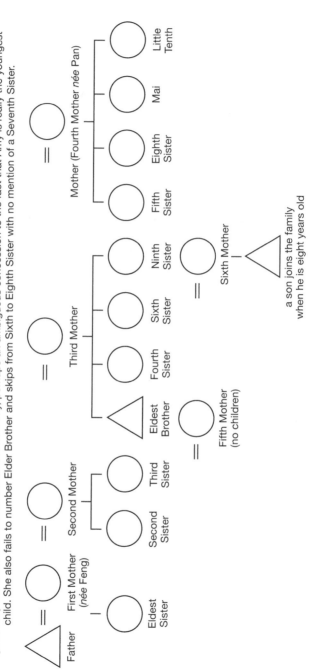

to 2002, I spent another two years in a now-familiar city, conducting dissertation research, while also continuing to file away details for this book.

I've wandered down the lane where the Lings used to live in every season. Gnarled trees rise through small square openings in the sidewalk. Buried roots strain upward and crack the pavement. Rows of gray one-story brick houses line either side of the *hutong*, their roofs patterned with curved tiles like fish scales. Windblown seeds have lodged between tiles, and dry weeds sprout toward the sky. Carved doorjambs, whose peeling paint once brilliant red exposes weathered wood, are high and awkward to step over. In the shortening days of autumn, I have watched a toy peddler, like a bit character in one of Ling Shuhua's short stories, craft small figurines of brightly colored dough on bamboo sticks, in front of where the old gates stood. In the numb cold, I have watched an old woman poking around the base of a winter-bare tree, searching for discarded pieces of coal. How many hot summer days have I rounded the corner from the bustling thoroughfare of Dongdan Street—with its Hong Kong franchise stores spilling sale-priced jeans and waves of air-conditioning onto the sidewalk and its wedding photo boutiques with racks of frilly white dresses and ornate red *qipao*—to the welcoming calm of this leafy, residential lane? The *hutong*'s quiet is increasingly rare, as sections of town all around fall to modernization, the noisy razing of old and construction of new buildings that has risen apace with economic reform. As I cast quick glances through the doorways of old homes, divided in a ramshackle manner into multiple family dwellings after the revolution, I realize my grandmother's blind eye to the inequality that sustained her family's privilege. Her heroic narrative of educated female emancipation overlooks the servants' cotton-soled shoes that hurried through their rooms and the calls of the street peddlers and rickshaw pullers outside her family's courtyard compound.

In China, I also found my family's proclivity toward "fiction" embedded in the language I learned haltingly to speak. Chinese laugh at American directness: how naive, how unsophisticated to wear one's heart for all to see. What I often misinterpreted as dishonest hiding behind language is a cultivated ability to move between formal and informal registers. In deciding when, where, and how to say something, the speaker has in mind a goal comprising more than words. The wintertime imperative, for example, of "wear more clothes" may mean: you pathetic foreigner, you don't know how to dress properly for the weather; you look worn down and should take better care of yourself; or let me fuss over you because I need to ask a favor. Set phrases or images are repeated not as subterfuge but often to express honest emotion or moral conviction.[3] Suppressing my American desire for exposé and working toward an understanding of these equally meaningful levels of language, I moved beyond the quest for a single immutable truth.

By learning to admire the raconteur's virtuosity, have I reasoned away their betrayal with too much academic ease? Am I no longer so bothered by the stories, never flush with one another, because I have also learned to lie, to tell a story when I know in my heart that it didn't happen exactly that way? I tried many times to explain to my grandmother that I was writing this book, but I did not explain my interpretation of her life, in which she is no longer always the hero. I started this book on multiple occasions, each time bearing new evidence that changed the entire undertaking. As I tried, over the years, to inhabit the lives of Amy and Shuhua, the pride behind their stories struck me as powerfully as the defensiveness. My sense of betrayal has dissipated, but the narrative holes and irreconcilable contradictions have not. Truth, whether that means getting things right or getting everything down, will never seem easy again.

Born at a distance, I am the first in generations of women in my family to have access to a line of women, talking and writing about themselves. In China, my grandmother and great-aunt, like my mother, never met their grandparents. Generalized assumptions about Chinese women might attribute this breakdown in generational communication to daughters given away in marriage to their husbands' families and seen as contributing nothing to their parents' genealogical line. Historical reassessments show, however, that a woman's inheritance rights and relationship with her birth family varied widely over historical period and geographical region, as the case of my grandmother's mother will show. The unprecedented mobility of women in late imperial China took her far from her parents' home, just as immigration separated my grandmother from hers.[4]

I once told myself that my grandmother and great-aunt and many previous generations of Chinese women must have faced the same daunting silence into which Virginia Woolf dared to let fly a questioning voice: "I have no model in my mind to turn about this way and that. Here am I asking why women did not write poetry in the Elizabethan age, and I am not sure how they were educated; whether they were taught to write; whether they had sitting-rooms to themselves; how many women had children before they were twenty-one; what, in short, they did from eight in the morning till eight at night."[5] I assumed that Western writers like Virginia Woolf had blazed the way for all women, but I have since learned that the supposed literary silence of Chinese women is simply a story reinforced by such assumptions. Courtesans and elite women of the Ming and Qing dynasties had access to the written word and often to an institution of publishing—manuscripts in hand-copied or block-printed form that were passed between families and studios—unknown in Western women's history. Writing was not universally viewed as an acceptable calling for Chinese women. But they did write.[6]

What I have to thank Woolf for is that, in a cross-continental correspondence with Ling Shuhua, she urged her to write an autobiography in English. I may never have had the patience to learn Chinese and read Ling Shuhua's stories in the original if I had not experienced that first taste in my native English.

With the late Ming poet Wang Wei's search for a mooring as a model of emotional cartography, I intend this book to be a set of stories that speak to personal and public ways of thinking about feminism, our relationship with the past, and the creation of border-crossing identities. Wang Wei, orphaned in childhood, grew up to be a courtesan and talented poet. In old age, she called herself "Daoist Master in the Straw Coat." In the middle of the seventeenth century, she traveled on a little boat loaded with the books of her library on the waterways of central China. She visited freely with male literati, exchanging verse with them. She wrote in the preface of her collection *Poems from Shaded Halls*, "Not having been born a man, I cannot right all wrong that prevails under heaven; instead I had to work within the confines of one room."[7] This modest remark reveals that, while aware of female inequality, she did possess a room of her own, on a boat adrift in endless space. The spirit of her wandering life and defiance of female norms guides the story I tell.

I

MOVING HOUSE

· *One* ·

Origins

*M*y grandparents' house in Indianapolis intimidated me as a child. Stranded atop an empty expanse of green lawn, it exuded a sterile 1950s sense of stability. Once-modern amenities (an intercom system provided the only entertainment, allowing my sister and me to have secret conversations) mingled with Chinese books, paintings, and artifacts captured behind glass. Our Christmas celebrations there felt formal, almost staged. My grandparents sat together on the sofa, while my sister and I quietly opened our presents. The sparsely decorated plastic Christmas tree stood next to a folding screen of black lacquer, cold to the touch, inlaid with colored stones creating a panorama of figures at a Chinese festival. I had to remember to thank them for the cotton Chinese pajamas with knotted cloth buttons called frogs that I knew I would receive every year.

A single object in that orderly home drew me to it. I tiptoed into the study to gaze at it in the curio case. Kneeling on a beige upholstered stool, I pressed my nose to the glass, eyes level with a polished peach pit carved in the form of a boat. It rested frozen in time, susceptible to my daydream mode of investigation. I imagined life inside, my hand on the tiller and a plate of fish on a worn wooden table. This talisman and my grandmother's story about the lady in the moon, a Chinese fairy tale about a runaway woman that contradicted what I'd heard about a man in the moon, stand out as the images of China I contemplated most intimately in childhood.

Only years after they left this house for an apartment in San Francisco did I hear a more detailed origin story from my grandmother. Her father Ling Fupeng was born in Panyu, meaning his daughters also recorded this town in Guangdong's Pearl River Delta as their hometown. Shuhua wrote that she was born in Beijing but spent several years of early childhood in southern China with her mother and sisters. Amy told me she was born in Panyu and moved north with her mother one year later, after her father rose to become mayor of Beijing. Ling's official travels or the Boxer Rebellion, which besieged Beijing in the summer of 1900, several months after Shuhua's birth, may have precipitated the temporary return of his family to the safety of Panyu. Regardless of the brevity of their stay in the south, the sisters identified themselves as Cantonese, an important distinction in a country as regionally diverse as China.

Guangzhou is one of China's largest southern ports. For over a thousand years, it has bustled with trade. Panyu lies to the city's southeast, now just an hour's bus ride away. Travelers from India and the Roman Empire first appeared at the Guangzhou docks in the second century CE. Arab traders arrived during the Tang dynasty (618–909). By the seventeenth century, British ships sailed into the port in search of tea, ivory, porcelain, and silk. The city's prosperous reputation and the fertile land of the Pearl River Delta had for centuries lured immigrants from northern China. They bent to the arduous task of rice planting, dividing the land into a palette of green terraced paddies. The industrious reaped the bounty of two or three harvests a year. When overcrowding, drought, opium peddled by the British, and civil war brought famine and violence to the region, the brave packed lavish dreams into ships that set sail for the famed Gold Mountain across the Pacific. Far from the Ming (1368–1644) and Qing (1644–1911) imperial seats of power in the north, the Cantonese became known as defiant wanderers and traders.

At the turn of the twentieth century, the wealth of the region's leading families was legendary. The banners of elegant shops filled curving streets and alleys. Markets overflowed with abundance: ripe bananas, faded vermilion clusters of lychees, radiant mangos, miniature orange trees bearing dainty fruit in blue and white porcelain pots, sprigs of plum blossoms, heavy-headed chrysanthemum, squealing pigs, large flashing fish in metal tanks, and turtles and frogs crawling over one another. Away from the commotion of the streets, the conversation of the silk-clad rich spilled out from open-air teahouses, toward the outlying town of Panyu, idealized in my grandmother's memory as a pastoral retreat.

From this lush landscape of family origin, the Ling household would move to the dry northern plain where the Manchu capital of the Qing dynasty was situated. The dusty streets of Beijing extended in grid-like geometry from the emperor's residence, the Forbidden City. A rectangular red wall with a moat at its base surrounded this palace enclave. Inside, a central north-south axis aligned the halls for official ceremony, each entryway facing toward the auspicious south. Outside, the crush of activity in the maze of *hutongs* between major thoroughfares humanized the pervasive order of officialdom. Peddlers sang out their wares with the thick, throaty *r* of the local dialect. Rickshaw pullers strained to convey their passengers through the crowd. Street stall vendors tempted passersby with sugar-glazed red haw berries speared nine high on wooden sticks, baskets of crunchy, yellow-brown pears, sweet yams whose thick aroma wafted from the metal roasting barrel, and hand-warming bags of dark, smooth chestnuts. Smoke rose toward the gray sky from round chimneys of squat brick compounds, built around inner courtyards where a few ancient and twisted pine trees might stand and where the Ling children learned to play new games.

Many of the stories in my grandmother's repertoire recalled the grandeur of her privileged childhood. When I first heard these stories as a college student, they struck me as fairy tales of a place mysterious and far away. I reacted with a yearning for the exotic similar to that revealed in Vita Sackville-West's introduction to *Ancient Melodies*, which recommends Shuhua's autobiography for its "Arabian Nights quality."[1] Years later, the limits of this interpretation led me to question what gets left out of idealized fantasy or nostalgic remembrance. I began to wonder instead if the sisters' preoccupation with the days of their youth represented a desire to recapture a state of perceived innocence. Did they entertain a nostalgia that would draw them

Rock garden in winter, Beijing, ca. 1910. Shuhua is second from left,
Amy second from right, and Shuping on the far right.

back, through years of compromise, to an imaginary homeland—the revolutionary moment of their youth? Is what my grandmother felt when she told her stories even the warm-hued, tender sort of nostalgia I used to associate with them? Nostalgia can also be a childish tyrant, nonsensical and naughty in its games. It had lured me into longing for a past I could only pretend to know firsthand and only hear through translation.

Ancient Melodies purports to be autobiography, but several of its chapters first appeared in Chinese as fiction. Ling Shuhua published the short story "Moving House," which eventually became the third chapter of her English-language memoir, in a 1929 issue of the *Crescent Moon* journal.

The story's protagonist Zhi'er is caught up in the commotion of a household preparing to move. Her mother, busy packing, pauses only long enough to tell the girl that she can't bring her pet hen on the steamer journey north. Zhi'er decides to give her pet and the eggs she hoped to hatch into chicks to Aunt Shi, the old woman who lives behind the family's ancestral temple.

Zhi'er has long been in the habit of escaping to the comfort of this neighbor's humble home. Aunt Shi, whose grown children live and work in town, teaches her simple household chores: how to feed the ducks or thread a needle. Zhi'er would help the white-haired woman with these small tasks and follow her to the fields, where they knelt with other villagers to fill baskets with peanuts pulled from the ground. Unable to imagine being separated from Aunt Shi, Zhi'er told her that Beijing lay just on the other side of the river. She repeated all of the stories she'd heard about the capital. She and her sisters planned to visit the emperor's golden house. She promised to pick up a piece of gold from the ground for Aunt Shi.

On the day before their departure, Zhi'er presented her hen to Aunt Shi, ignoring the sly comments of her family's servant about how fat and tender the chicken was. Later that evening the family had gathered for a final dinner when Aunt Shi arrived with two dishes cooked as a farewell gift. She lifted the country food from her bamboo basket and placed it on the table. The family servant watched Aunt Shi leave, before joking about her generosity in returning Zhi'er's chicken so quickly. Zhi'er demanded to know if Aunt Shi had killed her hen. No one responded, and her chopsticks clattered to the floor. The servant whose teasing had brought on her misery carried her to bed, red-faced and wailing.

In 1953, "Moving House" reappeared with the same title in *Ancient Melodies*. When Shuhua translated the Chinese into English, the only significant change she made was to the narrator's voice. The third-person perspective of Zhi'er in the original story becomes an autographical "I." This almost seamless translation from Chinese to English and from fiction to autobiography raises questions about the borderlands of history and memory. To what extent was the original story autobiographical? If the story of Aunt Shi and the hen actually took place, did Shuhua remember this fragment of childhood or only the incident as recounted by her mother or older sisters? These are a biographer's questions; dispensing with them may have been as easy for a fiction writer as the flick of a pen.

The first-person narrator of the English version of "Moving House" shows Shuhua translating across cultures, modulating her voice for a different audience. She shifted genre as she moved house from China to England. While autobiography in China dates back to the second century BCE with Sima Qian's inclusion of a self-authored biography at the end of his *Records of the Grand Historian*, it was considered a subcategory of the historical genre of biography. Most authors who wrote biographies of the self intended them as public historical records. They composed these narratives in a sparse and distant third person, rarely if ever including private or emotional reflections. Exposition that tended toward the subjective belonged not to history but to the realm of poetry and literature. Although examples of autobiographical self-examination exist, particularly in the Ming dynasty efflorescence of Chinese autobiography, most writers in a society that valued modesty and objectivity in historical recordkeeping avoided authoritative use of personal experience.[2] Even the famous social critic and writer Hu Shi, who emerged in the 1930s as a pioneer of modern Chinese autobiography, emphasized the importance of historical objectivity. He believed autobiography should "generate materials to be used by historians and pave the way for literature."[3] The writing may be poetic, but the subjective world of emotions is more decorously exposed in fictionalized accounts than self-revelation. In England, the European tradition of the Christian confessional and a desire for accessible narratives of life in "the Orient" encouraged the type of autobiography that *Ancient Melodies* became. Vita Sackville-West's nostalgia for an era before the Chinese drove the British from their treaty-port enclaves emerges in her introductory praise of the book as "delightful sketches of a vanished way of life on the other side of the world."[4]

The biographical veracity of "Moving House" fades in importance beside the story's emotional point. The experience of moving house brings an unsettling combination of excitement and disorientation. When Shuhua first wrote the story in 1929, she had already moved from Panyu to Beijing, Kobe, Tianjin, Kyoto, and Wuhan; but from the distance of London in 1953, the girl's sobs must have cried from the page as a prediction of a fate of uprootedness sealed in childhood.

Lessons in moving learned young accustomed the Ling sisters to transmigration. The journey from southern China to the northern imperial capital marked the first of many transitions they would go through in their lives, familiarizing them with the emotions of residency in a locale that is not one's native place or *yuanji*. The cultivated longing for Panyu that Shuhua described having had as a child in *Ancient Melodies* could just as easily describe her feelings as an adult, writing the story in England: "Viewing such beautiful scenery on a fine day when I was by myself, I always had a sense that I was missing something. I would feel a longing for certain places in my native country, where I imagined myself sitting silently on a rock. A little bit of departed sorrow dropped gently into my heart; it was like a pebble thrown into a pond: the smooth surface of the water gives a tiny leap upward, and small and big circles appear suddenly one after another and then suddenly vanish."[5]

As the sisters traveled, they carried with them, in battered metal trunks, wooden crates, and well-strapped suitcases, physical reminders of a home-land. My parents' moves seemed relatively devoid of drama in comparison, although they inherited the ancestors. In all of the different midwestern homes we lived in, their portraits presided over our lives. When my grand-mother gave the pair of paintings to my mother Mei, she told her they were portraits of the grandfather and grandmother she had never known. As a newborn, I lay on my parents' bed under the ancestor portraits. In lonely hours of childhood spent lurking around the house, I would sneak into the midday quiet of the dining room and stare up at them in their new place over the table. My impressive ancestors, in elaborate costume, sat sternly on throne-like chairs and stared back at me with flat, impassive eyes.

I grew up in St. Louis, where I thought of race as black and white, between which I found no easy place of belonging. Born at the end of the 1960s, the daughter of a Canadian father and a mother who considered her-self Indiana Hoosier first and Chinese American second, I learned a local version of the American obsession with identity. When my mother called herself oriental, like the living room rug, I didn't think twice. But, when she proudly called herself a Hoosier, that regional badge of Indiana natives, I winced. When one travels west from Indiana to St. Louis, somewhere across the plains of Illinois, past the town of Pekin whose high school sports mascot was the Chink until 1981, Hoosier translates into redneck.

A few days after moving into my college dormitory in California, "You're *hapa haole*, aren't you?" hit the side of my face. I realized the labels had shifted once again as I learned of my new regional proximity to Hawaii and its term for half-Asian. I began a mission to become a real *hapa*, whatever that might be, instead of a fake, not one who was just passing.

In my search for signs of Asian authenticity, I preyed upon the ancestor portraits. The importance of their presence multiplied with the distance I traveled from my childhood awe. They proved I had some claim on being Chinese American. Proof to me at least, for I had encountered questioning looks when I showed up at events organized by Asian American groups, where I felt as mongrel as my family's mu shu pork served in steamed pita bread. I had come across a closed community, intent, as far as I could tell, on policing the categories of "real" and "fake." Feeling as if I didn't look or talk or even eat the part, I attempted to craft an identity that would provide evidence of my belonging. Obliging always of my moods and phases, my mother took a photograph of the ancestor portraits and sent it in the mail. I had spent hours in life-drawing classes as a college student. Now several years later, I slid the photograph into the frame of a mirror. I compared their faces with my own, and decided to paint the female ancestor into a self-portrait.

Her masklike visage was made up with a smooth surface of white paint and a demure dab of red for lips. She sat on the flat representation of a chair in a beige space with no perspective. She posed with her arms resting on her lap, hands hidden in the long sleeves of her robe. I squeezed small mounds of oil paint onto my glass palette and began to mix colors. I held the photograph between the fingers of my left hand while I painted with my right. I squinted at the details of my face and hers, until they dissolved into shapes and shadows, until paint thinner started to smudge the emulsion of the photograph. I forgot the hunger of my search for identity, lost in the sensuous gesture of an oil-filled brush over canvas.

When I stepped back, I found that I sit stiffly in a straight-back wooden chair, pushed toward the left side of the canvas. I sit with my shoulders angled to the side and my unsmiling face looking straight ahead. My head and long hair cast a purple shadow on the cadmium wall behind me. In the corner, my great-grandmother's portrait hangs on the same plane of red. There is a strange lack of depth in the room. Her two-dimensional form and throne-like chair start to float forward. We stare into the same distance, cannily eyeing the viewer with a similar suspicion.

Around that time, a Chinese American acquaintance of my parents visited their home, and my mother showed him her ancestor portraits. He laughed, "Mei, those aren't your grandparents. You can buy pictures like that almost anywhere." To me, this information came too late. The generic portraits had already worked their magic. I had learned to look, knowing nothing about them, and to see myself in them. It did, however, seem quite likely that they were fake. It was just like my grandmother to draw upon the resources at her disposal to pass off a glorious picture of her past.

I had been given another layer of irony for self-portraiture at arm's length. For my mother though, this news from a virtual stranger standing in

Self-Portrait, *Sasha Welland, oil on canvas, 1995*

her dining room turned her into a child betrayed yet again. She had grown up obedient to the silence and secrecy of her parents' house, modeled after their filtered image of what a good 1950s American girl should be. They meant to protect her, but instead, they alienated her with empty symbols—ancestors embodying absence, the web of extended family that was never there.

· Two ·

Ambition

$\mathscr{I}$f Amy handed down fake ancestor portraits, Shuhua also claimed a familial connection her daughter suspects is partially apocryphal. A painting album given to Shuhua by her father contained a self-portrait of the artist Xie Lipu, in which he appears as an old man wrapped in white robes sitting under a tree. Shuhua publicly maintained he was the maternal grandfather of her father Ling Fupeng.[1] Xiaoying remembers her mother describing him as a more distant relative.

Xie Lipu was the penname of Xie Lansheng (1760–1831), a native of Nanhai, Guangdong. At the age of thirty, he passed the imperial examination, the pinnacle of a state exam system that brought bureaucratic office and social prestige. Instead of accepting an official appointment in the capital, he returned to Guangdong and devoted twenty years to work as an editor and lecturer in the local *shuyuan*, an academy where young scholars studied. He retired at the age of fifty to become a painter. At seventy, he collected all of the academic books he had published and set them on fire. As flames licked at the bindings, he declared they were not real books but useful only in preparing for the imperial examinations.[2]

According to *Ancient Melodies*, Xie Lipu's youngest daughter married Ling Zhaogeng, the son of a successful merchant in Panyu. Ling had passed the district examination at the age of fourteen but postponed taking the provincial examination in order to study foreign languages from local European merchants and missionaries. He moved on to algebra, geometry, and careful observations of foreign steamboats. When he was twenty-three, he hired a group of men to build two boats from drawings he'd made. In one design, steam powered the boat; in the other, a wheel produced a propelling current of air. Shuhua remembered a great-uncle describing Ling Zhaogeng's triumph: "On the day of the maiden voyage people swarmed into our village from neighboring towns to watch the event. We dined together that day in the hall of your ancestor temple. . . . He looked very handsome that day, wearing a white silk shirt—his eyes were shining."³ Two years later, in 1859, a son was born to Ling Zhaogeng. Ling Fupeng had not yet begun his studies when his father died. His widowed mother was left to supervise the boy's education.

The Chinese civil service examinations dated back over two thousand years, but the empire-wide system, which survived until 1905, was first consolidated during the Tang dynasty, with the first exam held in 622 CE. The system was designed to select capable men for government service according to intellectual merit, rather than bloodlines or wealth. In the Qing dynasty in particular, labor markets loosened and social stratification became more fluid than ever through intense competition. Family fortunes rose and fell, and peasants, artisans, and merchants all hoped to rear sons who might succeed in the official examinations and lift their family into the scholar-official elite. Theoretically, the system remained open to all men, but only families with enough money to hire a tutor or send their son to school could dream of cultivating a child worthy of the colloquial title "budding genius."⁴

Ling Fupeng spent much of his youth like other boys who carried the weight of family aspiration, committing the classics to heart. After memorizing the texts, students read commentaries on them and learned to write poems and essays modeled after those they had studied. Stories about a talented young scholar's advancement toward glory pervade Chinese history and literature. Shuhua and Amy grew up hearing family tales about their father's competition in the imperial system. His trajectory defined the movements of their family, from south to north, and led his daughters to eventually produce their own versions of the legacy they had inherited. They fed their youthful ambitions with a sense of family pride and drew hopeful inspiration from myths about women who disguised themselves as men to sit for the exams.

Their father passed through many stages. The first level consisted of the "youth examinations," held twice during every three-year period. Although intended for boys in their teens, older men clinging to the dream of literary talent and public office shaved their beards, falsified their age, and filed into the examination hall next to boys young enough to be their sons. The "youth examinations" began at the district level. Magistrates administered five day-long tests on the Confucian classics. Successful candidates from each district advanced to the prefectural examinations, a similar battery of testing. Finally, the names of candidates eligible to take the qualifying exam appeared on a "golden placard." These students carried the title *shengyuan* or "student of the government district school." In popular terms, they were called *xiucai*, "cultured talent" or "budding genius." They had already secured a significant level of social prestige, a grant from the government for further study, and exemption from corporal punishment. The Ling family announced their son's title in 1885. They pasted a red sign bearing the characters *shengyuan* over the entrance of their house. Ling Fupeng was twenty-six.

Around this time Ling Fupeng took the *zi* or "courtesy name" of Runtai, and his family arranged his marriage. His first wife was a woman with the surname Feng. With his future promise as a scholar, his mother would have been able to send a matchmaker to the best families. The chosen woman moved into the Ling household in Panyu while Fupeng continued to study, for the provincial examination. He probably spent much of his time away from home in Guangzhou to attend classes in the *shuyuan*. The academies, which also date back to the Tang dynasty, formed a support system for scholarship in major cities and towns across China. Originally funded by the emperor, high officials and wealthy families gradually assumed patronage for these centers of education and scholarship. Many *shuyuan* housed extensive libraries and the carved wooden blocks used to print books written and compiled by affiliated scholars.

Ling Fupeng spent much of his twenties and early thirties developing the calligraphy for which he would later be noted and perfecting his knowledge of the "eight-legged" essay. All essays written in response to the examiners' question had to contain eight main headings and adhere to a convention of balance and antithesis, while not exceeding seven hundred characters. Over centuries this style had grown increasingly formulaic, meaning students were expected to master volumes of examples. Kang Youwei, a spokesman for reform at the end of the Qing dynasty, participated in the Guangdong provincial examinations the same year as Ling Fupeng. He complained, "I spent much of my time in preparing for the examinations and in learning to write 'eight-legged' essays, and consequently I learned very little."[5] The eight-legged essay became a subject of intense criticism; detractors claimed its rigidity hindered original thought.

At the age of thirty-four, Ling Fupeng entered the provincial exams in September of 1893. Official examiners arrived in Guangzhou from Beijing to oversee the process and assigned each candidate to a tiny, numbered cell. On the night before the exam, cannon fire announced the opening of the honey-combed compound, and thousands of men queued up amid the glow of lanterns and flickering shadows. Inspectors checked their provisions—ink, inkstone, brushes, water, earthenware pot, dumplings, and bedding—twice. Any inspector who discovered hidden notes received a reward in silver. After three days, the candidates' papers were collected and recopied by clerks to prevent any bias an examiner might have if he recognized the calligraphy. The examiners selected successful papers through several rounds of elimination. Ling Fupeng and his peer Kang Youwei emerged with the title of *juren*, "exalted or recommended man."

Early in the spring of 1895, Ling Fupeng set out for the imperial examinations in Beijing. According to Amy, he traveled by river and the Grand Canal, China's manmade inland waterway, in a small hired boat. The boat's owner and a male servant accompanied him. When the wind died or the river narrowed with silt, they paid local men along the riverbanks to pull the boat with thick ropes looped over their shoulders. The weather grew colder as they moved further north. When the ink in Ling Fupeng's inkstone froze, the servant held it against his body until the ink flowed freely again. This river journey seems outdated, considering Kang Youwei made the trip by ocean steamer. The image of Ling Fupeng (quite likely Amy's creation) at an unsteady table practicing brushwork as his boat passed through fields and villages serves as a romantic counterpoint to Kang Youwei's travels. As his steamer sailed through the North China Sea, Japanese troops boarded and searched it. Humiliated by the helplessness of the Chinese, Kang felt his outrage intensify. For years, he had been sending letters and memoranda to the Qing court urging economic and military reforms he believed would strengthen China against foreign coercion.

Many of the thousands of candidates who converged on Beijing in April 1895 were more passionate about the subject of foreign encroachment than the form of their eight-legged essays. The British had defeated Chinese troops in the Opium War of 1842, followed by further losses to the French and British between 1856 and 1860, the French again in 1884, and finally the Japanese in 1894 to 1895. On April 15, 1895, in the midst of the examination process, the terms of the treaty between China and Japan reached Beijing. They stipulated that China give up southern Manchuria and Taiwan and pay Japan an indemnity from silver reserves. Kang Youwei and his protégé Liang Qichao launched into immediate action. Kang drew up a petition to protest acceptance of the treaty, and Liang summoned examination candidates from native place associations around the city to sign it. He appealed first to candidates from their home province of Guangdong. Eighty of the Guangdong examinees agreed to sign, followed by signatures of all of the candidates from the neighboring province of Hunan. Ling Fupeng's name does not appear in the Guangdong section, proving either his loyalty to the emperor's government or his absence from the Guangdong guesthouse when Liang came around. The "Ten Thousand Word Petition" called for rejection of Japan's terms, transfer of the capital to a more secure location, training of troops, and reform of laws and political institutions in order to strengthen the nation. Signed by some 1,200 provincial graduates, it was submitted on May 2. The public endorsement of this antigovernment stance by so many examination candidates represented an unprecedented expression of organized dissent.[6]

They did eventually turn their attention to the exams that had brought them to Beijing. On the appointed day, Ling Fupeng and *juren* from various provinces proceeded to the *Gong Yuan* or Public Halls, where the metropolitan examination was held every three years. Enclosed within high walls were long rows of nearly 8,500 cubicles, ten feet in height and five feet square. Inspectors again searched the candidates' provisions. They also had to change into clothing provided by the examiners to ensure notes could not be smuggled inside a sleeve or hidden pocket. A random character, corresponding to the one the candidate would use on his papers instead of his name, appeared on the door of each cell. On the first morning, examiners delivered questions approved by the emperor and sealed the cells with a piece of paper to remain unbroken for three days. Deputies patrolled the narrow passageways between the cells night and day. Stories abounded of candidates collapsing from exhaustion or hanging themselves with their own clothing.

After the posting of an imperial edict listing the three hundred names of those who had passed, Ling Fupeng joined this group as they entered the palace for the first time. They processed to a hall at the center of the Forbidden City to sit for the palace exam. At desks arranged before the yellow cloth-covered stairs leading up to the emperor's throne, they wrote another day of essays. Most passed this exam, conducted primarily to ensure that none had passed the metropolitan exam as a fluke.

On April 22, the process culminated in the court exam. The candidates, dressed in white robes, entered the palace and assembled in a wide terrace at the foot of a marble ramp carved with a dragon and swirling clouds. Bowing their heads to the ground, the candidates received their test papers. The questions, prepared by the emperor and his advisors, required them to draw upon their knowledge of the classics in a discussion of current affairs. They had until sundown to finish their papers.

The examiners spent days debating their selection of *jinshi*, "finished or entered scholars." They delivered the top ten papers to the emperor, who ranked them. These ten names were announced in a ceremony conducted before the emperor in the largest hall of the palace. On May 5, after the top five names echoed through the gilded hall, Ling Fupeng heard his name announced.

This honor granted Ling Fupeng admission to the Hanlin Academy. Prince Gong, trusted advisor of Empress Dowager Cixi and head of the Zongli Yamen office for management of foreign business, chose him for his masterful calligraphy to serve as one of two first secretaries to the court. His name and native place were carved with the other *jinshi* of 1895 on a stone stele in Beijing's Confucius Temple. His entry into officialdom conformed to the standard against which the behavior of Kang Youwei, who declined the position offered to him as one of the top ten *jinshi*, seemed unusual. Of his decision to return to Guangzhou, Kang wrote, "Since I had decided to make teaching and writing my career in life and was satisfied to live the rest of my life as a commoner, I had no inclination to be an official. Even taking the examinations was for me an act of compromise, and I had done it in obedience to my mother's command."[7]

For Ling Fupeng, however, the achievement represented a high point. In *Ancient Melodies*, Shuhua recorded her father reminiscing about this moment of his career. A blooming wisteria caused him years later to recall the fragrant flowers outside the inn where he stayed during the 1895 examinations: "I love the smell of this wisteria so much. . . . It takes me back in feeling to those youthful days when I came to the capital to try my luck in the Court examination. When my name was put up, I felt full of hope, all the world was looking and waiting for me."[8]

Imperial law barred women from entering the examination system. Tang dynasty poet Yu Xuanji expressed her frustration over this official prohibition in "On a Visit to Chongzhen Daoist Temple I See in the South Hall the List of Successful Candidates in the Imperial Examinations."

> Cloud capped peaks fill the eyes
> In the spring sunshine.
> Their names are written in beautiful characters
> And posted in order of merit.
> How I hate this silk dress
> That conceals a poet.
> I lift my head and read their names
> In powerless envy.[9]

Her poetic yearning testifies to centuries of educated Chinese women who learned to read and write classical poetry from their parents, brothers, or family tutors. In the late Ming and Qing dynasties, appreciation of women's literary activity grew, and significant numbers of women writers emerged. The courtesan poet occupied the center of Ming perceptions of talented women, while in the Qing, virtuous and cultivated women writers of elite families claimed this aesthetic and political space, fashioning themselves as precocious poets or learned moral instructors.[10] Through poetry societies, they offered literary instruction to one another, printed their texts, and in certain cases sought a public readership.[11] Family members viewed their talents as important virtues, which helped nurture morally upright sons and brothers. A daughter's erudition heightened the standing of her natal family's tradition of *jiaxue*, "family learning." A daughter trained well in household management, weaving, and the classics promised to make a good wife for an aspiring scholar. Likewise, courtesans trained in poetry and song employed these skills to enhance their attractiveness to educated male patrons, through whom they might gain access to greater social mobility.

Since women could not compete in the exam system, the ultimate purpose of educating them became a point of debate. Their learning brought honor but only if not used to question their responsibility to family duties. Some critics judged their poetry as derivative, echoing the voice of women created by male writers who preceded them in shaping literary history, but women's remove from the "dust" or taint of overtly political life also led many to argue they wrote more brilliantly and elegantly than men. Upper-class women often wrote about loneliness, boredom, suffering, and abuse, but they did not doubt whether they could write. Men borrowed the poetic female voice to express emotions disallowed in public writing, creating a stylized form often invoked in times of political misfortune. For example, a male official who lost his standing with the overturn of a dynasty might adopt the voice of a woman betrayed by her lover to signal his dispossession from power. Yu Xuanji provides a model of this spurned voice, although her lament, unlike that of male poets, is emphatically not allegorical. Whether seen as vital partners in male learning or threats to the stability of Confucian order, women played an important role in stories about the examination system.

Amy's version of Ling Fupeng's success, told from the distance of San Francisco, linked her to Chinese history through her father, but also through a wily grandmother. The story became more about this woman than her *jinshi* grandson. She began with a genealogical sketch. Ling Fupeng's grandfather was the second son of a man named Ling. This Ling had three sons, but the first son had died young, so the second son inherited all of the family's property. He married and, together with his wife, also had three sons. Amy qualified this accounting of offspring by saying, "In those days, the girls didn't count. Don't ask me. I don't know anything about the girls." While genealogists did not usually record daughters because they would be married off, women in the capacity of mothers could gain recognition for their shrewd managerial and investment skills. In Amy's story about Ling Fupeng's mother, she took control of the family business when her merchant husband passed away. Contrary to modern accounts depicting all pre-twentieth-century women as unrelentingly oppressed by Confucian patriarchy, they often wielded considerable influence at home and in local economies.

Her father's widowed grandmother became the matriarch of the Ling family. Along a narrow lane in Panyu, lined with tile-roofed buildings and enclosed by gates at either end, stood the ancestral temple, where incense burned in front of her husband's portrait. In a large hall, under the gaze of watchful ancestors, the clan gathered for meals. If a Ling left in search of greater glory but came upon hard times, Amy explained, he could always return to the family lane for food and shelter.

A sloping hill lay nearby. The grandmother had heard about potential buyers who wanted to turn it into a burial ground. To verify these rumors, she called upon the landowner. The man confirmed he was trying to sell the land, but thought it too good for a cemetery. As they strolled across the red soil, he pointed out how the slope faced south and had plenty of moisture and sunlight. He gestured toward mature olive trees on the top of the hill as proof of the fertile growing conditions.

"What is this land good for if you don't sell it for a cemetery?" she asked.

"If I had the money, I would plant it with peanuts," he replied.

To buy the land, she sold all of the shops owned by the Lings. She invested her money in the peanut operation and had every able-bodied family member planting peanuts. At harvest time, almost forty people kneeled on the ground and pulled up rooted clusters of peanuts under her supervision. They sat on squat wooden stools to shell the nuts, until the ground was covered in a layer of broken shells and papery skins. Large cloth bags were filled with the naked kernels, ready for roasting.

One step ahead of local competitors, she decided to sell not just peanuts but also peanut oil. She built a mill with two circular grinding stones and a water buffalo to pull each one in opposite directions. Once the oil had been filtered, they sold it in Guangzhou. Assessing her great-grandmother's business venture, Amy concluded, "Very, very successful. That's why she could put her grandchildren everywhere she wanted them to study."

When Ling Fupeng was a boy, the peanut matriarch took a liking to him, especially since his father, her inventor son Ling Zhaogeng, had died so young. She noticed that he preferred running wild with his friends to studying, so she asked him what he wanted to do when he grew up. With confidence, he told her he would become a merchant like his grandfather. She responded with a proposal. In China, custom dictated that the old year's debts be paid by New Year's Eve. Several shopkeepers in Guangzhou owed her money, so she sent her teenage grandson to collect these debts. Clutching the list of addresses his grandmother had given him, Ling Fupeng arrived at the home of the first debtor. A gatekeeper took his card inside. After several minutes, the gatekeeper reappeared and told him to wait while the master of the house collected the money. The boy waited for hours outside the door. His dream of returning with a purse full of coins faded. He finally fell asleep on the doorstep, his arms and head resting on his knees. Hours later, noisy firecrackers greeting the first light of New Year's Day woke him.

He shuffled home with downcast eyes. His grandmother asked him, "How much did you collect?"

"Nothing," he mumbled.

"Did you ask them?"

"Yes."

"Do you still want to be a merchant?"

"No."

She explained the only route to success was to study and take the examinations. She hired a tutor, and Ling Fupeng turned to his studies with new determination. Amy told me with delight, "The grandmothers knew how to get something."

Her story follows a cultural convention established by the legend of how Mencius's mother guided him, in the fourth century BCE, toward becoming a renowned philosopher. They first lived near a cemetery, and the young Mencius learned to act out scenes witnessed at the tombs. His mother moved them to a house in a marketplace, and Mencius began to imitate the salesmen. Finally, she found a new house next to a school, and her son became enamored with the scholars' manners. "This," she said, "is the proper place for my son." When he left school early one day, she took her knife and slashed the finished cloth on her loom. She instructed him, "Your neglecting your studies is very like my cutting the cloth."[12]

Attesting to the similar influence of a powerful woman in her family's history, Amy concluded, "My father said I look exactly like his grandmother. I never had the chance to meet her, but that's the story. My father said his success was all due to her."

This version of family history, when I told it to Shuhua's daughter, surprised her. The story she had heard from her mother roamed far from the peanut farm of Amy's account. According to Shuhua, the grandfather of Ling Fupeng and father of the maritime inventor Ling Zhaogeng was a pirate who sailed the South China Sea near Portuguese-held Macao. In a raid on a foreign ship, he snatched a girl from the deck and brought her into his household as a wife. His family called her *huangmao tai*, "yellow-haired wife." After her arrival, their fortunes began to rise, so they believed she had brought them luck and treated her well. Ling Fupeng's decision to compete in the exams instead of becoming a merchant disappointed his family. However, his grandmother assured his success by sewing gold ingots into the pillow he took north with him when he went to sit for the imperial examinations. In Shuhua's portrait, the grandmother was no peanut matriarch but rather a talismanic Spanish or Portuguese woman.

My grandmother frequently recounted visiting the Confucius Temple as a child. She and her siblings wandered through rows of carved stone steles, one for each year of examinations, searching for their father's name. When they finally arrived at the right stele, they touched the three vertically stacked characters of their father's name, evidence of his achievement and chance of being remembered by history. They read aloud the accompanying place name, identifying him as a scholar from Panyu, Guangdong.

My grandmother told me, "His name was carved in the Confucius Temple, in Beijing. If you ever go to Beijing, go to see that temple. When we were kids, we would go see his name. We were so proud. We'd go home and say, 'We saw your name.' So, that's a record. I don't think the Communists got rid of that. If they're short on space, they may get rid of that, too. I don't think they destroy history though."

The first time I visited the Confucius Temple, I rode there on a bicycle, a sturdy Flying Pigeon rented for a daily rate to tourists. Bundled in layers of winter clothes, I pedaled from the south of the city to the north, through the bicycle traffic of Dongsi Street. The other tourist spot in Beijing near the Confucius Temple is the Yonghegong Lama Temple, and I remember first drifting through its well-kept presentation of Tibetan Buddhism. Its glittering buildings, painted in rich hues of blue, red, and yellow, delayed the possibility of disappointment, and it was late in the day when I entered the neighboring temple-turned-museum, drab in comparison, of the old imperial order.

After stepping over the high wooden doorframe of the front gate into the first courtyard of the walled compound, I was immediately confronted with the rows of stone slabs. They seemed neglected, not as immense or magnificent as I had imagined. The graduate student with whom I was staying had written her master's thesis on my great-aunt Ling Shuhua and provided me with a rough diagram of how to find Ling Fupeng's stele. I pulled it from my backpack as I walked through the rows. I wandered, lost, trying to match characters on the paper to faintly legible tracings on the stones. An elderly man, wearing black pants and a high-collared jacket buttoned over the bulge of a sweater, emerged from an office. Noticing my bewildered assessment of the stones, he tugged the brim of a black cap over his cropped gray hair and approached me. A white badge identified him as part of the Confucius Temple work unit. He spoke a little English, and between his English and my broken Chinese, I managed to convey what I was looking for. He took my diagram in his bent fingers and led me to a row of steles not far from the office building. Carefully pacing down the row, he stopped in front of a stele with a thick horizontal crack running below its decorative headpiece.

In the late afternoon light, he couldn't find Ling Fupeng's name but assured me he had found the right year. As he stood there beaming, more proud of the discovery than I felt, I had to take his word for it. I couldn't spend much time contemplating what the possibility of a name carved in stone meant because the sun was setting. I took a couple of pictures, which later came out blurry and underexposed, and said goodbye to the helpful old man.

Several years passed before I visited the Confucius Temple again. In 1994, I had been living in Beijing for over a year, working as an English teacher in the industrial suburbs west of the city. My Chinese skills had improved, and I could recognize the characters of Ling Fupeng's name. When I arrived at the temple, I remembered the general vicinity of the stele and the year Ling Fupeng had entered the Hanlin Academy. I had forgotten about the identifying crack. As I roamed through the rows, I got lost again. The year 1895, according to the Western calendar, was not much help as I read the years carved into the steles according to the years of various emperors' reigns. Giving up the already half-hearted search, I walked around the dusty grounds with the other tourists, Chinese and foreign, touching instead the twisted trunks of almost leafless old scholar trees.

In the summer of 1997, six and a half years after my first trip to China, I returned with yet better Chinese and a roll of black and white film in my camera to take pictures of my great-grandfather's stele. I hoped to take a focused, well-lit photograph, to prove to my grandmother that her father's name remained. In the intervening years, Beijing's tourist trade had picked up, and the quiet, shady street where Confucius Temple lies now boasted a string of gaudy storefronts offering Buddhist statuary (complete with glowing pink electric lotus blossoms), icons, prayer beads, and incense to passersby on their way to the Lama Temple. In the afternoon heat of August, I stepped through the familiar front gate. Improvements had been made since my last visit. I handed the attendant a glossy color ticket and made note of the large brass plates bearing explanations of the imperial examinations. Bamboo scaffolding covered with yards of coarsely woven plastic cloth cordoned off a section of the steles. The jarring sound of a metal drill bit on stone stuttered from the makeshift construction site.

This third time, knowing that 1895 translates as the twenty-first year of Emperor Guangxu's reign, I found the stele with the long crack near the top by myself. I knew I had the right year, but as I searched for Ling Fupeng's name, I realized that the wear of time and weather had wiped the stone almost clean. I squinted at the gravelly surface, but only a few characters remained distinguishable. A huge flat piece of the stone's face, a planar expanse similar in shape to the map of China, had chipped and fallen away. I compared my great-grandfather's stone tablet with others nearby and found that the surface of some had been recarved with neat rows of characters, freshly etched in white dust. The process of restoration appeared less than systematic, and it occurred to me that donations given by families descended from *jinshi* must have paid for the touch-up job. While I stood under the shade of the old trees, taking pictures of the stone that had eluded me once again, a horsefly stung me. I tried to muster some feeling of filial reverence. Instead, I left scratching at the hot patch of raised flesh near my shoulder, turning my back on the one fact of my story that held the promise of being set in stone.

When I showed my grandmother the photographs I took that day, she grew excited. "Yes, that's it," she exclaimed, but as she peered more closely at the image, she added, "That stone used to be on top of a turtle, on the back of a big, stone turtle." The turtle, symbol of longevity and stability, no longer holds up her father's name, and the thick crack running through the stele suggests an attempt to destroy the past it represents.

· Three ·

Disappointment

$\int$huhua and Amy's mother, Li Ruolan, was born to a poor scholar and a farmwoman, who gave her a name meaning "like an orchid." My grandmother spoke of her in sparse detail, but Li Ruolan comes to life in a chapter of Shuhua's autobiography titled "My Mother's Marriage." At the age of sixteen, she helps display treasured paintings to a distinguished scholar. Her fingers, as she unrolls the scrolls, open and close like white orchid petals, captivating the family's guest.

The time is the late 1890s, and the place is Guangzhou, the home of the wealthy Pan family, who built their fortune by shipping tea, silk, ivory, porcelain, fur, feathers, oil, drugs, toys, and perfume to the West. Their ships then brought back clocks and watches, steel, iron tools, headache powders, and woolen cloth to sell in the shops they owned in Guangzhou. The Pans lived in a large residence and had paid a handsome sum for a famous calligrapher to write several elegant characters for the sign over their front door. The door opened onto a carved wooden screen, in front of which a porcelain vase displayed seasonal flowers: peonies in spring, lotus in summer, chrysanthemums in autumn, and plum blossom or pine branches in winter.

The girl with orchid in her name was not born into this family. Her parents lived in a village west of Guangzhou called Sanshui, meaning "three waters," where a confluence of rivers flowed into the Pearl River. Her father carried the family name Li from his father, who had become a *juren* after passing the provincial exam. Ruolan's grandfather chose, however, to remain in his native village, close to his elderly parents. When he died, he left only a reputation of filial behavior and a book collection, but Ruolan's father married the daughter of a prosperous farmer who had admired the old scholar Li. Her dowry provided a few hundred acres of rice fields. A capable wife, she hired workers and managed the farm, so her husband could pursue the quiet lifestyle of a scholar. They had a son and two daughters. Ruolan, the youngest, was her father's favorite. When a cousin invited him to a birthday celebration in Guangzhou, he took the four-year-old to show her off. After a seafood banquet and many toasts to long life, the tipsy revelers decided to stroll along the harbor. Strings of lights illuminated the ships for some unknown foreign holiday. Ruolan jostled through the crowd, drawn by the twinkling lights reflected in the water. She reached for her father's hand but found only strangers surrounding her. As she frantically turned around, an old woman snatched her up and ran quickly down a dark alley.

When her father discovered her missing, he ran panic-stricken through the streets, searching the face of every child who crossed his path. Neither he nor his relative could find Ruolan. On the third day of looking, he collapsed from exhaustion, and his cousin sent him back to Sanshui in a cart. "My Mother's Marriage" recounts his death of a broken heart a year later.

Ruolan had fallen into the hands of a child slave peddler. The old woman sold the pretty young girl for a healthy sum, not as a slave or future courtesan but as companion to a childless young widow. Madame Pan's husband had been the first son of the wealthy merchant family. When he died not long after their marriage, her father-in-law discovered she was literate and astute at accounting. She helped him run the family's affairs, until she fell ill from the pressure. Hoping to lighten her loneliness and fatigue, her father-in-law bought Ruolan to accompany her. Delighted with the little girl, Madame Pan treated her like a daughter and educated her in reading and writing. Every morning, the little girl attended lessons with a tutor.

Ruolan's birth mother, after months of continued searching and futile inquiries, finally heard about her daughter's new life with the Pan family. She arrived at their front door and appealed to Madame Pan to let Ruolan return home. Madame Pan put the choice to the little girl, who could no longer remember much of her former life, and Ruolan asked to stay in Guangzhou. The two women arranged that her mother would come to visit her at the Pans, and that together they would make future decisions about her life. In the absence of a father figure, they agreed that when the time came, their daughter would have the right to pick her own husband.

Shuhua recounts this story as biographical fact, but it reads like a fairy tale. Ruolan grew into a beautiful young woman who attracted numerous suitors. Madame Pan instructed their gatekeeper to turn away all matchmakers. Her mother-in-law, however, received a visit one day from a nephew smitten with Ruolan. As a young man, he had gone to San Francisco, where he started a successful business, and recently returned home as a "sudden rich" to find a wife. Many families courted him for their daughters, but he had his eye on Ruolan. The older Madame Pan excitedly brought her nephew's proposal to her daughter-in-law. The younger Madame Pan replied, to the old woman's horror, that she had to consult Ruolan before any decision could be made. When Ruolan heard the news, she sobbed at the prospect of being carried off to a foreign country. Encouraged by her birth mother to take pride in her scholarly grandfather Li, she declared she would not marry a man who could only read half a page of Chinese characters. Gossip about her refusal spread, and the older Madame Pan snidely remarked to her relatives, "I suppose I shall live to see Ruolan married to a Prime Minister or a Cabinet Minister."[1]

The following spring, orchids, peonies, and narcissus bloomed in the garden as old Mr. Pan prepared to receive a distinguished guest. The visitor, the calligrapher whose characters graced the sign over the family's front door, had taken leave from official duties in the capital to visit his parents' grave in the south. He refused dinner invitations from other local families but accepted the Pans' offer because the father of Ruolan's foster mother had once been his tutor. He'd also heard that Mr. Pan owned a sizeable collection of work by the artist Xie Lipu. After dinner, Ruolan was called to help with the valuable scrolls. She entered the room in a powder blue silk coat and black satin trousers. As her fingers nimbly unrolled the scrolls painted by the visitor's great-grandfather, he found himself more entranced with the girl than the paintings.

A few days later an elderly female cousin of old Mr. Pan arrived with a marriage proposal from the high-ranking guest, Ling Fupeng. She explained that he was already married to her niece from the Feng family, but she suffered from tuberculosis and, according to doctors, would not live long. Ling's ailing wife herself then called upon the Pans, bringing a personal guarantee to treat Ruolan well and four cases of expensive food as gifts. The woman's sincerity touched Madame Pan. She convinced herself that Ruolan's position as a concubine would be softened by having a prominent scholar, with a kind wife, for a husband. The student-tutor bond between Ling and her father made the match seem even more desirable. She discussed these advantages with Ruolan, and they decided to accept. Ling's wife sent four more cases of presents, this time containing jewelry and rolls of silk and brocade. In exchange, Madame Pan sent a man's hat, boots, and robe and a set of scholarly implements—fine brushes, a carved wooden brush stand, and a heavy inkstone. She brought in dressmakers to tailor new clothes for her foster daughter. Although she'd been consulted in the decision, Ruolan wept at the thought of entering a stranger's home. Three days later, the girl and her chests of wedding gifts set sail with the Lings for Beijing.

If Shuhua's account ended here, one might assume the heroine lived happily ever after. However, "My Mother's Marriage" comes to a swift, unexpected end. In the final paragraphs, as throughout the story, Shuhua refers to her father as Mr. Ding and his first wife as Madame Ding. Ju-lan is an earlier form of romanization for Ruolan (such discrepancies are common in translations from Chinese), but why did she write "Ding" when she used "Ling" in English as her surname? This slight change of an initial consonant suggests a subtle acknowledgment of the small, but purposeful, inconsistencies she makes in names and facts throughout *Ancient Melodies*, a hint that it shouldn't be taken for its autobiographical word.

> A journey from Canton to Peking took about a month in those days. On the day after their arrival a young woman with a little girl came to see Madame Ding, and told her that she was her husband's concubine; the little girl was his daughter. She had decided to come and live in the house. Madame Ding knew that her husband had a concubine living outside, but she did not expect that she would decide to come to live with her. In those days it was not seemly for a wife to refuse to let her husband's concubine join the family; a virtuous woman ought to be broad-minded in this matter. Madame Ding did not know what to do; she had to let the young woman move into the house.
>
> Now, Ju-lan could not see any romance in living in a house with a man who had three wives. Besides, the young woman said that as the second madame died before she came to join the family, she ought to be called the Third Madame, and as Ju-lan came after her, she ought to be the Fourth.
>
> Ju-lan was greatly disappointed, and Madame Ding was very sorry to see all this happen. She apologized to Ju-lan and said often: "I am sure the heavenly gods will have mercy on us; they will let you have a son."
>
> Madame Ding died the next year before seeing the arrival of Ju-lan's first daughter. Ju-lan thought it was one of the gods' mercies that Madame Ding had not lived to be disappointed of the hoped-for son.[2]

With this unraveling denouement, Shuhua sketches a fuller picture of the family before Ruolan entered it only to discover how she had been duped. In addition to Ling Fupeng's tubercular first wife, a second had already passed away and an outside concubine came to join the family, demanding she be called Third Madame. Ruolan found herself pushed to the lowest rank.

The story presents a fairly typical picture of elite Qing family relations. A man began his married life while still a student struggling to achieve official position, a process that required long periods away from home. His first wife remained responsible for maintaining the household and preserving family virtue. While traveling, it was expected that he would seek relations with other women, often of a different social class, who then might join the family as concubines, particularly if no sons had yet been born to carry on the family line.

Amy never tired of telling how her father rose through the examination system. She repeated the story regularly, relishing each time it turned to the peanut matriarch. Yet, of her mother, she uttered only the most generic praise, even or especially when questioned for more detail. She said she was a kind woman. She was a generous woman. She dispensed free tea in the *hutong* outside their house in Beijing. When I asked about the circumstances of her parents' marriage, Amy tersely stated she would never have dared inquire about such a private matter. Without Shuhua's story, Li Ruolan would be little more than the distant woman in the fake ancestor portrait or the image of a woman wearing a fur-lined silk robe in the pair of photographs my grandmother kept of her parents. Amy celebrated the story of their father's achievement and his grandmother's intelligence, but Shuhua seemed more drawn to the story of their mother's disappointment. This divergence on what warrants public record added to the tension that held the sisters together.

After years of compliance to the warning issued by Shuhua's daughter, I finally mentioned *Ancient Melodies* to my grandmother. Rather than responding with the anger I expected, she said she'd never read the book. She claimed to know only what others said about it. Her expression, however, beneath her face powder and penciled eyebrows, tightened as she reflected upon her sister's writing career. She had read some of Shuhua's stories in Chinese but disliked them because of the negative depiction of mothers. Incensed by the memory of fiction that read like thinly disguised autobiography, she explained

Ling Fupeng and Li Ruolan, Beijing, ca. 1900

her sister's compulsion to write this way by casting the relationship between Shuhua and their mother as an antagonistic one. Even though Shuhua claimed in *Ancient Melodies* to be the youngest child, Amy really was. She said her parents spoiled her as the baby of the family, arousing her older sister Shuhua's jealousy. She accused Shuhua of devising plots to win their father's confidence by tattling on their mother. When Ruolan went to do the household shopping, Shuhua would tell their father that she was gambling with friends at the mahjong table. Amy ended her attack on Shuhua's uncomplimentary depictions of their mother with an overblown defense. She described how Li Ruolan helped foster government orphanages and donated a large portion of her mahjong winnings to the Chinese Red Cross. Amy announced the end of our discussion on the topic by asserting, "Everyone in Beijing loved her. You can't say that about many people!"

I don't believe that Amy knew nothing about her mother's youth and marriage when her sister seemed to have known so much. Her silence on the topic propped up her insistence on one mother, one father. May Fourth–era criticism of traditional marriage practices combined with assimilated U.S. social norms led her to conceal the position of their mother as a concubine. Although I have never heard her budge on this point, she once told my father another story altogether, in which Ruolan was a courtesan. At the age of ninety-eight, she sat alone with him at the dinner table. She described the elaborately painted boat on which her mother had worked as a young woman. Her father came on aboard and pointed to the most beautiful girl. "I want that one," he said, and Li Ruolan left with him.

An interview Ling Shuhua gave in 1986 to a Taiwanese researcher suggests the two sisters had conversations about how to suppress this information, which Amy considered highly sensitive. In a question related to a story called "A Happy Event" about a new concubine entering a household—a story that also ended up directly translated into her autobiography *Ancient Melodies*—the interviewer asked if the main character, a girl named Feng'er, wasn't really the author herself. Shuhua answered, "Feng'er is half me, and the five wives in the story were really four wives. Due to the fact that my sister Shuhao was a doctor in the United States, we didn't want to let foreigners know the real facts of the old-style Chinese family system of wives, so we changed my mother's rank. My father had four wives in total, and my mother was the third."[3] So, did Ling Fupeng have six wives as "A Happy Event" and the "Note" in *Ancient Melodies* indicate, five wives as Shuhua told her own daughter, or four wives as she described in this interview? Her playing with the numbers might have prevented Chinese audiences from making direct links between her stories and personal life. But the addition of two extra concubines would have only made their family seem more bizarre to foreign readers, the cause of Amy's worries once the stories appeared in English. Nonetheless, biographical accounts of Ling Shuhua in Chinese literary sources now all rely upon *Ancient Melodies* for their information and number her father's wives at six, placing Shuhua as the daughter of the fourth.

Just as I don't believe Amy's feigned naïveté, I also doubt "My Mother's Marriage." It is generic like the "yellow-hair wife" story in mythic proportion, with its hard-luck filial scholar, father dead from a broken heart, wicked child slave peddler, magical adoption into benevolent wealth, and fair maiden blossoming like her namesake flower before a distinguished suitor. Both of the sisters' treatments lead me to suspect a more difficult truth exists. Did Ruolan really come from such a doubly illustrious background, combined offspring of the scholarly Li family and the prosperous merchant Pans? Is it possible she was sold instead to a brothel, as the story Amy told my father suggests, where Ling favored her among the other courtesans? In a short biographical account of Ling Shuhua, Chinese literary scholar Chen Xueyong writes that her maternal grandfather's gambling debts forced him to sell Ruolan to the Pans.[4] Perhaps she was sold as a maid, who was later sold again by the Pans as a concubine? Increased social mobility, which blurred lines between the respectable and servant classes, became a hallmark of the Qing dynasty. Women especially found themselves susceptible to becoming saleable property for families fallen upon hard times, but just as respectable women faced the threat of descending into slavery, so might lower-class women ascend through marriage as a concubine. And precisely because of this split understanding of women as stabilizing moral mothers and chaste wives on the domestic front but sexually available for men on the road, the virtue of women in the inner chambers of home had to be firmly protected.[5]

I grasp after the inner world of the real Ruolan but come up empty-handed. There are only two objective facts I can stand behind: she was Cantonese and one of several concubines to Ling Fupeng.

Literary critic Rey Chow has interpreted several of Shuhua's stories about traditional Chinese women as narratives of "virtuous transaction."[6] The woman enters a transaction with patriarchal society when she follows the "virtuous" role ascribed to her, but rather than finding her desires fulfilled, she discovers them crushed. She becomes a victim of her own efforts. "My Mother's Marriage" follows the pattern: Ruolan, exercising the rare freedom to choose her own husband, rejects the "sudden rich" suitor and marries the distinguished scholar, only to find herself in the ignoble position of Fourth Madame. Rather than using her talent to besmirch her mother's reputation, as Amy would claim, Shuhua wrote about the absurdity of a system in which women, exchanged in a commotion of jewelry and silk, found themselves trapped by socially conditioned aspirations. She drew upon their mother's life

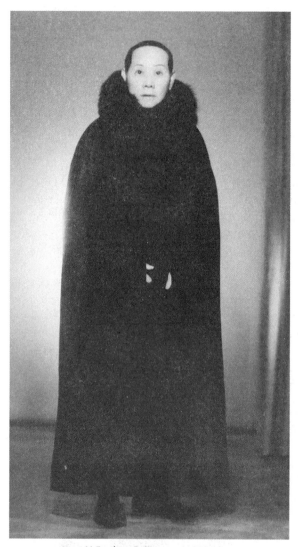

Li Ruolan, Beijing, ca. 1930s

to write about the frustration of women in old-style households, just as Amy's shame about their mother's origin led her to construct a bright facade over the past.

My imagination raced the first time I saw a solitary photograph of Ruolan. I don't know why Amy decided, after so long, to bring it out of the drawer or box where it had been stored. It stood for a while on the small table next to the couch where she kept her magnifying glass for reading. It then vanished until I noticed it later on top of her dresser. It is a small, black-and-white studio photograph of her mother displayed in a simple gold frame. Her hair has been pulled back tightly from a plucked brow. She is wrapped in a dark floor-length cape with a fur collar fastened at the neck. Three fingers peek out from the somber triangle. Her theatrical gaze is fixed, powerful, and unsettling in the intimacy of my grandmother's bedroom.

While privy to a shared past, the sisters shaped it to their personal inclinations. The two proceed from entirely different principles. One framed the story of Ruolan in the conventional, authoritative language of the biography of an exemplary woman: virtue looks like this. The other plotted the disclosure of subjective experience: deception feels like this. The sisters originated, so to speak, from the same place. They both tried to protect their mother from humiliation, by proving that the daughters of a woman with no sons could succeed in a changing world.

· *Four* ·

Courtyards

A length of paper lay next to a porcelain jar of brushes on a red lacquer table. The room's paper windows were painted with lilacs and wisteria. Li Ruolan sang a ballad, seven characters to a line, from one of the Cantonese songbooks strewn throughout her room. In the song, a sixteen-year-old girl lays down her brush. She remembers her maid's description of a beautiful garden behind the family home. She impulsively calls the maid and asks the way to the secret garden. Finding its hidden entrance, she wanders down shaded paths lined with flowers. When she returns to her room, she falls asleep and dreams of meeting a young scholar in the garden's peony pavilion. The man embraces her, until suddenly she awakes from the joys of cloud and rain to find herself alone. Obsessed with her vision, she slowly wastes away in the seclusion of her chamber.

Li Ruolan sang while stroking the fur of a cat asleep by her side. The ballads provided an escape from the complex relations of the large household in which she'd become enmeshed. In her first years in Beijing, she gave birth to one daughter after another, Shuzhi, Shuping, and then Shuhua. According to Shuhua's account in *Ancient Melodies*, her birth brought disappointment. When Ruolan went into labor, she quietly sent their gatekeeper to fetch the midwife, an old woman who delivered a daughter on March 25, 1900. Ruolan cried to her maid, "Don't tell people about the baby coming, that will only make them say she's got one more."[1] Three days later, the midwife reappeared to announce the third-day ceremony. Family members gathered to see the baby being bathed and threw money into the basin. The midwife collected the coins for her fee and left the young woman alone with her squalling baby. Around this time, Ling Fupeng brought another concubine, Fifth Mother, into the family.

Beyond the walls containing these domestic dramas, political tensions in the capital intensified as foreign powers stepped up commercial and territorial demands. With their expanding influence in treaty ports along China's eastern seaboard, the influx of Christian missionaries accelerated. In response, the antimissionary movement of the Boxers United in Righteousness burst out in Shandong province; their recruits included peasants, artisans, and itinerants from poverty-stricken areas plagued by flooding, drought, and political instability. These populist troops of rebellion forged a military philosophy from various tenets of local folk religions and Chinese martial arts. In the first months of 1900, Boxer troops spread throughout Zhili, a geographic area consisting of modern Hebei province and the municipalities of Beijing and Tianjin, looting and burning missionary establishments and killing Chinese Christians. They aimed to oust all foreigners from China.[2]

At first the Qing government reacted ambivalently to the Boxers' activities, alternately offering protection to foreigners and support to the Boxers for their display of loyalty to the dynasty. In early June, groups of their ragtag militia in red or yellow turbans, sashes, and leggings began appearing in Beijing and the nearby coastal city of Tianjin, where they attacked the foreign legations. On June 21, Empress Dowager Cixi officially recognized the Boxers and issued a declaration of war against the foreign powers, which had recently commandeered a Qing fort in preparation for military conflict. A joint force of soldiers from Japan, Russia, Britain, the United States, and France swiftly and brutally retaliated with gunboats and relief troops funneled from Tianjin into Beijing. By the end of the summer, they had defeated the Boxers, taken control of Beijing and Tianjin, and driven the Qing court into exile.

The Ling household suffered disruptions due to Ling Fupeng's connection with the imperial government. In *Ancient Melodies*, Shuhua writes that in the conflict Ruolan lost all her wedding gifts, the pearl and jade earrings, bracelets, and hair ornaments sent to her by her husband's first wife. Ling Fupeng joined other officials in the effort to settle the terms of a peace treaty. In the Boxer Protocol, eventually signed in September 1901, the Qing government conceded to the foreign powers an indemnity payment four times that of Beijing's annual budget. This sum, amounting to $333 million at the exchange rates of the day, to be paid in gold with interest over the years, further strained China's domestic economy.

During these upheavals, twenty-four-year-old Ruolan discovered she would have another child. In the spring of 1901, five months into the pregnancy, she miscarried a baby boy. Despondent, she did not get out of bed for three months. Of all the adults in the family, only Fifth Mother, who had no children of her own, regularly sat with her and helped look after her three young daughters. When Ruolan finally rose from her bed, she declared, "Even a brave hero or a strong man cannot overcome his fate."[3] Through Shuhua's literary usurpation of Amy's position as the youngest child, her birth became her mother's tragedy. However, Ruolan's fate as a mother of daughters was actually sealed several years later in Panyu, where Ling's concubines and children retreated for several years. She gave birth to Shuhao, her fourth and final daughter, in the Ling family's hometown on September 10, 1904.

> *Ling Fupeng:* courtesy name Runtai, sixty-three years old, Panyu, Guangdong, *jinshi* in the second-to-last civil service exam held by Emperor Guangxu, Administrative Official in the Ministry of Finance, Prefectural Magistrate for the Defense Administrative System of Beijing and Tianjin, Prefectural Magistrate of Baoding, Director of Salt and Hemp Distribution in Tianjin, Governor-General of Zhili under imperial rule, Assistant Chairman of the new political congress, Assemblyman in the provisional constitution meetings and participatory government.[4]

I discovered this biography in a 1922 copy of *Assembled Biographies of Recent Officials and Gentry*, a thin volume covered in frayed blue silk. Ling Fupeng's entry warrants three vertical lines of text in the classical style devoid of punctuation. My translation of those dense lines reveals an undated list of the various posts he held. I have tried to produce a chronology that corresponds to national history and his daughters' stories, but I can only conjecture when he was where, doing what, and how his official activities affected the lives of his wives and children. I have found it difficult to understand what political beliefs he held, wedged as his career was between imperial rule and modern reform. He hovered in the margins of more influential men's lives. Governed more by pragmatism than strong conviction, he maintained alliances with politicians and painters of various stripes.

Shuhua described him as a tall man with broad shoulders and a long, distinguished face. On ordinary days he wore a favorite blue gown and black satin cap topped with a tiny red ball. When Amy characterized their father, she lowered her voice, emphasizing certain words with a throaty rumble: "He was a very *powerful* man. When he said no, it meant *no*. He was six feet high, *big*. I don't know how much he weighed. He was very *heavy*."

As the Qing dynasty faltered under foreign pressure and Chinese calls for reform or revolution, Ling Fupeng's politics followed those of other *jinshi* who continued to support the old system but also saw the need for change. In 1898, his Cantonese peer Kang Youwei had advocated a constitutional monarchy modeled after the Japanese joint imperial and parliamentary structure, headed by Emperor Guangxu. Shuhua recalled, in an interview, that Kang Youwei visited their Beijing house during her childhood. She once mischievously asked him to write a few characters for her in his famous calligraphy. He asked her how big she wanted the characters, and she replied, "As big as you can write!"[5] This encounter suggests that Ling remained on friendly terms with his fellow scholar.

The places and positions listed in Ling Fupeng's biography indicate that following the Boxer conflict he became a member of the northern Zhili clique headed by Yuan Shikai. After Empress Dowager Cixi had suppressed her nephew Guangxu's support for Kang Youwei's reform movement, Yuan became closely allied with her. As governor-general of Zhili, he emerged as one of the two strongest provincial leaders in the early years of the twentieth century. Yuan pushed his own set of reforms in response to the regional disorder wrought by the Boxer Rebellion. He focused on strengthening urban centers and, borrowing from Western and Japanese models, created modern schools, police, and prisons. Under his command, the Beiyang Army in the north developed into an efficient military unit with officer-training schools, foreign instructors, and state-of-the-art weaponry.[6]

Under Yuan Shikai, Ling Fupeng held a variety of positions in Zhili's main cities. In Baoding, Ling Fupeng was likely involved in building up the city's police and military academies, established in 1902 and 1904. Both employed Japanese instructors to teach modern surveillance and warfare methods. As prefect or mayor of Tianjin, Ling supervised reform of the criminal justice system. In conjunction with Yuan's push to develop a model prison system, Ling Fupeng was dispatched in April 1903 on a study mission to Japan, where he investigated prison facilities in five cities, including Tokyo and Osaka. On the basis of Ling Fupeng's report, the Tianjin police chief and other local officials pushed for a new kind of prison to replace Chinese jails, which were cramped, filthy, and rampant with abuse. The stone and iron fortress of Tokyo Prison—with its long corridors of cells radiating out from central watchtowers, glass windows, running water, and electricity— influenced their plans. They envisioned a modern facility, located outside the city limits, capable of housing five hundred or more inmates, and outfitted with medical and recreational facilities. Completion of the prison compound took three years, but an attached *xiyi suo* or workhouse opened in July 1904. Those convicted of misdemeanors worked off their sentences while learning a trade.[7]

In China, as in other countries where rule by a king or emperor gave way to modern institutions of nation-state governance, prison sentences gradually replaced banishment or bodily punishment. Prisons in China based on Western models, often imported via Japan, became a modern symbol of national prestige, while simultaneously drawing upon traditional Confucian beliefs in the transformative power of moral education. Revisions to the Boxer Protocol pushed late Qing officials to adopt such changes; the United States, Britain, and Japan had agreed to consider relinquishing extraterritorial rights in China if the Qing government instituted certain legal reforms, including the abolition of corporal punishment and development of a modern prison system.[8]

In 1905, Ling took another investigative trip to Japan to examine prison regulations, facilities, training methods, and financing. The proposal he submitted after this study mission included recommendations for training prison personnel, improving prison buildings, and expanding *xiyi suo* facilities. The rehabilitative workhouse system, adopted directly from Japan, had been publicized as one of the Zhili prison program's great successes. Similar facilities soon appeared in cities throughout the province. In an attempt to clear city streets of beggars, petty thieves, and derelicts, Ling Fupeng and his colleagues set up vagrant workhouses, free meal stations, and poorhouses. Between 1904 and 1908, they established twenty-five *xiyi suo* throughout the province to train "apprentices" in weaving, dyeing, and the manufacture of baskets, clothes, hats, and shoes.

In 1907, the Qing government recalled Yuan Shikai to Beijing, making him a grand councilor. This move reinforced their authority and curtailed the growth of Yuan's power by disrupting communication between him and his troops. Around this time Ling Fupeng also moved to Beijing, perhaps in alliance with the former governor-general. Ling continued to travel between Beijing, Tianjin, and Baoding for many years, but after his appointment as prefect or mayor of Beijing, he finally summoned his family back from Panyu to the capital. This reassembled household provides the setting for the sisters' most recurrent childhood stories.

They lived to the east of the Forbidden City, in a quiet residential area with wide tree-shaded lanes. Their front gate opened onto Ganmian Hutong, Dried Noodle Lane. Four connected courtyards extended north, one after another, to a back entrance on Shijia Hutong or Historian Lane. Long rooms with covered walkways in front lined the four sides of each courtyard. Carved wooden balustrades and eaves painted on the underside with flowers and opera scenes decorated the outdoor corridors. Date, persimmon, and pine trees grew in the courtyards. The southernmost courtyard housed the austerely furnished rooms used by Ling Fupeng to receive visitors and conduct official business. Since his first wife and concubine had already died, Third Mother held the most senior position among the remaining concubines. She lived with her son, the only boy in the family, and three daughters in the second courtyard. Shuhua, Amy, and their two older sisters lived in the third courtyard with Ruolan and childless Fifth Mother. The fourth courtyard contained their father's private quarters and book-filled study. Ling's private secretary, gatekeeper, tailor, servants, and their families also lived with them. A small gate in each courtyard opened onto a path that ran up the east side of the compound to the kitchen, the servants' quarters, and a large garden in back. A gardener tended its trees, grapevines, flowerbeds, bamboo grove, and rocks creating artificial mountains. Here the children played, collected insects, ate the fruits of summer and autumn, and stood still on the rocks in winter before a photographer's camera.

Ling Shuhua opens *Ancient Melodies* with her impression of the residence: "No one can now tell me how many rooms or courtyards it really contained, but I remember little children often lost their way when they walked out alone from their own courtyard. I always failed to find out exactly how many people lived in that house, because the births and deaths of my half-sisters and brothers and the number of new and old servants were never certain."[9] As a writer, Shuhua uses this house as a stage, first for her fiction and, in later years, for dramas from her childhood. That it should appear quaint or delightful on its surface is part of its ruse.

Critics of Ling Shuhua's Chinese short stories have praised her evocation of life in *jiu jiating*, old-fashioned elite households, and criticized the traditional, and hence antirevolutionary, nature of such subject matter. A

"Our House in Beijing," Ling Shuhua, illustration for Ancient Melodies, *1952. Courtesy of Chen Xiaoying.*

1928 review of her first collection of stories characterizes its world as one of "madams, young ladies, administrators, female students, and young and old masters, which touches upon youths whose lives have been corrupted."[10] In these stories, she writes in the third person, but with an intimacy that reveals troubled emotions below the surface. She experimented with literary forms of psychological realism, which were entering the Chinese canon through translations of Western fiction, to explore the position of women in families that, if charming on the outside, were rotting from within.

"The Lucky One," first published in a 1926 issue of the literary and political journal *Contemporary Review*, presents one version of a *jiu jiating*. Acquaintances of the story's main character, Old Mistress Zhang, all proclaim her "Number One" in good fortune. At the age of sixty-nine, she has successfully married off four sons and seen the birth of eight grandsons. The pregnancy of her eldest grandson's wife provides the promise of a great-grandson. Her three married daughters live in other towns with their husbands' families. She can't keep the number of their children straight. Since she never learned to read, she relies upon her husband to tell her what their letters say.

Old Mistress Zhang's husband respects her judgment to such a degree that he has given her control of the family income. Her children and grandchildren desire her opinion, heed her advice, and strive to outdo one another in caring for her. As a confident first wife, she exhibited no anger when her husband married each of his two concubines, stating that "it was improper for a man to be without two or three wives and that only people of low birth quarreled out of jealousy."[11]

One afternoon, her maid accompanies her to the courtyard where several grandsons lie recovering from measles. When she realizes that she has forgotten to bring snacks purchased for the boys, she sends the maid back and continues strolling alone. She suddenly overhears the voices of her eldest son and his wife coming from a window. They heatedly discuss the division of household property, enumerating the schemes of each son and daughter-in-law to ingratiate themselves with the old woman. When her maid returns, Old Mistress Zhang directs their path past the window. Only when she coughs loudly does the conversation inside stop. Her face remains composed, but her gait falters. The maid cautions, "This courtyard rarely sees the sun, so the ground is covered with lichen. Take it carefully and slowly, Mistress."[12]

Old Mistress Zhang represents the most powerful position a woman in this type of household might achieve. Yet, in Shuhua's story, the machinations of her children abruptly expose the hollowness of her luck. When the facade of the Ling house on Ganmian Hutong crumbles, uglier rivalries are played out in a drama of family disintegration. Several of the chapters in

Ancient Melodies focus on tensions between the concubines, who emerge as more prone to self-pity, tears, and anger than Old Mistress Zhang.

Third Mother was mother to the family's only son. Although Ling Fupeng never granted her the status of wife, she used her position as senior concubine to bully the others. Li Ruolan, resigned to her subordinate fate and adept in survival skills, arbitrated their fights. Emotional Fifth Mother turned bitter when Ling Fupeng praised the beauty of a female prisoner who arrived in his court one day. Shuhua recounts the fallout:

> It was said that when father honestly answered Fifth Mother that the woman prisoner was really pretty, Fifth Mother said something which hurt Father's pride, and he threw a cup of hot tea over her new dress. . . . She ate some opium that night. The whole house was upset; fortunately she was saved by a good doctor. My mother believed this was one of the reasons that Father thought of having another new mistress.[13]

Fifth Mother survived her suicide attempt, but deathly overtones shade the background of *Ancient Melodies*. Shuhua opens her memoir with the tale of an execution and their father's role in it. Although this is one of the few stories by Shuhua that overlaps with a childhood account told by Amy, confirming the impact of the event on their early lives, their versions diverge on significant facts. It must have occurred in 1910 or 1911, the last years of the Qing dynasty, and together the sisters' renditions convey their father's tenuous position as scholar-official turned reformer, caught between the old-fashioned street spectacle of capital punishment and modern criminal science.

In the first chapter of *Ancient Melodies*, titled "Red-Coat Man," Shuhua sits on the shoulders of her father's bodyguard, Ma Tao. As they trotted down the street, he pointed out a large crowd approaching them and told her they were lucky to see a "Red Demonstration." A man wearing a red coat rode by in a horse-drawn wagon. He was singing at the top of his lungs, encouraged by the shouts of the crowd. Shuhua wondered whether he was a famous actor, until Ma Tao explained he was a convicted criminal on his way to the execution ground. Soldiers pushed the man from the wagon and led him to a table with burning incense and candles. People handed him cups of wine, and he sang even louder. Then, guns were fired into the air. Soldiers cracked their whips to drive the crowd back. After the commotion cleared, Shuhua saw the man's body, beheaded, its blood soaking the red coat where it lay in the dust.

In a narrative jump to a trial scene, she connected the execution back to her home on Ganmian Hutong. As mayor, her father served as judge of final appeal in cases from the municipal districts of Beijing. Officers would bring prisoners to the central hall of their front courtyard, where Ling Fupeng waited behind a large table. In Shuhua's description, "The seal of the Mayor as big as a human skull, wrapped in yellow satin, was on the table, and big brushes and an ink slab beside it. Behind Father there stood many soldiers, in black and yellow uniforms with red tassels on their caps. Numbers of minor officers and secretaries sat on either side of Father in their robes, each according to his rank."[14] Ling's wives and children would secretly crowd behind a wooden screen in the hall to listen to the trial.

One day, they heard that a young woman convicted of murdering her mother-in-law would appear in court that afternoon. They rushed to their hiding place behind the screen and watched the guards lead in a striking beauty. In a powerful voice, she addressed Ling Fupeng as Blue Sky Lord and stated her case. She killed her mother-in-law because her mother-in-law had been killing her with exhausting work and abuse. Shuhua explained that her mother would repeat this story years later. Rather than feeling sympathy for the woman's plight, a common one for daughters-in-law, Li Ruolan described her as a foxlike woman who almost tricked their father into postponing her sentence. The prisoner's lament, however, did not sway Ling's secretaries, and she met the same fate as the Red-Coat Man. Fifth Mother's fight with Ling Fupeng over his appreciation of the prisoner's beauty then provoked him to bring another concubine into the household. By airing her grievances publicly, much as the female prisoner had, Fifth Mother engineered her own downfall.

In Amy's account, the case revolved around a murder mystery that enthralled Beijing when she was six years old. Newspaper headlines announced that a body had been found. The dead man had been involved in shady dealings, and the police suspected foul play. But his corpse bore no marks indicating the cause of death. After the police came up empty-handed, Ling Fupeng took over the case. Rumors about the mysterious death circulated through the streets, spreading paranoia about an unknown disease or malevolent supernatural forces. During this time, Ling played the role of street detective because he was forced to leave home in disguise. He had just initiated a public works project that included widening major streets. He had become the target of intense hatred from citizens whose houses were subsequently slated for destruction, and several assassination threats had already been delivered to their gatekeeper. Before stepping out of the house, Ling removed his blue robe and changed into patched trousers of coarse canvas and a wide-brimmed straw hat. Dressed as a commoner, he walked the streets mulling over the evidence.

Ling entered a teahouse and sat in a corner with a pot of tea, listening to the conversations of nearby tables. He overheard two men discuss their theories on the murder mystery and strained to catch their words. One of them, pointing to the back of his head, described a vulnerable spot at the base of the skull. It was possible, he said, to stick a long needle through this point into the brain, causing sudden death but leaving only a tiny mark. Ling walked, sweating, to the morgue. He pulled off the straw hat to reveal his face to the attendant and ordered him to shave the dead man's head. Together they examined the base of his skull and found a small needle mark. Ling Fupeng sent police to search the man's house, and they discovered a long needle in his wife's sewing basket. After hours of interrogation, she broke down and confessed. She cursed her husband for beating her and said he deserved to die. Ling Fupeng presided over the woman's case and sentenced her to death.

Amy remembered the case, as well as her desire to witness the execution. At meals, she stole cakes, slipping them into her pocket. She used this stash of sweets to bribe a servant into taking her to the execution. He carried her on his shoulders, and they saw the woman paraded through the streets with her head locked in a wooden cangue. The crowd cursed and spat at her. Guards led her to a shallow pit surrounded by police, who removed the cangue from her neck and pushed her into a kneeling position. The executioner wiped his hands on a bloodstained leather apron. With one swift blow of his heavy sword, her head fell into the pit.

Amy recalled blood pouring onto the ground and then tears on her cheeks, "I cried all night. I just thought of all that blood and couldn't sleep." I told her that Shuhua had described a similar event in one of her stories and asked her if her sister had gone with her. She looked at me incredulously and replied, "No. The artist sister never wanted to see anything like that. Only me. The artist sister, she always stayed at home."

One sister described the execution of a man singing to a crowd in the face of death, the other a disgraced woman covered in spittle. Both told of trials with defiant female defendants sentenced to death in spite of the abuse that provoked their violent crimes, and of the surprising lack of sympathy their fates elicited. The sisters' reactions differ from my original impulse to write all these women off as victims of traditional Chinese culture. The women they present, while not necessarily more sympathetic, embody both the callous disregard and courage necessary to survive. They learned not to look away when tragedy came calling.

In an ironically titled chapter of *Ancient Melodies,* "A Happy Event," Shuhua recounts how Sixth Mother entered the household after the fight between Father and Fifth Mother over the beautiful prisoner. As a maid braided Shuhua's hair into pigtails, the little girl remembered overhearing the day before that Fifth Mother had begun weeping and refused to eat. She ran into the courtyard to play with the other children and caught a glimpse of Fifth Mother storming toward her room. Suddenly, an explosion of firecrackers drew their attention to Sixth Mother's entrance. Crowding behind the adults, the children whispered, comparing the woman's face to that of a horse or donkey. One of the sisters chimed in, "If she were on the stage, I don't think people would feel she would look fit to be my mother's maid."[15] Too short to get a good look, Shuhua listened intently to the older girls' gossip. When her mother bowed to the new concubine and presented her with a gift wrapped in red paper, shame washed over her.

As their father left the hall, Third Mother unexpectedly shouted out for the children to kneel in front of him. They ran to his study and fell to their knees. Embarrassed by the excessive display, Ling Fupeng told them to get up, but then the servants, Shuhua's mother, and Third Mother followed suit. As he tried to lift them from the floor, Fifth Mother also knelt before him. Third Mother began to laugh so hard at her that she couldn't stand up. The children and servants joined in giggling. Father tried to end things by distributing small gifts of money to the children. Third Mother, still laughing, noted the mothers expected larger amounts. Fifth Mother grinned, adding, "What sum do you want? Better say it now, today your words are like gold and jade, tomorrow they will become mud and rotten rags." When Shuhua's mother rebuked them for their greed, Third Mother responded, "Why should one feel ashamed? You see it is perfectly true. A tip is money, money is everything."[16]

Ling Fupeng then asked Fifth Mother to grind his ink, but she refused to do it, saying he had "a new one" to wait on him. Instead, she took Shuhua to a performance of "Wandering in the Garden, Stirred by a Dream," the two most famous scenes of the *Peony Pavilion* opera. On returning home, Shuhua refused to go to her mother's room and stayed with Fifth Mother, lying in her bed and eating fruit. "I asked her to explain the play we had seen. I did not understand why the pretty girl, who had met the scholar only once, could not live without him afterwards; why she should fall ill and die so quickly; and what disease had made her die. I kept asking round and round, which must have bored Fifth Mother, for she said to me: 'I hope you will not ask these questions any more. Little children need not bother to understand them.'"[17] Sixth Mother moved into the rooms on the east side of the fourth courtyard with Ling Fupeng. The sight of her face covered in dead-white powder made Shuhua frightened to venture to her father's library.

In a later chapter, "A Scene," Shuhua sits on the floor reading her mother's songbooks, when Sixth Mother's maid runs into the room to announce that a fight had broken out between Third Mother and Sixth Mother. Ruolan, who had been napping, dressed quickly and ran past the bright red pillars of the walkway toward the next courtyard. Ling Fupeng called to her, "Go quickly to them, it would be no joke if one of them were killed. Third Mother always wants too much, while Sixth is particularly afraid of losing face."[18] When they arrived upon the scene, they found Sixth Mother beating her head against Third Mother's chest. She yelled, "I don't want to live any more. What would be the use of living, just to be the object you have made up your mind to torture to death? Kill me, kill me!"[19] Ruolan and several maids pulled the two women apart, but they continued to hurl insults. Third Mother accused Sixth Mother of being a "woman of cheap bone . . . one of those cheap horses ridden by all sorts of men," who should treat her with more respect because she had helped bring her from the brothel into an honorable household.[20] Sixth Mother declared she felt no shame for her past, since she had only been keeping herself from hunger and cold. She called Third Mother the cheap one for using her husband's money to keep a lover, "a pale-faced young man in her own bed." Enraged, Third Mother slapped the younger woman's cheeks and screamed she was the one using the family's money to support an illegitimate son outside of the family. Ruolan led Third Mother to her room.

Shuhua returned to her bedroom to find her father hiding there from the fight. Brush in hand, he was writing characters. After he finished two long scrolls, he hung them on the wall. He lit a cigar and stood back to admire his calligraphy. He lectured Shuhua, "Those new-fashioned people certainly have missed something as they adopt the Western way. They don't respect character writing. You see, character writing is the best way to make one's heart at peace. One concentrates one's mind on doing it, though it is easy, but it occupies one's whole mind, for one must use one's eyes and hand as one is doing it."[21] He then asked Shuhua to go get her mother to help light his opium pipe. Ruolan instructed her to reply that she had a headache and couldn't leave her room.

Shuhua describes discovering, as a child, a kind of aesthetic pleasure at seeing such dramas acted out in their house: "Their actions reminded me of figures on the stage. They interested me. I thought Third Mother was like the woman . . . who murders her husband and then fights with her brother-in-law. Sixth Mother was very like the woman who treats her mother-in-law badly in the absence of her husband."[22] In a chapter called "A Plot," Ruolan and Fifth Mother sit back to watch an intrigue involving First Sister. She was the married daughter of Father's first wife who came to visit from Guangzhou with her husband and his two concubines. She and Sixth Mother had become friends during an earlier meeting in the south and schemed to bring Sixth Mother's son into the family. During her arrival feast, First Sister turned the conversation with her father to the topic of children and lack of sons in the family. She convinced him that Sixth Mother's son had reached the age to begin his studies and that he should join the family to do so. She then blocked any objections from Third Mother, who had given birth to the family's only son, by playing to her material greed. She invited her to a mahjong game that evening and let her win a large sum. The following day, a boy arrived at Ganmian Hutong from his grandmother's house to begin lessons with the family tutor. Although his mother said he was six years old, the maids whispered behind their hands that he was really eight or nine, implying that he had been born before Ling Fupeng met Sixth Mother. "He looked like a strange dog entering someone's house by mistake," observes Shuhua.[23]

Shuhua describes herself as the good little girl, the "little pussy cat in the corner" in whom adults confided.[24] She wrote, in English copyedited for publication, of a younger self trying to make sense of the adult world she witnessed. Her sister Amy, in her dinner-table stories, relished instead the freedom she gained as a precocious youth. She attracted attention with her antics and loved being spoiled. Beneath the brave face of her stories, however, lies a sense of abandonment within a large household where children competed for the favor of adults and concubines for that of their husband.

Amy gained her father's notice by being an inexhaustible eater, so it is fitting that the one Chinese fairy tale I remember her telling me as a child recounted an escapade of reckless ingestion, the story of the lady in the moon. I imagine my grandmother as a young girl at a temple fair. She scrambles to catch a view of the makeshift theater set up by traveling puppeteers. As brightly dyed donkey-skin puppets move their jointed limbs across the screen, the children follow their shadows and listen to a tale punctuated by the beating of a small drum.

At a time when ten suns shone in the sky, scorching the earth, Heaven dispatched the Divine Archer Houyi to help its parched inhabitants. He shot down nine of the ten suns and restored the earth to a green and temperate place. Wandering by the side of a stream, he met the maiden Chang'e, and they fell in love. To remain with her, Houyi relinquished his immortality. They married, and the archer defended his wife's village from wild beasts that came down from the mountains.

The emperor, hearing of Houyi's bravery, sent him to investigate a strange streak of light in the sky. He followed it to Mount Kunlun, home of Queen Mother of the West, Daoist goddess of immortality, who asked him to build her a palace. Houyi constructed a magnificent structure of jade and fragrant woods and was rewarded with an herbal elixir that gave eternal life. Upon returning home, Houyi hid the herbs in a jar above a rafter in his house.

One day Chang'e noticed an unusual white light in the roof rafters. A delicious odor permeated the room. She climbed up a ladder and discovered the hidden jar. Curious about what her husband had hidden, she stuffed the ball of herbs into her mouth. Suddenly, she sprouted wings and began flying around the room. When her husband came home, she feared his wrath and flew out a window into the night.

She climbed toward the moon's cool light. When she finally alighted on its surface, she observed a barren landscape with only a few acacia and cinnamon trees. Breathing hard from her flight, she began coughing violently until she vomited up the covering of the immortality herbs, which changed into a rabbit companion, white as the purest jade. She drank dew from the acacia blossoms and nibbled on cinnamon before settling into her new home. She had flown past her husband and gained the immortality he'd relinquished for her. But a cold and lonely existence on the moon served as punishment for her appetite.

Amy's rebellious eating stories included the early memory of accompanying her mother on a trip to Panyu. Her mother had been sent to tend to the Ling ancestral temple. After a short train ride to Tianjin, they boarded a ship and sailed for Guangdong. Ruolan had sewn the money for the temple repairs into the lining of Amy's clothes. She instructed her daughter to cry loudly any time soldiers came on board to inspect the passengers. "We went on a steam ship," described Amy.

> I liked Guangdong very much. The food in Guangdong is very good, lots of fruits and vegetables. We came back on a steam ship carrying bananas from Hong Kong to Tianjin. I smelled the bananas and went downstairs and got a whole bunch. I took it to our stateroom. And I lied down and began to eat one banana after another banana for both meals. I ate every single banana in the bunch. Then I got very sick, and my mother thought I might have typhoid fever. I ran a very high temperature. When we got back to Tianjin, I was much better. And I was all better when we got back to Beijing. I don't eat bananas any more.

Censures against excess and overindulgence existed particularly for women, but the male act of eating was one of empowerment. The eater gained strength by ingesting the variety and largesse of the world. Like the emperor, who held extravagant, ritualistic banquets to demonstrate that he ruled materially as master of all under heaven. Like Amy, who declared at the dinner table, "I eat everything."

For Amy, the genre of bold digestion framed her stories of childhood mischief and need. While she probably didn't peel the first banana with conscious intentions, she discovered through eating a way to win the concern of her mother. Beneath her storytelling gusto lies the hunger of a child in a divided household, a craving met momentarily by returning to moments of devoted sickbed care. Shuhua recalled a similar joy in being sick, "My happiest memory of my early childhood was when I was ill. My mother sat on my bed to attend me, so that I could talk to her and look at her as much as I liked."[25]

When Amy spoke about her family relations, a sense of detachment crept in with the often-repeated phrase, "I was very lucky." She claimed to have been lucky in childhood. When questioned about a professed closeness with her father, she confessed, "Well, I was afraid of him. I was very close to my mother." Of her mother she said, "I was very lucky. My mother was very nice to me." However, she admitted rarely sharing her mother's company. When not going to temples or opera performances with her friends, Ruolan was busy attending to the household duties of tea tasting, shopping, supervising servants, or planning the menu for family meals. True to her nuclear family version of genealogy, Amy rarely mentioned the large number of children in the household and called her half-sisters and half-brother, the children of the other mothers, cousins.

She revealed the formal relationship she had with her parents by describing how servants raised the family's children. Several women, rather than a single woman complementing a father figure, filled the role of mother for her. While her mother's family origins and those of her father's other concubines remained unspoken, the women who cared for her came mostly from different classes and sometimes regional backgrounds than the family presented in her picture of a distinguished Cantonese scholar's household. She explained,

> I was raised with a milk *amah*. My mother didn't have enough milk. My *amah* was younger than my mother. She fit her child on this side, fit me on the other side, and she still had milk to spare. She treated you like her own daughter. She left the house when I was about five years old. She did nothing but feed me. We had a room for her. She had her baby there. And she ate the best food. You had to feed her first. She was northern Chinese, not Cantonese.

Amy marked the cultural difference between herself and her *amah*. However, the sometimes-narrow distinction between her mother, the other mothers, and the maidservants of the household emerges in Shuhua's stories, particularly at moments such as Sixth Mother's arrival, when Ruolan, along with Third and Fifth Mothers, kneeled with the servants before Father.

Amy did not dwell in the corners of the house on Ganmian Hutong, rehearsing its dramas, as her sister had. Instead, in her pared-down report of childhood, she insisted on a lucky penchant for play. Unlike Shuhua, she got along with everybody by avoiding the tensions between them. "No problem at home because I liked to play all the time. I didn't bother my parents. I played with our cousins. I played tennis with the neighbor boy. The artist sister never played. She sat down and wrote and painted all the time. Ever since she was five years old. She didn't bother anybody. Nobody bothered her." Amy followed this statement by saying she never spent much time with her family, amusing herself instead with solitary games, jumping rope, or kicking around a *jingzi*, a common Chinese toy fashioned from a tuft of feathers affixed to a coin through the hole in its center. The solitary image of her alone in a courtyard on a cold spring morning, concentrating on the rhythmic clink of the toy against her shoe as it is kicked into the air, lingers after the confidence of her words has passed.

· *Five* ·

Mountains and Walls

𝒮huhua woke up late one morning to find the courtyard empty. She ambled down the path to the garden and sat on a rock, envisioning the events she had slept through. Father stuck his hands in the pockets of his blue robe and strode out the front door held open by the gatekeeper. Mother climbed into a curtained sedan chair to light incense at a Buddhist temple and buy tea. Old Zhou the gardener picked up his basket and grabbed his daughter's hand. They slipped out the back gate to collect some seedlings from a friend's greenhouse. Alone on a hot summer morning, she had nothing to do but imagine what lay on the other side of the wall. She saw the man riding a horse in the jerky black-and-white film their uncle had taken the children to see. She saw the candy salesman from the temple fair, the camels described by the gardener's daughter, and a store full of elaborate foreign clocks like those she had heard about in the palace. In her mind, she embarked on an adventure in the world outside the narrow confines of home.

A similar little girl appears in Ling Shuhua's story "The Phoenix," first published in 1930 in the *Crescent Moon* magazine and later in her 1935 collection *Little Brothers*. The girl's name is Zhi'er, the same as the protagonist of "Moving House," one of the stories that later became autobiography.

Zhi'er wandered around an empty courtyard, finding only their old black cat asleep in the sun. She drifted into another courtyard, where Zhang Ma sat silently mending clothes, and watched a blackbird land on a tree. When she asked Zhang Ma the bird's name, the woman showed little interest in conversation, continuing her work. In search of her pet dog, Zhi'er walked around the greenhouse and noticed the small back door had been left open. Seizing the opportunity, she slipped through the door.

She saw a flock of children crowd around an old man striking a gong. She joined them to watch him mold creatures from different colored doughs. His tiny Monkey King on a stick brought squeals of laughter. When he crafted a beautiful multicolored phoenix for a little girl, Zhi'er desperately longed to have one as well. The man made three more, two of which he quickly sold. Zhi'er called out to claim the third one but then fell speechless when she realized she had no money. A stranger in a black vest standing behind her stepped forward and bought it for her.

Zhi'er didn't know what to say. The toy maker packed up his supplies, and the children dispersed. She wanted to run home and show the phoenix to her sisters, but the strange man began talking to her. She followed him as he strolled out of the *hutong* to a bigger street. He gently stroked her braids, asked questions about her family, and offered to be her good friend. She replied, "You are my good friend!" He offered to take her to his house, explaining he kept a real phoenix there. Excited by the prospect of seeing such a magnificent bird, she promised to be well behaved on the way.

The inventory of marvelous things she observed expanded as they walked through the city: automobiles, a band with trumpets and drums, and store windows filled with unfamiliar items. The good friend showed no annoyance, like most adults, with her questions. They exited the city gate and crossed the bridge out of town. Frightened by some large approaching animals, Zhi'er hid behind her companion. Having never seen camels before, she fancied them as the magical creatures ridden by the prince in a fairy tale she had heard. As they entered a wooded area, he told her they were getting close. He promised to help her catch a phoenix of her own, and Zhi'er began to believe he was an immortal. Suddenly, he dropped her hand and fled. Zhi'er heard her family's servant Wang Sheng call her name. He and the gardener ran up and tugged her ears. As Wang Sheng pulled her home in a rickshaw, she cried in protest, asking after her good friend. Rather than feeling relieved at being taken back, she smelled the tobacco from Wang Sheng's pipe and felt like vomiting.

Narrated through the eyes of a child, "The Phoenix" almost convinces the reader of the stranger's goodwill and the existence of a mysterious phoenix, symbol of rebirth. As Zhi'er takes in the sights of the city streets, she forgets her family's stifling courtyards. The inner female world of the girl emerges in sharp contrast with the outer world of the male stranger.[1] The servants' arrival just in the nick of time infuriates her, for they seem so ignorant of the adventure they've disrupted. Lurking behind the child's dream are the ominous and vaguely sexual intentions of the stranger in the black vest. Whom should the reader trust? Childhood innocence is fraught with the perils encountered in any real quest for freedom. Shuhua's narrative remains ambiguous, yet reluctant to give up Zhi'er's imagination of heroic proportions.

In Amy's stories of herself at this age, she sought freedom by dressing in boy's clothes. Her hero's daring, curiosity, and confidence endeared her to those around her and paved the way for explorations outside the normal domain of girlhood. This period and place in her memory represented life at its most promising. Her eyes danced as she told me, "Life was more fascinating then. People didn't know I was a girl. I always dressed like a boy. I just liked the boy's outfit. I liked the boy's freedom. See, the girl didn't have much freedom in China. I don't think my mother had anything to say about it. I was kind of spoiled I think. I was the youngest, so they just let me do what I wanted."

Along with the watch, the car, the prison, and the government school, the bicycle was a modern status symbol, and Amy learned to ride one at a young age. Afraid of others making fun of her, she got up early every morning and pushed the sturdy black bicycle out of the garden shed. In the gray light of dawn, she wobbled and fell clattering beneath the trees of Ganmian Hutong. One morning, she made it to the end of the street, and then continued. She pumped her legs with growing confidence, past Tiananmen, where she turned south and headed out the front gate of the city wall. She glided joyfully down a shopping street, observing it gradually come to life on either side. When she looked ahead again, a farmer on his way into town to sell eggs stood directly in her path. He carried two baskets of eggs, hanging from opposite ends of a bamboo pole balanced across his shoulders. She lost control and smacked into one of his baskets. The pole spun around and fell from the man's shoulders. She landed in a sticky mess of broken eggs. The farmer began shouting a string of curses. Amy wiped splattered egg from her face and quickly said her mother would pay for the eggs. She gave him their address and rode home as fast as possible. From a hiding place behind a screen in the first courtyard, she saw him come to the house and collect the money from her mother.

Amy claimed to have once convinced the two drivers of her father's carriage to let her squeeze into the narrow space beneath their legs. The horses pulled Ling Fupeng's carriage into the palace that morning. After he had stepped out, he turned to give instructions to the drivers and saw how his daughter had managed to smuggle herself in. He marched her to a corner, where he made her sit all morning on a big wooden chair. Amy saw her father and other officials kowtow three times to the boy emperor Puyi. She had never seen her father kowtow to anyone, let alone a child, and the sight shocked and amused her. In the carriage on the way home, she sat across from him and began to mimic the ritual, laughing and bowing three times in front of him. His gazed at her sternly and told her never to talk about what she had seen.

In spite of the distant relationship Amy seemed to have had with her father, she traveled with him on several occasions. "I went with my father," she said, "wherever he wanted to go. He took me because I dressed and acted like a boy. I liked to ride horses. Traveling in China, you either went by sedan chair or horseback. I was the only one who liked horseback riding. I hated sedan chairs. Two people carried you, bouncing you up and down. I like the horse. You can control the horse." She described in detail a trip she took with him on a retreat to a Buddhist monastery. Ling Fupeng did not share Li Ruolan's faith in Buddhism, but he went to temples to escape obligations in the capital. Only his personal secretary and a few servants accompanied him. In Amy's story, she was the sole child, dressed in boy's clothing, allowed to go.

They took the train to the city of Tai'an in Shandong province, at the base of the sacred Mount Tai. Sedan chair bearers carried her father up the mountain. Following behind on horseback, Amy guided her horse between rivers flowing on either side of the trail. When they stopped at the bottom of a steep waterfall, she picked up a handful of transparent pebbles and put them in her pocket. At the temple, the chief monk let her father reside in his quarters for several weeks. Sometimes they traveled down the mountain to visit officials in the city below. She said of these trips to Tai'an, "He didn't take me, but I followed. I liked to follow him. My father very seldom talked to me. But when he talked, he meant it. Every word of it."

Even during these retreats from the capital, Ling Fupeng brought work with him. Amy explained, "He always had a lot to do, but I liked to eat with him. He often ate something special. And I said to myself, I like to eat. I want something special, too." She continued,

> One day, I smelled something really good in the temple. I was about six or seven years old. I followed the smell to the kitchen. I went in thinking, their food tastes awful good, if it's only vegetable it couldn't be that good. Buddhists don't eat meat. They eat chicken and eggs on the first and fifteenth of the month. The rest is all vegetables and tofu. They don't eat pork or beef, but I saw lots of hams hanging from the kitchen ceiling. I asked, 'Why do you have all those hams?' I discovered that's why the food was so good. Tofu itself has no flavor, but their tofu was very good because they seasoned it with that ham. They didn't show you the ham, they took it out.

The youngest daughter of the Ling family described herself as a determined and curious child, with the attitude and resources to outrun a traditional girlhood.

Shuhua escaped by curling up in bed on dark winter mornings while the wind howled outside her window. "I let myself be carried away by my imagination: I could see gods and fairies sailing in the sky with their beautiful robes flying in the wind, all coming to attend the heavenly concert. What a joy to think I was one of them!"[2] This scene opens "My First Lesson in Painting," a chapter in *Ancient Melodies* in which Shuhua claims the same privileges that Amy earned by dressing as a boy, but through a different route.

Her child's eye roamed the bedroom. The morning light illuminated flowers painted on the paper window. Sparrows under the eaves outside gently touched their beaks to the ink flower buds. Water boiled in a kettle on the coal-burning stove, its low sound accompanying the plucks of her mother's needle through fabric stretched taut on an embroidery hoop. She wandered from this interior scene to the garden outside, to sit on the rocks and admire the bright colors of the Forbidden City and the receding purples of distant hills. Shuhua recalled what she did next.

> I moved round the garden aimlessly. Then I picked up a piece of charcoal from the ground. This made me think of ink, which my sisters had, though I had none. The white wall was just in front of me, so I tried to draw something on it with the charcoal. I forget how long I worked on the wall. I remember that on the first occasion I drew everything that came into my mind—landscapes, animals, and human figures—till the white wall was covered with my drawings. The next day I went to draw on another new wall; then it became a habit, and I went to draw something every day.[3]

One day Wang Zhulin, a court artist who was her father's friend, saw her uninhibited drawings on the wall. Impressed, he offered to tutor her. Moved by this praise of his daughter, Ling Fupeng asked Shuhua to kneel before her new teacher. The story of his grandfather Xie Lipu, the scholar who burned all of the books written in his youth and turned to painting, had kindled his passion for art in middle age, especially as the demands of his official career fatigued him. Ling Fupeng harbored the hope that one of his children would carry on the family tradition. He welcomed the opportunity to dote on a gifted daughter, especially since Third Mother's son had not shown any talent with a brush.

Shuhua's father encouraged her study of painting by promising to give her a prized portfolio of his grandfather's paintings after she grew up. Wang Zhulin taught her to mix colors and to paint rocks and plants. He gradually filled her painting desk with bamboo-handled brushes, pretty boxes, thick sticks of compressed ink, inkstones, and rolls of paper. Sometimes Ling Fupeng invited her to dine alone with him and her older brother, much to the dismay of Third Mother. Once when Shuhua was too sick to accompany her father to meet a famous painting collector, Third Mother lashed out at Ruolan: "Why, you will lose a good chance to show your daughter off. If I were she, I would go with him even if I could only drag myself as heavily as a worm."[4] When Wang Zhulin had to leave Beijing, he suggested that Ling

Fupeng ask Miu Suyun, painting instructor to the empress dowager, to teach Shuhua.[5] Ling expressed doubt that the proud and aging artist would want to teach a little girl. In *Ancient Melodies*, Shuhua wrote that Wang explained it didn't matter whether she actually taught her or not: "What I mean is that I wish to send my pupil to her just for the purpose of seeing something and listening to something—in other words, to make her see the life of an artist, not just what the artist does in painting, but everything in her daily life, her manner, her speech, her taste in art, and all her surroundings as well as what she does in painting."[6]

Shuhua's tutor defined an artist's training according to the Confucian rituals at the center of Chinese conceptions of civilization, in which the term for writing, *wen*, was the same as for culture. Achievement in the linked arts of writing and painting provided the cultural refinement necessary to become fully human. These rituals prescribed forms of correct behavior for every occasion, which, practiced correctly, led to a superior moral and artistic sensibility. By including this overheard speech in "My First Lesson in Painting," Shuhua documented the early entry of the idea of an "artist's life as art" into her consciousness.

The sisters both believed they held a special place in their father's affections, each following after him, in their separate ways, with the desire to experience a privileged realm to which even their mother had no access. In an early draft of "My First Lesson in Painting," Shuhua noted the discomfort she experienced as a child riding in a carriage to visit her new painting instructor, Miu Suyun, for she knew that her mother, as a concubine, could not call upon such a respected woman.[7] Amy prided herself on being the boyish cross-dressing hero with transparent pebbles in her pocket, fearlessly astride a horse scrambling up the side of Mount Tai. Shuhua reveled in being the budding artist hero, even writing the following words into the mouth of an effusive First Sister: "I am not at all surprised that you are the artist of the family. You have Father's nose, Father's eyes, and the same shaped face as Father. I am sure you have also got his talent and his skillful hand for brushwork."[8]

The ebullience of childhood radiates from these stories. They tell the tale of a young girl in the quest for "something special, too." These memories form a significant point of return. Amy retold these stories again and again, with undiminished enthusiasm. The main protagonist in many of Shuhua's short stories—including four that she wrote first as fiction in Chinese and then translated into English with herself as the autobiographical narrator—is a preadolescent girl. The first half of *Ancient Melodies*, which itself ends just as her formal schooling has begun, focuses on this period of youth.

Biographies and autobiographies usually begin with the circumstances of the subject's parents, birth, and childhood. The discipline of writing a continuous life forces a search for self, in which the origin myth grows important, with vital clues about the adult the child will grow into. Yet it's difficult to know whether those clues were so obvious in actual childhood. The adult narrator more likely planted them there for the sake of continuity, an orderly explanation of how the person of today sprang from the past. The raw testimonies of a child or the explanatory accounts of the adult are both legends to the same map, but neither can be fully trusted.

The mountain of my grandmother's youth no longer exists as it did in her memory. When I traveled to Mount Tai in 1993, I also took the train from Beijing to the city of Tai'an. Over the May Day holiday, a three-day weekend at the university where I taught, I joined a group of foreign teachers to climb this most famous of China's five sacred mountains. On Thursday evening after class, we boarded the train in Beijing and rode overnight in a packed, hard-seat car. After a sleepless night amid the cramped, shifting bodies of the train car, we stumbled into the gray dawn at Tai'an.

On Saturday, we passed under a wisteria-covered stone archway inscribed with calligraphy reading, "The place where Confucius began to climb." We began to climb, together with thousands of others. Groups of students and families, mostly Chinese tourists on holiday, rested along the side of the path. My students in Beijing had told me I was crazy to climb Mount Tai during the May Day weekend. They warned me the route had been so crowded the previous year that several students had been pushed over the edge. I felt sure they had been teasing me, especially during the leisurely first half of the climb. We made frequent stops to rest, picnic, eat at the various makeshift food stands, marvel at the calligraphy carved into the cliffs, and take photographs. At the temples along the way, elderly peasant women lit incense and prostrated themselves before Buddhist and Daoist religious icons. Winding around these mountain temples, the roughly paved path gradually grew narrower and so steep at points that we found ourselves puffing up stone steps, which, by some back-breaking feat, had been laid into the side of the mountain.

As the chill of evening approached, we arrived at the midway point of Zhongtianmen (Half Way to Heaven Gate) to find the guesthouses either full or without license to accept foreign guests. Our Chinese work cards did little to persuade wary registration clerks to overlook the rules, and we refused to pay for the overpriced three-star hotel reserved for foreigners. After we had given up on sleeping that night, we searched in glum silence for a place to eat. In a well-lit noodle shop, we ate as slowly as possible, cradling the warm soup bowls between cold hands. While the kitchen staff played a loud game of cards, slapping down cards with exaggerated impatience, we lingered.

Back on the path, still crowded in the middle of the night, the flickering flashlights of other climbers and dangling bare bulbs of the occasional teashop lit our way. As I dragged my feet up the steep steps, I thought of my grandmother on horseback following behind her father's sedan chair, but I found it hard to reconcile this romantic image with the paved path, the tourists, the souvenir stalls, the new cable car near the summit, and the tough grandmother pilgrims with backs bent from years of hard work. I found no tranquil temple courtyards, waterfalls, or beautiful transparent pebbles, and as I climbed through the night and shivered at the summit with thousands of others wearing rented People's Liberation Army coats, I wondered if she had only dreamed of accompanying her father on retreats to Mount Tai. And then I wondered if it was here at the summit that the students had fallen to their death the previous year. Among the hungry, exhausted crowd, it no longer seemed an impossible scenario. Huddled against the cold on rocky outcrops, we all waited for what turned out to be a disappointing sunrise. The gray, misty sky slowly grew lighter. A faint outline of distant mountain peaks rose out of a sea of mist and clouds. Rows of crops, buildings, and roads gradually appeared, filling the valley and stretching out to meet the horizon.

Chasing after my grandmother's childhood has yielded many moments of futility. The path is littered with obstacles: exhausting stretches of rough-hewn stone steps, hotels that do not accept foreign faces, and peddlers of tacky knickknacks, those plastic emblems of promise and disillusionment. Yet, I understand the impetus of her story and the aura surrounding it. For I too remember my childhood stance toward the world, wonder stuck in my throat and eyes open wide to dreams of adventure. As the metaphor of Mount Tai was to the imagination of my grandmother as a girl in China, the promise of the open road was to me in America.

When I was seven years old, my parents crammed our white VW camper van full of boxes, provisions for a year, and we began the great summer's trek west from Missouri to southern California. My father had a year's sabbatical, and we were moving to the land of sun, smog, and the La Brea tar pits. The day my father drove the van home from the used car lot, I fell in love with its compact sink and refrigerator, camper pop-top, and musty beige plaid curtains. My four-year-old sister and I were packed into the back seat, between the boxes, with our stuffed animals and an invisible line drawn between us. My parents sat in front with sunglasses on, consulting maps, deciding where to stop for food and gas, and concocting games to keep us entertained. As

Diana Ross and the Bee Gees poured from the radio, my sister and I waved at truckers and watched the scenery whiz by.

That same year, my mother gave me my first camera—a simple box-shaped mechanism not much different from the Kodak Brownie she had owned as a girl. With my gray, plastic, one-speed camera, its lens forever focused to infinity, I had only to stand far away enough from my subject on a reasonably sunny day and press the shutter. I learned to load the film, wider than 35 mm and only twelve frames per roll, by feeding its paper leader onto a black plastic spool inside the camera. The peculiar chemical smell that filled my nose when I ripped open the wrapper of a new roll of film and the process of directing my family into the viewfinder on top of the camera made me feel like an adult. I had control of the camera obscura, that darkened attic of family memory, its trail of paper images pressed between pages of forgotten scrapbooks.

I took blurred and bizarrely framed photographs, up through the branches of redwood trees, down into the depths of canyons, and out at the tiny figures of my parents and sister poised against a desolate desert horizon. Finally, there is a picture of me. Enamored with horses that summer, a suitable obsession for our journey through the American imaginary of the West, I pleaded to ride a horse every time we saw one. At Bryce, my father gave in and together we rode into the canyon, led down a dusty, narrow trail by a park ranger. I sit in my jeans and sweat-suit jacket, on an old horse with blinders whose reins I clutch between my fists. I stare directly and slightly down at my father who held the small box camera against his chest, his chin tucked as he gazed down into the viewfinder.

What do we really know of childhood? My grandmother had photographs from her childhood, staid images made early in the development of photographic technology, when exposures took minutes and posing was a serious affair. In America, she became an amateur photographer, with a darkroom in her basement and tubes of oil paint for hand tinting family photos, but the still image was not the idiom she relied upon to recount her early years in China. Her stories were in her tongue, her eyes, and her animated face as she talked. Her memories resided in mimicked voices and in her voice repeating the demands of a younger self. Beside her father at the dinner table, "I like to eat. I want something special, too." Her opinion on modes of transportation, "I like the horse. You can control the horse." Later, at her older sister's wedding, "Don't you ever engage me out to a man I've never met. I'll run away, and you'll never find me." As a writer rather than a talker, Shuhua's words create scenes with a painterly aesthetic, with a sense of movement like a scroll unrolling. My memory depends instead upon the photographic image.

I made my pilgrimage to Mount Tai too late in life, searching for facts instead of magic. Its false promise was revealed just as my math professor father's explication of quantum electrodynamics had accounted for the mirage-like puddles of sky, shimmering on the hot pavement, glimpsed out the windshield of our VW van. The all-American metaphor of the open road as an escape from the past, of movement toward a newer and truer self, was as accessible to my grandparents (unable to rent apartments or swim in certain pools because of their foreign faces) as the hotels on Mount Tai were to me. My grandmother and I remember our childhoods in the language of our culture and our times. In spite of our kinship, our idiomatic inheritance is not the same. I have a father, with a stretch of road reflected in his glasses, who indulged my desire to ride a horse, and a mother, with memories of her childhood gaze out the window of a westward-moving Silver Zephyr train, who bought me a camera like her Kodak Brownie so that I could record the trip from my viewfinder. My family never took home movies; we were a nuclear family of the still image. Our emotions are captured within a rectangular frame by the mechanical, spiraling wink of the camera's dark eye.

Mothers and fathers represent personal symbols of the past, figures to explain our particular conformity or rebellion. No different in this autobiographical impulse, and encouraged by the Chinese tradition of ancestor worship and a diasporic desire for connection to home, Shuhua and Amy engaged in this search for themselves as they recounted the formative experiences of their parents' lives and their parents' influence on them. Their two sets of stories stand contentiously side by side, a sibling rivalry fed by the competition they witnessed between the mothers of their household.

However, they were not unique in their attachment to the metaphor of youth; a vision of fledgling vibrancy, imagination, and health rejuvenating an ailing China would become the badge of their generation. Many of Shuhua's fellow women writers would foreground childhood and youth in their stories, and most would later be criticized for failing to mature, for writing only when they were young and only about this period of their lives. Some explain this failure in terms of an intensity that could not be sustained. The effort required to explode onto the scene burned out quickly.[9] But for Amy and Shuhua, whose lives spanned almost the entire twentieth century, the continual return to their youngest days suggests multiple strategies of survival, after the "modern girl" image lost its currency in Chinese politics and after their departure to foreign countries. Their youth became, in many respects, *the* formative experience that would influence, define, and destabilize the rest of their days. They observed the lives of the women in their household stagnating within the walls of a besieged culture, and they took the first narrative steps of placing themselves on the other side of that wall. These stories later served as a source of strength to draw upon in moments of redefinition, a means of establishing a fixed identity that carried them into an uncertain future. For Shuhua in England and Amy in the United States, stories of childhood reinforced bonds of culture with a distant homeland.

In Shuhua's story "The Phoenix," the girl protagonist Zhi'er secretly ventures into dangerous city streets and ends up in a search for a phoenix, the bird of rebirth, which in the end fails to reveal itself as either wonderfully or deceptively fantastic. The sisters' stories likewise embody a search without an end, driven by the need to make sense of movement through time and space, from a traditional past to the promised future of female emancipation and between China and the West. Their stories of childhood create a respite, a *yuanji* of the imagination, a native place to return to, and an infinite and expansive moment in time in which they recognize themselves as defiant and unquestionable heroes. Huddled under the thick blankets of winter, listening to the gusting wind blow through the hollow bamboo sticks of summer awnings still covering the courtyard walkways, their imaginations soared.

In the last scene of "My First Lesson in Painting," Ling Fupeng lectured Shuhua on famous artists. With serious eyes and a faint smile beneath his long drooping mustache, he instructed her on remaining headstrong: "If you want to be a great artist in the future you must remember my words: never do any picture which you do not like to do. Paint everything for your own sake. You should not try to please anyone, even though he may be your father."[10]

After dinner, my grandmother carefully wiped her mouth with a napkin. She reached slowly for a toothpick and methodically used it to probe the gaps between her teeth. Removing the sliver of wood from her mouth, she looked at me contemplatively. Then suddenly, her eyebrows lengthening, she pointed the toothpick between her bony fingers straight at me and declared, "I was born to fight. You wouldn't understand. I grew up fighting."

II

CASTING OFF

·Six·

Lessons

$\mathcal{A}$ moon gate in the back garden of the Ling household led to the family tutor's quarters. At the center of his small courtyard, a grotto of tall, white rocks rose like a mountain, flowers blooming at its base. Willows and bamboo formed green walls on two sides. The sisters' older brother attended lessons in the tutor's study every day. As a young girl, Shuhua often stood in the arc of the moon gate listening to the tutor chant texts. His loud, clear voice spilled into the courtyard, followed by her brother's as he struggled to recite the lines.

One morning she was so focused on their words that she didn't notice when it began to rain. The tutor emerged from the study, saw her wet dress, and called her inside. Shuhua sat in back while her brother finished reading. A tarnished bronze incense burner and a pair of flower vases stood on a narrow table below a portrait of Confucius. The only other furnishings were the tutor's bookshelves, his large wooden desk, a tea table, and her brother's small desk.

Ling Fupeng brought her back to the study that afternoon and instructed her to kowtow. She kneeled on the stone floor in front of Confucius. Her father and the tutor agreed that she should learn some poems and short essays before starting on Confucius's *Analects*. The tutor commented, "I won't let her work hard; she is so very small and delicate. I have not the heart to see a little girl study hard." Ling Fupeng concurred, "I don't expect very much of her; I think a girl like her does not need to learn much. If she can learn how to compose a short poem on her painting when she wants to, that is quite enough."[1]

A chapter of *Ancient Melodies* titled "Tutor Ben" records Shuhua's early education within the tradition of *jiaxue*, "family learning." The imperial examination system, finally abolished in 1905, no longer provided a career option for her brother, but Ling Fupeng arranged for his son to study at home because many new schools no longer taught Confucius. The Chinese

Ministry of Education officially removed the Confucian classics from school curriculum in 1912. Ling Fupeng wanted his son to have an education similar to the one he had received as a boy. According to Shuhua, her persistence in surreptitiously following her brother's lessons convinced her father to let her study alongside him.

When I first read "Tutor Ben," I understood Ling Shuhua's initiation to the classroom as a hard-won achievement, her confrontation of traditional Chinese patriarchy. I didn't pick up on the other clues in *Ancient Melodies* that her father, rather than opposing his daughters' educations, may have encouraged their erudition as a symbol of the family's status. In other chapters, Shuhua writes about her older sisters going to school, presumably one of the girls' schools run by missionaries or the Chinese government after the Qing court sanctioned formal education for women in 1907.[2] Shuhua read books of "solid nourishment" under the guidance of these sisters. Her brother bragged that the girl to whom he had been betrothed wrote poetry. While serving in Tianjin, Ling Fupeng had become an official advisor to teachers' colleges for both men and women. The anomaly of Shuhua's situation in "Tutor Ben" is not that she studied at all but that she stayed at home to study classical texts because her father's outlook on the nation's crisis led him to return to Chinese cultural values.

Shuhua and Amy arrived after their father's hope for an illustrious line of sons had grown thin. In their stories, he encouraged their precociousness. While Shuhua had a brother beside whom she studied, Ling Fupeng did not consider him capable of literary achievement. When Tutor Ben proclaimed that with Ling as her father and a great-grandfather like Xie Lansheng, Shuhua should have no trouble learning to write poetry, Ling Fupeng responded, "But her brother never did compose a decent poem." Modern presentations of Confucian patriarchy highlight the overwhelming importance of patrilineal descent, yet in *Ancient Melodies* Ling Fupeng glories in the achievements of his maternal grandfather and hopes that his daughter will be the one to continue them. Amy told me, in her blunt way, that her brother wasn't very bright. She described the difficulty he had learning the alphabet when he began studying German. As he paced the courtyard reciting the letters, she used to taunt him by singing them out more quickly than he could.

In Amy's version of her early schooling, Tutor Ben had no such endearing nickname. Instead of being charming or encouraging, he was a strict, old man who stroked his long, white beard in a slightly wicked way. He forced her to stand rigidly while chanting long strings of words she didn't understand. When she faltered, he rapped her knuckles with a bamboo rod until they burned. Amy never mentioned different expectations for sons and daughters. In her story, all the children were thrown together in the same class with little regard to their gender, age, or ability. Always the hero, she declared that only she had enough dedication to endure the tutor's rigorous demands. Her version outdoes her sister's. She becomes the only student.

> We had an old man who my father hired. He taught us all the Chinese we needed to know. I was four years old when I started. There was my sister and one of my brothers, the one who died young. He taught us three, but finally just me. The others didn't want to be taught by him. He was very shrewd. Not shrewd, but how do you say it? Very strict, see. You study Confucius's four books. You have to recite it from the first word to the last word. You can't know what it means at that age, but you have to memorize it. If you don't memorize Confucius's four books and Mencius's five books, you're no good.

The sisters' lessons in classical Chinese represent a final moment in a tradition of scholar-official families educating their daughters at home. Around the turn of the century, Western missionaries and Qing reformers suppressed this history of learning because their female liberation narratives required an understanding of traditional women as uniformly oppressed. Their emphases on breaking from the past in order to produce modern, professional women effectively erased premodern *cainü*, "talented women," who, while small in number, had been highly literate.

Christian missionaries who arrived in China in the late nineteenth century were often rebuffed by elite families and therefore had little access to learned women sequestered within such households. They interacted mainly with lower-class women. Based on these experiences, missionaries routinely described Chinese women as ignorant and illiterate, even when they knew that elite women were often well educated. The blanket claim that Chinese women lacked knowledge bolstered their mission of Christian enlightenment.[3]

At the same time, late Qing reformers promoted a new Chinese nation that would radically depart from a tradition in decline. Women's emancipation became central to their platform. In order to prove the need for female liberation, they derided the literary achievements of traditional women. For example, Kang Youwei's protégé Liang Qichao announced in 1897 that their writing amounted to nothing but "ditties on the wind and the moon, the flowers and the grass . . . [and] cannot really be called learning at all."[4] He equated the *cainü* tradition with a soft and sentimental Chinese past, precisely what had to be overthrown to create a strong forward-thinking nation. In "On Women's Education," he insisted on the importance of educating women as the mothers of future citizens.[5] In a collusion of East and West, the image of the traditional Chinese woman as synonymous with feudal oppression gained increasing power throughout the twentieth century.

Although Amy associated memorizing the books of Confucius with the very process of learning to read and write in Chinese, Confucian patriarchy would soon be blamed for an egregious lack of women's education and for conditions that enforced female submissiveness. In their dismissal of elite women's classical erudition, Chinese reformers singled out one female scholar in particular. Ban Zhao, born into a scholarly Han dynasty family, pursued learning from a young age and gained recognition in the court along with her brothers. She eventually became tutor to the future Empress Deng. In 106 BCE, she published a book on female behavior titled *Nüjie* (Instructions for women). Later, extremely literal interpretations of this work as a Confucian text promoting female docility reduced it to a rulebook consisting of the "Three Obediences," requiring a woman to obey her father before marriage, her husband after marriage, and her eldest son after her husband's death; and the "Four Virtues," advising women to be chaste, restrained in speech, graceful in deportment, and devoted to needlework and other domestic chores. However, the historical context in which Ban Zhao wrote does not support these interpretations of her as a Confucian moralist and traitor of women. Court intrigues, violence, and murder rather than Confucian filial piety provided the backdrop for Ban's upbringing, and the teachings of militarist Daoists figured much more prominently in her education. *Nüjie*, rather than promoting female submissiveness, may have provided a set of survival skills for women. These techniques, made to appear as "virtues," trained them in the art of self-defense within a hostile environment of intense power politics.[6]

Traditional folk tales, poems, and operas seem, in fact, to belie what now passes as conventional wisdom about the powerlessness of traditional Chinese women. Historical female characters provide profuse examples of virtue, but also wit, intelligence, and influence. A common theme in these stories is cross-dressing, through which women disguised as men succeed on the battlefield or in the court examinations. The influence of characters like woman warrior Hua Mulan, whose story of replacing her father in the army first appeared in a sixth-century CE poem, seems obvious in Amy's delight in dressing like a boy. Yet, unlike these traditional characters who temporarily adopt male roles in order to aid society or a parent in need, Amy did so to partake in adventures that would have been off-limits otherwise. She told me, "My father treated me like a son," rooting her success as a professional woman in the independent spirit she developed as a girl dressed in boy's clothing.

In *Ancient Melodies*, Shuhua describes her introduction to this genre of stories. When her Great-Uncle Wu visited Beijing from Guangdong, he kept a pile of books on his bedside table. The two books from the pile that she remembered the most clearly contained stories of intelligent and capable women who disguised themselves as men, escaped to the capital, and won honors in the court examination. She borrowed the books and asked her mother to sing the stories aloud. In the evenings, the children, mothers, and maids gathered around the stove to listen to Ruolan's simple tune bring these heroines' exploits to life.

Great-Uncle Wu's love of a book called *Flowers in the Mirror* left an especially strong impression on Shuhua. In this eighteenth-century novel by Li Ruzhen, the main character Tang Ao travels to a variety of remarkable lands. When he and his brother-in-law Merchant Lin arrive at the Country of Women, they discover the men wearing skirts, mincing about on bound feet, smiling coyly, and attending to domestic affairs. The women wear hats and pants, take concubines, and govern all political affairs. When Lin approaches the emperor with his merchandise, she takes a fancy to him. Attendants drag him to a private chamber where they dress him in women's finery. His ears are pierced, his face powdered, and his feet bound. Li Ruzhen sets this utopian fantasy during the reign of Empress Wu (684–705 CE), the notorious first female ruler of China who usurped the throne from her son. Although Empress Wu is a historical figure, the twelve decrees for women's welfare, including female imperial examinations, she issues in *Flowers in the Mirror* are fictional. In these examinations, the main category for competition is poetry. Great-Uncle Wu read aloud poems in the book written by women with court positions. When Shuhua responded that she wanted to disguise herself as a man and take the examinations, he told her the system no longer existed, but that exams of all kinds would be open to women by the time she grew up.

Shuhua held onto her great-uncle's promise and linked future success with redemption of her mother's fate. "How many mornings I got up with a hope that I might go to take a court examination one day, as my father had in the old days. If I passed it, how happy my mother would be. She would be admired by everyone in the family. Then nobody would dare to say: 'She had no son!'"[7]

Western missionary activity and internal nationalist calls for reform had changed the circumstances of women's education in China by the time Shuhua and Amy began their studies at home. American Protestants first arrived in southern China in the 1830s. As evangelists, they considered Chinese women, mothers of the next generation, valuable converts. Local norms of gender division made it difficult for male missionaries to approach Chinese women, so their female counterparts became vital to the enterprise, although they also had little access to elite women. These independent women in high-collar dresses conducted house-to-house visits, bearing the message that

Christianity led to the higher status of women in the West. Ironically, the labor market at home often did not provide an acceptable channel for their social outreach energies. Only abroad did they participate in a fuller range of evangelical, educational, and medical activities. Many of the first female missionaries in China accompanied husbands, but single women increasingly filled the ranks. For example, by 1900, women made up almost 60 percent of the total American Protestant missionary force of 2,785, which included 811 single women, compared to 400 single men.[8]

Female missionaries focused on establishing schools for girls as part of their goal to foster a Bible-reading community of Chinese converts. They established boarding schools, modeled after those in the West, which physically removed Chinese girls from family relationships and trained them to be "Bible women." The Church of England's Society for Promoting Female Education in the East established the first girls' school on the mainland in 1844, and by 1896 at least three hundred missionary girls' schools existed, mostly in treaty ports and foreign concessions along the east coast.[9]

Around the time of the 1895 reform movement, elite Chinese took a new interest in Western knowledge. The McTyeire School, founded in 1892 in Shanghai, became the flagship example of a missionary school for upper-class families' daughters. Amy remembered this Methodist-run institution as a rival of the government-sponsored girls' high school she would attend. Chinese pushed for programs of broad liberal education, and missionaries adapted to these demands in order to continue with their evangelical work. Teachers at McTyeire instructed students in Western languages, literature, and science, in addition to Bible studies. In the late 1890s, Chinese reformers established their own private girls' schools, often openly accepting advice and aid from Christian foreigners.

Of the new professional fields opened up to this generation of girls, medicine became one of the most prominent, and female missionaries played an important role in this development. Most missions ran a small hospital, clinic, or dispensary to provide Western medical care. Female physicians again gained access where men could not, since cultural prohibitions prevented male doctors from treating women. The first female medical missionary began work in Beijing in 1873. By the turn of the century, women made up a much higher proportion of the Western medical force in China than they did at home. Female graduates from U.S. medical schools experienced discrimination in establishing professional careers at home but found practice in China open to them.[10] The precedent established by these physicians paved the way for Chinese women. Amy's strongest role model would be a Chinese woman who had attended medical school in the United States. This woman had followed the lead of even earlier female medical students. In

1896, Kang Aide (Ida Kahn), the adopted daughter of unmarried missionary Gertrude Howe, and Shi Meiyu (Mary Stone), whose Christian father had sent her at a young age to study under Howe, received their medical degrees from the University of Michigan and returned to China with great fanfare. Reformer Liang Qichao wrote a biography of Kang Aide that promoted her as a modern Chinese woman. Amy may also have heard through her father about Jin Yumei, the first Chinese woman to receive a U.S. medical degree in 1885, who was asked by Yuan Shikai in 1907 to supervise a women's medical department in Tianjin. These women helped make medicine an acceptable female calling.[11]

The missionary focus on Chinese women had a limited impact until Chinese nationalists also began to endorse women's education and oppose practices such as footbinding. Footbinding, while sometimes likened to Western corsets, appalled missionaries and symbolized for them the degraded position of women in Chinese society. This custom, which became the norm for elite Han Chinese women during the Ming dynasty (1368–1644 CE), encompassed a variety of traditions. In its most extreme form, older women bound a girl's four smaller toes toward the heel with cloth strips to restrict growth and create an arched shape. To Westerners, this practice opposed nature, but in imperial China, the bound foot signified genteel status, civility, and culture itself through rituals of bodily adornment. When Manchu invaders from the north overthrew the Ming in 1644 to establish the Qing dynasty, they attempted to prohibit the custom but ran into profound opposition from Han men and women.[12] Only as the Chinese empire came under attack by foreigners did native reformers denounce footbinding as the epitome of a tradition that had to be eradicated in order to build a modern nation. A British missionary established the first antifootbinding society in 1874. Nine years later Kang Youwei started a similar non-Christian society in Guangdong. In the ensuing years, foreign and Chinese women united behind the cause, advocating "natural feet" and encouraging women with bound feet to endure the painful process of unbinding them.[13]

In addition to foreign provocation for women's emancipation, a minor strand in Confucian thinking, developed over several centuries, had attempted to reinterpret the classics in a way that insisted on the same standards for men and women. This indigenous argument for gender equality informed Kang Youwei's thinking. His masterpiece *Datong shu* (Book of the great community), completed in 1902, presents a utopian anticipation of progress toward an Age of Universal Peace, a society free from divisions of nation, class, race, and gender. He even broaches the issue of sexuality, noting that homosexuals and heterosexuals alike should be permitted to sign short-term, renewable marriage contracts.[14]

Kang's *Datong shu*, however, was not published until 1935, and essays by his student Liang Qichao, which tied the women's movement to nationalism, became more influential. In his 1898 "A Suggestion to Establish Girls' Schools," Liang declared, "With men's and women's equal rights, the United States has become powerful; with women's education spreading, Japan has become strong; to build a prosperous nation and an intelligent people, we have to start with women's education."[15] Liang looked to models elsewhere and latched onto the social equality of women as an important element of nation building. His subsequent use of tradition as a foil to the modern nation-state silenced past female figures of power, all those passionate poets, managerial experts, peanut matriarchs, and grandmothers who, in Amy's words, "knew how to get something." For male intellectuals in semicolonial China, the struggle of the oppressed woman became one they could champion without appearing to indulge in a solipsistic discourse of self-emancipation.

This attention to women's advancement as a measure of China's modernity spilled into the burgeoning women's press of the early twentieth century. In publications like Shanghai's *Nüxue bao* (Journal of women's studies), launched in 1903, female essayists entreated readers to fight for women's rights because such changes would strengthen the nation. For even the most radical, the socialist or anarchist, women's liberation remained part of a larger revolutionary nationalism. In Charlotte Beahan's review of the women's press at the time, she notes their constant awareness of developments in the West. Their incentive to fight emerged from a desire to measure up to foreign women and surpass their achievements.[16]

The actual advancements of Western women were often not as thoroughgoing as assumed by Chinese women; this ongoing process of international imagination became an important aspect of twentieth-century feminism. British suffragette Emmeline Pankhurst would find inspiration in the 1912 actions of the Women's Suffrage Alliance in Nanjing. While on trial for window-breaking protests in London, she expressed a similar kind of measuring up: "Is there anything more marvelous in modern times than the kind of spontaneous outburst in every country of this women's movement? Even in China—and I think it somewhat of a disgrace to Englishmen—even in China women have won the vote, as an outcome of a successful revolution."[17] She referred, in exaggerated fashion, to the brief existence of women delegates in the Guangdong Assembly, or perhaps she truly believed that Chinese women had already won their revolution.

In spite of this early twentieth-century connection between women and nationalism, whenever I have tried to weave the sisters' stories together with significant national events, the pieces refuse to form a coherent picture. Amy and Shuhua vaguely allude to historical incidents but do not adhere to their chronology. The history of men of power and politics forms a distant back-drop to their everyday life. I shouldn't be surprised at how hard they have made it for me to connect them to conventional dates and political markers; the challenge they present is one of learning what needs to be rewritten for a fuller understanding of the past.

There is the disconcerting detail, for example, that Amy once slipped into our conversation. As late afternoon rays of California sun illuminated her powdered face, I listened carefully because I was wildly pleased to be having a conversation with her in Mandarin. After returning to the United States from my first two years in China, I had looked forward to speaking with my grand-mother in her native language. I wanted to prove myself to her. After many attempts, over weeks, then months, to start a conversation in Chinese, I finally gave up. Amy refused to believe that I could speak more than the most basic of phrases. She would say with painstaking slowness to me, her grand-daughter with a foreign face, "*Ni xi bu xihuan chi zhongguo fan?*" (Do you like to eat Chinese food?). Then one day, she let her guard down. I said some-thing casual in Chinese, and she suddenly began to tell me a story in Chinese. She told me about a time when fighting broke out in Beijing. She and her family hastily gathered a few belongings, slipped out the door to a carriage waiting in Ganmian Hutong, and departed the city. Soldiers in the streets displayed bloody heads speared on wooden poles. A body had been subjected to a grisly act she called *tianhuo*, heaven's fire. The victim's stomach was cut open, filled with oil, and lit on fire. When Amy saw horror creep across my face, she repeated these details. She liked to remain in control, springing these hidden traps.

I sometimes think I dreamt this conversation. I forgot to take notes afterward, notes on the anomalous irruption of history into her girlhood and of Chinese into our conversation. I can find no record of the conversation in my journals. It appears in my memory like one of the dreams I have in the first weeks after my return to the United States from a separate life in Beijing, dreams in which I and everyone else, regardless of their linguistic ability, speaks Chinese. When I told my mother about the *tianhuo* story, she con-firmed that she had heard similar ones as a child. She classified them as the "be glad you live in America" type of story.

When I asked my grandmother what caused this violence, she shrugged her shoulders. She was just a child. I conjecture that it took place in March 1912 after the revolution and overthrow of the Qing court. Bloodshed occurred in numerous riots and revolts leading up to the boy emperor's abdi-cation. Most of the fighting took place in southern provinces. Violence broke out in Beijing, in the form of an army mutiny, only after the establishment of the new Republic. In my reconstruction, the severed heads displayed on poles in Amy's story belong to executed mutineers. In a time of hope that the transition from dynastic rule to Republican government would lead China to become a modern nation, the spectacle of violence paraded through the streets represented the intrusion of one period into the next. Only one year earlier, a scholar veteran of the Ministry of Punishments had implemented a new criminal code abolishing the public exposure of heads and corpses, obviously ignored in the mutiny.[18] The Red-Coat Man of the old system marches on, taunting death with a brave song.

Meanwhile, Li Ruolan fled with her daughters from Beijing to a small house somewhere in the Hebei countryside, probably near Baoding, where an aunt lived. There were not enough beds for everyone, so Amy slept in the bottom drawer of an empty chest, pulled out trundle-like and padded with extra clothing. The quick escape, the anxious whispers of adults, and then a dresser drawer for a bed, to her, made up the elements of an adventure, one that her American-born descendents could not face with such courage. But, as I imagine a girl, tucked into a wooden box with her mother's coat cushioning her body, I am struck by the tender vulnerability of a child, breathing heavily in her sleep and traveling through troubled dreams in a coffinlike vessel.

To arrive at this moment of revolution though, I must first back up. Liang Qichao's promotion of a national parliamentary government had eclipsed Kang Youwei's hope for a constitutional monarchy. Cosmopolitan Sun Yatsen, a doctor first educated by missionaries in Hawaii, emerged as the political actor who tipped the balance toward the downfall of the Qing dynasty. Embracing the traditional rebel model of the Triad society, Sun first formed a secret revolutionary group in 1894. After a thwarted attempt to take over the Guangzhou government offices, Sun initially took refuge in Japan, where he eventually joined with other likeminded Chinese to form the Revolutionary Alliance, based on a loosely defined platform of nationalism, democracy, and concern for the people's livelihood. Aided by funds Sun raised from overseas Chinese in Japan, Singapore, Europe, and the United States, they launched years of attacks on the Qing government.

By 1911, the Manchu-governed dynasty had been weakened by scattered revolts, worsening economic conditions, and lack of support among its own officials. In October, a spontaneous rebellion occurred in the tricity area of Wuhan. A hidden bomb belonging to a revolutionary study society in the Russian concession of Hankou accidentally exploded. When authorities investigated, they found membership lists containing the names of soldiers from the local imperial army, about a third of whose troop members had secretly joined revolutionary societies. Troops in all three of Wuhan's cities mutinied, igniting a string of revolts and anti-Qing defections in provinces around the country. This revolutionary fervor included ardent women who formed their own corps, such as the Northern Expeditionary Dare-to-Die Regiment, which included student volunteers from Tianjin, and the Chinese Women's Espionage Training Institute, organized by prostitutes in Shanghai.[19]

On December 29, 1911, Sun Yatsen was elected provisional president of a fledgling Chinese Republic. In its new capital of Nanjing, provincial delegates assembled to form the National Council and negotiate an interim constitution. The last of the Chinese dynasties came to an end when the boy-emperor Puyi abdicated the throne on February 12, 1912. The following day, Sun resigned from the provisional presidency, which the Nanjing Council then conferred on Yuan Shikai, the former Qing official widely considered the only figure capable of unifying the new nation with his combination of military backing and administrative experience. Almost immediately Yuan Shikai took advantage of the situation. Using the pretext of a violent army mutiny in Beijing, which some guessed Yuan instigated to prove his indispensability in the north, he convinced the National Council to allow his inauguration to take place in Beijing, a city central to his power base. Shortly after a mother and her children fled the city in a horse-drawn carriage, Yuan assumed presidency, on March 10, 1912.

Ling Fupeng served in the National Council as a delegate from the Zhili region. My grandmother displayed a photograph of her father, taken in 1912, on top of the television in her San Francisco apartment. Clutching the white gloves of a Western statesman, he posed at the base of a sweeping staircase painted onto the photographer's studio backdrop. A tuxedo replaces his Chinese robe and hat. When asked about this image, Amy explained, "When the Republic came to China, they asked my father to be the speaker of the Senate in 1912. He got everybody together and helped form the Senate represented by eighteen provinces."

The provisional constitution issued by the Nanjing Council called for national elections to fill two chambers of Parliament, the Senate and House of Representatives. After the elections, the majority party would select a premier, and Yuan Shikai would resign in order for new presidential elections to be held. In late March, armed members of the Women's Suffrage Alliance charged the chambers of the Nanjing Council to demand the vote for women of the new Republic. Guards forced them back into the visitors' gallery. The following day, the women entered the chambers again, after breaking windows, raising blood-drenched fists, and fighting off guards who blocked their

Ling Fupeng at the National Council meetings, Nanjing, 1912

way. On the third day of their protests, sufficient measures had been taken to prevent their entry.[20]

Sun Yatsen reorganized the Revolutionary Alliance into a political party called the Guomindang, or the Nationalist Party. Thirty-year-old Song Jiaoren, a long-time member of the Revolutionary Alliance, became its leading force. Over three hundred newly formed parties competed for parliamentary seats during the national elections held in late 1912. Song Jiaoren's campaign, which warned against the ambitions of Yuan Shikai and called for a true democracy, helped the Guomindang defeat their three largest rival parties. Wide consensus held that Song would be chosen as the new premier.

News of these events seeped into the consciousness of Ling Fupeng's children, who knew their father was involved. In *Ancient Melodies*, Shuhua remembers asking Li Ruolan for an explanation of the emperor's sudden departure from the throne. "I learned only that the revolutionary people had taken his place. The President and a number of his followers had moved into the palace. Some of them, Mother said, were my father's friends. This fact made the beautiful palaces feel less mysterious."[21]

Even as these changes occurred, Li Ruolan's oldest daughter entered a marriage arranged by Ling Fupeng and a friend of his whose son was close in age to Shuzhi. This friend held profitable stakes in the new railroads beginning to crisscross the country, and the two fathers agreed their children made a good match of families. As Amy put it, "My sister married into the railroad." She explained that soon after the wedding, Shuzhi departed on a train to a northern town near Harbin, where Shuzhi's husband ran a cigarette factory and sold his product mostly to Russians.

Shuhua's chapter in *Ancient Melodies* titled "Two Weddings" dates her sister's wedding to 1912. She dramatizes the transition of the times by comparing her brother's wedding ceremony with that of Fifth Sister. Both were married in the same year at the age of seventeen. I suspect that Shuhua concocted her brother's wedding as a fictional device that provides symmetrical contrast; a newspaper source gives his age in 1913 as fifteen, which would make him only fourteen on his wedding day. But if we follow the chronology of "Two Weddings," Eldest Brother, only son of boastful Third Mother, married early in the year. The Republic had just formed, and Sun Yatsen still served as the provisional president. The wedding presumably occurred just before an army mutiny would send them scrambling to the countryside. He had also been betrothed to the child of one of Ling Fupeng's close friends, in an agreement made eleven years earlier, when Eldest Brother was six years old and his bride-to-be only five.

Ling Fupeng consulted the ancient calendar to select an auspicious date for the wedding. The family prepared the red wedding gown and headdress and displayed them in the house before sending them to the bride. The younger girls pushed a blushing Eldest Brother forward to look at them and teased him about the beautiful bride he would soon see for the first time. When the day arrived, red silk banners festooned the main hall. Eldest Brother wore a blue gown and black satin jacket and stood in the courtyard waiting for the sedan-chair carriers to depart for the bride's home. His mother complained about how ordinary his gown looked. She blamed the newly established Republic, which prohibited her from wearing the Qing costume of an official's concubine and her son from wearing a Mandarin robe.

Overhearing Third Mother's grumbles, Eighth Sister took Shuhua aside and whispered, "Little Tenth, now you see why I said a Republic is fair to everyone. Those who have sons are no better than those who have none. You see, a country with an emperor encourages mischief. If Third Mother could wear Mandarin costume today, she would look down on everyone else in the house."[22] Eighth Sister also ridiculed Third Mother's delight that President Sun Yatsen had sent the family a wedding present. She told Shuhua that the president was an ordinary man who had once been a country doctor. Awed by her sister's knowledge, Shuhua asked if she, too, wanted to be a leader. Eighth Sister responded, "Of course I want to become a leader. You know I want to study medicine and become a doctor, then I shall know many people and shall be a leader to reform China. I will reform our family, too!"[23] Eighth Sister, like Amy, wanted to study medicine, a calling that attracted many reformers early in their careers.

Eldest Brother's bride wore a red silk veil that covered her entire head, but Fifth Sister's groom wanted an updated ceremony, with the bride in a white Western gown and himself in tails. As a man of the new Republic, he wished to ride in an ordinary carriage to pick up his bride. Father laughed when his friend anxiously presented all of his son's requests regarding the ceremony. Mother frowned, however, when she told Fifth Mother about the conversation. She did not want her daughter to wear the color of death on her wedding day. In a compromise, she arranged for Fifth Sister to wear a pink veil with red flowers and a coat and skirt cut from pink embroidered silk. The ceremony took place in a hotel reception room. A Western-style orchestra played Christian hymns and military marches in the background. In spite of all the modern trappings, Fifth Sister reacted much as Li Ruolan had on the eve of her own wedding. She cried bitterly for days before her marriage to a man she had never met. One evening Shuhua and Eighth Sister snuck out of bed to eavesdrop beneath her window as their mother comforted her. When Eighth Sister could no longer bear listening to them, she grabbed Shuhua's hand and dragged her back to their bedroom, where she threw herself onto the bed and sobbed. On the day of the ceremony, the bride with a wreath of red flowers holding her veil in place and the groom in his top hat bowed, in Confucian manner, to their parents, relatives, and friends. The stern announcement of each bow by the master of ceremonies reminded the younger sisters of an old-fashioned funeral.

Amy recalled that on the day before Shuzhi's wedding, she sat in the corridor outside her sister's bedroom and cried. Her mother flung open the door and pulled her into the room. "Why are you crying?" she demanded, even though her eyelids were also red and swollen. Amy pointed at her sister's tear-streaked face. "Stop it, you are being silly girls," her mother scolded. Amy looked at her mother and said, "You have so many girls, but you don't know how to protect them. I don't want to be your daughter any more," before running out of the room.

On the day of the wedding, she stayed with her mother in a back room as the clamor in the banquet hall rose in waves with each toast. Between courses they helped Shuzhi change into different gowns before sending her out again to pour wine into the tiny toasting cups of her father's guests. They drunkenly cheered the bride as she wove her way between the crowded tables. The next day Amy confronted her father, threatening, "Don't you ever engage me out to a man I've never met. I'll run away, and you'll never find me."

Amy told me that Shuhua's marriage had also been arranged when she was young. One biographical source for Ling Shuhua indicates that her father made a verbal agreement with Tianjin Police Chief Zhao Bingjun, a colleague from his prison reform days, that Shuhua would marry his son when they reached a suitable age.[24] Amy confirmed that Shuhua was nine years old when their father promised her away. "So you see," Amy concluded, "I was the only daughter not engaged out. I told my father, 'I want to be a doctor.' He said, 'How much is that going to cost me.' I said, 'I won't use a penny of your money.'"

· Seven ·

Mist

Shortly after Shuzhi's train, bound for a cigarette factory in the north, pulled out of Beijing, Shuhua boarded a ship. It was April 1912, and she stood shortest among the Ling children pressed against the rail. Their reflection wavered in the dark water below. Turbines slowly spun to life, and the still water at the ship's aft churned into a steady white spume. The faces of their collective reflection vanished beneath the rushing water.

The first school that Ling Shuhua attended was not in China. Her formal education began at the end of a journey through the Yellow Sea, around the south of Korea, and into the waters of the Pacific Ocean. After years of studying with the family tutor in Beijing, Shuhua traveled to Japan where she and several of her siblings enrolled in school. Whether Ling Fupeng or any of the mothers accompanied the children to Japan is not clear from either of the sisters' accounts. Both vaguely indicate that their parents remained in Beijing or Tianjin. Shuhua writes in *Ancient Melodies* that she and four sisters lived in Kyoto, the hometown of their father's friend Mr. Matsumoto, who had initially suggested the idea of their schooling in Japan. Amy told me that they were sent to Yokohama. A newspaper account placed them in Kobe.[1] Getting the children out of the capital may have been a precautionary move, due to the recent unrest in Beijing. Although sending them to a foreign country might seem a brash decision, the Ling children followed a route traveled before them by several waves of Chinese students as well as their own father, eastward from the urban centers of China's seaboard to the modernizing and increasingly powerful nation of Japan.

After the Boxer Rebellion of 1900, Qing reform programs sent study missions to Japan, such as Ling Fupeng's prison investigation tour, and after 1905 provided state sponsorship for Chinese students to enroll in modern Japanese schools. In the mid-nineteenth century, Japan like China had faced encroaching Western powers. In 1853, Commodore Matthew Perry's gunboats in Tokyo Bay forced the Shogun into a series of unequal treaties, which

93

gave the United States jurisdiction over areas in Japan and tariff controls. These imperial designs were then reenacted by Britain, Russia, and Holland. In 1868, an internal revolt overthrew the Shogunal government. The Meiji Restoration replaced the old government with new officials who established a constitutional monarchy. Meiji thinkers of this period quickly adopted Western ideas, transforming them into a vision of Japanese modernity and national sovereignty. Their efforts attracted the attention of Chinese struggling to reform their government and strengthen resistance to Western imperialism. Like the Europeans and Americans, the Japanese began their own program of imperial conquest. Their 1895 victory in the first Sino-Japanese War allowed them to secure Taiwan and acquire foreign concessions in Chinese cities like Tianjin. An 1896 treaty gave Japan all the same privileges held by Western powers in China. Even with this military tension between their countries, when the Japanese defeated the Tsarist armies of Russia in the 1904–1905 war in Manchuria, the admiration of Chinese intellectuals for Meiji Japan grew.

The victory of an Asian nation over a Western power eclipsed Japan's recent aggression toward China. It served, in the minds of Chinese students and reformers, as a clarion call for national strengthening. Thousands of students, some on provincial scholarships and some self-financed, flocked to Japan. The island nation provided many young Asians a space for intellectual exchange. Among the intellectual circles in the Tokyo-Yokohama area, revolutionaries discussed the concept of Asia, which until then had been a relatively insignificant label applied to them from the outside by Europeans. They conceived of Asia united not by geographic proximity or race but by peoples who had lost their countries to Western invaders. The short-lived Asian Solidarity Society organized in 1907, for example, attracted Indian, Chinese, Japanese, Vietnamese, and Filipino members to meetings held in a Tokyo Unitarian church.[2] However, while Japan gave birth to such pan-Asian sentiments, it also served as a breeding ground for Chinese nationalism, which would soon find itself at odds with Japanese imperial ambitions.

In Japan, many Chinese students experienced a sense of intellectual and political freedom enhanced by their collective gathering abroad. Debate buzzed throughout the Chinese quarter, where study groups published newspapers advocating anti-Qing revolution. They promoted internal strengthening against foreign invaders, modernization through scientific thought, and social and political reorganization. They condemned tradition as superstitious and backward. Art students criticized the formulaic court styles of late Qing painting. They sketched from nude models in the studios of Japanese copy masters of European realism. Men in Tokyo cut off their long, braided queues in symbolic defiance of the Manchu government then still in power. Some studied ballroom dancing as an expression of modern cosmopolitanism, and this urbane superficiality drove at least one disillusioned Chinese student out of Tokyo to a small town in northern Japan. In self-enforced seclusion in Sendai from the frivolity of waltzing intellectuals, Lu Xun, who would become China's most preeminent twentieth-century writer, continued his education in medicine.

Women also enrolled in Japanese schools and participated in political activities. Several flamboyant female leaders, who spearheaded the movement for women's rights, emerged from this early twentieth-century period. He Zhen, a feminist and anarchist, believed that women's liberation depended upon a radical departure from the traditional family, as well as economic independence from male dominance and the unequal distribution of wealth under capitalism. She served as editor and publisher of the Tokyo-based newspaper *Tianyi* (Natural justice). The cover of the July 1907 issue declared, "The destruction of established society and the realization of human equality are our main aims. In addition to a women's revolution, we advocate racial, political, and economic revolution."[3]

The revolutionary Qiu Jin also began her activist life during a two-year stint in Japan. After submitting to an arranged marriage and giving birth to two children, she fled her family at the age of twenty-six and boarded a ship for Japan in the summer of 1904. In Tokyo, Qiu Jin stood out because of her militancy and habit of wearing Western men's attire. She claimed as role models Madame Roland of the French Revolution and Sofya Perovskaya, the Russian revolutionary who was executed for her involvement in the assassination of Tsar Alexander. She published articles calling for revolution and equality for women, carried a short sword, and practiced bomb making and marksmanship. After this period of political awakening, she returned to China, began publishing *Zhongguo nübao* (Chinese women's journal), and ended up beheaded at thirty-two in 1907 after being implicated in a political assassination. She joined the ranks of the female martyrs she so idolized.[4]

It was at this time, as political opinions of Chinese overseas students in Japan filtered back to China, that Ling Fupeng traveled to Japan on his prison reform missions of 1903 and 1905. Ling Fupeng forged his connections with Japan at the height of an intellectual exchange characterized by the idea of *tongwen*, "common culture," referring to the social and cultural traits shared by China and Japan. For many Chinese, *tongwen* promised a pathway to the success of Japan's synthesis of East and West in building a modern nation.[5] Shuhua and Amy's father viewed Japan as a crucible for Asian modernization, and his acquaintance with Chinese and Japanese officials who traveled between the two countries influenced his decision to send the children to Japan for schooling.

Ling Fupeng's friend Mr. Matsumoto, mentioned by Shuhua, was quite possibly Matsumoto Kamejiro, a well-known Japanese language teacher to Chinese students at a popular school in Tokyo and from 1908 to 1912 at the Beijing College of Law and Administration.[6] As Chinese who had studied in Japan gradually replaced the temporary workforce of Japanese teachers in modern Chinese schools, Matsumoto returned to Japan in 1912, perhaps as chaperone to the Ling children on their steamer voyage.

By the time of their arrival, the trend of Chinese students enrolling in Japanese schools had reached its peak and begun a downward turn. After the founding of the Republic, Chinese reformers increasingly turned their backs on tradition and even on the idea of synthesis exemplified by Japan. *Tongwen* lost much of its former appeal, and Chinese students eventually packed up their Tokyo dreams and sailed home. Lu Xun, for example, was motivated to return by an illuminated slide from Japanese-occupied Manchuria. In a Sendai classroom darkened for a lantern show of war slides, he witnessed the apathy of Chinese who stood by while Japanese soldiers shot fellow Chinese accused of spying for the Russians. Shifting his commitment from medicine to literature, Lu Xun devoted himself to a spiritual instead of physical healing of his country.

The sisters' accounts of the Ling children's sojourn in Japan are brief and insubstantial. For a long time I assumed that Amy, at age eight, traveled along with her siblings because she sometimes mentioned details of their life in Japan as if she had been there. One day when I asked her about the Chinese community in Japan, she finally told me that she had stayed behind in the care of the aunt who lived near Baoding in Hebei province. She was considered too young to undertake the long trip. In *Ancient Melodies*, Shuhua writes that she was nine when they arrived in Kyoto, where they lived for two years in the house of their father's friend Mr. Matsumoto, who took care of all arrangements for them. Another source indicates she was twelve in the year 1912 and that her sisters enrolled at the Common Culture High School in Kobe, a school for Chinese students established by reformer Liang Qichao.[7] Regardless of this discrepancy, Shuhua traveled abroad at a young age, in circumstances certain to leave a deep impression.

Shuhua sets up her stay in Japan with a sentimental chapter of her autobiography titled "My Foster-Parents." She describes her introduction at the age of eight to one of her father's close friends and his wife. Uncle Chao had traveled widely and excelled in all of the traditional scholar-official arts: music, chess, calligraphy, and painting. His wife played the *guzheng*, a seven-stringed harp, with great skill. Shuhua charmed the couple, whose only daughter had died at a young age. With Ling Fupeng's approval, they decided to adopt her. After exchanging gifts in a ceremony marking their bond of affection, Shuhua spent long days with her foster mother, playing in her well-tended garden, learning to play classical Chinese music, and flying home-made kites. Shuhua wistfully notes that the warmth and attention she received from her foster mother contrasted with the invisibility she experienced in her own family. Uncle Chao had once served as a private secretary to Yuan Shikai in the Beiyang Army. This thin biographical information matches with the career trajectory of Zhao Bingjun, the Tianjin Police Chief who had worked with Ling Fupeng under Yuan Shikai, and whose son Shuhua had been betrothed to by her father. If her foster father was really this Zhao, could it be that the informal adoption ceremony, which she describes with the delight of being chosen from her siblings for the privilege of such refined company, was actually a ritual to confirm that one day she would become their daughter-in-law? Perhaps, like Amy's purposeful forgetting of her father's other concubines and reference to her half-sisters as cousins, Shuhua hid the traditional arranged marriage lurking in her background behind the romantic fantasy of talented and loving foster parents. Such a beautiful veneer seemed better suited to a memoir that aimed to charm. In *Ancient Melodies*, one year after meeting her foster parents, Shuhua departed for Japan, leaving behind not only her real parents but also the melancholy tunes of her foster mother's harp and the farewell song she played on their last night together.

> My heart is broken, my mind troubled,
> Our love is deep, deep, deep,
> So deep, how can I bear to part.[8]

Shuhua collapses her time in Japan into one short chapter about their arrival in Kyoto during the Sakura Festival. She describes the attractions, women in graceful kimonos, colorful paper lanterns, and cherry trees that bloomed into powder pink clouds. She dwells on the image of a traveling monk in a straw hat whom they observed amid the trees. Carrying a bamboo flute, he slowly walked down the hill. Mr. Matsumoto told them that such monks had no home or personal property but wandered the countryside playing the flute and resting wherever people gave them food. Eighth Sister sighed with envy for this roaming lifestyle as he explained how ancient Japanese heroes used to disguise themselves as this type of monk, traveling from place to place until they found adventure.

Of their daily life in Japan, Shuhua writes only that they lived in a two-story house with paper windows, which opened onto mountains whose peaks nestled in the clouds. Although Chinese communities existed in Kyoto and Kobe, they were not as large as those in Tokyo or Yokohama. The Ling children began to learn Japanese upon arrival and attended classes with Japanese students of their same age. Regardless of their improving language skills, I imagine they felt stares at their Chinese clothing and overheard comments about them that marked their difference. The first Sino-Japanese War still lingered in recent historical memory. A gradual shift began for the Japanese, who had once seen China as the center of the cultural world but now gained an increasing sense of dominance in the region. Chinese students in Japan also anxiously acknowledged the success of Japanese modernization in relation to China's continuing vulnerability. In the streets, taunts sometimes stung the ears of overseas students who had grown sensitive to the humiliation of China at the hands of their host country. A common slur used to refer to boys or men who wore the Manchu hairstyle, shaved in the front with a long pigtail in back, was *chanchan bozu*; the syllables *chanchan* phonetically mimic the Chinese language or Chinese names as they sounded to the Japanese (*chan* is also a diminutive term used for children), and *bozu* is a disrespectful term for a monk or young boy.

The Ling children had probably heard about the activities of their older overseas counterparts in Tokyo. The bifurcated attitude of these intellectuals toward Japan would influence the sisters' future ways of thinking about nationality. The selective vision that enabled Chinese student activists, from the martyred Qiu Jin to the emerging writer Lu Xun, to view Japan even with its recent military aggression against China as a safe haven for intellectual development involved a paradoxical stance unique to an era of nascent ideas about nationhood. Later observers would interpret the concept of *tongwen* or "common culture" as a Japanese fiction to trick the Chinese into cooperating with Japanese imperialism, but many Chinese had once embraced it with hope and optimism.

Shuhua foreshadows a tragic event and their consequent departure from Japan in her "Sakura Festival" chapter. One night before turning out the light in their new room with bedding arranged on a tatami-mat floor, Eighth Sister sang one of her favorite songs in a low voice:

> Flower, yet not a flower,
> Mist, yet not a mist;
> It comes at night and
> Before dawn it goes away:
> Like a dream in spring it never stays long,
> As morning cloud vanishes without a trace.[9]

Shuhua remembers that, at the time, she appreciated the haunting melody of her sister's song but not the meaning that would later become apparent. As the two girls lay together in the dark, the moon shone through the branches of a pear tree, tracing a delicate shadow on the wall. A breeze lofted the curtain into the air and scattered a few flower petals across the floor.

According to Shuhua's one-paragraph account that opens the following chapter in *Ancient Melodies*, Seventh and Eighth Sisters drowned one summer day while playing in a waterfall on a high mountain. Immediately after the accident, Mr. Matsumoto cut short their education in Japan. He sent the surviving children back to their parents in China. Shuhua concludes, "I left Japan full of regrets; all my beautiful visions in that country vanished as suddenly as morning clouds from the sky."[10]

Amy's mention of the years her siblings spent in Japan was almost always a footnote to her matter-of-fact report of the brother who died young. Asked about her siblings, she usually described three older sisters, Shuzhi, Shuping, and Shuhua, and then added on the brother who drowned in a waterfall in Japan. The blame she often placed on Japan as the instigator of suffering at home in China may have begun with this fragment of tragedy, lodged in her memory by whispered stories about the accident. She told me that if she had been sent to Japan she would have died in that waterfall. Of all the children, she said, she was the most daring. She would certainly have wanted to play in the water.

The spare, surreal quality of the sisters' accounts made me wonder how they experienced the deaths. I replayed in my mind the scene of the drownings. Mr. Matsumoto scrambled down the bank and pulled the cold bodies out of the water. He pounded on their chests and listened to their blue lips. Guilt and terror stiffened his face. Several days later, he stood on a pier, directing the dockworkers to handle the child-size wooden boxes more carefully. The rest of the children silently marched up the gangplank, holding their breath against the sharp, fish-smelling water. Their eyes searched the shore for something familiar: a tree, a building, or a face. With a final glance back, they entered the boat that carried them and the still bodies of their sisters and brother back to China.

Several years after I recreated this scene, a Japanese researcher who has written on Ling Shuhua sent me a copy of an article she found in an August 11, 1913, issue of the *Kobe Shimbun* newspaper.[11] In antiquated Japanese diction, a local Kobe reporter recounts a drowning on the previous day of four Chinese children, three girls and one boy, in the lower section of a famous local waterfall. A twenty-minute walk up a steep hill to the east of Kobe, the Nunobiki Falls rush down a rocky mountain face in a stair-step pattern of four linked waterfalls. The long stream of water cascading between lush, green trees resembles a continuous bolt of flowing cloth, which gives the falls its name meaning pulled fabric. The final fall is the tallest, where the white water unfurls over a forty-three-meter drop.

According to the article, at five in the afternoon of August 10, 1913, a man named Nakamura Kamezou passed by the falls on his way home and spotted the bodies of three young Chinese beauties and a drowned boy. They were floating in the rapids of the dark, blue water at the base of Namidagataki or Teardrop Falls, the name the author gives, with poetic allusion, to a segment of the lower falls. Shocked, the witness Nakamura reported what he'd seen to the police. They then brought in a doctor to inspect the bodies. He guessed the girls were fifteen, sixteen, and seventeen years old, and the boy thirteen. A crowd gathered to observe the sad scene and expressed sympathy for the drowned siblings. The girls all wore Chinese summer clothes of light colored silk and silken underwear. The oldest girl had a light blue, silk sash tied around her waist. However, the journalist draws our attention to the important clue that although they all wore jackets, they had taken off their trousers. Their trousers and four silk umbrellas were found beneath Tanigawa Bridge.

The police interviewed witnesses who had seen four young people resting at a nearby teahouse at 3:00 p.m. They wanted to eat ice cream, but the teahouse had none, so they bought a postcard of the Nunobiki Falls and continued their climb. They went through a black gate near the falls, after they had been observed at 4:00 p.m. by office workers who saw them walking around in front of their building. One of the workers told them not to proceed further up the mountain, and they turned around and came back down through the gate. Approximately one hour later, their bodies were found in the turbulent water at the bottom of the falls.

Although the reason for the deaths could not be stated with absolute certainty, the article surmised from the police evidence that the boy, who was totally naked, had shed his clothes to swim in the pool at the base of the falls. He got caught in the pounding water, leading his sisters one by one to take off their trousers and jump in to try to save him. They didn't have time to remove their jackets. The bodies of the two older sisters were stiffer than the youngest girl, causing the police to speculate that they had jumped into the water first. The oldest sister had a wallet with two yen and Chinese books in the breast pocket of her jacket.

The deceased are listed with their confirmed ages as a boy Ling Shujia (fifteen) and three girls Ling Shuying (eighteen), Ling Ruiqing (seventeen), and Ling Darong (sixteen), the children of Ling Fupeng, who had been living in Kobe at an address in the Shimo-yamate-dori section of the city. Earlier in the afternoon, the son of the family had gone out with his three older sisters to visit the Ikuta Shrine. When they didn't return home, their family

Postcard of Nunobiki Falls, Kobe, ca. 1910s. Courtesy of Anker Nielsen.

tutor went to find them but heard on the way to the shrine about some Chinese who had drowned in the Nunobiki Falls. He immediately went back to the house to tell their mother, a thirty-nine-year-old woman with a maiden name of Xie, and two remaining sisters Ling Shuping (fifteen) and Ling Shuhua (thirteen). Together they went to the Nunobiki police station, where they were shocked to hear the story of what had occurred from a police officer. City officials arranged for the corpses to be sent back to their house.

The Ling children had been sent to Japan for their studies in May of the previous year. The daughters Shuying and Ruiqing had been in the second year at the Common Culture High School, and Darong in the first year. They had all been beautiful and intelligent, and the oldest daughter especially loved her fifteen-year-old brother, causing her to leap in after him, which led to this tragedy of Chinese beauty lost in the tearful Nunobiki Falls.

This melodramatic piece of journalism, infused with a tone of melancholy beauty and told from the perspective of a Japanese observer with ready access to a surprisingly modern-sounding police record, fills in details missing from the sisters' versions and my imagining of what happened. They lived in Kobe. Four children died in the falls. Their names were Shuying, Ruiqing, Darong, and Shujia. The three eldest attended the Common Culture High School. They had a family tutor. At least one parent, Ling née Xie, most likely Third Mother, had traveled with them to Kobe. She—not Mr. Matsumoto—collected the bodies, which had been discovered by a stranger on his way home. They had wanted to eat ice cream. The girls wore light-colored, silk summer clothes. They bought a postcard of Nunobiki Falls. They walked through a black gate but turned around when told to go no further up the mountain. They laid down their silk umbrellas under a bridge. The boy stripped and jumped into cool water. A waterlogged book remained in the breast pocket of the oldest sister even after her lungs filled with suffocating water.

The character for *shu* used to print the name Shujia in the *Kobe Shimbun* article is the one 淑 containing the three-drop water radical on the left side and means maidenlike, the water connoting purity, fluidity, and femininity. If the only son of the family had temporarily been given a girl's name to fool death from stealing him away prematurely, the trick did not work. Only Shuping and Shuhua stayed home that day. Only two survived.

How was the return from Japan of six reduced to two explained to Amy, the youngest daughter who had been left behind? In *Ancient Melodies*, a quiet transition occurs after the paragraph that swiftly recounts the drownings. Before the accident, Eighth Sister had figured as Shuhua's favorite. Shuhua had looked up to her as the sister who boldly challenged tradition, declaring,

"I will reform our family, too!" Shuhua expresses no explicit grief over the death of Eighth Sister, but in the chapters that follow the return from Japan, Mai—the pseudonym given to Amy—appears as the predominant sister. Shuhua writes of her, "She was witty and eloquent, which often reminded me of Eighth Sister; therefore I also became one of her admirers."[12] Like Eighth Sister, Mai aspired to become a doctor. A replacement stepped into the void, assuming many of the characteristics of her predecessor. Shuhua deals with the loss through this subtle narrative transition, telling of the strengthened bond between herself and Amy in the cold aftermath of death.

Shuhua told a more superstitious version of the deaths to her daughter. Before Eighth Sister left the house on that fateful morning in Japan, Shuhua borrowed a comb from her. She was never able to return it. The memory of this simple object, the last thing they exchanged, haunted her the rest of her life. She refused to ever lend a comb to anyone, believing it would bring bad luck. Even in the ways Amy and Shuhua mourned, they diverged in dramatic and characteristic ways. Amy expressed her grief through anger at the Japanese. Ghostly images caught Shuhua unaware.

· *Eight* ·

Amid Ghosts

$\int$huhua awoke in a moonlit room and saw a young woman standing by the side of her desk. The woman held a wooden comb in her hand. She dragged it across her scalp and down through her hair, smooth as water, in a single stroke until it pulled free at the ends. Shuhua sat up in bed. Peering through the dark, she could only see the elegant profile of the woman's face. She blinked and tried to shake off the transfixing vision, but the woman continued to slowly comb her hair. Shuhua shrank down and pulled the covers over her head. The next morning, sun blazed through the windows, but the late night apparition lingered in her memory.

They had settled in the rapidly growing port city of Tianjin. After Shuhua returned from Japan, Amy left her aunt's house in the Hebei countryside to rejoin the family. Ling Fupeng thought the Tianjin schools were better than those in Beijing and had built a Western-style house there. Together under one roof again, the family's recent tragedy muted the tensions between the mothers. The children moved gingerly through rooms filled with an unspoken absence. As they gradually explored their new living space, they discovered a house haunted by *guizi* of all kinds, wandering ghosts, bedroom specters, foreign devils, and dead neighbors.

They lived next to the city's public burial ground. From their front gate, they could see low rolling hills spotted with raised mounds of earth. In a chapter of *Ancient Melodies* titled "Ghost Stories," Shuhua explains how they learned that the ground beneath their house had once been part of the graveyard. When workmen cleared the site for construction, they dug up several graves and moved the coffins. Rumors circulated about an exhumed coffin that two workmen had opened. They found a young woman inside. Her complexion was flawless, and she wore a fashionable new dress. As soon as the sun hit her body, it evaporated, leaving behind only a patch of water. Her dress became ash and blew away. The Ling children and servants in the household began to see the beautiful woman standing in their garden. Not even the male servants would enter the courtyard after dusk. They heard footsteps on the staircase at night and the sound of someone flipping the switches of the newly installed electric lamps. Lights flickered on and off in empty rooms. Some saw a tall, ghostly man with a beard sitting on the steps leading to the parlor. This master of the house replaced Ling Fupeng, who was often out of town on official duties.

Five rivers and the Grand Canal flow into the Hai River at Tianjin and then east out to the Yellow Sea. Crisscrossed by this confluence of water, the city rests on marshy land just above sea level. In the early twentieth century, the streets often flooded during summer months. Long an important shipping center in northern China for grain and salt (as well as opium after the Opium Wars), Tianjin had grown by 1914 into a treaty port divided by various interests. Nine foreign concessions—German, Belgian, American, British, Russian, French, Japanese, Italian, and Austro-Hungarian—with export-processing factories and customhouses lined the east and west banks of the Hai River. They ran from the south, where a racecourse and country club drew the patronage of foreign residents, to the north, where a bustling area of small merchants and handicraft shops butted up against the old city. The main thoroughfare changed names as it crossed concession borders, from Kaiser Wilhelmstrasse to Victoria Road to Rue de France. A hodgepodge of architectural styles defined the concessions, where Victorian homes mingled with French colonial, Italian marble balconies faced the Corinthian columns of Meiji modernism, and Russian onion domes stood out against the skeletal towers of the French Catholic cathedral torched by the Boxers. The Chinese city, once a rectangular walled fortress nestled in a corner below the intersection of the Grand Canal with the Hai River, had flourished in the Qing dynasty, but foreign troops destroyed much of it when they suppressed the Boxer Rebellion in 1900. An area near the old city bordered by Japanese, French, and Chinese municipalities was called the "Three Who-Cares" district because none of these governments regulated its growing business in prostitution, gambling, and opium. To the north of the old city, across Jin Gang Bridge and past the ironworks and cotton mills, lay the Hebei district developed by Yuan Shikai during his tenure as governor-general of Zhili province. The sisters' descriptions lead me to believe they lived in this section of the city, home to many modernization-minded government officials.[1]

According to Amy, Ling Fupeng owned two houses in the city, a small, old one in the German concession purchased during his early days in the Tianjin city government and the newly built residence north of the river. She described for me the second house, the one where she lived, on several occasions. Each time the house took on more fabulous proportions. It was a one-story Chinese house. It was a two-story Western house. It was three-story amalgam of Chinese and Western styles. Her constantly mutating picture captured the mixed conditions of the city itself. Shuhua writes that they lived in a two-story Western-style house, constructed around a courtyard with a small Chinese house half hidden behind a grotto of tall garden rocks. Amy remembered the house as round on the outside, with a modern screened-in porch wrapping around the first floor. European furniture filled some of the rooms, whereas others were decorated in a traditional Chinese style. With the architectural details always shifting, their Tianjin house has grown in my mind into a space of twisting corridors, mismatched rooms, and stairways with carved banisters of dark wood that lead nowhere.

Ling Fupeng had the house built on a large plot of land he owned on the outer edge of Hebei district. Amy told me that the foreigners, with their concessions in the heart of the city, occupied the best land in Tianjin, leaving the low-lying sections to the Chinese. Dampness seeped into every corner of their new home. The remainder of her father's land holdings, she explained, proved to be so marshy that he had them filled in and sold off to slick entrepreneurs. A red-light district of hastily constructed buildings sprouted up nearby, a zone of danger in her story equivalent to the cemetery in Shuhua's account.

In "Ghost Stories," the mothers and children moved into the new house without Ling Fupeng. As they settled in, several policemen stopped by. The new police chief had been trained in the Beijing Police Academy when Ling, as mayor, oversaw its functioning. Concerned that the household of women and children might feel anxious about living alone on a sparsely populated street, he arranged for a small police station to be built near their house. This arrangement comforted the mothers, and the children grew fond of the friendly policemen who frequently passed by the house, but this small show of power did nothing to protect them from the surrounding presence of death.

When the sisters accompanied Li Ruolan across Jin Gang Bridge into the commercial area of the old city, the streets grew crowded. Wealthy foreigners and Chinese barked orders at rickshaw pullers. Children gripped the handles of overloaded carts and wobbled along in the stream of traffic. In the hazy distance, smokestacks spewed black smog into the sky above the dirty water of the Hai River. Scrambling after their mother, Shuhua and Amy passed factory gates where famine-starved workers, dislocated from the countryside by flood or drought, lined up for work. They felt hungry stares press into their backs as they disappeared behind the heavy curtain covering a shop door.

Several months before their family's tragedy in Japan, a more public death had taken place in China. In the spring of 1913, the nation's newly elected representatives began traveling to parliamentary duties in Beijing, where Yuan Shikai had moved the capital. On March 20, Song Jiaoren, leader of the recently triumphant Guomindang, stood waiting on a train platform in Shanghai when a man emerged from the crowd and shot him at close range. He died two days later. The Shanghai police found and arrested the gunman, as well as a man named Ying Kuicheng who had hired the assassin. In Ying's home, detectives discovered secret communications sent to him by the secretary of Yuan Shikai's cabinet. The seized documents—containing instructions such as "destroy Song and receive merit"—implicated Zhao Bingjun by name and Yuan Shikai by association and motive. At the time, Zhao Bingjun served in Yuan's cabinet as the minister of internal affairs and provisional premier.[2] The assassination successfully removed a rising politician who had threatened to curtail Yuan's ambitions.

Public anger erupted over the revealed plot. The Shanghai judiciary called for Zhao Bingjun to appear in court. This once close colleague of Ling Fupeng declared his innocence and tried to pin the blame on a cabinet secretary who went into hiding in the foreign concession area of Qingdao. Zhao avoided prosecution but took a forced leave from his position as premier. On July 16, 1913, Yuan Shikai called for his official resignation. Guomindang members, infuriated by Song Jiaoren's assassination, attempted to establish a second revolutionary government in Nanjing, only to be defeated by Yuan's military force. In a new appointment with the Beijing police, Zhao Bingjun helped Yuan Shikai launch a campaign against the Guomindang. Yuan declared martial law on July 21, 1913. By October of 1913, soon after Ling Fupeng's wives and children had settled into the house in Tianjin, Yuan forced the members of Parliament to elect him to a five-year presidential term. He then dismissed all of the Guomindang's newly elected parliamentary members and banned the political activities of the party as seditious to national order. Sun Yatsen fled once again for Japan.

In December, Ying Kuicheng, who had escaped from prison in Shanghai, showed up in Beijing to ask Yuan Shikai for the merits promised him for carrying out the plot against Song Jiaoren. On secret orders from Yuan Shikai, a detective trailed Ying and knifed him to death on a train traveling from Beijing to Tianjin in early January 1914. Unaware of the behind-the-scenes arrangements, Zhao Bingjun, who now served as the military governor of Zhili, put out a warrant for the arrest of Ying's murderer and complained to Yuan Shikai that after this incident no one would be willing to "do things for the president." Yuan feigned innocence and in February gave Zhao Bingjun a new appointment as leader of the Tianjin municipal government. Days later, Zhao Bingjun ate poisoned soup delivered to his office in Tianjin. Suffering immediately from diarrhea and dizziness, he lost consciousness. Blood seeped from all his orifices, and he died in what many suspected was another assassination arranged by Yuan Shikai to silence the last person with direct knowledge of the Song affair.[3]

My grandmother told me that in Tianjin they lived next to the family whose son Shuhua had been engaged to at the age of nine, meaning they lived next door when death arrived in the final unfolding of this political intrigue. Amy concluded her story about Shuhua's engagement by saying, "This son turned out to be no good, and his mother called off the engagement, saying he didn't deserve Shuhua. His mother liked Shuhua. She was also an artist." The public disgrace that followed Zhao Bingjun after his indecorous end caused his wife to break off the marriage pact between her son and Shuhua. Shuhua's foster mother, who had once strummed for the sleepless girl a bittersweet parting song on a seven-stringed harp, now permanently severed their kinship tie to save her from the shame of a dishonored family.

Contracts once arranged between fathers were left to the final judgment of the women who remained behind, which begs the question of what Ling Fupeng was doing while the political careers of his former colleagues from the Zhili clique rose and fell. He did not break completely from Yuan Shikai, as some of the Zhili clique did out of commitment to the Republican ideals that Yuan had betrayed. He most likely fell in with those who saw dictatorial bureaucratic centralization as a necessary preliminary to reform, and then gradually retreated into the background in the manner of a traditional official who withdraws from the corrupt world of political life to focus on moral self-realization.

Ling Fupeng received an assignment from Yuan Shikai in early 1915 to supervise repairs on the Qing imperial tombs. Yuan had begun grasping after imperial symbolism in an attempt to justify his rule in the public's eye.[4] In *Ancient Melodies*, Shuhua remembers Ruolan saying their father's assignment was a "very fat job" because the government had promised a large amount of money for upkeep of the tombs.[5] Shuhua explains, without giving details, that Yuan chose their father for the job because he knew Ling Fupeng had lost a lot of money during his tenure as mayor of Beijing. With graves surrounding his family in Tianjin, Ling Fupeng wandered down the sacred passageway followed for centuries by Qing imperial funeral processions. He became an aging official sent to the countryside while the death throes of an old order, resurrected by Yuan in ersatz fashion, convulsed the country.

In "Ghost Stories," the morning after seeing the woman with the comb in her bedroom, Shuhua began to describe her vision to a rapt audience. She elaborated certain details to make the story more compelling, borrowing narrative techniques from supernatural tales she'd heard. She described how she'd scratched her hand in the dark until it felt painful. When this effort did not cause her to wake up, she explained to her listeners, she knew the woman was a ghost. Telling ghost stories quickly became the children's favorite activity. One afternoon they gathered to hear a maid spin a new story. As they clutched each other with horror, Third Mother's youngest daughter began to tremble uncontrollably, as if possessed. The incident spooked Third Mother so badly that she went to the Catholic church in the French concession and asked a priest to draw protective signs. She hung the yellow pieces of paper over each doorway in the house. The children refused to sleep unless the lamps stayed lit throughout the night.

The mothers began to play long rounds of mahjong after dinner. Without Ling Fupeng at home, they grew indulgent and allowed the children to play card games at a table next to theirs. These activities turned the household schedule upside down. The mothers and children noisily placed bets throughout the night. They drove away their shadows with the game's regulated motions, chopping the night into manageable portions and starting all over again with each washing of the tiles, until exhausted they retreated one by one to their beds in the early morning. In spite of the seeming disarray of their haunted household, Shuhua writes of these days in Tianjin, "It seems to me, as I recollect it now, that all our mothers were on better terms with each other when Father was away from the house."[6]

Beyond the family's garden, the children played in the public burial ground at the city's edge. In the summer, a carpet of green grass crept over the exposed earth of new unmarked graves. By autumn, the dry blades bent and cracked under their running feet. Shuhua describes in her chapter "Tianjin in Autumn" how she joined the games of pauper children she met in the graveyard. They were coal pickers who gathered whatever pieces of unburned coal they could find by the nearby train tracks. In her favorite game, they would grab each other's waists to form a train that climbed up and over the hillocks of graves. They also lit matches and watched the flame leap from their fingers to the grass, burning like bright red snakes. One of Shuhua's new playmates smiled as she imagined the flames warming her parents, who had been buried in flimsy robes.

When Ling Fupeng returned from his tomb repair assignment, Sixth Mother ingratiated herself with him and arranged for her bedroom to be connected to his sitting room. Third Mother quarreled bitterly with her and eventually moved out of the house to live with her married children. Ling Fupeng put up little protest. Childless Fifth Mother, Li Ruolan's faithful confidante, turned to Buddhist meditation and left the household for confinement in a nunnery. After her departure, Shuhua writes, "I was resentful towards Father. I no longer felt happy when I was with him. His attitude towards life seemed all wrong. . . . Mother always tried to see Father as little as possible. She said what was the use of pretending. I felt ashamed of myself for doing it every day. We only met Father at meal times when the food was put on the table. After dinner I left quickly."[7]

As their traditional household fell apart, Li Ruolan hired a tutor to bring Shuhua up to speed on the coursework taught in the top Tianjin government schools, which only accepted students who had completed the official junior high curriculum. One of Ruolan's friends knew a recent graduate of the highly regarded Tianjin First Girls' Normal School. This young woman agreed to coach Shuhua for the entrance examination. Shuhua stayed at home to study the Chinese classics, mathematics, and history. Amy was sent to the junior high school.

Attending school excited Amy at first, but she soon grew bored. She passed notes with other girls and read popular novels hidden behind the history book propped up on her desk for recitation. One day as she ran to join her classmates in the yard, the teacher called her name. "I know your father is in a high position and you may seem privileged on the outside," he said, "but inside you are really just a stupid girl." Amy described her response:

> I quit junior high because I liked to play all the time. The teacher called me in and bawled me out. "Little Ling," he said, "*Congming lian, ben duchang*, you've got an intelligent face, but a very stupid stomach." I said, "Is that so? I quit." I went home, and my father asked, "What are you going to do now?" I said, "I'm going to study at home." He said, "What are you going to study?" I said, "History, geology, all those courses they take in high school." He said, "You go and find the teachers you want, and I'll pay for it." I thought that was very nice, so I got teachers who taught me chemistry, physics, mathematics. I studied at home the whole year.

Just as Amy returned home to study, Shuhua tested into the First Girls' Normal School. In the early Republican educational system, high school included one preparatory year, followed by four years of course work. Based on her test scores, Shuhua entered the second-year class, which would allow her to graduate in three years. She and her classmates received instruction in an updated program of arts and sciences. The required classes for male and female students were similar except that boys studied agriculture and girls received instruction in home economics, gardening, and sewing.[8]

"Little Liu," a short story Ling Shuhua first published in 1929, opens with a vivid depiction of a girls' school, likely based on her own experience. The narrator reflects back on an incident that occurred during her second year of high school. During afternoon recess, she and her friends gossiped about an older student named Chu, who had recently begun auditing their classes. The leader of the pack, Little Liu, promised to tell a great story about "Duck," the nickname she had given the new student because of her lumpy figure and the way she walked on recently unbound feet. Little Liu asserted that Chu was not only recently married but also pregnant. When questioned on the veracity of her claim, she retorted, "I might as well tell you the whole thing. This morning as I was getting off my rickshaw, I heard this rickshaw puller cursing like the devil: 'Damn rickshaw seat's got this filthy puke all over it. A woman having her morning sickness out in public, that's got to be news!' I took one quick look, that cursing rickshaw puller turned out to belong to Waddles!"⁹

Provoked by Liu's revelation, another girl added, "If you ask me, things are getting out of hand at this school—letting married women come to a girls' school!" They nodded with indignation and discussed the possible ridicule of their school as an "Institute for Cultivating Good Wives and Wise Mothers." Finally, they prepared a plan for their afternoon sewing class, in which they would "build the walls and clear the fields," military terms they'd recently learned in a history lesson. When the teacher walked in, Little Liu stood up and asked her to give them some ideas of things to sew for a baby. Heads turned toward their pregnant classmate, until Chu threw her needlework on the floor and cried out, "What are you all staring at!" She ran out of the classroom crying, and after a brief moment of silence, the girls began to shout, "Hooray for General Little Liu." Their attempt to differentiate themselves from traditional women came at the expense of a woman struggling to go to school in spite of the fact that as a pregnant wife, she was expected to stay at home.

A year after Shuhua started school, Amy took the exam to enter the third-year class along with her sister. Shuhua writes that she and Amy were in the same class and that she admired Amy for her schoolyard wit and her nickname, the "foreign doll," given by classmates because of her large eyes. Amy described instead their sibling rivalry:

> I went back to school. I wanted to enter Shuhua's class. They told me I wasn't qualified. I said, "I am too!" They gave me an examination, and I got over 90 percent. They had no way to postpone me. The only thing is they put me in the same class as my sister. Shuhua didn't like it because she was about four years older. At the end of the year, when the reports came out, she hated it because I was number one. She was number three. Shuhua always thought she was the smartest in the family. She *always* had that notion. I didn't think she was the smartest, but she could paint and write. Her compositions were real good. But I said, "You don't know the other things. I think I'm better at the other things."

Beginning in the fall of 1915, they boarded at school together. Shuhua continued to excel in literature and art, and Amy gravitated toward science. The Ling sisters fell on either side of one of the era's most pressing intellectual debates, whether reform in the realms of culture or science could heal a nation whose political and economic order was unraveling in the face of imperialist threat. In this debate, the question of evolution versus revolution captured the popular imagination. When news of Darwin's theory had reached China, his claims about the survival of the fittest made disturbing sense to thinkers in a country besieged by foreign invaders with superior might. Self-critical fears of racial degeneration gave rise to social Darwinism and the specious theory that if China faced the danger of gradual extinction, the Chinese should will themselves to adapt into citizens better equipped for the future. Whether to do so by ministering to the Chinese body or spirit became the dilemma that drove Lu Xun, for example, from the scalpel to the pen. One revolutionary lauded Lu Xun's transformation in a way that captured the contradictions of social thinkers motivated by a biologically deterministic model. He declared that Lu Xun had evolved from an evolutionist to a Marxist, or "from the theory of evolution to the theory of class."[10]

Behind this dream of a social progressivism that would strengthen China's ability to compete with the West lurked a shadow of fin de siècle, decadent cynicism. This antiprogressive strand of thought equated civilization with disease and degeneration; decline was inevitable and could be reversed only by returning to natural instinct.[11] In 1919, Lu Xun bluntly stated, "We Chinese since antiquity have been going against nature, hence the withering of human capabilities, and the standstill of progress."[12] Many writers, like Lu Xun, who had experienced family financial decline in childhood used bourgeois family sagas to convey a sense of decadence, as does Shuhua in her memoirist chapters "Ghost Stories" and "Tianjin in Autumn." Shuhua's Tianjin chapters rest on the edge of an aesthetic attraction to the morbidity of an overly mature civilization and a desire to expose its injuries. Like other women writers, she faced the symbolic problem of what femininity represented. As Chinese theorists adapted Western Decadents' idea of a degenerate female gender, they linked this concept to national salvation: if China wished to evolve into a virile nation, the Chinese people would have to rid themselves of a weak and feminized culture. Amy could seek progress through scientific investigations of natural processes, such as cellular regeneration, that would revitalize society, but Shuhua remained attracted to a feminine aesthetic and found it more difficult to jettison this cultural past, in spite of its association with China's decay. From her perspective, the past appears tinged with terror but also a sensual pleasure in the exquisite sorrow of decadent culture. The gleaming promise of test tubes and stethoscopes to guide

China toward social health attracted Amy, while Shuhua lingered in a bedroom studio filled with old paintings, burnished memories, and the haunting presence of a beautiful female ghost.

In Amy's story of two classmates with bound feet, she emphasized how she set them on the road to modernity. The girls were twin sisters from the countryside whom Amy convinced to unbind their feet. Amy made a fist to show me how the toes of their feet had been forced to curl under, and then she slowly straightened her fingers to demonstrate their gradual progress back to a natural state.

Each spring the First Girls' Normal School held an athletic exhibition that parents were invited to attend. Chinese schools had begun to adopt physical education for girls based on Western pedagogical ideas that linked physical and mental strength. As early as 1903, the editor of Shanghai's *Journal of Women's Studies* had called physical education the most basic category of women's education because it would enable them to overturn a male ideal of feminine beauty rooted in physical weakness.[13] Even as a young girl, Amy loved sports. She had moved on from her early morning bicycle rides to tennis matches with a friendly opponent recruited from a boys' grade school on Ganmian Hutong. At school Amy led her classmates in running laps and learning how to dribble a basketball. As spring approached, the gym teacher gave her star athlete two tasks: organizing her classmates for the annual sports meet and convincing the twin sisters with bound feet to participate.

After class, the girls lined up in rows on the playing field to practice the sequence of calisthenics they would perform for their parents. Each wore a light blue cotton blouse and short black skirt. Amy stood in front of the group, calling out the counts for the coordinated movements. After they had finished the routine, they gathered in a huddle under a tree to discuss the event their class would host. Amy blurted out her suggestion for a relay race ending at the school kitchen. The last team member would have to run to the kitchen, pick up a plate of hot food, and then run back to the starting line before the food had stopped steaming. The girls laughed at this idea and quickly agreed on it. As they wandered back to the dormitory, Amy noticed the two twins Li Ying and Li Yun sitting by themselves. They had been dismissed from gym because of their bound feet.

By the time Li Ruolan gave birth to her daughters, many prominent reformers lectured against footbinding, and the practice gradually decreased in most urban centers. In the countryside, however, gentry families continued the practice, fearing poor marriage prospects for a daughter with the large feet of a peasant. Amy had heard stories about women who endured the painful process of unbinding their feet. When she saw the Li twins alone on the bench, she felt determined to liberate them. She marched over to them and asked, "Wouldn't you like your parents to see you in the athletic exhibition like everyone else, so they can be as proud of you as all the other parents will be?" They stared at her with disbelief. After a long pause, Li Ying said, "We can't." Amy replied, "What if you unbound your feet?" Li Yun whispered, "It hurts." Her sister added, "Mother says we won't be able to marry if we have big feet. Like you." "Who cares," Amy shot back and walked away.

The next afternoon, she found the twins alone in a classroom studying and asked if they had thought any more about unbinding their feet. The sisters exchanged glances. Li Yun said, "We're not as brave as you city girls." "However," Li Ying announced, "we will try." Amy knelt by their desk and held Li Ying's small foot in her palm, weighing it before she carefully slid off the embroidered slipper. As she untied the binding strip and began to unwind it, the smell of rotting flesh rose from the cloth. Flakes of dead skin peeled away. While Li Yun unwrapped her sister's other foot, Amy ran to fetch a basin of cold water for her to soak her feet in.

That weekend, Amy crossed Jin Gang Bridge to the Da Hutong shopping district and bought them each a pair of the smallest black leather shoes she could find. Each week Amy cut their binding cloth shorter and helped them wrap the strip of cloth as loosely as they could stand. After the daily practice for the sports meet, Amy met them behind the classroom building to encourage them to walk on their tender feet. Over the course of the spring, their curled-under toes began to straighten. Each time one of them needed larger shoes, Amy would walk with them over the bridge, following their slow steps toward the store where she had bought their first leather shoes.

Eventually, the twins joined their classmates in the athletic exercises, but neither could run very well. Li Yun moved with a limp because one of the bones in her foot had been fractured and never straightened completely. On the last afternoon before summer vacation, Amy went to the large sleeping room in the dormitory to gather her belongings. She saw one of the twins sitting on a bed, her shoulders protectively hunched over something in her hands. As Amy approached, she saw one of the satin slippers embroidered by the girls' mother. Li Yun held the small, beautiful object, which no longer fit her foot, in two cupped hands. When she heard Amy behind her, she quickly slid the shoe into her basket and continued folding the rest of her clothes.

· Nine ·

Into the Streets

*C*louds of gnats hovered in Tianjin's damp spring streets, but delicate orchids bloomed in Shuhua's mind. She distracted herself from the port city's depressing smokestacks with memories of the garden behind their courtyards on Ganmian Hutong. She longed for the days in Beijing when the gardener Lao Zhou let her accompany him to the weekly fair at Longfu Temple. Merchants at each of the stalls they visited greeted Lao Zhou and provided him with specially reserved food for his flowers. The farrier invited them in for tea, but Shuhua waited outside to watch horses having their hooves trimmed. With a basketful of hoof trimmings for his orchids, Lao Zhou directed her toward the butcher, where they picked up pig, sheep, and cow offal for the peonies and bamboo. A grocer had saved scraps from bean and peanut plants. Lao Zhou explained that the chrysanthemums would benefit from this vegetable nourishment. They collected chicken bones and offal for the roses and headed home at dusk with one final purchase, a pair of crickets in a dried gourd shell, for Shuhua. As the sun sank behind the Western Hills, the old gardener dumped the hoof trimmings clattering into a large ceramic jar and poured warm water over them. In three days time, the soup would be ready for Shuhua to feed the orchids. After her morning lessons, she wandered through the greenhouse. The straw curtain had been rolled up to let sunlight shine through the paper windows. She spooned the liquid into pots of lavender, pink, yellow, and light and dark green flowers.

By contrast, their house on the wide, empty street of Tianjin's Hebei district was drained of life. Third and Fifth Mothers had made their separate departures, leaving Sixth Mother to gloat. There were no more all-night mahjong tournaments. Ruolan lived in small quarters in a building separate from the main house. She kept to herself, stitching small pieces of embroidery or softly singing Cantonese opera tunes. Neither Shuhua nor Amy mentioned their older sister Shuping when recounting their years in Tianjin, so she must have left for schooling or marriage elsewhere. When the family's youngest

117

daughters returned home for summer vacation, they settled in with their mother and tried to study through the hot, humid days of July. Ling Fupeng's absences continued off and on. He had responsibilities in the seaside town of Qingdao in Shandong province where he was dispatched in late 1915, as Amy suggested in her description of his tour of duty in the once German-held city.

China had declared neutrality in World War I, but Japanese troops landed on Chinese territory and launched a successful attack on the German concession in Shandong. In January 1915, the Japanese minister to China arranged a secret meeting with Yuan Shikai. He delivered a document on thick, white paper watermarked with dreadnoughts and machine guns. The document, the infamous Twenty-One Demands, ordered China to vastly extend Japanese rights in Manchuria, Inner Mongolia, Shandong, China's southeast coast, and the Yangzi River valley. Yuan's government leaked the secret demands to the foreign press, but the West offered no assistance. After protracted negotiations, Yuan consented to a slightly modified version of the demands. This decision sparked protests, strikes, boycotts against Japanese products, and intense opposition to Yuan's leadership. Angry patriots declared May 7, 1915, the date of his acquiescence, the "Day of National Humiliation."[1]

In Qingdao, Ling Fupeng must have helped oversee the transfer of power and witnessed what his fellow examination candidates had feared most when they arrived in Beijing in 1895. Japanese soldiers and administrators moved their operations into the solid Bavarian buildings recently deserted by the defeated Germans. Meanwhile, Yuan Shikai's advisors suggested that the people desired a restoration of the imperial mandate, and on January 1, 1916, Yuan declared himself emperor. This move turned out to be a gross political miscalculation, and province after province declared their independence from Beijing. Yuan Shikai died in June, leaving the early ideals of the Republic in shatters, and the country slid into an era of warlord rule.

In Qingdao, Ling Fupeng's hope descended into resignation, but his daughters' lives remained relatively unaffected by the mounting tensions. The plethora of publications that began to appear in Tianjin and other port cities energized them. In addition to their schoolwork, they were exposed to many new offerings, such as accounts of Marie Curie's 1898 discovery of radium; translated works by Western writers like Zola, Goethe, Flaubert, Turgenev, Tolstoy, Chekhov, Ibsen, Wilde, and Mansfield; journal pages devoted to women's education and rights; and popular press stories full of love, scandal, and sleuthing detectives.

Early in the century, a new literature movement had begun promoting the use of *baihua* or vernacular language, which more closely approximated spoken Chinese than classical literary construction. Loanwords from foreign languages, as well as conventions such as punctuation marks, entered Chinese at an unprecedented rate. In 1903, Liang Qichao launched the journal *New Fiction* with a manifesto declaring that a revolution in the realm of fiction would improve national morality.[2] Slowly increasing rates of literacy, particularly among women, provided a larger reading public. The development of the *fukan* or literary supplement to newspapers and journals became an important outlet for literary production. Concession areas in Shanghai, but also cities like Tianjin, whose extraterritoriality provided relative freedom from the censorious eye of the Chinese government, gave rise to a lively publishing scene. In addition to the publications of "new literature" proponents, popular fiction poured forth to meet a new market demand for entertainment literature.[3] Shuhua augmented her knowledge of the classics with these new perspectives on writing.

Shuhua and Amy graduated from high school in 1917, just as the rain started to fall. Two separate typhoons hit Tianjin that summer, and floodwaters swelled until dikes burst on each of the city's five rivers in September. Fields, streets, and buildings flooded within hours. On the first floor of their house, water lapped against chair legs and sent them fleeing upstairs. By the time it reached the top landing of the stairway, a raft with fluttering Red Cross flags floated toward their cries. An evacuation team of soldiers and fishermen helped them abandon the drowning house. Amy remembered being lifted out of a second-story window into the arms of someone standing precariously in a wide, flat boat below. An oarsman with a long punting stick pushed them between roofs and chimneys. Snakes, rats, and dogs swam through the filthy water. Cats and chickens clung to trees and the tops of walls. The broad shopping avenues had turned into canals. Boats, doors used as rafts, and bobbing heads dotted the watery thoroughfares. Swimmers dove through store windows to salvage what they could. Farmers from the surrounding areas tried to recover some of their crops. They anchored junks over their fields. Young men stripped and jumped into the water with reaping knives. Kicking ten feet down to the bottom, they cut off as many stalks as they could before rising to the surface for air. The Ling family crowded into the small house in the German concession, which was on higher ground, until the water in the Hebei district house receded. It left in its wake a trail of sodden clothing, a layer of pungent silt across the floors, drowned mice in the cupboard, and teacups lodged in the garden. The disaster left six million homeless and starving. Refugees crowded into shanties covered with mats of braided reeds and straw.[4]

As the city struggled to recover, Shuhua entered a two-year "Household

Program of Study," also at the Tianjin First Girls' Normal School. This program, the equivalent of junior college, provided continuing classes in standard academic subjects, combined with instruction in home economics and "self-cultivation." Amy told me that when she and Shuhua graduated from high school, many of their classmates received job offers at a local elementary school. Because Amy was too young to become a teacher, their headmistress encouraged her to attend a physical education school in Shanghai to train as a gym teacher. Already determined to study medicine, Amy rejected this suggestion. She continued her studies in science at home with a tutor. Comparing her educational trajectory with Shuhua's, she said, "Her schooling was more regular than mine. She went straight through. I went off and on." For both of them, events of the next few years would influence their future trajectories.

After the national humiliation of Yuan Shikai's agreement to Japan's Twenty-One Demands, teachers and students on college campuses in major cities fervently discussed how to save the country. Overseas students returning from Japan, the United States, and France upheld "Mr. Democracy" and "Mr. Science," personified names for the ideas they had studied abroad. They preached everything new: new youth, new culture, new literature, new learning, and new women.[5] The last concept, in particular, captured the imagination of female students, who debated arranged marriage versus free love, filial piety versus individualism, Confucianism versus democracy. They passed around copies of Qiu Jin's collected poems. In 1918, when *New Youth* magazine ran a complete vernacular translation of Ibsen's *A Doll's House*, they rushed to bookstores to buy the issue. Its heroine Nora became as potent a representative of female defiance as Qiu Jin. The play was widely read and even produced, its climactic scene repeatedly reenacted with Nora announcing to her husband that she will leave him and their children because she has realized she is nothing more than a puppet playing a role. She declares, "I believe that first and foremost I am an individual, just as much as you are—or at least I'm going to try to be."[6]

After Yuan Shikai's failed attempt at monarchical restoration, another military leader tried to reinstate the boy emperor Puyi. Rival warlords reacted by bombing the palace. A low-grade civil war, which made China even more vulnerable to foreign aggressors, continued with a renegade south battling against the entrenched power of the north. To finance these skirmishes, warlords relied heavily on loans from Japan. In secret pacts, they made an increasing number of economic and military concessions. As news of these dealings leaked out, anti-Japanese sentiment spread, especially among merchants threatened by the competition of Japanese goods in an unfair market. They forged an alliance with new culture intellectuals to organize for patriotic, anti-Japanese action.

When World War I ended on November 11, 1918, spontaneous celebration broke out in Beijing. Hopes ran high that the Paris Peace Conference would overturn the covert Sino-Japanese treaties and agreements signed during the war. Leading intellectuals optimistically extolled Woodrow Wilson's Fourteen Points for their insistence upon self-determination and open diplomacy. As the negotiations unfolded, the chief Japanese delegate announced that Japan had secured secret consent from Britain, France, and Italy in 1917 to retain ex-German rights in Shandong province. Furthermore, the warlord government in Beijing had signed an agreement in 1918 confirming Japan's position in Shandong. Outraged by the possibility that the Great Powers would honor these acts of secret diplomacy, student groups, commercial organizations, labor unions, and overseas Chinese associations sent an onslaught of indignant telegrams to the Chinese delegates in Paris. They urged them to defend China's national rights, or in the words of one telegram, ensure that "China be saved from those perils into which traitors have betrayed her."[7] In the final days of April 1919, the news from Paris grew disheartening. Student groups in Beijing began organizing protests.

Although the circumstances differed, the students' collective opposition to the government's foreign policy drew on a tradition of scholarly dissent, such as the petition of the 1895 examination candidates organized by Kang Youwei. British philosopher and social critic Bertrand Russell, who would soon give a series of lectures in China, observed the tendency of educated Chinese to become reformers or revolutionaries rather than adopt the comfortable cynicism of some of their Western counterparts. John Dewey, an American philosopher from Columbia University, had arrived in China just days before the students' demonstration and wrote home, "To think of kids in our country from fourteen on, taking the lead in starting a big cleanup reform politics movement and shaming merchants and professional men into joining them. This is sure some country."[8]

When definitive news of China's failure to regain Shandong reached Beijing, leaders called a mass meeting of students from the city's universities and colleges. In the emotionally charged assembly hall, participants gave speeches and presented plans of action. A law school student, overwhelmed by the moment, cut open his finger with a knife and wrote "Return our Qingdao" on the wall in blood. On May 4, 1919, over three thousand students gathered in Tiananmen Square. Between impromptu speeches, they chanted slogans: "Externally, struggle for sovereignty, resist the Great Powers! Internally, throw out the traitors!" They hoisted a pair of sarcastic funeral scrolls for the government's three most pro-Japanese officials: "The names of Cao

Rulin, Lu Zongyu, and Zhang Zongxiang will stink a thousand years; the students of Beijing mourn for them with tears."[9] When they marched from the square to the extraterritorial Legation District, the police at the gates refused to let them enter. Radical elements shouted for demonstrators to converge on the house of the traitor Cao Rulin. When the official, who had escaped out the back door into a getaway car, failed to make an appearance, rocks flew from the crowd. Cao's house was set on fire. Another breakaway group chased down Zhang Zongxiang and beat him up. At the end of the day, thirty-two students sat in jail.[10]

On May 5, students in Tianjin heard about the events of the previous day. Like their peers in many major cities, they began a citywide organization modeled after the Beijing Student Union. When news spread that a student injured during his arrest in Beijing had died several days later, students nationwide rallied with increased determination. In coalition with merchants and other community groups, they drafted petitions urging the government not to ratify the Versailles treaty. They lectured in the streets, organized strikes, and launched a general boycott of all Japanese goods.

With the encouragement of their teachers, Shuhua's class joined what came to be called the May Fourth Movement. Classmates elected Shuhua to be one of the four secretaries in their school's newly formed student union. She remembers, "I had to write down all the plans, all the letters, or write speeches when we were going to a demonstration or to places where we knew we could get a large audience."[11] The First Girls' Normal School joined five other local girls' schools to form the Tianjin Association of Patriotic Female Comrades. The association boasted more than six hundred members, the youngest only thirteen years old, and published a weekly journal titled *Awaken the World*. Xu Guangping, who would later marry Lu Xun, served as one of the editors. Sixteen-year-old Deng Yingchao, future spouse of the Communist Party Premier Zhou Enlai, led the association's speech-writing corps.[12]

In "My Teacher and My Schoolmate," the second to last chapter in *Ancient Melodies*, Shuhua describes an event that motivated her class to take to the streets. She fuses this moment with her first sense of a possible career as a writer. When news of two workers killed during a strike in a Japanese-owned factory reached their school, Shuhua and her classmates also went on strike.[13] They marched out of class and positioned themselves on local street corners, where they gave speeches about the factory incident. Later in the day, they took up the chant "Encourage the use of native goods!" and went from store to store to ask owners to close their doors for a day of protest. After they returned to school, their Chinese teacher gave them the assignment to write about their demonstration. He selected what he considered the best essay and sent it to the *Tianjin Daily*. The following day Shuhua saw her first piece of writing in print, but only after their teacher read it aloud in class. She recalls the moment: "I realized it was my article; my face flushed, my heart beat fast, and later tears came into my eyes. I did not dare to look at anyone."[14]

Amy described standing on a chair in the middle of the street to shout boycott slogans through a megaphone. In her recollection of the protest activities, she emphasized the superior persuasiveness of female activists: "Those boys from Nankai [Middle School] didn't know how to talk, so we girls took the protest over. We were very effective because we rang doorbells. We told people, 'Don't buy Japanese.'" After students in Beijing, Tianjin, Shanghai, Guangzhou, and many other cities walked out of their classrooms to demonstrate in the streets, the Beijing government took action. They dispatched police patrols in the capital to disperse the lecturing bands of students and their audiences. When the city's prisons could no longer accommodate all the detainees, they converted the Beijing National University Law School into a temporary prison. When the students held there exceeded one thousand, the School of Science became another makeshift prison. With many of the male students thus detained, female students took their place. They assembled at the president's palace to denounce the use of school buildings as prisons, request the release of all students under arrest, and demand freedom of speech. Merchants and workers, particularly in Shanghai, were angered by the mass student arrests and staged strike actions of their own. Finally, the three most notoriously pro-Japan officials resigned, and government authorities released the students.[15] At the end of June 1919, in a largely symbolic gesture, the Chinese delegates in France refused to sign the Treaty of Versailles.

I have traveled twice on the orange double-decker trains along the Beijing-Tianjin line. Each time I failed to find the house where the sisters lived. On my first trip, I wandered lost in the streets of Tianjin. A narrow lane filled with the squawking cages of a pet market encircled the French Catholic cathedral, where Third Mother once procured yellow protection signs. Old brick buildings butted up against new tiled ones. A new shopping mall lay across the street from a wasteland of discarded rubble. Where the map indicated a major thoroughfare, I found an endless stretch of construction. People pushed their bicycles around mounds of bricks, deep ruts, and open trenches.

In spite of my disorientation, I managed to find one tourist attraction, the Memorial Hall of the Young Comrade Zhou Enlai's Participation in the Tianjin Revolutionary Movement. The museum is housed in a two-story stone building, previously Nankai Middle School. Zhou Enlai attended classes in this school during the same years Shuhua and Amy began their studies at the First Girls' Normal School. He emerged as a student leader in Tianjin during the events of the May Fourth Movement.[16]

The city had refused to accommodate my historical desire, but here in the sepulcher-like museum, I finally felt at home. I lingered in the still, hot air of the second-floor classrooms and gazed at photographs and memorabilia covering the walls. I felt I had learned how to interpret the hopeful faces of this moment in time. I came upon the dark printing plate, hand crank, and interlocking gears of a printing press cordoned off in a corner. Zhou and his compatriots had printed the daily bulletin of the Tianjin Student Union on it.

The layout of the Memorial Hall of the Young Comrade Zhou Enlai guides its visitors through the standard narrative of the Chinese Communist Party, in which the May Fourth Movement occupies one moment in China's revolutionary progress toward Communist victory in 1949. The story's most iconic representation appears back in contemporary Beijing at the center of Tiananmen Square. Four main panels, carved in marble bas-relief, surround the pedestal of the Monument to the People's Heroes. Their scenes reconstruct a linear version of history by linking together Lin Zexu's 1840 burning of British opium stores in Guangzhou; the May Fourth student movement of 1919; the guerilla war against the Japanese during World War II; and Mao Zedong's final 1949 victory over the Guomindang. In this trajectory, May Fourth activists became socialist revolutionaries.

When I returned to Tianjin years later, a friend who had grown up there guided me north through the former concession areas in another fruitless search for the house, close to a cemetery or red-light district, described by the sisters. He did lead me, however, to the site of the First Girls' Normal School. The old campus forms one section of the current Tianjin Academy of Art. Next to a playing field and cracked cement basketball courts, old dormitories stand in a neglected row. On the second floor of each gray brick building, five doors open onto a long balcony. Weathered red paint coats the wooden railings and eaves, decorated with carved European heart designs and stylized Chinese potted plants. In the middle of shrub-lined paths connecting classroom buildings stands a statue of the sisters' former schoolmate Deng Yingchao. She later married fellow Tianjin activist Zhou Enlai and became the first vice president of the Chinese Communist Party's All-China Federation of Democratic Women. Cast in bronze, atop a square pedestal of black marble, she sits stiffly in a chair with her hands folded in her lap, overseeing this corner of the old campus. Those who did not follow this particular path of

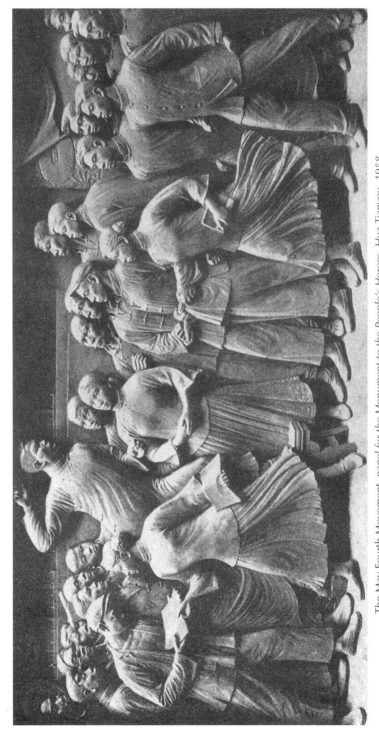

The May Fourth Movement, panel for the Monument to the People's Heroes, Hua Tianyou, 1958

revolution have fallen from the mainland historical record, but they all once marched together out of the gates of this campus.

The students' urgent sense of purpose in 1919 provided a name for a larger ongoing social, cultural, and political movement. The May Fourth Movement's leading proponents, students in their teens and twenties and professors in their thirties, came from an intellectual elite with backgrounds vastly different from China's majority. They had received a hybridized form of education that also set them apart from previous generations of scholars, and they applied a panoply of new and borrowed ideas to their mission of saving the nation.

In Shuhua's chapter "My Teacher and My Schoolmate," her patriotic Chinese literature teacher, who had encouraged his students to strike and then write about the experience, grew critical of the student movement when its leaders adopted the slogan of "Down with Confucianism." Their protest against the study of Chinese classics infuriated him. Early in the movement, he had corrected his students' speeches, petitions to the government, and articles to newspapers, but now he lectured them against turning a blind eye on their cultural heritage. He expressed disdain for arrogant overseas students recently returned to China. "To their minds, even the moon would look more lovely in Europe or America than the one we see here. I don't blame them if they only admire their [Western] success in the scientific world, but I cannot see what is in their minds when they praise their philosophy and literature."[17] Pointing out the imperialistic designs of these "civilized nations," he argued that the roots for a modern democratic nation could also be found in the writings of Mencius. Shuhua notes the influence of her early home studies in her reaction to the debate: "I understood more of the Chinese classics than most girls in the school. I especially liked Mencius."[18]

When Shuhua's writing continued to impress her teacher, he encouraged her by giving her a copy of the teachings of Zhuangzi, the famously imaginative and unconventional Daoist philosopher. Shuhua carried the book with her everywhere and forced herself to wake up at four o'clock every morning to puzzle over select passages. She remembers becoming completely caught up. "I talked less to my mother and my sister," she writes. "My father was away, though sometimes I wished I could talk to him, because I remembered he was interested in something that was similar to what I was thinking at the time."[19]

After observing Shuhua's devotion to this outmoded text, her classmate Guo Longzhen approached her to talk about it. Guo had established herself as a leader in the student movement. She was widely admired as one of the original members of the Awakening Society, which was devoted to continuing student activism and intellectual debate after the summer of 1919. She and Shuhua sat on a bench in the school garden, and Guo expressed her concern about their teacher's wavering belief in the movement and his influence on Shuhua. Shuhua convinced her to read a passage from Zhuangzi in which he sarcastically comments upon Confucius. The next day Guo encouraged the rest of their classmates to read the underlined parts of Shuhua's book.

In "My Teacher and My Schoolmate," Shuhua discusses a passage from Zhuangzi that she spent many mornings trying to fathom. Unlike utilitarian theories and the scientific rationality that dominated debates of the day, its lines suggest the intangibility of meaning itself: "The fish trap exists because of the fish; once you've gotten the fish, you can forget the trap. The rabbit snare exists because of the rabbit; once you've gotten the rabbit, you can forget the snare. Words exist because of meaning; once you've gotten the meaning, you can forget the words. Where can I find a man who has forgotten words so I can have a word with him?"[20] For a student talented in painting and writing, this passage challenged a belief in words or pictures as lasting or fixed. Shuhua already worried that neither could save the nation, having told her cousins, "I think painting cannot help China out of her difficulties. It is an occupation for peace time."[21] Yet in years to come, she would find her way as a writer, one of the neotraditionalists of the Beijing School, whose reaffirmation of Chinese tradition and its validity in the modern world allowed it the same claims to universality as Western culture. Decades later, as she neared the end of her career, she would look back on her May Fourth experience and say, "There are some anthologists who, with good intentions, have firmly grouped me with the May Fourth Movement players; this unexpected flattery surprised me, for at the time of May Fourth, I was a high school student, still infatuated with ancient paintings and poetry and anything to do with classical Chinese art."[22]

Young women of the Ling sisters' generation searched for ways to cross the divide between traditional and modern expectations. May Fourth rhetoric told them to awaken to their duty to society, but the outlets for their ambitions remained limited. They had no reliable map for how to proceed once their consciences had been stirred. In 1923, Lu Xun offered a bleak assessment of women's options in "What Happens After Nora Leaves Home?" an essay referring to the main character in Ibsen's *A Doll's House*. He concluded that a Chinese Nora had only three choices—to starve, to "go to the bad," or to return home to her husband. He offered only one way for the awakened Nora to survive: "To put it bluntly, what she needs is money."[23]

Amy located herself differently from Shuhua within the May Fourth scene. She emerged as the practically minded sister. She wanted to study medicine, a field of established patriotic worth, but her attraction came from a dream of becoming an independent career woman. When asked why she wanted to study medicine, she said nothing about saving the nation. Instead, she asked me, "Do you know how women used to give birth?" After a dramatic pause, she answered her own question. "They had two people to help them, one to hold this hand and one to hold the other. And then she would scream her head off, yelling 'I'm dying. This child is killing me.' I wanted to help women. I thought there had to be a better way." She planned to forgo marriage after completing her training in order to open a women's clinic.

Life at school allowed female students to consider alternatives outside the family. A new Chinese term, "singlehood," described women's desire to resist marriage and lead a single, professional life. This idea aroused strong social criticism. Articles denouncing singlehood claimed that it could lead to same-sex love or insanity, as well as potentially harm the nation's reproductive abilities.[24] Yet Amy persisted in her admiration of an exemplary woman named Dr. Ding who, like Kang Aide and Shi Meiyu, had attended the University of Michigan. Dr. Ding returned to China to open a private hospital. When Amy told Shuhua about her dream, Shuhua made fun of Dr. Ding, saying she was an ugly woman with a face covered in pockmarks. She said no one would ever marry her. Amy replied, "It doesn't matter to me. It doesn't matter to her patients."

The Ling family spent two summer vacations, in 1919 and 1920, at Beidaihe, a seaside town in Hebei province originally developed as a beach resort by British railroad engineers in the 1890s. At this cosmopolitan vacation destination, where both foreigners and Chinese gathered, Amy's plans to attend medical school took shape. The Lings stayed in a house owned by one of Ling Fupeng's friends from the Zhili political scene. The two sisters could run out the front door onto the beach, while the adults watched horse races at the neighboring track from a second-floor balcony. Amy recalled the parties her father hosted. He and his guests drank dark German beer from a wooden keg packed in a tub of melting ice on the balcony. The foreigners Amy met the first summer included a young Indian woman from a wealthy family who practiced speaking Chinese with her and an American woman who taught at Qilu Medical College on the campus of the Shandong Christian University in Jinan. Many foreign vacationers knew the American teacher because she ran a small drugstore for them in the summer at Beidaihe. Amy slipped into the store and pretended to look over the items for sale. She glanced nervously at the woman from behind shelves of aspirin, tooth powder, and sunglasses. She bought a bathing cap and ran back out to the beach. On the following day, she worked up the nerve to ask the woman if she indeed taught at Qilu as she had heard. She asked, "Do I have a chance to enter that college?" The woman asked how much English she knew, explaining that half of the classes were taught in English. Amy shrugged her shoulders, and the woman told her, "Then you have to study English."

When the sisters' Feng cousins, nephews of First Mother, visited Tianjin the following winter, they broached the issue of how Shuhua and Amy would continue their studies in the coming years. A train passed by the house, and Ruolan complained about living so near the station. Feng Xianguang seized the opportunity to tell her that her youngest daughters should attend university in Beijing. He urged them to leave: "Tianjin is not the place for Uncle to live in. What nonsense to have to see those warlords every day. He cannot enjoy such a life. Now they are trying to draw him into their group; it simply does harm to him."[25] When Ling Fupeng decided to follow his nephew's advice, the two sisters were thrilled at the thought of returning to Beijing. In this hopeful moment, with which Ling Shuhua ends *Ancient Melodies*, the grit and oppressiveness of Tianjin in her memory finally lifts.

> Both Mai [Amy] and I were excited when we heard Father's decision. I remember in the evening she and I went into the garden chasing the two large dogs up and down the artificial rocks for a long time. The garden was lighted by the electric lamps; the young trees, the rocks, the flowerbeds, the Western-fashioned steps and balconies were then covered with white snow; they looked extraordinarily fascinating, which I had never noticed before.[26]

· *Ten* ·

Romance

$\mathcal{T}$he sisters returned to Beijing, where their family moved back into the house on Ganmian Hutong. Not far away, the northern gate of the Forbidden City had been thrown open to the public. Students gathered to read and chat on benches in the Imperial Garden. Young women strolled arm in arm over paths paved with multicolored stones, past pavilions where they might overhear the discussions of student leaders from the nearby Beijing National University. On the other side of the wall, the fifteen-year-old emperor Puyi still lived in the inner court of the palace.

In the fall of 1921, Shuhua and Amy enrolled in the women's college of the newly formed Yanjing University. Amy focused on English, determined to learn enough in one year to apply to medical school. Shuhua expressed an initial interest in zoology, not out of a newfound love of science, but because she'd heard Goethe once studied the subject. A Chinese version of Goethe's *The Sorrows of Young Werther*, translated by writer Guo Moruo, had just appeared in bookstores. The novel became wildly popular among educated youth enthralled with the idea of romantic love. Shuhua explained,

> Goethe read zoology, so I followed his example in every way. In addition, my sister studied medicine, and zoology had a course in dissection. Who knows if I could have worked with her? But an English teacher who'd read my essays strongly believed I could develop in literature and lent me some books by St. Francis of Assisi (another enthusiast of animals and the natural world) and guaranteed that after reading them I would change my mind. I did later switch departments.[1]

Yanjing University was founded by a joint board of American missionaries who consolidated four missionary schools in Beijing, including the North China Union College for Women. They intended to build an institution that could compete with the famous coeducational Beijing National University. Henry Luce, born to missionary parents in Shandong and later founder of

Time magazine, spearheaded fundraising efforts in New York for the construction of a new campus. In the meantime, the women's college remained at its former location on Dengshikou. Once a market street famous for its stalls of glowing paper lanterns sold during the annual Lantern Festival, Dengshikou now housed Christian charities such as the Salvation Army. Ganmian Hutong lay within easy walking distance.[2]

When Amy and Shuhua attended classes in the women's college at Dengshikou, the realization of a central Yanjing University campus remained in the future. Male teachers and administrators continued to reside at the men's college, while their female counterparts taught at the women's college. The curriculum included classes in religion, and many students tolerated Bible study as a means to a Western-style education. Amy remembered that a mixed staff of American Methodists and Presbyterians ran the college. Students attended chapel every morning after breakfast. Since Amy was one of the youngest students, the principal assigned her a job no one else wanted, ringing the morning bell outside the dormitory. "I was very young," she explained. "I was very active. I got up early and rang the bell. At six-thirty we were supposed to have breakfast. Then we went to the chapel. From seven to eight, we had to go to chapel, to listen, pray, and read the Bible."

Shuhua left no direct record of her Yanjing experience, but others described candid dormitory discussions about the issues that concerned them. Many had reached what their parents considered a marriageable age and tried to come up with ways to escape the fate of an arranged marriage, like the one Shuhua had avoided after Zhao Bingjun's death. In their rebellion against Confucian family mores, young students dreamed of freedom in the form of romantic love. A 1926 article in *Xin nüxing* (New woman) magazine described the typical girl student: "Her hair has been cut by half. To her loose short hair is fastened an ivory butterfly [ribbon]. Her breasts inside her snow-white gauze shirt are very flat, obviously she is wearing a tight brassiere. . . . Under her short and open [split] black silk skirt are a pair of short legs in white silk stockings. Further down are her dark high-heeled leather shoes, which make her limbs wave and writhe when she walks."[3] Bobbed hair, introduced from Soviet Russia, raised hemlines, and book bags became part of the style associated with the *modeng gou'er*. This transliteration of "modern girl" entered Chinese from the Japanese term *modan gaaru*, which connoted transgressive young women dressed in Western fashion who were liberated, bold, flirtatious, wage earning, and visible in city streets.[4]

The previous year, a group of these Chinese modern girls had crowded into the Beijing National University auditorium to listen to foreign scholars invited to China by the Society for Lectures on the New Learning. When Shuhua and Amy moved into the Yanjing dormitory, they likely heard older girls discuss the lectures given by British socialist Bertrand Russell. His traveling companion Dora Black, who provided a living example of a modern Nora, had captured the imagination of many young Chinese women. She and Russell lived together during their year in China, although it was widely known they weren't married. During their months in Beijing, Black visited the Beijing Girls' Normal School several times to lecture on her belief in socialism. Her positive assessment of Bolshevik progress in Russia diverged from Russell's opinion. After the lectures, the students eagerly questioned her about marriage, free love, and contraception. In his autobiography Russell wrote of the open discussion of love and sexuality in these question-and-answer periods: "Nothing of the sort would have been possible in any similar European institution."[5]

On Friday afternoons, the sisters left their dormitory and walked home to spend the weekend with those family members remaining in the household. But new attractions in the neighborhood also drew them into the crowds of nearby streets. A few blocks away, the Zhenguang (True Light) Cinema, first organized in 1919 by a university student, had begun screening films. Amy and Shuhua went early one Sunday to see an American silent film praised by the Chinese press. The Zhenguang projected full-length features, bringing Hollywood hits like D. W. Griffith's thirteen-reel, three-hour *Way Down East* to Beijing audiences. Recalling the introduction of Hollywood to China, the writer Lao She would later comment, "The barriers and taboos that set Chinese boys and girls apart for ages were crushed over night. A single ten-cent ticket brought the young to the very door of a new world where romance and adventure were as common as chopsticks and tea cups."[6]

As the opening frames of *Way Down East* lit up the screen, an interpreter on stage began to give scene-by-scene narration in Chinese above the noise of the projector. Shuhua and Amy struggled to read the prologue to the film's action as the English text flickered by: "Since the beginning of time man has been polygamous—even the saints of Biblical history—but today a better ideal is growing—an ideal of one man for one woman. Today woman brought up from childhood to expect ONE CONSTANT MATE possibly suffers more than at any point in the history of mankind, because not yet has the man-animal reached this high standard—except perhaps in theory."[7]

A white face surrounded by a glowing halo of wispy hair appeared in the spotlight. The silent film star Lillian Gish played Anna Moore, a poor young woman sent to Boston by her aging mother to ask their rich relatives for help. To the dismay of her urbane cousins, an eccentric aunt takes Anna in, dressing her in elegant clothes for an evening ball, where she attracts the attention of the slick Lennox Sanderson. After a brief courtship, Lennox lures her into a fake marriage. She agrees to his request to keep their relationship secret, until she becomes pregnant. When she announces this development, Lennox reveals their marriage to be a fraud. Anna's face silently contorts, and she swoons to the floor. Alone in a cold boarding house, Anna gives birth to a baby who dies hours later. Anonymous in the Zhenguang Cinema audience, Shuhua felt tears stream down her cheeks. On screen, Anna finds work in a new village, where a local family adopts her until they learn of her shameful past. Rejected, she flees into a brutal winter storm and faints on an ice floe, which moves downriver toward a waterfall. Amy yawned with impatience. A flash of handkerchief caught the corner of her eye, and she glanced over to see her sister wiping her face. When Shuhua begged Amy to go with her to see the film again the following Sunday, Amy laughed at her emotionality. "Why do you want to go to that thing again?" she asked. "It's so sad, you just sit there and cry and cry. I don't like to keep thinking about those sad things all the time."

Melodrama captivated one sister while it exasperated the other. The events of the May Fourth era, in which women expressed their grievances in public and strove to leave the past behind, conditioned both of their responses. Amy repeatedly told this story—Shuhua's endless tears and her mockery of them—to differentiate herself from her sister. Committed to the rational promise of science, she rejected what she saw as emotional weakness. However, Anna Moore's search for home in a world of patriarchal morality treacherous with a sham marriage, infant mortality, and the threat of a watery death struck a chord with Shuhua, who surely saw their mother's fate partially projected in the flickering light.

A man who had fallen in love with Anna Moore saves her at the last minute from going over the waterfall. *Way Down East* closes with their marriage, a happy Hollywood ending that contrasts with the May Fourth ideal of singlehood and marriage resistance held by independent-minded Chinese women. The confrontation of traditional gender mores became a popular theme in Chinese short fiction of the 1920s. Male and female writers, including Ling Shuhua, created protagonists who experiment with romantic desire in same-sex relationships.[8] Five years after she first moved into a Yanjing dorm room, Shuhua published her story "Once Upon a Time," which provides vivid and suggestive detail about life in a girls' school. It evokes schoolgirl intimacy with a sensitivity that drew on her experience and observations as a student.

The story opens with the character Yingman in a school courtyard yelling, "Juliet, Juliet, Romeo seeks thee Juliet!" She is calling a fellow student, Yunluo, to come to their rehearsal of *Romeo and Juliet*. The play will be performed in celebration of the school's ten-year anniversary, with Yingman and

Yunluo cast as the star-crossed lovers. After their final rehearsal, Yingman accompanies Yunluo back to her dormitory.

> Sitting under the lamp, she watched Yunluo undo her hair and plait it into a loose braid, then change into her imported pastel pajamas with snowflakes embroidered along the cuffs and collar. . . . "Juliet, shall I massage your back for you?" Yingman said with a grin as she went over to Yunluo, gazing at the ivory skin of her exposed chest, then down past the large collar where she could make out the faint curve of her soft, slightly protruding breasts. Her small arc-shaped mouth, now slightly agape, was so adorable; two dimples appeared at the corners of her mouth and then two more on her cheeks. She looked more enticing now than she had in the play when she was on the verge of kissing Romeo.[9]

After their performance the following night, Yingman stays over in Yunluo's bed. The two girls wake in each other's arms, gently kissing and whispering. They soon become inseparable, and everyone on campus refers to them as Romeo and Juliet. One evening as they sit together gazing at the moon, Yunluo says that her older brother has written that he wants her to marry someone he knows. Yingman responds, "People make their own destinies. Why can't we be together forever? Look at the primary school instructors Miss Chen and Miss Chu, haven't they been living together for five or six years?" The girls swear their love to each other but part during summer vacation, when Yunluo returns home to the south. At the start of fall term, she hasn't answered any of Yingman's letters. Yingman, worried that her lover has been prevented from travel by fighting in the south, continues to wait until she overhears some classmates gossiping and learns that Yunluo has married.

Amy's college roommate was Li Dequan, a third-generation Chinese Christian whose father was a minister in Hebei province. After class, they often strolled down Wangfujing Street, weaving their way through the bustle of shoppers. They practiced new English phrases, giggling when people turned to stare at them. Crunching their teeth into sugar-glazed haw berries speared on long wooden sticks, they gazed at windows displaying the latest Western fashions, drop-waist flapper dresses, cloche hats, beaded handbags, and high-heeled shoes. On their way back to the dormitory, Amy would drag her roommate on a detour, down a side alley east of Wangfujing. She wanted to inspect the progress on the buildings of the new Peking Union Medical College (PUMC), a project of the Rockefeller Foundation. On the day Amy and Li Dequan saw the roof of the central building completed, Amy turned to her and said, "After I study English, I'm going to go there. I just *love* that building."

It was during the year at Yanjing that Amy adopted her English name. On the first day of class, their English teacher, an American named Alice Frame, asked the students to stand up one by one. When Amy rose and called out her name in Chinese, Miss Frame assigned her a new one in English, and Ling Shuhao met her future American self in the two easy syllables of Amy.

At the end of the year, Amy decided to apply to Peking Union Medical College instead of the more provincial Qilu she'd previously considered. After she sat for four days of written examinations in biology, chemistry, physics, and mathematics, only a test of her spoken English remained. She recalled for me the anxious moment of facing her examiner, Dr. W. W. Stifler, in a medical exam room with tongue depressors and cotton swabs in jars on the table behind her. She said to him, "You have to go very slowly because if you speak too fast, I will not be able to catch all your words." She was so unsure of her performance that she asked Miss Frame to write a letter on her behalf. A few days later, Miss Frame received a reply from the doctor, saying she didn't have to apologize for Miss Ling, who had passed the exam with a superior score.

In the spring before Amy left Yanjing University for PUMC, her class put on a presentation of "Chinese culture" for foreign philanthropists being shown around the associated schools of Yanjing. She and a classmate named Bing Xin dressed up in the old-fashioned clothes of a bride and groom and performed a traditional Chinese wedding ceremony in the school auditorium. Both Amy and Shuhua had shared English and literature classes with the twenty-two-year-old Bing Xin, who had recently published stories and short pieces of fragmentary poetry in the literary supplement of the Beijing *Chen bao* (Morning post). She became one of the first women to emerge on the literary scene after May Fourth. After graduating with a degree in literature one year later, Bing Xin would travel on a scholarship to Wellesley College in Massachusetts.[10]

Bing Xin later married a fellow overseas student, a sociologist named Wu Wenzao who had also returned to China. At their wedding she wore a white, knee-length wedding gown. However, in her 1922 reenactment of a traditional ceremony, Bing Xin wore red. Amy played opposite her as the groom. Staged for a foreign audience, their masquerade performed a parody not only of traditional marriage practices but also of the all-male Beijing opera, in which men played both male and female roles. Amy stood alone, wearing a long, gray robe, black silk cap, and fake mustache and beard. She feigned wedding day nerves, wiping her brow, as a petite figure in red silk demurely crossed the stage. The red veil covering Bing Xin's face trembled as she walked. Amy turned around and cried out in mock surprise upon seeing the bride. They faced each other and began a series of slow, formal bows.

They bowed to one another. They bowed to their parents. They bowed to the ancestor portraits hanging on the wall. The visitors assembled in the hall whispered about the beautiful costumes and quaint customs of the Chinese. The bride and groom bowed to the audience, who burst into applause. Behind a prickly beard and a musty red veil, the two performers had begun to laugh uncontrollably. Amy raised a shaking hand to the veil covering the bride's face. She lifted the silk and shrieked at the sight of Bing Xin making a face at her. They bowed quickly one last time. Convulsed with laughter, the newlyweds dashed off stage.

· Eleven ·

Gatherings

$\mathcal{D}$uring Shuhua's third year at Yanjing University, a dynamic instructor created a buzz on campus. Eager students crowded into the classroom where Zhou Zuoren delivered his innovative and eclectic lectures on "New Literature." Shuhua wanted to enroll in the class, but her home department of foreign languages and literature prevented her from adding it to her schedule. She began to read Zhou Zuoren's essays on her own.

Zhou Zuoren was Lu Xun's younger brother and a well-known essayist and translator of Western literature. He lectured at several Beijing universities and introduced students to contemporary Chinese stories and poems written in *baihua* along with translations of ancient Greek and Roman poetry, Russian novels, and modern Japanese fiction. Bing Xin remembered him likening early Greek epigrams to bees, whose sting drew blood. As different philosophies, "art for life" and "art for art," developed, Zhou aligned himself with the life school, declaring that art and literature "should have contact with life through the writer's feelings and thoughts."[1] In a 1922 essay, he advocated an "Ancient/modern/Chinese/foreign school" that integrated heterogeneous influences to create a local form of modernity.[2]

He also helped found the Association for Literary Studies, whose members aimed to reinvent the role of literature in society. In the past, a *wenren* or man of letters painted or composed poetry to escape from the demands of official duty, creating amateur works for friends. New literature proponents, however, developed professional publication outlets in newspapers and magazines. Writing in vernacular Chinese, they promoted a national literature that could hold its own on the international stage. In 1921, the Association for Literary Studies had published in their monthly journal a manifesto that called for a writers' union: "The time has passed when literature was taken as amusement in periods of elation or diversion in periods of depression. We believe that literature is also a kind of labor and, furthermore, an urgent kind of labor for man. Persons engaged in literature should consider it a life-time occupation."[3]

Bing Xin recalled the vigor of the publishing scene at the time:

> In the wake of the New Literature Movement, all sorts of new periodicals were appearing like mushrooms after spring rain. Not only did these carry diatribes against imperialism and feudalism, there were also introductions to and criticism of foreign literature, as well as short stories, new poetry, and prose, all in the vernacular. Then, our thirst for knowledge was at its height, and we greedily devoured these periodicals outside our lessons and even hid them under our textbooks, openly stealing glances at them.[4]

Writing had become a tangible career option, and Shuhua was drawn to Zhou Zuoren's model of balancing traditional and modern aesthetics. In a letter dated September 1, 1923, she explained why she hadn't been able to enroll in his class and asked if he had any spare time to mentor her. She described herself as a quick study, adept in new and old learning, and boldly stated that she wanted to be a writer:

> During the past few years, I've firmly committed myself to becoming a future female writer, and so I've diligently studied three national literary traditions, Chinese, English, and Japanese. I want to look for an advisor, but there are very few proficient in these three languages. As you, sir, already know, there really isn't a single one among the teachers at Yanjing University besides you. Summoning my courage, I ask if the gentleman can accept me as a student. There are too few Chinese women writers, so the thoughts and lives of Chinese women have not yet made themselves known to the world. In terms of contributions to humanity, this is truly irresponsible. What are the gentleman's thoughts? Is he willing to accept a female comrade in this type of undertaking?[5]

He agreed to her proposal, and five days later she sent him one of her notebooks containing preliminary manuscripts. Conventions for *baihua* writing were still developing, and in her accompanying letter, she asked him to correct her mistakes: "I've studied the use of English punctuation marks, but the new Chinese punctuation is foreign to me. I don't know if it's the same as English or not."[6]

In 1924, Shuhua's final year at Yanjing, she published her first *baihua* story in the *Morning Post* literary supplement. "A Daughter's Lot Is Too Miserable" appeared on January 13 by Ruitang, Shuhua's birth name and one of the many pennames she used during her early career. The story takes place in spring. Two cousins sit by a window overlooking a courtyard abloom with flowers, bees, and butterflies. Pale young Wanlan tells her cousin, "Auntie asked me to persuade you not to always stubbornly talk about equality and freedom."[7] While showing her the photo of a potential suitor, Wanlan emphasizes the importance of finding a husband before her youth passes. Her cousin listens in silence until she finally interrupts in exasperation and reveals to Wanlan something she recently learned. Wanlan's fiancé has been fooling around behind her back with his mother's maid. When Wanlan's future mother-in-law discovered the maid was pregnant, she merely decided that if the maid gives birth to a son, she will welcome her into the family, meaning that after her wedding, Wanlan will have to accept the maid as her husband's concubine. To make matters worse, Wanlan's parents have knowingly hid this information from Wanlan and conspired to speed up the wedding preparations to seal the marriage before the impending birth. Shocked by this revelation, Wanlan listens to her cousin's advice that she make a clean break from her fiancé, which is still possible since she hasn't entered his household yet.

A year passes, and again two women sit by the same courtyard. Wanlan reclines in sickly repose, and from her hairstyle it is clear she is married. One of her father's concubines helps her drink some medicine, and Wanlan recounts how her illness arose from the disaster of her marriage—her refusal to share a bed with her husband and his reaction of nightly forays to the courtesan quarters. She sighs with regret that she didn't heed her cousin's counsel, causing Third Mother to disclose the story of this cousin's death, a fact withheld from Wanlan when her health declined.

Three male friends proposed to Wanlan's cousin at once, but she refused them all. In cruel response to her rejection, each published poems in tabloid newspapers insinuating that they had had their way with her. This public besmirching began to affect her father's business, and she became sick with anger. After she entered the hospital, the rejected suitors continued their malice and spread rumors that she was pregnant but didn't know with whose child. She died shortly after.

Third Mother then relates the deception, by Wanlan's father, that led to her marriage, and Wanlan bursts out in a speech that demonstrates Shuhua's youthful flare for the melodramatic: "Women have no laws to protect themselves and have been used by men as their playthings for thousands of years. We both understood this too late. If only we'd known earlier of this family's perpetual darkness and learned from youth to be determined not to marry this kind of confining man, then we wouldn't be where we are today."[8] Wanlan concludes by comparing a daughter's fate to a willow catkin weighed down by floating flower petals. With this metaphor of the catkin, Shuhua employs a traditional literary symbol for a particular kind of *cainü*, the precocious female poet-genius, whose muse she partially courts.

Days after the publication of Shuhua's story, an anonymous critic submitted a letter that challenged the author's moral standing by asserting a connection between the story and her personal life. The *Morning Post* chose not to publish the attack, the circumstances of which Shuhua describes in a letter dated January 20 to her teacher Zhou Zuoren.

> Respected Mr. Zhou:
>   I received a copy of the submission to the *Morning Post* that you sent, and for this I am grateful. . . . Recently I was happy to have written this story. I meant to do nothing more than convey the situation of Chinese women's inequality; I didn't consider that it would raise reckless conjecture. . . . The first half of the letter really has nothing wrong, but what follows contains some wild fabrications, the most disgusting of which states that I've already been married and divorced. In terms of the incident involving a person named Zhao, it was not like what the author claims. When I was a child in Japan, my father and Zhao Bingjun (the two of them were sworn brothers) made a verbal agreement, but after he died, this thing passed like the wind. . . . The writer of the submission has shown that he has a heart to ruin a person's reputation, because whether or not a woman has already married (not to speak of the many guilty of hiding the truth from others) really results in different treatment if she is still in school. With regard to my current reputation and wellbeing, this insinuation would not be insignificant. Fortunately, the sharp-minded report-ers at the *Morning Post* sent the submission to seek my confirmation. . . . A few days ago I wrote my story because of the "woman question." I didn't think that someone would go so far as to "draw a snake and add feet to it."
>
>   —Written by the student Ling Ruitang[9]

By depicting the dilemmas faced by women, Shuhua found her personal life subject to scrutiny. The accusation that she had been divorced revealed the risks of pursuing the life of a writer. For me, this incident also raises the ques-tion of what her father, who had once promised her to a friend's son, thought about her new literary career.

Years after the fact, Shuhua claimed that her father disapproved of the new vernacular style that threatened to replace classical Chinese. She insisted that she hid her *baihua* writings from him and that he knew nothing about her literary activity. This assertion has become a standard feature of biograph-ical synopses of her career.[10] I suspect, however, that she exaggerated her father's conservatism in these later accounts to make her struggle as a woman writer more dramatic. (Amy would similarly claim, "We were always number one in grades, but our father did not pay one cent for our schooling." On different occasions, Amy maintained that scholarships or a sympathetic neighbor helped pay her school fees.) Shuhua's penname Ruitang disguised nothing from her family since it was what they had called her as a child, and as Ling Fupeng retreated in retirement into the life of a traditional *wenren*, his friends included prominent artists and writers from traditional and modern schools.

The European-educated scholar Gu Hongming, erudite in Latin, Greek, and English, but also a staunch critic of Westernization and defender of Confucian values, was a frequent guest in the courtyards on Ganmian Hutong.[11] In 1919, he had written articles denouncing the vernacular literature movement, which perhaps influenced Ling Fupeng's opinion on the matter. However, by the mid-1920s, one of the most active *baihua* proponents also made visits to the Ling household. Hu Shi had begun advocating for Chinese language reform while studying overseas in the United States and continued to promote the cause as professor of philosophy at Beijing National University. Shuhua began a correspondence with him in 1925 that spanned many years. In her letters, he emerges as a family friend who sometimes shared books with Ling Fupeng.[12]

In Shuhua's descriptions, Ling Fupeng appears a mercurial figure, at once a patriarchal authority and a doting father who delights in her artistic precocity. A photograph of him during this period shows a man who bears almost no resemblance to the one pictured in his Nanjing Council studio portrait. Standing on a bridge in Beijing's Western Hills, he cuts a slight figure, dressed in a pure white robe and wide-brimmed straw hat. Having grown a long, sparse beard, he leans on a bamboo cane. Shuhua's participation in the artists' circle he helped cultivate in Beijing indicates more that she played willow catkin to her father the retired scholar. In the early 1920s, a teacher at the Beijing Art Academy organized a club for his friends. Made up of poets, calligraphers, painters, and scholars, the group's most famous member was the ink painter Qi Baishi, who'd been a farmer and carpenter before he learned to read and write. The club gathered every month at different locations throughout Beijing. They would share a meal and then move to a room where painting materials—different types and sizes of paper, brass paper weights, brushes, sticks of ink, inkstones, and porcelain bowls of water—had been laid out for them. They spontaneously created individual and composite works, with a poet often adding a few lines of calligraphy to a friend's painting. These meetings occasionally took place at Ling Fupeng's home, where Shuhua could mingle with her father's friends and join in their painting sessions. Even while attending classes at Yanjing, she devoted time every day to painting and calligraphy. She sometimes visited the studio of an acquaintance made through her father's connections, a woman whose husband's family possessed an impressive art collection. The two women enjoyed viewing and discussing paintings together. In February 1923 they decided to jointly host an artists' party at the Ling residence to celebrate the birthday of Song dynasty poet Su Dongpo.[13]

In addition to several well-known older artists, they invited American painter Mary Augusta Mullikin, who lived in China from 1920 to 1945. In Mullikin's description of the event, Shuhua glowed as the behind-the-scenes organizer. "The gathering was held in the home of an elderly Confucian scholar, yet contrary to usual Chinese form, his brilliant artist daughter was the hostess. . . . This day was in itself a masterpiece, the creation of our young hostess, Ling Jui T'ang [Ruitang], unobtrusive, never interfering or seeming to guide, yet appearing just when needed with happy suggestion and friendly word."[14] Mullikin characterized the male painters as slightly unkempt, with long hair, beards, and fingernails. Some puffed on foreign cigars. She also noted that several female painters, including herself and Ruitang, joined the men in the suite of rooms prepared for them to indulge their artistic whims. After dinner at three in the afternoon, followed by bowls of tea, melon seeds, lychees, and sesame cakes, they continued painting into the evening, prolonging her sense of "a Chinese intellectual Bohemia where artists claim a classic freedom."[15] Shuhua gave Mullikin two paintings signed as the work of Ling Ruitang. One of them, a pine tree executed on the taut silk of a circular fan with a bamboo handle, served as counterpoint to an inscription in the elegant, precise calligraphy of her father.

Like Mullikin, Shuhua also later wrote an essay remembering the casual ease of the gathering that flowed that day from painting to painting, as wine and tea were poured. She had helped prepare the painting materials with care, laying out the paper and grinding the ink herself. Pots of narcissus, sandy vermilion plum blossom, and miniature magnolia stood in the corner. Gently warmed by a stove, their fragrance mingled with the scent of tobacco and brewing tea. Even Qi Baishi, who usually hated when people came to his studio begging for paintings, generously gave away one after another, even fulfilling the request of a female servant. Suddenly, someone called out, "Let's do a group painting!" Eight different painters lent their hand to a piece titled "Nine Autumn Plants." Shuhua liked the result so much that they dedicated it to her. The plump and animated poet Yao Mangfu patted his stomach with appreciation for the day's provisions and wrote,

> On the tenth day of the first month of the year [in the Chinese calendar], we gathered together and painted this picture. Banding painted the apple blossom, Mengbai the chrysanthemum, Shizeng the yellow hibiscus, Zhiquan the pine, Baishi the Scarlet Autumn Visitor, Xiao'an the cassia, Mangfu the orchid, and Gongbei the morning glory and the water-weed. When we finished it, Shuhua asked for the painting, and we gave it to her.[16]

At the same time that Shuhua moved easily in this world of classical aesthetics, she continued to publish in the *Morning Post*. Five stories and essays appeared in 1924 before her graduation in July. During this period, the newspaper's editor-in-chief Sun Fuyuan, a literary impresario who called himself "a writer without works," turned what had once been the publication of Liang Qichao's Progressive Party into a showcase of new Beijing writers. He paid particular homage in early issues to the brothers Lu Xun and Zhou Zuoren. After Sun's departure, the reputation of the newspaper's literary supplement flourished under the direction of romantic poet Xu Zhimo. He would assume the editorship in 1925 and become an enthusiastic advocate of Shuhua's writing.[17]

Xu Zhimo had studied literature at Cambridge under the sponsorship of China enthusiast Goldsworthy (Goldie) Lowes Dickinson. During two years in England, Xu met literary luminaries such as E. M. Forster, Thomas Hardy, and Katherine Mansfield. Basking in a newly discovered poetic spirit, he fell headlong for a young, Western-educated Chinese woman; Lin Huiyin, who would also become a writer, was only sixteen when she first met him in London. Absorbed in this infatuation, Xu neglected his first wife from an arranged marriage, who had recently traveled to England to join him. Behind the poet's thrall of emotions lay the selfish cruelty of his modern strivings. He walked out on his wife one morning, abandoning her pregnant in a foreign country whose language she did not speak.[18]

In 1922, Xu Zhimo returned to China. His decision to leave his wife, publicized as China's first case of modern legal divorce, became a popular topic of discussion. He made his way to Beijing and reconnected with Chen Yuan, another intellectual and writer recently returned to China after ten years in Britain. He and Xu Zhimo had met previously in London, through a common friend in the small group of Chinese students there who debated politics, economics, art, and science over cheap boiled meals, followed by walks around Clapham Common.[19] Chen Yuan was also known by his given name Tongbo and published under the penname Chen Xiying. He left China at the age of sixteen to study literature at Edinburgh University and later politics and economics under Harold Laski at the London School of Economics, where he aided H. G. Wells with material on Asia for *Outline of History*, his two-volume survey of world history. Back in China, Chen Xiying became a professor in the English department of Beijing National University, where he lectured on the authors he'd studied in Britain. Shortly after Xu Zhimo gave an October 1922 lecture in Beijing titled "My Personal Impressions of H. G. Wells, Edward Carpenter, and Katherine Mansfield," he persuaded Chen Xiying to join him in a translation task close to his heart.[20]

In England, Xu Zhimo had been granted a short visit with Katherine Mansfield, who was seriously ill with tuberculosis. Warned by her husband

John Middleton Murry not to tire her out, Xu climbed the stairs to her bedroom. She wore bright green stockings, a burgundy velvet skirt, a pale yellow silk blouse, and a string of tiny pearls around her bare neck. In a high breathy voice, she agreed to Xu's request for permission to translate her stories into Chinese. He left completely enraptured. In January 1923 in Beijing, he learned of Mansfield's death at thirty-five, less than six months after he'd seen her in Hampstead. The following month he published "Elegy to Mansfield" in *Effort*, a weekly magazine edited by Hu Shi. Xu revised the poem for an essay about his "immortal" twenty minutes with Mansfield, in which he wrote,

> I had the honor of being granted by her in person the right to translate her works. Now that she is dead, I must treasure all the more this task entrusted to me. . . . My good friend Chen Tongbo [Xiying], who must be better versed in European literature than anyone else in Peking, has lectured on Mansfield at Peking University, in his course on the short story. Lately he, too, has promised to do some translations of her work.[21]

This essay appeared in the May 1923 issue of *Xiao shuo yue bao* (Short story magazine), along with his translation of her story "An Ideal Family." The magazine's frontispiece featured the first stanza of Xu's elegy beneath a portrait of Mansfield. Readers responded immediately to the essay's romantic description of the dedicated writer whose life had been tragically cut short. In 1924, a special Katherine Mansfield issue of *Short Story Magazine* published translations by Xu Zhimo, Chen Xiying, and the magazine's editor in chief.

Xu Zhimo and Chen Xiying worked together again to bring the Indian poet Rabindranath Tagore to China. Previously, the Society for Lectures on the New Learning had invited John Dewey, Bertrand Russell and Dora Black, American educator Paul Monroe, and German philosopher Hans Driesch. (Chen Xiying also wrote a letter of introduction for U.S. birth control advocate Margaret Sanger during her visit to China in 1922, putting her in touch with the president of Beijing National University.[22]) With the Tagore invitation, they welcomed for the first time a literary figure, and more importantly one from an Asian tradition. Although best known for his Bengali lyrics, the 1913 Nobel Prize winner also wrote fiction, essays, and plays, and had gained recognition as a painter, musician, and educator. When Tagore arrived in 1924, he brought a small delegation of eminent Bengalis, a historian, an artist, and a philosopher, to cultivate cultural connections between China and India. He announced his purpose in China as "a pilgrim to pay respects to Chinese culture."[23] Xu Zhimo worshipped Tagore and his use of natural imagery as spiritual expression. In the year before Tagore's historic trip to China, Xu Zhimo, Chen Xiying, Hu Shi, and several other friends formed a casual dinner and discussion salon named after Tagore's book of prose poems titled *The Crescent Moon.*

The Crescent Moon Society first began meeting at number 7, Stone Tiger Lane, in an old Qing dynasty building, where Xu Zhimo had been given living quarters by his mentor Liang Qichao. Each member paid five yuan a month, which allowed him to eat, drink, read, meet friends for discussion, or join in entertainment like billiards and musical concerts at the club. They enjoyed group meals together twice monthly. While the poet Wen Yiduo later commented that he preferred a more "Latin Quarter" sensibility than the gentlemanly atmosphere of the Crescent Moon gatherings, they moved Xu Zhimo to write his poem "Number 7, Stone Tiger Lane," which opens with the line, "There are times when our little courtyard ripples with infinite tenderness."[24]

After a delay due to illness, Rabindranath Tagore finally arrived at the Shanghai dock in April 1924. As the tall, gaunt man with a full, white beard and flowing, white hair descended the gangplank, Xu Zhimo waited at the water's edge to greet his hero. He traveled with Tagore to Nanjing, Jinan, and Beijing and translated for him at public lectures. Photographed together wearing long robes and turbans, Tagore rests his hand on Xu Zhimo's shoulder. When Tagore lectured in Beijing at the expansive grounds of the Temple of Heaven, Lin Huiyin, the object of Xu Zhimo's affections in England, lent a steadying hand to the senior poet as he climbed the stage. She stood by his side while Zhimo translated on the other. The gossip that trailed the young couple glamorized them in the eyes of the public, with one commentator describing the three figures on the Temple of Heaven stage as "an amiable picture of green pine, bamboo, and plum blossom."[25] In spite of the praise heaped upon Tagore and his argument for Asia's spiritual civilization over Western materialism, he also provoked critics who attacked his message as ineffectual in the face of colonial oppression. The writer Guo Moruo went so far as to call his peaceful preaching "the morphine and coconut wine of those with property and leisure."[26]

Shuhua did not attend Tagore's lecture at the Temple of Heaven. She had read two of his poetry collections, *The Crescent Moon* and *The Gardener*, and hesitated to ruin her feeling for his verse by seeing him in person, especially at such a large venue. Finally, convinced by friends' accounts confirming the visionary reality of Tagore, she sat in the audience as he lectured at the women's college of Yanjing University on May 6. Shuhua watched with amazement when afterward a large number of female students approached the stage. Tagore exuded a calm attraction, even for the most reluctant of students, something she had never witnessed before at a public lecture. The Beijing English Teachers Union hosted a tea in the auditorium lobby, and students continued to flock around Tagore. When Shuhua grasped his hand, she gazed at his silvery white beard, long nose, and mystical eyes and felt transported into a book of Song and Ming dynasty paintings.

Tagore drew her into a conversation about Chinese poetry and art. He asked whether she preferred Chinese or Western painting styles, and she responded,

> Chinese painting is somewhat older, perhaps with slightly deeper experience than European painting. The good thing about Chinese painting is that it can really lead one to become lost in thought. . . . European painting emphasizes realism a little too strongly. The popular new Parisian style of the last few years is also very strange, making people feel unable to discern anything at first; only after careful examination do they come to know it for the first time. Real artwork shouldn't cherish method. The more informal, the more apparent the brilliance of its brushwork becomes; a piece that induces enthusiasm truly contains a kind of inextinguishable spiritual power.[27]

Tagore nodded and smiled.

The poet's gentle manner impressed Shuhua so much that she immediately returned to her room and recorded the afternoon in a journal entry. A week later, "My Idealized and Realized Mr. Tagore" appeared in the *Morning Post*. She begins the essay by comparing Tagore with Maupassant and Shakespeare, whose works she claims are too old and distant from Chinese sensibility to arouse genuine sympathy. She extols Tagore for achieving an art delicate in spirit and faithful to a common Asian heritage. Finding in him a model of how to break from tradition without merely copying Western styles, she writes, "When Tagore's poems first appeared, attacks came from all sides, because he neither followed ancient Indian poetry nor imitated Europe; he loved nature, so nature became his teacher."[28]

On the day Tagore made such a strong impression on Shuhua, she also met another writer who would have an even more profound affect on her life and career. During the reception following Tagore's lecture, someone introduced her to Chen Xiying. He wore wire-rimmed spectacles with round circles of glass centered over each eye, and his smooth forehead gleamed below a shock of bushy black hair combed straight back.

Shuhua hosted her own tea in honor of Tagore two days after his lecture at the Yanjing women's college. In later reminiscences about the event, Shuhua did not mention whether Chen Xiying was among the invitees. She did, however, note that Xu Zhimo, Lin Huiyin, and Hu Shi all attended. She had planned to buy some European-style snacks at the nearby Dong'an Market, but her mother told her she couldn't let Chinese people lose face before such an important guest. Ruolan proceeded to order baskets of wisteria, rose, and turnip cakes and hired a worker to grind fresh almond milk, which the guests consumed in large bowls. Shuhua walked up to Tagore and playfully announced, "Today is a painting party. Do I dare ask if you can paint?" A Yanjing teacher by her side quickly tugged at her sleeve to indicate she shouldn't be so forward. But Tagore immediately sat down at the table where Shuhua had set out a thin piece of sandalwood and painted a Buddha with lotus flowers. After he finished and thanked her for the opportunity, a musician picked up his stringed *pipa* and began to pluck some classic tunes.[29]

Xu Zhimo's reputation as a poet increased after the publicity he received from Tagore's tour, as did rumors about his lack of restraint, since he'd recently become enamored with the wife of a Chinese military officer. Tagore's visit to Beijing also brought Shuhua more firmly into the fold of writers with whom she would grow intimately associated. By the time she graduated from Yanjing University in July 1924, she'd become a regular member of the Crescent Moon Society—she and Lin Huiyin being its only two female participants. Shuhua even took her father along once to the society's new location, rented rooms on Pine Tree Lane, to prove to him that it was no regular club, but a cultural salon. Xu Zhimo, who'd recently given a lecture at a girl's college and cited Mansfield along with Virginia Woolf, Jane Austen, and the Brontë sisters as examples for the students to emulate, dubbed Shuhua the "Chinese Katherine Mansfield."[30] The comparison stuck, undoubtedly influencing Ling Shuhua. She developed as a stylist of less plot-driven stories than before and continued her focus on the psychological lives of women and children.

Xu Zhimo still claimed strong feelings for Lin Huiyin and had become dangerously attracted to another man's wife, but he was also drawn to Shuhua as the Beijing counterpart to his Hampstead sylph. During the fall and winter of 1924, Zhimo and Shuhua exchanged a flurry of letters, now believed lost. That she agreed to become Zhimo's correspondent demonstrates a certain respect for him as a writer, since just months earlier she had mocked the current craze for writing love letters in the *Morning Post*. In one of a series of essays titled "Jottings to Kill Time," she gives a satiric answer to an American friend who asks why Chinese girls gloat about the number of love letters they've received but still refuse to answer them. In a quick economic analysis—since she notes, with equal cynicism, that Americans best understand things in terms of money—she explains how the letter recipients have calculated the cost of stamps and paper and decided that they can't be bought for a handful of coins.[31] Beyond this deflation of epistolary romance, however, the tendency of her affections remained unclear. Another Crescent Moon translator of Katherine Mansfield was also looking for a woman whose talent could measure up to Mansfield's. Chen Xiying waited with more patience than Xu Zhimo was ever capable of.

· Twelve ·

Modern Medicine

$\mathcal{I}$n the fall of 1922, Amy moved into a three-story dormitory for women students at Peking Union Medical College. The stolid, stone face of Oliver Jones Hall, funded by a benefactor from Liverpool for the missionary college that once occupied the campus, stood alongside grand new buildings designed by the Rockefeller architect. As eighteen-year-old Amy climbed the stairs to her room, she felt a sense of accomplishment. A competitive group of students had taken the entrance exam for the PUMC premedical program. Amy described many of the applicants as older university students. "I remember one man graduated from St. John's University in Shanghai and also had a degree from Nanjing University. Some of them didn't pass the exam. Anyway, I entered the premedical school. It was very difficult, but I did it. You saw my picture in the yearbook."

And there she is, with a serious expression, her brow slightly furrowed, in a class portrait posed in front of the leafy shrubs surrounding a campus building. A row of students in Western suits and ties sits cross-legged on the ground. The students standing in the row behind them wear long Chinese robes. Amy stands in the middle of the back row, one of three women in a class of twenty-one.

I first began to understand the nature of my grandmother's determination one Sunday afternoon not long after my grandfather died. We sat eating steaming bowls of wontons in her apartment high on the seventeenth floor. Pungent cilantro filled my nose as I blew on a spoonful of broth and watched my grandmother eat. She joked that she had shrunk with age, but still she possessed an amazing appetite. Across the plastic-covered table, she bent over slightly and placed her lips to the rim of the bowl. With her chopsticks, she slowly pushed a wonton from the bowl into her mouth.

A dumpling slipped from the grip of my chopsticks and splashed back into the bowl when she told me I should consider atom splitting as a logical

151

career choice. "What is your major? Pick something more challenging than English, something with more future. Anyway, atom splitting is a woman's field. You're suited to do that kind of thing." She explained that scientific research is a very exacting process and requires more patience than men have. "Men are always too busy, running this way or that way."

Her urgings could be classified as "grandmotherly advice," but with a twist. The twist came when, in the same breath that she asked me when I planned to get married, as if hoping to hurry my unfortunate, single days along, she would tell me I must first get a PhD or write a book. She extolled the importance of a woman remaining financially independent and prided herself on having been so since her marriage. My grandmother's words quickly dispelled any stereotypical image of passive Asian womanhood.

William Warren Stifler, the professor who administered Amy's English exam at PUMC, had come to Beijing from the physics department at Columbia University. He'd been recruited to direct the three-year premedical course, established as a temporary measure until Chinese schools developed basic science curricula deemed adequate to prepare students for PUMC. The lure of Rockefeller money and a high-ranking position in an ambitious institution on the other side of the Pacific drew many accomplished professors to PUMC's classrooms and laboratories. A largely American faculty, filled out by a few British instructors and some Chinese scientists who had studied abroad, provided an education in Western scientific medicine. Beneath roofs of green glazed tiles, their students sat at microscopes in sparkling classrooms outfitted with the latest equipment.[1]

John D. Rockefeller Sr. had first considered founding such a school in 1909, when his philanthropic advisor convinced him to sponsor an Oriental Education Commission. This science-minded advisor urged Rockefeller to build upon the foundations laid by medical missionaries in China. The report made by the commission after traveling to Japan, India, and China supported this goal of creating a medical school of international stature in China. In 1914 and 1915, the Rockefeller Foundation sent two China Medical Commissions composed of leading scholars in medicine to conduct further investigations. They toured missionary medical schools affiliated with three U.S. universities—the University of Pennsylvania in Guangzhou and Shanghai, Harvard in Shanghai, and Yale in Changsha. They were dismayed by a general lack of standards. Union Medical College in Beijing, the joint enterprise of six American and British missionary societies, left the best impression. In addition to its central location, the college had several functional buildings and the advantage of being the only missionary school recognized by the Chinese government. In 1915, the recently incorporated Rockefeller Foundation purchased the college and spent six years and nearly ten million dollars expanding and upgrading the campus.[2]

The Rockefeller China Medical Board tried not to alienate their predecessors. John D. Rockefeller Jr. issued an open letter to all missionary groups in China, pledging that PUMC would "select only persons of sound sense and high character, who were sympathetic with the missionary spirit and motive."[3] In action, however, the PUMC planners opposed many of the practices of populist missionary medicine. Missionary doctors often emphasized quick cures because immediate results attracted converts. The traditional repertoire of Chinese medicine, highly refined in herbal and acupuncture treatments, included little surgery. Missionary doctors, even those with only a basic grasp of surgical procedures, easily impressed patients who suffered from maladies incurable by Chinese medical practitioners. The leadership of the Second China Medical Commission wanted to move away from the quick fix and its reliance on surgery. They put their resources behind the idea of a world-class institution that would provide advanced training in scientific research for an emerging professional class of Chinese doctors.[4]

The model they selected, the Johns Hopkins University School of Medicine, epitomized a recent revolution in U.S. medicine, which transformed the field into a highly specialized, upper-middle-class profession concentrated in urban centers. At the turn of the century, a wide range of medical standards persisted in the United States. In addition to medical schools run by universities or colleges, privately operated schools trained doctors in rudimentary techniques. Very few schools of either type required training in chemistry, biology, or physics prior to admission. This system produced a large number of doctors who could provide basic treatment to many sectors of the population, but also a fair share of quacks. In the early 1900s, Johns Hopkins developed a curriculum that embraced European, particularly German, standards of scientific rigor. In 1910, Abraham Flexner, the younger brother of a Rockefeller Foundation trustee, published an exposé of American medical colleges and named Johns Hopkins as the only medical school headed in the right direction. With the Flexner Report as a catalyst for reform, foundations provided support for major universities to upgrade their programs. Proprietary schools disappeared, most medical colleges began to require at least one or two years of prior undergraduate education, and laboratory research methods became essential to a general medical education. As a result, the quality of medical care gradually increased, but a basic level of care was less widely available.[5]

The China Medical Commission made two other important decisions. They opened admission to both men and women, which presented little difficulty since women in China had worked actively in medicine for several decades. However, the question of whether instruction should be carried out in English or Chinese caused considerable debate. Eventually the trustees agreed that all courses, except Chinese of course, would be taught in English. They believed that if they wanted to hire the highest caliber of faculty from the United States, they could not expect them to learn Chinese. A more theoretical argument advanced the case for English as an emerging international language of scientific communication.

In the fall of 1921, John D. Rockefeller Jr. and family traveled to China for the long-awaited gala opening of the PUMC campus. The design of the buildings, completed under consultation with the architect of Harvard's Medical School, adapted a Chinese palace style and prompted one member of the Second China Medical Commission to compare them to the Forbidden City.[6] The elegant lines of the roofs, with figurines of mythical guard animals perched atop each corner, curved toward the sky. Opposite the two-hundred-and-fifty-bed hospital complex lay the old palace of Prince Yu, now converted into a modern residence for the PUMC director. In a pun substituting the prince's surname with the Chinese word for oil, *you*, locals soon began calling the Rockefeller institution the "Oil Prince's Palace."

On the day of the dedication, faculty dressed in academic regalia processed across the courtyard. A U.S. Marine Band played atop the steps of Prince Yu's palace. Chinese officials in silk robes, John D. Rockefeller Jr. in a tuxedo and top hat, somberly dressed missionaries, and foreign dignitaries from around the world filed into the auditorium. Amy had stood outside the gate that day, with her roommate Li Dequan, to watch the guests' honorary medals and satin sashes gleam in the sun. Now she walked through the front gate as a member of the class of 1928. If she completed three years of premedical coursework and advanced to the medical college, she would graduate with a doctorate in medicine in 1928.

At the opening ceremony, Rockefeller asserted that Americans only aimed to "point the way" for the medical school, which he believed would eventually be run by a predominantly Chinese faculty and board of trustees.[7] However, the rhetoric of the resident director of the China Medical Board veered toward a "Yellow Peril" assessment of the school's purpose when he proclaimed, "Either those who have little or nothing must be enabled to improve their conditions at home, or they will eventually go to the country of those who have, and in such numbers as to cause a violent upheaval in the country they invade."[8] Criticism of the project seemed to come only from Bertrand Russell, who was living in Beijing at the time. He pronounced that Americans in China would always remain missionaries, if not of Christianity then of Americanism: "What is Americanism? 'Clean living, clean thinking, and pep,' I think an American would reply. This means in practice, the sub-

Peking Union Medical College staff and students assembled in the forecourt of the hospital, September 1921. Courtesy of the Rockefeller Archive Center.

stitution of tidiness for art, cleanliness for beauty, moralizing for philosophy, prostitutes for concubines (as being easier to conceal), and a general air of being fearfully busy."[9] The hospital did nonetheless treat a variety of patients, including Chinese officials, psychopathic cases transferred from the prisons by local police, indigents gathered by rickshaw teams, nearby laborers who'd heard about the free treatment available, and eventually a pneumonia-weakened Bertrand Russell.[10]

Amy became a student of American pep. While her sister hosted parties for artists, she juggled a rigorous schedule of classes in biology, chemistry, mathematics, physics, Chinese, and English, to be supplemented in the second and third years with anatomy, biochemistry, physiology, and pharmacology. She and her classmates studied late into the night, hunched over their desks in Oliver Jones Hall. The dorm mother, a middle-aged woman from Sichuan, urged them each night to turn out their lamps at midnight. If she failed, she would shuffle out of the room with a dramatic sigh. Minutes later, they would hear her on the stairs as she climbed back up with plates of hot pickles and crunchy rice crust as snacks. As one of the editors of the yearbook, Amy wrote a short vignette of student life in 1924, called "Catching the Early Train."

> One day Miss Wang came to visit, and we were having an animated conversation when a classmate came in and said, "I don't mean to interrupt, but which train do you plan to catch tomorrow?" I replied, "I'm going to catch the five-thirty morning train." As soon as Miss Wang heard this, she immediately stood up to go, saying, "You'd better start getting your things together. If I don't leave, you won't catch that train tomorrow morning." Upon hearing her, I couldn't help but laugh and explain, "Good sister, I'm not catching the train, sit down, and I'll tell you. Our 'morning train' means we get up early at five o'clock to study. . . . If we don't get up at five or stay up until midnight, we can't finish our homework.[11]

This dialogue appears in one of the two books my grandmother possessed as a record of her years at PUMC. A thin, black volume contains the yellowed pages of her laboratory notes. Entries in English in a neat cursive hand are accompanied by charts, measurements, and drawings of cells seen under the microscope. The other, slightly thicker and covered in a soft, patterned blue silk, is *The Unison*, the bilingual yearbook produced by the students of PUMC in 1924. The pages devoted to the class of 1928 list their colors as red, white, and blue and their motto as "knowledge for service." In one of the photographs of student activities, I find my grandmother sitting on a step as a member of the Basketball Team of Medical Girl Students. Amy—still Ling Shuhao or Little Ling to her classmates in Chinese—also shows up in a paragraph insisting that extracurricular activities did not distract from their studies: "On the contrary, during the first year in the Medical School, overburdened as we are by the heavy schedule; yet every one of us maintain a very good standing in the class work. In this respect, Miss Ling Shu-hao, Messrs. Chin Kuan-yu and Cheng Yu-ling deserve special mention for their high intellectual attainments."[12]

Calligraphy by *baihua* reformer Hu Shi graces the yearbook's frontispiece. The "Round the Year" calendar of events lists the holidays of Christmas and Easter as well as Chinese New Year, with the Chinese National Holiday falling four days after the Christian Association testimony day. The college song, written by Lorin Webster, an English teacher at the school, applies the spirit of an Ivy League fight tune to the message of how "to serve our dear old China."

> PUMC forever,
> The College of Our Choice,
> Let us not now, aye, never, aye, never,
> Forget our mother's voice.
>
> Hurrah for PUMC
> The College of Our Choice
> Tis here we learn such precepts
> As makes our hearts rejoice.
> We've learned the truths of science,
> We've learned to study men.
> We've learned to know each other;
> We part to meet again.
>
> She's taught us ills to lessen,
> And how disease to cure,
> By killing all bacilli
> We heal the rich or poor.
>
> It's ours to help the wretched
> To guard the public health,
> To serve our dear old China
> Without a thought of wealth.[13]

Lorin Webster taught Amy's second-year English class. He had arrived with his wife and son in the fall of 1923. On the first day of class, Amy realized she had seen him before. In the last weeks of summer, she often visited her Feng cousins, who lived on Jinyu Hutong just north of PUMC. The younger brother, fast-talking Feng Gengguang, had become manager of the

Bank of China and patron to the Chinese opera star Mei Lanfang. When the actor, dressed in the gowns of the female characters he played, rehearsed in the Fengs' courtyard, the brothers invited friends and relatives to watch. A large persimmon tree shaded their garden, and while the adults drank tea, Amy sometimes climbed it. Sitting in the top branches, she watched the people in the alley below. She saw a foreign man in a straw hat weaving his way through the street hawkers. A rickshaw puller, straining with his fare, almost ran into the bewildered man and cursed at him. The man picked his straw hat from the gutter and hurried away. Amy's gaze followed him down the narrow passage, until her mother shouted at her to come down before she fell.

After her first year at PUMC, Amy worried that she couldn't speak English as well as many of her classmates, so she asked Lorin Webster if he would tutor her. One Saturday afternoon, Dr. Webster arrived at Ganmian Hutong and announced with pleasure that he'd never visited a Chinese home before. Ling Fupeng greeted him, and with Amy translating, thanked him for helping his daughter. The men sipped tea in the sitting room, until Ling Fupeng picked up a thick package on the table between them. As he removed a book from the brown wrapping paper, Amy explained that she had found a copy of the Webster's dictionary in a Wangfujing bookshop. Her father had been impressed to learn that her English teacher was a descendent of the original compiler. He held out the book for him to sign the front page. After Dr. Webster laid down his pen, Ling Fupeng left them to review the week's grammar lesson. Several months into their Saturday lessons, Amy's teacher dispensed with their textbook and simply chatted with her in English, asking questions about things he'd observed in Beijing.

Dr. Webster grew to feel at home in Beijing, but his wife and son rarely strayed from the confines of their American-style brick house in the faculty compound. Mrs. Webster, inept at communicating with the Chinese servants arranged to help her, never adjusted. Combined with some prodding from her husband's home department at Columbia University, she convinced him to return at the end of the school year. Dr. Webster threw a farewell party for his students, during which he jumped on top of a trunk in their living room and belted out an impassioned round of the English songs he had taught them. Surrounded by his family's waiting luggage, they joined in to sing "Yankee Doodle Dandy," "Jingle Bells," and "Onward Christian Soldiers."

The next day, a car arrived to take the Websters to the Beijing train station. Amy rode along so that she could help them board the train for Shanghai, where they would transfer to a ship. Dr. Webster looked back at the PUMC gates as they closed behind the car. Mrs. Webster spoke enthusi-

Shuhua, Ling Fupeng holding a grandson, Amy, and Lorin Webster and wife, Beijing, 1924

astically about the few days they would spend in Shanghai before sailing home. Although Amy had never been there, she answered questions about the city and explained that the best stores could be found on Nanjing Street. Streams of people on either side of the car peered through the windshield. The enclosed space grew hot and stuffy.

The still air in the cavernous station felt oppressive. As Dr. Webster directed the loading of their luggage onto a cart, he suddenly clenched his chest and crumpled to the ground. A crowd gathered. Mrs. Webster sank to her knees at his side, his son ran for the driver of the car, and Amy frantically tried to assess what had happened in medical terms. By the time they arrived at the PUMC hospital, he had died of a heart attack. Amy walked Mrs. Webster back to the family's empty house and sat with the grief-stricken widow in silence. She recalled the songs in that room the night before, before death stranded her teacher in a foreign country, far from the green summer hills and church bells of his boyhood. When his wife finally lifted her swollen eyes and said she wanted her husband's body cremated, Amy slipped out the door with relief to deliver the message to the morgue. PUMC held a funeral ceremony in the auditorium on July 7, 1924, and several days later Mrs. Webster and her son finally left Beijing carrying a small urn of ashes. Amy wrote an article for *The Unison* eulogizing Lorin Webster. He became etched in her memory as the friendly father figure who had delivered American culture firsthand to her doorstep.

In the second year of her premedical course, Amy began to study anatomy. PUMC found it difficult to obtain cadavers for instruction. Although the Chinese government had legalized the dissection of human bodies in 1913, the execution grounds served as the main supply source for medical schools.[14] While waiting for specimens, their anatomy teacher used life-size charts, a human skeleton hanging in the corner, and animals. For their first assignment, they dissected a cow's eye. Amy slipped on a white coat and sat at the bench with a round orb staring back at her from the black wax of the dissection tray. Fat clung to one side of the eye, like a gummy clot of yellow sleep, where it had been ripped from its socket. Amy slipped a scalpel through the cornea and lifted out a lens. Holding the small transparent disk in front of her face with a pair of tweezers, she saw the classroom reflected upside down. She set aside the lens and probed deeper through the vitreous humor.

In pharmacology class, they cut open the underbelly of a live frog and peeled back clammy flaps of skin to observe the vasoconstrictive effects of different drugs on its blood vessels. Their young instructor pointed with a needle at the frog's wildly beating heart. Students liked Chen Kehui for his thorough explanations and admired his U.S. training. He had spent five years at the University of Wisconsin, where he received a PhD in biochemistry and physiology. He dressed meticulously, always wearing a shirt and tie under his white lab coat. I imagine Amy transfixed by his precision as he tapped out powdered drugs from their vials onto squares of paper. Her resolve and intelligence had already impressed him.

Chen had cleaned the blackened glass covers of street lamps in his village to pay monthly fees required by the local schoolteacher. After emerging as a star pupil, he left his home in Zhejiang province for nearby Shanghai, where he studied at the missionary-run St. John's High School. In 1916, he received a scholarship to enter the third year at Qinghua University in Beijing. Qinghua, with its American faculty, had been established as a preparatory school for Chinese men who would eventually study in the United States. Eight years after the U.S. government levied a heavy indemnity for losses suffered in the Boxer Rebellion, Congress decided to remit the money still due and applied the balance to a scholarship fund for Chinese to enroll in U.S. universities. Between 1912 and 1929, Qinghua sent more than a thousand students abroad on Boxer indemnity scholarships—a project to civilize the barbaric Boxer, the image of the Chinese that predominated in the United States.[15]

Chen Kehui arrived in Madison, Wisconsin, in 1918. After receiving a bachelor's degree in pharmacy, he transferred to the School of Medicine. He improved his English by joining the Hesperian debating society. A former French soccer coach at St. John's had taught him to play Western instruments, and Chen joined the R.O.T.C. band. Wrapped in the gleaming coil of a tuba, he marched through snow flurries on the football field.[16]

After completing his PhD in physiology, Chen Kehui began studying for a doctorate in medicine but returned to China in 1923 because his mother's health had taken a downturn. For years in Madison, he had washed dishes in a Chinese restaurant and sent his wages home for a younger brother in Shanghai to buy the ginseng their mother believed would cure her of an unknown ailment. He suspected the expensive root wouldn't help but continued to send the money. As soon as he arrived home, Chen accompanied his mother by train to the famous PUMC hospital. The director of obstetrics and gynecology diagnosed her with cervical cancer. He treated her with a new procedure that used a radium needle to attack the cancer with radioactivity, and she lived for over another decade. After she returned home, Chen Kehui remained at PUMC where he had enthusiastically accepted a position as senior assistant in the department of pharmacology.

One winter afternoon, Amy hurried across the courtyard toward her dormitory and ran into Chen Kehui. She addressed him formally. He paused and then told her to call him by his American nickname, KK, the initials of his name romanized as Ko Kuei. They stood facing each other and awkwardly shuffled their feet in the cold. Finally, KK invited her to dinner at the Beijing Hotel. Amy blushed as she thought of the girl who'd been caught late at night in the dormitory parlor sitting on a male classmate's lap. Gossip about the vaguely scandalous incident had spread throughout the school. She looked up and said she couldn't go to dinner without a chaperone. Then, she invited him to tea that weekend at her family's house.

In a small room off the one where her father received guests, Amy and her teacher sipped tea. Amy asked about his research and pressed for stories about the United States. KK returned frequently for tea on weekend afternoons but always politely rose to leave after his cup had been filled for the third time. Remembering these meetings, my grandmother told me, "My family was very modern to let us bring our boyfriends home. In China, you weren't supposed to have a boyfriend."

K. K. Chen had begun analyzing a medical material recommended by his uncle, an herbalist. Over dinner once, he became intrigued by his uncle's claims about Chinese medicine and asked him for a list of the ten most toxic preparations. His uncle placed *mahuang* at the top of the list, explaining that it came from a perennial shrub that grew along the Great Wall and had been used in China for over five thousand years. Classified in Emperor Shen Nong's herbal treatise as one of 365 staple drugs, *mahuang* reduced fever and stimulated circulation. KK located an herbal dispensary near PUMC. As he opened the door, he breathed in the familiar pungent smell of the boiled medicines his uncle had prescribed during his childhood. An elderly man pulled out one of the hundreds of small drawers lining the back wall and measured a packet of *mahuang*.[17]

In the lab, KK distilled the herb into a liquid and injected it into a dog. Aided by Carl Schmidt, a research associate from the University of Pennsylvania, he documented a sharp increase in the dog's heart rate and a rise in blood pressure. Excited by these results, the two men isolated the herb's effective alkaloid, ephedrine. Further research demonstrated the cardiovascular effects of ephedrine when taken orally. As soon as Chen and Schmidt published their results, the Eli Lilly pharmaceutical company in Indianapolis immediately ordered several hundred pounds of *mahuang* from a contact in Shanghai and put ephedrine on the American market by 1926. Doctors in the United States and Europe used the drug to treat asthma, hay fever, and whooping cough.[18]

K. K. Chen, Madison, Wisconsin, 1921

News of their research reached Rabindranath Tagore during the poet's 1924 visit to China. The indigenous literary forms Tagore espoused as a writer complemented a larger belief in maintaining India's cultural institutions, including the practice of traditional medicine. When he heard about K. K. Chen's *mahuang* experiments, Tagore requested a meeting. In a PUMC laboratory, the bearded poet listened as KK explained the details of his study. He left encouraged that the Indian formulary might also yield a medicine whose efficacy would be widely recognized.[19]

Within the year, PUMC became the center of an event with greater political implications. In 1924, Feng Yuxiang, known as the "Christian General" because of the religious beliefs he preached to his troops, married Amy's former roommate Li Dequan. In October, Feng attacked the dominant warlord and seized the capital, creating a power vacuum in northern China. Sun Yatsen decided to take advantage of this sudden political realignment. In November, Sun left Guangzhou for Beijing, with the hope of securing support from northern generals to reinstate him as president of the Republic—a final bid to renew the dialogue between north and south that had broken off in 1917 and to create a centralized government able to fight for national sovereignty.

As he traveled, Sun Yatsen issued his *Manifesto on Going North*, which called for abolition of the unequal treaties that granted extraterritorial privileges to Western powers in treaty-port concessions. In Shanghai, he attacked the British in print. In Kobe, he resurrected the idea of the "doctrine of Greater Asia" and expressed support for Soviet Russia's rejection of colonial aggression. By the time Sun reached Tianjin, ailing health required him to negotiate with the northern generals from his bed. He failed to win their backing, and the generals continued to support their handpicked candidate, who would uphold all existing treaties in exchange for official foreign recognition. A defeated Sun Yatsen traveled in a private train car to Beijing, where he was taken directly to the PUMC hospital. Surgery confirmed that he suffered from advanced liver cancer. Sun Yatsen died on March 12, 1925. His wife and son wanted a Christian burial, and a Protestant service was conducted for family and friends in the PUMC auditorium. The public observed a second ceremony, staged in front of the Forbidden City.[20]

While Sun Yatsen's body lay in state, KK made his regular Saturday afternoon appearance at Ganmian Hutong. He and Amy assumed their usual places in the sitting room. KK carefully placed his teacup on the table and asked, "Have you heard about the Qinghua scholarships?" "Of course," Amy replied, "but they are only for male students." He explained that this year Qinghua University would host a nationwide competitive examination for five female scholarships. Previously, Qinghua had given ten scholarships every other year for women to study in the United States, but the awards were suspended in 1920. A string of protests by female students across the country criticized the patriarchy of the all-male institution with slogans such as, "Why is Qinghua among the few institutions maintaining the so-called male superiority?" and "Co-education should be established at once!"[21] In 1925, the administration decided to reinstate five of the female scholarships. KK encouraged Amy to apply and offered to pick up the necessary forms the next day when he would be giving a lecture at Qinghua. He assured her that she had as good a chance as anyone.

He also told her that he would leave for the United States at the end of the summer. He worried that political unrest in Beijing would disrupt his research. Following the advice of several PUMC faculty members, he had decided to return to Madison. He planned to complete his unfinished credits there before transferring to Johns Hopkins to continue his research on Chinese herbs as a third-year student in the medical school. In describing this meeting, my grandmother remained coy about whether KK encouraged her to sign up for the Qinghua exam as a way to follow her ambitions or continue their courtship.

Amy's hopes sank when she saw the minimum age requirement of twenty-one. Making a quick decision, she recorded her age as twenty-two, falsifying it by two years for good measure. Amy didn't tell anyone in her family about the exam, except her sister. Shuhua tried to discourage her. "What's the use?" she said. "You'll just lose face." Shrugging her shoulders, my grandmother told me she'd retorted, "I'll lose my own face, thank you." Soon after submitting her application, she discovered that several other women in her dormitory were also secretly studying for the exam late at night. Hoping to narrow the competition, no one had spread the news.

Amy described for me the momentous occasion:

> I took the Qinghua examination in 1925. It was a nationwide exam. There were five hundred people. They all wanted to go to the United States. I'd heard so much about the United States, so I wanted to see it, too. Qinghua is not in Beijing, but five or ten miles away, in the country. You have to stay there to take the examination for a whole week. You live in the boys' dormitory, and they give you the examination in two very big halls. Five hundred girls from all of China took the examination. They'd all heard of this chance. I never heard of it until KK said, "Do you want an application? You have to apply."

Students from the McTyeire School in Shanghai, who had spent one year studying exclusively for the Qinghua exam, arrived in a big group and occupied several dormitory rooms. On the Friday before the examination would begin, Amy told her mother that her room at home was too hot, so she was going to the dormitory at PUMC to study. Carrying a bag of clothes and books, she hired a bicycle rickshaw outside their house. After they went through one of the northern gates of the city wall, crowded streets gave way to fields and tree-lined roads. Arriving at her assigned room of ten students, Amy hung her mosquito netting over a bed in the corner and sat within the white mesh to review her books one last time.

For five mornings in a row, she ate a bowl of scrambled eggs and rice in the cafeteria. In the testing halls, a proctor handed out the exam papers, and she wrote algebraic equations, descriptions of molecular reactions, and essays on Chinese and international history. Exhausted at the end of the week, she made a detour on the way home to a small village outside the city wall. The village's water chestnuts were famous, and she bought a bunch for her mother. She made up an excuse for how she'd gotten them.

In spite of the pessimism Shuhua had expressed about Amy's chances, she wrote a letter on Amy's behalf asking for help with a recommendation. In July 1925, Shuhua painted a fan with a scene of Hangzhou's famous West Lake, which she sent to Hu Shi with a request.

> After my younger sister Shuhao took the Qinghua exam, she heard three judges would make the final decision. The other students attending the exam had already found people to introduce their moral character and educational background to the judges by the time they sat for the exam. Fan Yuanlian is one of the judges, and I remember you know each other. I don't know whether or not you can write a recommendation letter to Fan for Shuhao? She graduated from [Tianjin] Beiyang Girls' Normal School, studied science at Yanjing University, and then graduated from the preparatory course at PUMC, where she's already completed two years of formal coursework. She's known at school as a good student and in 1922 and 1923 received honor scholarships. That she has for years been a leader in women's physical education speaks to her healthy, lively demeanor. These are all facts. You won't laugh at me bragging about my own people, will you? If you don't know Fan, please know it was just a hope.[22]

When Amy told me the story of asking Hu Shi to serve as her character reference, she told me he wanted to know why she had lied about her age. When she explained the situation, he laughed and said, "You shouldn't be kicked out just for your age." She asked her cousin Feng Gengguang to serve as a financial guarantor. As with Hu Shi, she asked him to say nothing to her family.

A week later, a telegram arrived at their door announcing that she had been chosen as one of the five scholarship students. When her parents heard the news, they wanted her to turn down the scholarship and stay in Beijing.

But exhilarated by the chance to study abroad, Amy raced around the city making preparations. When she consulted her professors at PUMC on where to study, they recommended the medical school at Western Reserve University for its intimate size and quality of teaching, and Amy sent her scholarship information to the Cleveland address they provided. In late July, she picked up a small leather-covered passport with her photograph stamped by the Ministry of Foreign Affairs in Chinese and French.

She bought a large steamer trunk and packed her books. Realizing they could not dissuade her from leaving, her mother, father, and older sister Shuzhi each gave her a traditional Beijing winter coat lined with fur. She folded the three coats on top of her books and Chinese dresses. Shuhua assured her that she would be able to buy ready-made Western clothes in Shanghai before her ship departed. On her last night at home, Ling Fupeng threw a farewell banquet and toasted to the success of his youngest, most modern daughter in her medical studies abroad. When my grandmother pushed back from the dinner table after telling me once again about her father's examination success or her own scholarship triumph—for this, not

Passport photograph of Ling Shuhao (Amy), Beijing, 1925

sad farewells, is what she loved to tell best—she raised her voice proudly, "Every examination I had, I passed. It was difficult, but I did it."

Shuhua traveled with Amy on the train to Shanghai. They arrived in the city two months after a series of strikes had led to the violent May Thirtieth Incident, in which police fired into a crowd of protesters that included students. Insulated by months of rigorous studying, Amy only vaguely remembered the strikes and protest marches. She said they blurred with the memory of strikes occurring throughout her entire youth. She worried instead about getting to Shanghai in time to board the August sailing ship on which the Qinghua scholarship students' passage had been arranged. She feared Western Reserve wouldn't accept her as a student because she hadn't received any response yet.

When Amy and Shuhua stepped off the train, they found that a friend of their father had sent his car to pick them up. They asked the driver to drop them off at the Shanghai YWCA, instead of the home of an older sister my grandmother called Ella. When I asked for more information about this sister, she told me that Shuping had attended school in Shanghai and adopted the English name Ella. She'd become a good dancer and a chain smoker. Their father had married her to a wealthy playboy living off of his inheritance. Ella spent her time arranging dancing parties with pretty Chinese girls for American businessmen in Shanghai. According to Amy, Shuhua considered her lifestyle petty and sad and refused to stay with her. In *Ancient Melodies*, Shuhua briefly mentions an older half-sister, a daughter of Third Mother, who sounds very similar to the Ella of Amy's description. She had attended a fashionable finishing school in Shanghai called "The East and the West" where she learned English, French, singing, and ballroom dancing.

When Shuhua and Amy met Ella for lunch the next day, she gestured at Amy with a long cigarette holder and sighed over her lack of sophistication. She couldn't believe that Amy planned to go to the United States without knowing how to dance. Ella extracted from Amy a feigned promise to buy a pair of dancing shoes before she departed. As they left the restaurant, Ella reminded her of the proper heel height for dancing, measuring a space between her thumb and forefinger. As she waved goodbye, Shuhua hurried Amy down Nanjing Road to the Yong An Trading Company, where they wandered among racks of Western-style dresses. Laughing over Ella's advice, Amy said, "Never mind. Dancing is a waste of time. There are better things to do." Shuhua watched in the dressing room while her sister tried on slips, skirts, and blouses. Nothing fit, and she didn't have time to have anything tailored. She would have to show up in the United States wearing Chinese clothing.

In the small YWCA room she shared with Shuhua on the night before her departure, Amy had trouble sleeping. She lay in the dark staring at the ceiling. I imagine light piano notes from the hotel ballroom across the street drifting through their open window. Amy closed her eyes and saw her stylish sister lighting a cigarette. Ella raised one of her plucked eyebrows and blew out a thin stream of smoke. The piano player picked up the beat, and the dancing couples across the street swirled into a blur. Amy saw her reflection in the dressing-room mirror. The Western dress hung loosely on her thin body. She said aloud, in a phrase she would repeat often in the future, "I never danced in my life. I never learned dancing. No time for that." In the distance, she heard the voice of their Feng cousin. Fragments of his speech about the direction Ella had taken drifted through her mind, "A school for fashionable girls only . . . it will not help China at all. . . . I am glad that Shuhao decided to study medicine. I'm sure she will be a good doctor."

Amy woke a few hours later, with the pale light of dawn at the window. Shuhua shifted in her sleep, and the bed frame creaked. Amy smelled the thick blanketing comfort of dough being fried by a street vendor. She remembered the sight of her sister at home through a doorway, painting at her desk, and their mother in the kitchen cooking her favorite meal: lamb with mushrooms, walnuts, bamboo shoots, and leeks sizzling over the fire.

· *Thirteen* ·

Crescent Moon

$\mathscr{P}$ink lotuses choked the lake at Beijing University as I circled it in July 1997. The campus had been home to the centralized Yanjing University when it opened its gates in 1926, a year and a half after Ling Shuhua graduated with a "Golden Key" award. An American architect enamored with the Forbidden City had designed the original campus buildings in an adapted palace style. Even the dormitories, shaded by willow trees, possessed a stately presence with their curving tile roofs and decoratively painted wooden eaves.

Leaving campus, I wandered in and out of neighboring bookstores until I found the one I was looking for and descended into a sweltering basement. I had recently discovered a new anthology of Ling Shuhua's short stories printed in Beijing. After years of official mainland suppression of her writing due to its bourgeois tendencies, publishers had finally begun to reissue her work. I fell into a habit of searching out new reprints. When I first lived in China in the early 1990s, it had been virtually impossible to buy Ling Shuhua's books. Only bookshops in Hong Kong or Singapore sold her two-volume *Selected Works*. In a hot underground catacomb of books, I scanned the modern literature section. No luck. On a display table, I found piles of paperbacks from a new series featuring essays by twentieth-century writers. I opened a book by another May Fourth woman and noticed on the inside flap a list of the twenty-five authors in the series. Ling Shuhua's name appeared near the bottom of the list. I searched through the piles on the table, but even with help of a shop assistant, I failed to locate the book with essays by Ling Shuhua.

I had a fellowship that summer to study Chinese at Beijing Normal University. In my class of twelve, two-thirds were Chinese American undergraduates. Local instructors drilled us in grammar and vocabulary every morning in small groups. Our head teacher had grown up in Beijing but now lived in the United States, where he taught university-level Chinese. When we met as a class for one hour before lunch, he stood at the head of a large table to lecture on our reading assignments. Our three "native" instructors, all female, sat on a sofa at the back of the room. I gradually developed a vague antipathy for the head teacher, which reached its peak the day he announced we wouldn't be reading the only short story in our textbook written by a woman. With a dismissive wave of his hand, he explained that he didn't like her writing.

Each week we wrote an essay on an assigned topic, memorized it, and recited it in front of class for a grade. I dreaded this exercise. My Chinese sounded flat and clumsy next to the easy tones of my classmates who had grown up speaking it at home. One Friday I recited an essay I had titled "What about Hu Shi's Sisters?" We'd read an autobiographical article by the famous *baihua* reformer, in which he reminisces about his early education in the classics. Our teacher praised the article, reliving through it his boyhood love of heroic men like the good fellows in *The Water Margin*. In my essay, I raised the example of my great-aunt and described the book, *Flowers in the Mirror*, that had inspired her to believe that one day she might compete in the imperial examinations.

The following week, I had an individual Chinese clinic with the teacher. He looked at me with a strange smile and asked why my great-aunt had read *Flowers in the Mirror*. I understood the implication of the question and answered, "Because she was Chinese." He blinked behind thick glasses. Waiting through a familiar pause of surprise, I knew I was being reassessed according to this piece of genetic information. I would be more authentic in his eyes, but never as authentic as my perfectly accented classmates.

Not long after, one blazing summer afternoon, our class toured the Lu Xun Museum. Located next to a small compound where Lu Xun lived between 1924 and 1926, the museum houses his photographs, manuscripts, diaries, and letters. In the bookstore, our teacher bought a set of the complete works of Lu Xun. He allowed each student to borrow one volume from him. Our assignment was to pick a short essay or story to read on our own and then discuss with him during our individual sessions. From a long essay on Chinese New Literature, I picked a passage about May Fourth writers, in which Lu Xun compares Ling Shuhua to several other women writers of the period.

Opposite our teacher, I opened the book to this passage. In Chinese, I explained that Ling Shuhua was the great-aunt I had mentioned before. When I told him I had written my undergraduate thesis on her and other women writers to emerge after May Fourth, he laughed. I stared blankly at his earnest face and heard him say, "What women writers? There were no women writers." "Yes, there were," I snapped, beginning to spew names. I pointed to the paragraph in which his beloved Lu Xun critically assesses Ling

Shuhua. He carefully took the book and read the paragraph. He flipped to the end of the essay and read the short footnote on Ling Shuhua. "Interesting," he murmured, still looking at the text.

At the end of the summer, in my last individual meeting with him, we chatted casually about our plans for the fall once we returned to the United States. As our half hour neared its end, he pushed a book across the desk to me. "I found this at a bookstore last weekend," he said. It was the volume of essays by Ling Shuhua that I had hunted for, sweating in a basement bookstore. I awkwardly offered to pay him for it. "No, I'm giving it to you," he said. I left his room, both happy and ashamed, with the paperback peace offering on top of the notebook I hugged to my chest.

On January 10, 1925, Shuhua published a story titled "Intoxicated." It begins in the wake of a party: "It was late at night and the guests had departed. A drunken man in his thirties had collapsed and was sound asleep in a huge chair in the middle of the parlor. Next to the fire sat a tipsy young couple whispering to each other. A still, sweet aroma filled the air."[1]

The wife, Caitiao, asks her husband to cover their sleeping guest with a blanket and remove his shoes. The couple decides to stay in the room in case he should wake up and need anything. The husband gushes about the perfect atmosphere of their home—"even lotus petals would smell bitter by comparison"—and Caitiao's beauty. Caitiao grows impatient with his clichéd metaphors and raptly watches the sleeping man. His face strikes her as mellow and sensuous. Her husband asks what she would like for the New Year celebration, and Caitiao impetuously replies that she has a wish that will take only a second to fulfill, to kiss the face of their sleeping guest. Her husband argues that she is drunk. She tries to explain, "As you know I was born with a peculiar love of literature, and whenever I read a truly marvelous essay I always imagine how dignified the author looks. . . . But he . . . what really makes me adore him, well everything! . . . I've gotten to the point where I won't feel comfortable if I don't express this emotion."[2] Her husband hesitates, uncomfortable with his wife's taboo wish to *kiss*—he says "kiss" in English—but finally relents. As Caitiao crosses the room, her heart pounds wildly. Suddenly, she stops. Her face cools down, and her heart resumes a normal rhythm. She returns to sit next to her husband. When he asks her what is wrong, she hangs her head and responds, "Nothing. I don't want to *kiss* him anymore."

"Intoxicated" appeared in *Xiandai pinglun* (Contemporary review), a new Beijing weekly covering mainly politics, economics, law, and philosophy. Chen Xiying served as editor of the literature section and published regular commentaries on politics and culture. These short essays, which he called

"Idle Chats," ranged widely from criticism of Hollywood sentimentality to sarcastic sketches of Chinese manners, reflections on the link between literature and revolution, and support for a "Little Theater" movement in China based on community art troupes in Europe. With "Intoxicated," Chen began publishing a string of stories by Ling Shuhua, and *Contemporary Review* became her most important early publication venue. "Intoxicated" received wide recognition, marking her arrival on the Beijing literary scene. Zhou Zuoren praised the story in one of his essays, and the comic dramatist Ding Xilin, another participant in the Crescent Moon salons, adapted the story into a one-act play.

Lu Xun would eventually write about Ling Shuhua in an introductory essay for the *Compendium of Modern Chinese Literature*. In the passage I showed my Chinese teacher, he compares her to another woman writer of the period, Feng Yuanjun, who also wrote about the questions of marriage and love faced by women. In Feng's "The Journey," for example, two unmarried students secretly take a vacation and sleep in the same hotel room, in spite of the criticism they know they will receive if discovered. Lu Xun points out the writers' differences:

> Ling Shuhua's fiction . . . she uses a suitable amount of daring like Feng Yuanjun, but her courage of expression is not the same. Generally speaking she is very prudent and refrains from going too far in her description of complacent females in old-style households. Even though among her works there are those which jump the tracks, like "Intoxicated," to reveal the flickering influence of chance drunkenness in writing, in the end, she recovers her original path. This is good—it allows us to understand characters who are never the same as those in the stories of Feng Yuanjun [and others]. This represents one perspective on the world, revealing the psychology of the elite and illustrious class.[3]

Lu Xun's judgment seems lukewarm: she successfully captures the interior struggle of an elite woman with a modicum of rebelliousness. The boundary between marital and friendly affection remains intact. However, Caitiao's desire to kiss the sleeping man and her husband's consent hint at the erotic tensions of the modern girl, heightened in the end by her frustrated effort.

As boldly as Shuhua had written to Zhou Zuoren, she now began sending letters to the editor who had published "Intoxicated." She wrote to Chen Xiying that she would like to meet him and invited him to Ganmian Hutong. Chen Xiying came from a poor scholarly family in Wuxi, and when he arrived at the address Shuhua had given in her letter, he thought he'd made a mistake. Staring at the grand red doors, he finally summoned the courage to knock. Like KK, Xiying soon became a regular visitor.

Meanwhile, gossip circulated about the romantic improprieties of Xu

Zhimo. After Lin Huiyin became engaged to someone else, he fell for Lu Xiaoman, a glamorous twenty-year-old socialite married to a military officer. Xiaoman's husband had accepted a post in Manchuria and asked Zhimo to accompany her to parties during his absence, unwittingly opening the door for their affections to develop. In a long letter to Hu Shi, Shuhua expressed outrage at rumors about the nature of Zhimo and Xiaoman's relationship.[4] She thought they were ungrounded and threatened Xu Zhimo's reputation as a poet. She wrote on the same night that she had taken her father to the Crescent Moon Society, to show him how it differed from other clubs and seek his approval for her to officially join. An evening of interesting conversation ended awkwardly on the ride home. They shared a carriage with a banker who brought up the affair between Xu Zhimo and Lu Xiaoman. Shuhua refuted his claim that the two were lovers, only to have the banker scoff, in front of her father, that she lived secluded within her family's inner chambers.

Shuhua's letter to Hu Shi emphasizes that she believed Zhimo and Xiaoman had nothing to hide. In her opinion, they possessed the spirit of children and hadn't considered the public consequences of their actions. She also defended her own past actions:

> For example, when Zhimo and I exchanged letters, we half crazily, half foolishly told jokes to amuse ourselves. There was nothing we couldn't express to each other. . . . Since I want to have a taste of literary affairs, of course I cannot bear to build walls to enclose myself as common girls do. But when I sent him letters in return, baseless rumors proliferated. . . . From the beginning to the present, I've always thought of Zhimo as a writing friend, and he now also only takes me as a friend who accepts and understands his melancholy.[5]

Shuhua told Hu Shi that she had discussed with Xu Zhimo a plan for him to leave the country to extricate himself from potential scandal. She asked Hu Shi to encourage him to take this trip, for the sake of his position and the Crescent Moon Society. Then she reiterated, "I want to state that Xu Zhimo and I have always been literary friends." This clarification of emotions toward Zhimo opened the way for an increasingly close relationship with her editor at *Contemporary Review*. Xu Zhimo eventually extended his comparison of Ling Shuhua to Katherine Mansfield by likening Chen Xiying to Mansfield's husband, the critic-editor John Middleton Murry.

The publication of "Intoxicated" marked the beginning of an extremely productive year for Shuhua. In March 1925, Chen Xiying published another of her best-known stories, "Embroidered Pillows," in which a young woman painstakingly embroiders a pair of pillows. Her *amah* blots perspiration from her face while she sews the tiny stitches that make up a kingfisher with lotuses and a phoenix on a mountain of rocks. The cushions will be sent as a gift to a family whose son her parents hope to attract as a marriage partner. The young mistress labors intensively over these objects, which will represent her on the marriage market. After the pillows are sent, two years pass, without a response from the receiving family until she inadvertently learns from a maid's story that on the night the pillows were presented, a drunken guest at the party vomited on one of them. A mahjong player carelessly used the other as a footstool.

> She began to recall that when she had made the crest she had had to embroider it, then take it out, altogether three times. Once her perspiration had discolored the delicate yellow thread. She didn't discover it until she was through embroidering. Another time she used the wrong color of green for the rock. She had mistaken the color while embroidering at night. She couldn't remember why she had taken it out the last time. For the light pink of the lotus petals, she didn't dare just take up the thread after washing her hands. She had sprinkled her hands with talcum powder before touching it. The large lotus leaf was even harder . . . she had matched twelve different colors of green thread to embroider it.[6]

When the maid suggests to her mistress that she sew another pair of pillows as gorgeous as the damaged ones once were, she can only shake her head.

As I read and reread, with my imperfect Chinese and in translation, I wonder if I even like Shuhua's stories. Can I learn to approach them as literature rather than clues to a family I understand too little? The more I discover, the more I do not want to understand. I begin to hate these stories for their compactness and for the beauty of their stylized passages. Her sketches of self-imposed domestic constriction repeatedly collapse inward, like an opulent old house sinking into the mire. The maid in "Embroidered Pillows" reports, "The bird is said to have been raised in relief but now it's already been trampled and it's caved in."[7]

Several lines written to me in letters from Shuhua's daughter cross my mind. "My mother's shadow will be with me until I die."[8] And a month and a half later, "The more I see the letters written by my mother, the more sad I have become. I don't think I understand her at all. Her family background, her mothers, and the jealousy of all the children must have made them rather damaged."[9] I want her—the woman in the stories, the woman in my story—to kiss, to rebel, to change, to forgive. I ask myself, will she jump the tracks?

In the spring of 1925, Shuhua purchased a small blank scroll, less than four inches high but over four yards long. One evening after dinner at the Crescent Moon Society, Shuhua placed the scroll in Xu Zhimo's hand and asked him to take it to England. Lu Xiaoman's husband, upon learning of the letters his wife continued to exchange with Xu Zhimo, had threatened to kill him. Zhimo finally planned to leave for his second trip to Europe. He would take the trans-Siberian railway and spend the spring and summer months visiting friends and acquaintances from previous years abroad.

On the eve of his departure, in exchange for her blank scroll packed in his luggage, Zhimo entrusted Shuhua with two things. He asked her to occasionally visit Lu Xiaoman and encourage her to cultivate more literary habits such as painting and keeping a diary. In a later letter to Xiaoman, he wrote, "Of my female friends, Shuhua is my comrade."[10] He also handed over to Shuhua for safekeeping a small chest that he called his "Eight Treasures Box," which contained his diaries, letters, and notes. He usually carried these writings with him, but he feared for their safety during his travels or in the hands of Xiaoman, whose jealousy might be unleashed if she read his early diary entries about Lin Huiyin. As he bid his trusted "comrade" farewell, he proclaimed half in jest that if he didn't return she should use the contents of the box to write a novel based on his life.[11]

During Xu Zhimo's stay in England, he spread out Shuhua's scroll, opened an album of his own, and invited his hosts to contribute some artistic offering. In this manner, with a compact, brocade-covered scroll as her surrogate, Shuhua first traveled to the West and received an introduction to British writers and artists associated with the Bloomsbury group, who began to fill up her blank length of paper with small paintings and inscriptions.

Shortly after Xu Zhimo's departure, during the summer that Amy hurriedly prepared to leave for the United States, a student protest at the Beijing Women's Normal University led Chen Xiying and Lu Xun into a bitter exchange in print. Their "battle of pens" devolved over several months into personal insult and eventually entangled Shuhua in a peripheral way.[12] The conflict at the university had begun in 1924, when the chancellor expelled three students for returning to school late, ignoring their claims that unrest in the south had delayed them. The chancellor was the first female head of the school. In spite of her education abroad in Japan and the United States, she was a Confucian authoritarian and clashed regularly with students. In January 1925, the student government initiated an effort to oust her. The conflict came to a head in May, when the chancellor invited her staff to a meal where they decided to expel six of the most radical students, including two members of the Communist Party.[13] Lu Xun and his brother Zhou Zuoren, who both lectured at the university, supported the students. In frequent essays, Lu Xun denounced the expulsions and lambasted the chancellor as a ruthless mother-in-law who intimidated "helpless students of her own sex," as if they were "child-brides" coming into her household.[14]

Chen Xiying expressed private disagreement with the students' tactics—which included plastering school bulletin boards with humiliating personal attacks against administrators and hissing during lectures—and Lu Xun's support of them. Shuhua later recalled that although Chen Xiying did not know the chancellor or have any connection with the university, he opposed the manner in which Lu Xun provoked the students. She remembered that Lu Xun had gone so far as to throw the chancellor's suitcases out the front gate of the university.[15] Chen Xiying's remarks made their way to Lu Xun, who in mid-May equated the Crescent Moon Society with the chancellor's infamous banquet. He accused Chen Xiying of refusing to publicly comment on the topic. "I have only just learned that to refrain from writing is a way of showing one's social status," Lu Xun quipped.[16]

When Chen Xiying responded in print, he accused Lu Xun of "inciting students," "plotting to become college president," and "adding false antlers to his head," in other words, posing as a fighter to foment revolt.[17] Lu Xun denied these claims in an essay called "Not Idle Chat," a title mocking Chen's weekly column. He wrote, "As for certain 'men of letters' who pose as critics, their sole function seems to be that of a bodyguard—they gesticulate and hold forth, just to protect their master."[18] His assaults led Chen Xiying to defend himself against insinuations that he was related to the conservative minister of education or friendly with the chancellor, who both hailed from his hometown of Wuxi. Their battle continued throughout the summer, when the university was forcibly closed for several months, and into the fall, after the threat of violence against protesting students proved real. At this point, Lu Xun's criticism took a different but nasty tack. In an article on "pseudo-widows" or professional single women, he held up the embattled chancellor as an example of "morbid old maids" whose "love remains latent, or withers and becomes abnormal" outside of marriage and motherhood.[19]

Xu Zhimo returned from Europe in September, after Lu Xiaoman's husband granted her a divorce. When he saw Shuhua again, he pulled out her scroll and unrolled it to display the contributions he had collected on her behalf. Roger Fry had painted a horizontal, idyllic landscape of river, trees, and mountains in monochrome ink wash. Dora Russell (Dora Black had returned to England several months pregnant after her trip to China with Bertrand Russell and agreed, against her previously stated principle, to marry him) had added a version of a line from her 1925 feminist tract *Hypatia, or Woman and Knowledge*: "The dualism of mind and matter is essentially a masculine philosophy." For the next thirty-three years, Shuhua would continue to pass her little scroll around to artist and writer friends, who lent their hand to the growing collection. The juxtaposition of calligraphy, images, and styles provides a record not only of the individuals with whom Shuhua came in contact but also of the continuous travels of the scroll, its contributors, and Shuhua herself. The celebrated twentieth-century master of traditional Chinese landscape painting Zhang Daqian squeezed one of his additions, a pensive scholar sitting beneath a pine tree, between Roger Fry's brushstrokes and Dora Russell's cursive. Two of Xu Beihong's early horses, painted in 1925 during Xu Zhimo's visit with him in Paris, gallop through long grass. Jiang Xiaojian, another Chinese painter who studied for years in France, provided a still life of a wine bottle, glass, and cut baguette arranged on top of the newspaper *La Liberté*. The painter-turned-poet Wen Yiduo sketched a bust of Tolstoy, his head encircled by trees, in thick, quick strokes. A poem in flowing, grass-style calligraphy by Japanese novelist Tanizaki Junichiro would be added in 1927. One of the last additions now appears at the very beginning of the scroll, a bold four-character title reading "Spring Trees and Autumn Clouds," written by Zhang Daqian in Tokyo in 1959.[20]

The practice of keeping scrolls or albums in which friends of the owner would leave artistic offerings had been common among the educated elite of China for centuries. Shuhua's scroll documents the transnational circuit of modernism, while preserving an amateur ideal of Chinese art, which she managed to maintain alongside her professional career as a writer. In many ways, this aesthetic resonated with the philosophy held by a group of writers and artists in England admired by Xu Zhimo. The credo of the Bloomsbury Group drew upon a line by philosopher G. E. Moore: "By far the most valuable things, which we know or can imagine, are certain states of consciousness, which may be roughly described as the pleasures of human intercourse and the enjoyment of beautiful objects."[21]

Ling Shuhua cultivated this art of life as her autobiography slipped into fiction and her fiction back into autobiography. In my attempt to narrate her life, I've struggled with the contradictory impulses of biography: its transformation of a life into a bounded text and its responsibility to untidy realities. Nevertheless, it is through these records of artistic cultivation that I know Shuhua. The elegant and self-contained scroll, a beautiful object faithful in its devotion to art, is a token of the life she aspired to lead.

Shortly after Xu Zhimo's return to Beijing in the fall of 1925, he became editor of the *Morning Post* literary supplement. He and Shuhua pored over a book of prints by the English artist Aubrey Beardsley and chose one for the supplement's new masthead. In England, Xu Zhimo had come to admire the *Yellow Book*, a late-nineteenth-century British literary journal featuring authors of the Decadent school, such as Oscar Wilde and Max Beerbohm, and cover illustrations by Beardsley.[22] As Zhimo prepared his first issue, Shuhua assisted with the artwork. She sketched the Beardsley drawing they had selected onto the printing plate.[23] The bare back of a man wearing a toga faces the viewer. The silhouette of his face turns to the side, toward a graceful arm raised over vertical calligraphy reading *Morning Post Supplement*. Xu Zhimo gave credit to Ling Shuhua for her work but failed to mention the original artist. This omission created a minor scandal in which critics who recognized the Beardsley illustration accused Shuhua of plagiarism. Zhimo explained the mistake in the next issue and changed the masthead by the time his third issue went to press, but a taint trailed Shuhua's name for months.

In the October 1, 1925, issue with the controversial drawing, Xu Zhimo also published a story by Shuhua titled "The Night of Midautumn Festival." A newlywed couple happily prepares to eat their first festival dinner together. The evening is perfect until a phone call delivers urgent news about the health of the husband's foster sister. He wants to leave immediately to help, but his wife insists that he first eat the dinner. He hastily takes a bite of "Togetherness Duck," but it tastes greasy. He spits the piece out and rushes off to see his foster sister. He arrives minutes after her death and blames his wife for delaying him. She, however, angrily believes that his refusal to partake in their first ritual meal signals doom for their marriage. The ensuing argument leads to many years of discontent. The husband frequents the city's pleasure quarters and squanders all of the earnings from his family's grocery on gifts for the women there. His wife suffers two miscarriages, with the second one exhibiting deformities caused by syphilis. Yet, even after her husband moves in with relatives in Tianjin's "Three Who-Cares" district, the wife stubbornly clings to the belief that their fate resulted from a transgressed ritual she tried to perform properly.

Of the nine stories Ling Shuhua published in 1925, "Intoxicated," "Embroidered Pillows," and "The Night of Midautumn Festival" would later prove to be the ones most anthologized, as representative not just of her early period but rather her whole career. Critics have used this trio of stories to classify her as a member of the "*guixiu* school," writing by women of the inner chambers. While the term had once been used to honor traditional learned women, it now served as an insult a banker might use during a shared carriage ride to indicate a lack of seriousness or objectivity. Contemporary literary critic Rey Chow uses these same three stories, but to a different purpose, in her analysis of Ling Shuhua's "virtuous transaction" with literature. She points out how Shuhua's focus on the domestic economy of her female characters' daily existence lays bare its psychological terror. Shuhua's reworking of *guixiu* literature did more than paint women in leisurely repose: "The realm of the *guixiu*, seen in this light, is not the realm of a privileged class but rather a 'theater of the absurd,' where the most involved, dedicated, and passionate participation in a social contract becomes a matter of self-sacrifice, and where the more virtuous the woman is, the more thoroughly her aspirations and desires are demolished."[24]

The artistic training Shuhua received as a girl also influenced the aesthetics of her writing. Although she yearned for a modern life free of patriarchal tradition, her classical education represented a Chinese cultural history under siege by the West and a deep source of pride and pleasure. This tension influenced her writing style, in which epiphanic moments unfold with an economy of language, highlighted by painterly description. Shu-mei Shih, in her study of literary modernism in semicolonial China, argues that Shuhua's recuperation of a feminine tradition in order to undercut it through parody imbues the feminine voice with a subversive quality. This technique allows for a "hybridization of the vernacular and the classical, the modern and the traditional, so that they might become intermingled and interdependent."[25] Rey Chow demonstrates how Shuhua's use of *baihua* actually accentuated classical tendencies in her writing, in a way that garnered attention but also allowed commentators to undermine the serious gender critique in her stories. Chow describes the irony of this "virtuous transaction," in which Ling Shuhua's literary language fulfills a contract with a public aesthetic.

> In fact, one can go as far as saying that it is as she writes in *baihua* that the stylistic features of her classical literary training appear most distinctly. This is something that her readers hardly fail to notice. In the laudatory comments they make about her, it is often terms which allude to the atmosphere of classical Chinese poetry or painting, such as *ziran* [natural], *yinyi* [recluse-like], *juan-yong* [meaningful], *fengya* [graceful], *gupu yadan* [simple and refined], that they adopt. In the Chinese literary context, these terms are often used to suggest a writer's attainment of a high spiritual level, a *jingjie* [state of mind], which is the sign of a mature personal development. However, while these terms may put Ling Shuhua on a par with ancient poets and painters, they also depersonalize, and hence de-feminize, the social contexts of her stories.[26]

When Rabindranath Tagore asked Shuhua in 1924 if she felt more attracted to ancient or contemporary Chinese poetry, she answered, "Old poetry has no flavor. New poetry often has no inspiration and just tries to imitate European styles. This is boring and even worse dishonest."[27] In her fiction, she struggled with how to write in a way that expressed female experience, broke from a male-dominated literary past, and remained Chinese by resisting wholesale adoption of Western techniques. She subverted convention by using classically inflected language not to describe women's melancholy beauty but rather the trauma of their interior worlds. Don Holoch, one of the earliest Western critics to write about Ling Shuhua, calls her stories evocations of "everyday feudalism."[28] By contrast, her style as a painter of landscapes, birds, and flowers deviated little from classical tradition, perhaps especially after the incident involving the Beardsley copy. The flexibility with which she moved between modern aspirations and traditional aesthetics opens a space of ambiguity in the interpretation of her life, as protofeminist or retrograde bourgeois woman. Shu-mei Shih identifies this flexibility as a trait of the Beijing School's neotraditionalism.[29] This group of writers in which she places Ling Shuhua did not see the traditional East or the modern West in terms of direct opposition or linear progression, but as distinct resources that could be combined and synthesized, resulting in a form of biculturality that resisted nationalism and linear history.

Although Shuhua would continue throughout the 1920s and 1930s to produce a steady stream of short stories, most reviews of modern Chinese literature that include her work favor stories written in the years immediately after she left Yanjing University. They draw exclusive attention to her stories about elite women within domestic spaces—the ones Shu-mei Shih calls parodies of the traditional poetic Boudoir Complaint genre, in which a woman left by a lover or husband stands by the window to observe the outside world.[30] This critical focus overlooks Shuhua's stories featuring young children or schoolgirls as protagonists, as well as her stories set at school or in city streets. In the later canonization of modern Chinese literature, the narrow characterization of Ling Shuhua's repertoire reflects the limited range of categories applied to educated women after May Fourth. Shuhua's fiction was made to fit the category of *guixiu* literature, written for women, by women, and about women confined to the traditional inner chambers of home.

In her personal life, she strove to get out of exactly these chambers. After graduation, she had briefly contemplated taking a position as a family tutor. However, after interviewing for the job, she heard someone say, "A female family tutor is really just the same as a foreign governess. Society doesn't regard their position very highly." She declared that she wanted to "come out and do something." Worried that the job would make the literary world take her less seriously, she turned it down.[31]

Shuhua's struggles in the literary world continued when the plagiarism claims against her resurfaced in 1925. After she published her story "Temple of Flowers" in *Contemporary Review*, an article in *Jing bao* (Capital news) accused her of copying Chekhov's "At a Summer Villa."[32] The two stories bear a strong plot resemblance, and given Shuhua's admiration of Chekhov, she had probably read the story in question. However, in her version, she changes the temperament of the main characters and adds a perspective more sympathetic to the female character.

In Chekhov's version, a married man on his summer holiday unexpectedly receives an anonymous love letter requesting a rendezvous. Filled with uncharacteristic desire, Pavel Ivanitch dresses and goes to the appointed meeting place, only to run into his brother-in-law. Both men refuse to leave, but the letter writer fails to appear. Over dinner that night, Pavel's wife laughs at them. She sent them both the same letter to get them out of the house so she could clean it without disturbance. In Shuhua's story, the main character is a poet so bored with life that he's lost all inspiration. One day he receives a lyrical love letter. Using fresh, natural metaphors, the writer describes a Temple of Flowers to the west of the city. The next morning, the poet hires a rickshaw to take him to the temple. He anxiously waits, until his secret admirer arrives and turns out to be his wife. He had previously thought of her as a woman preoccupied only with embroidery and gossip, but now she teases him about his infidelity inspired by her poetic writing.

Shuhua performed a similar revision with her story about the Romeo and Juliet schoolgirl lovers. When Xu Zhimo published "Once Upon a Time" in 1926, it appeared with an introduction by author Yang Zhensheng. Yang explained that he had previously published a similar story of same-sex desire titled "Why Has She Gone Mad?" He had written it hastily and was not happy with the result. Many, including Ling Shuhua, believed that his protagonist went mad too quickly, so he asked her to write another piece based on his. Shuhua's version drew on her experience of dormitory life and presented the characters in a more compassionate light, in which their love is seen as normal rather than aberrant.

After various claims against Shuhua as a plagiarist appeared in print, Chen Xiying wrote an "Idle Chats" column on plagiarism. He declared that recent accusations of artistic theft had gone too far, since literary inspiration and borrowing is an important aspect of the creative process. Chinese, European, and Indian poets had all used flower metaphors to describe a beautiful woman, but it was hard to tell who had plagiarized whom. He asked, what would Ben Johnson, Tolstoy, and Shakespeare have done if unable to borrow the words or plots of others?[33]

The division between different literary societies, some of whose members had once been on friendly terms, deepened. In January 1926, the *Yu si* (Thread of talk) magazine, in which Lu Xun's essays frequently appeared, published a satire of certain Chinese authors that likened them to well-known European figures. It targeted Chen Xiying and other Crescent Moon Society members. The essay ends with a mocking chart of equivalencies, in which Chen Xiying is listed as China's Voltaire and Anatole France, Wen Yiduo as Alfred Tennyson, and Ling Shuhua as Aubrey Beardsley.[34] In the following month, Lu Xun denied Chen Xiying's claim that he had been the one to accuse Shuhua of plagiarism.[35]

That spring Hu Shi drafted a letter to his three "respected and beloved friends," Lu Xun, Zhou Zuoren, and Chen Xiying, appealing to them to stop their print battle. During a recent visit to Shanghai, a group of young readers had asked him what the writers were fighting about. He could give them no clear answer, since a once-reasonable debate had deteriorated into an exchange of curses including insults about each other's hometowns. He argued that their example of suspicion, hard-heartedness, and intolerance provided exactly the opposite of what young readers needed during difficult times.[36] His argument must have convinced the "three friends" for they finally desisted.

A more somber conflict captured public attention on March 18, 1926, when a student protest ended in violence. Rival powers vied for control of the north, and Feng Yuxiang's troops had mined the sea approaches to Tianjin as protection from the warlord who dominated Manchuria. This military tactic disrupted trade in what the Japanese considered their sphere of influence. They ordered Feng to clear the harbor, and he seemed ready to capitulate. Students marched on his office in Beijing and demanded that he reject the Japanese ultimatum. On the second day, police blocked demonstrators and opened fire on unarmed protestors, mostly students. They killed forty-seven, including two women.

On April 10, Shuhua published a story in *Contemporary Review* written in reaction to the student deaths. "Waiting" would be one of her few stories with any direct political reference. Hardworking Ah Qiu and her widowed mother have struggled for years to scrape by, but Ah Qiu has recently gotten engaged, and they joyfully clean the house and prepare a meal for her fiancé. When he arrives after his classes at the university, they will eat together to celebrate the anniversary of the couple's first meeting. They set food on the table and wait, but the boyfriend fails to appear. Hours pass, and the mother suddenly remembers what a neighbor told her about the students' petition to the government. She rushes out to the university and discovers that Ah Qiu's fiancé has been shot and killed. A group of supporters accompany her home, but she cannot find the words to tell her daughter what has happened.

On April 31, one day after Shuhua attended a memorial service held for the dead students, she wrote to Hu Shi:

> It's really, really not good here. If it weren't enough that blinding yellow dust mixed with the smell of animal dung swirls through the streets and whips at people, you also have to listen to troublesome, frightening lies, and you have to see the blood shed by good young people who have swallowed bullets. It

makes your stomach burst with anger, yet there's no concrete way to retaliate. Does this chaotic world foster our cowardice? Yesterday I went to see the memorial service at Beijing National University, where those bloody clothes were displayed. I looked at them and felt only a deadening cold numbness travel from my lips to my heart, and then to the bottom of my feet. . . . I've been thinking of writing some public words, to exert a sense of duty, but my heart is disordered and scared.[37]

In the same letter, she suggested that Ling Fupeng had given his blessing to her engagement with Chen Xiying. (A week and a half earlier, she had published a translation of Katherine Mansfield's "The Little Girl." The story captures a young girl's fear of her father's brusque, authoritative manner, but also her discovery of his latent tenderness.) Shuhua's letter to Hu Shi continued cryptically. Writing presumably about her relationship with Xiying, she stated that it "added another color to life and gave comfort, sympathy, and encouragement, offering a walking stick on the road of art." Xiying published another story by Shuhua in June 1926. A month later he married her in a courtyard ceremony held in Beijing, attended by several members of the local literary scene.

After their wedding, Xiying took Shuhua back to his hometown of Wuxi. He was the oldest of five children in a family that prided itself on a tradition of scholarship. His parents had spent most of their money on educating their children and lived in a small, damp old house. Xiying proudly presented his talented wife to them. By custom, as a new daughter-in-law, Shuhua was expected to serve snacks and tea to Xiying's parents and their friends who came to meet her. Resistant to this wifely role, she pretended to be sick and refused to get out of bed. She was also angry when she learned that Xiying sent almost three-quarters of his modest professor's salary back to his family. When Xu Zhimo and Lu Xiaoman married that fall, Shuhua envied their glamorous life.

Back in Beijing, Shuhua and Xiying moved into rooms at Hu Shi's residence, temporarily rented to them by Hu's wife while he traveled abroad. They each had their own study, and while mutual understanding about a life of writing supported their relationship, they did not serve as the other's first reader. Toward the end of her life, Shuhua would joke that it was easier to give Chen Xiying a beating than to earn his praise of one of her sentences.[38] Shuhua accepted a position in the division of painting and calligraphy at the Beijing Palace Museum, where she aided with cataloging and preservation. She also volunteered as an assistant teacher in the Yanjing University art department and published five new short stories in *Contemporary Review*. Xiying continued to lecture at Beijing National University and to edit *Con-*

*Ling Shuhua and Chen Xiying, Beijing, ca. 1926.
Courtesy of Chen Xiaoying.*

temporary Review until July of 1927, when political instability among the warlords in Beijing caused its editorial board to move south. Shanghai was a site of greater potential political conflict, but the extraterritorial status of its foreign concessions offered a degree of protection for beleaguered intellectuals and their publications. This difficult choice between two unstable situations hints at an escalating national crisis.

In the previous months, two warlords who controlled much of northern China continued to wrestle over Beijing and began a campaign to drive Communists and radical supporters of the Guomindang out of the city, since both groups threatened their rule. A financial crisis befell the city's universities and colleges, which depended upon warlord contributions, and professors often did not receive their salaries for months. Many intellectuals in Beijing began to move southward, albeit to cities that did not necessarily guarantee any greater security. Meanwhile, the United Front of the Guomindang and the Communist Party, joined in uneasy alliance to oust the warlords and imperialists and unite the country, had begun their Northern Expedition in July 1926. Two of their main offensive thrusts through central China proceeded successfully, and Guomindang Generalissimo Chiang Kaishek began a military push up the east coast. In March 1927, his troops marched into Shanghai, where the pro-Communist General Labor Union had coordinated a citywide workers' strike and armed insurrection against the warlords to show support for the Guomindang troops. However, following clandestine arrangements with secret society leaders and Shanghai industrialists, Chiang's forces merged with local anti-Communist paramilitary elements and destroyed the labor movement in a sudden reign of terror. Thousands of workers, labor organizers, Communists, and others suspected of leftist tendencies were killed in the streets or rounded up and executed in what became known as the "Shanghai Spring." On April 18, Chiang set up his own government in Nanjing, and by August scattered pockets of open military conflict began to break out between the Guomindang and the Communists.

Beginning with warlord attempts to maintain control through terror and then Chiang's coup in 1927, women who displayed any feminist tendencies such as opposing arranged marriage or having bobbed hair came under attack by the Guomindang right. One female leader described the violence inflicted on women:

> Every girl with bobbed hair who was caught was stripped naked, raped by as many men as were present, then her body slit in two, from below upwards. Often the girls were not more than fifteen or sixteen, and officers, giving interviews to eager British journalists from Hong Kong, said: "The bobbed haired girls are the worst; they are very arrogant and talk back defiantly. We have had to kill hundreds of them."[39]

The anti-Communist violence of the Guomindang often focused on the transgressions of liberated women, as described by another female revolutionary:

> More than 1000 women leaders were killed in that year alone [1927] in all of China—not all were Communists, some were bourgeois and there were many students, but all were revolutionary leaders. . . . After girl students were beheaded, their heads were put into men's coffins, and the gendarmes said:

"You have your free love now!" If girls and men happened to be killed at the same time their heads were exchanged on the bodies. The girls' bodies were always horribly mutilated.[40]

During this reactionary outburst of violence against modern girls, a warlord general in Shandong executed Guo Longzhen, Shuhua's former classmate from Tianjin, for leading a Communist demonstration. In *Ancient Melodies*, Shuhua memorializes Guo's earnest involvement in the student movement: "Simplicity and open-mindedness was one of her great charms, and it was also the great virtue which many leaders had in those days."[41] As instability threatened both their writing life in Beijing and their May Fourth ideals, Xiying and Shuhua sought a way out.

III

SEEKING A MOORING

· Fourteen ·

Arrival

$\mathcal{M}$y grandmother never talked about departures. She did not describe the scene of the SS *President Jackson* disembarking from the port of Shanghai with her and sixty-eight other Qinghua scholarship students on board, but in August 1925, the large steamer eased away from the dock where her sister Shuhua stood, growing smaller on the horizon. The students' gestures of final communication subsided, and they gradually left the ship's railing and went below to settle into the close quarters they would share for two weeks. The sixty-four male students slept in bunks, eight to a cabin. The five female students were assigned to a honeymoon suite. Their trunks and extra cots crowded around the nuptial bed. A chaperone named Miss Grace, a thirty-eight-year-old Chinese graduate of Columbia University, supervised their encampment. One of Amy's cabin mates had received as farewell gifts a large basket of canned delicacies and a pair of crickets in a dried gourd shell decorated with the carving of a miniature landscape. Seeing their only child off to America, her overwrought parents hoped the durable goods would soon be eaten but that the fragile insects would survive the ocean passage as a reminder of home. All of the women gathered around to watch her tearfully unpack the shiny cans and jars. They staved off anxious stomachs with the thought of the many fine shipboard meals they would enjoy together before dispersing to schools across a foreign country.

The Qinghua Alumni Yearbook, 1925–1926, provides the name, home province, field of study, and U.S. university affiliation for each woman in this group of cabin mates, labeled collectively beneath their photograph as the "Class of 1925 Girl Students":

> Chang, Miss Nyoh Tsung—Jiangsu, Music, Oberlin Conservatory
> Ling, Miss Shu Hao—Guangdong, Medicine, Western Reserve University
> Tang, Miss Luh Djen—Jiangsu, History and Government, Smith College

189

Tsang, Miss Wei Van—Jiangsu, Physics, Cornell University
Wong, Miss Violet—Guangdong, Business Administration, University
of Chicago[1]

As it turned out, the recipient of the food basket, Miss Chang from
Shanghai, lay in bed moaning with seasickness for most of the journey. She
ate only *xifan* (rice porridge), which the others brought her from the dining
room. In return for their ministrations, she handed over the basket's contents.
They huddled in the corner and rolled back oblong tin lids. Amy recalled
these stolen moments of pleasure: "She was sick with motion sickness and
stayed in bed all the time. She asked us to eat all her canned Chinese food,
fish, oysters, and abalone. I ate them all."

Of the five female students, Amy and Violet Wong came from Cantonese families and clung together. In the hours not sequestered in the ship's
honeymoon suite, they ran laps around the deck, cheered each other's skill at
games of shuffleboard, and strolled arm-in-arm in the sea air, wondering
aloud what would become of their lives in America. Instead of arranged mar-
riages, they had embarked on an independent journey. They discussed the
problems women faced. I learned of their frankness about sex as a college
student, when my grandmother shocked me one afternoon by giving me a
lecture on birth control. Prompted by a television show on teenage pregnancy
she had watched the night before, she sat me down on the living room sofa
and explained that certain things had not changed. On the boat from China
to the United States, she had discovered that some women still knew very
little about birth control. She told me that a woman on the boat—failing to
clarify whether this woman was a fellow student or simply another female
passenger—approached her, knowing she studied medicine, and asked what
she could do for protection since she hadn't brought anything on board. Amy
told her all she needed was cotton and vinegar. Describing for me the methods of the day, she wrinkled her nose in distaste and said, "You just put some
vinegar on cotton balls and put it up there." While, as far as I know, the
members of the "Class of 1925 Girl Students" were not sexually active during
a sea crossing mostly spent cooped up and chaperoned in a cabin adorned
with forlorn lace curtains, they told each other tales of romance. They
debated the merits of free love, as opposed to arranged marriage, and passed
on information about birth control.

After seventeen days at sea, the ship's passengers caught their first
glimpse of the Pacific Coast early on September 2, 1925. They stared at an
overcast sky and the lush, green islands of Puget Sound. As the ship
approached Seattle, the Qinghua students gathered on deck for a group photograph. The male students wore western suits, some sporting hats and bow

ties. Many wore a small, round pin with the Qinghua insignia on the left lapel of their jackets. The female contingent, minus one seasick cabin mate, stood in the middle of the tightly packed group. In front of them, a row of kneeling students held up two flags, one bearing the characters for Qinghua and the other emblazoned with the five-colored stripes of the Republican flag. Each stripe represented one of the five major nationalities imagined to constitute the Republic of China. First raised in 1912 over the Provisional Senate Building in Nanjing, the Republican flag had also flown over Yuan Shikai's government and the May Fourth student protests. In the fall of 1924, before his final expedition to the north, Sun Yatsen had ordered the Republican flag lowered in southern China and replaced with the Nationalist flag, which featured a white sun against a blue field and symbolized his belief in the Chinese nation-state as one of Han unity rather than multiracial citizenship.[2] The students holding the old five-bar flag stare down at it respectfully rather than at the photographer. The memory of departure remains inherent in the moment of arrival, although what has been left behind is already outdated in its utopian sign.

I study the image as I do many photographs from the past, searching within its frame for something more than semaphore. I seek the photograph's emotional message, the anomaly that makes it more than just a textbook illustration. Packed into the group portrait, the many individual narratives that briefly intersected during a two-week sea voyage stare out at me. The faces of three men in the back row are blurred, the motion of their laughter beyond the capture of a slow exposure. What private joke do they share? A few faces beam with smiles, but most compose themselves with a dignity befitting the occasion; at least one man has the suave demeanor of a film star with slicked back hair and droopy, half-closed eyelids. My grandmother, her hands clasped together and a brooch pinned at the base of her collar, squints into the future. She carries the ambition of becoming a doctor and returning to China to open a clinic for women. Violet Wong, in a dark cape, stands by her side. Several students sit on the railing. One is distracted by some activity on shore and stares at whatever lies just beyond the frame. His gaze reminds me of the customs officials, doctors, and Chinese dockhands who waited on the pier.

The history of previous Pacific passages would weigh upon these new arrivals in ways that their group portrait does not immediately reveal. I cannot tell whether their faces register an understanding of their own exceptionality as Chinese freely entering the United States. The long struggle of Chinese gold miners and laborers against discriminatory laws extended back for decades preceding the moment the SS *President Jackson* dropped anchor in Seattle. The Chinese Exclusion Act, the first U.S. law that prohibited the entry

Party of Qinghua students arriving at Seattle on the American Oriental Mail Litter SS President Jackson, September 2, 1925

of immigrants on the basis of nationality, was passed in 1882. This act made it unlawful for Chinese laborers to enter the United States for the next ten years and denied naturalized citizenship to Chinese who already resided in America. Six years later, Congress broadened the law to deny entry not just to laborers but also to "all persons of the Chinese race," except officials, teachers, students, tourists, and merchants.[3] Renewed indefinitely in 1902, the Chinese Exclusion Act continued for forty more years to frame a racialized national discourse on China and Chinese immigrants—an officially sanctioned attitude that justified acts of aggression. U.S. Treasury Department immigration officers broke into Chinese homes on the pretext of registration checks, an action that often led to harassment and deportation. Even official visitors, such as the Chinese delegation to the 1904 St. Louis Exposition, suffered suspicious questioning and rough treatment at entry ports. In 1905, the Qing Ministry of Foreign Affairs, appalled by accounts of mistreatment, refused to renew their immigration treaty with the United States. Merchants in Guangzhou, Shanghai, Xiamen, and Tianjin strengthened the protest by declaring a total boycott of American goods, damaging U.S. trade for several months.[4]

In 1924, one year before Amy's arrival in Seattle, an additional immigration law had passed. The National Origins Act legislated tight restriction on the immigration of Chinese women. Although the number of Chinese women living in the United States had always been small compared with that of male immigrants, the 1924 legislation virtually stopped their movement and further increased the gender imbalance of Chinatown "bachelor societies."[5] One congressman stated that this provision concerning women arose "from the fact that we do not want to establish additional Oriental families here."[6] The same 1924 law promoted the formation of families of European origin, by allowing European immigrant men to return to their home countries and bring wives back with them.

As they descended the gangplank, the Qinghua students strode free of the legislative acts that severely curtailed the movement of their fellow countrymen and women. On new ground, they waited on shaky legs for their turn to pass through the medical examination. The doctor pulled up eyelids to check for trachoma, listened for abnormal heartbeats, and shone his examination light in throats and ears. Miss Chang, still weak from the persistent nausea of her crossing, clung to the fancy, carved gourd containing the two crickets. While lying in their honeymoon suite, she and her cabin mates had listened to the insects' familiar song each night while drifting off to sleep. During her medical examination, Miss Chang set the cricket cage on a table. A customs inspector wandering by picked up the cage and yelled out, "Whose is this?" When she answered with a feeble "Mine," the inspector laughed. As

Amy tells it, miming the motions of the inspector, he said, "Not anymore." With a backward toss, he hurled the entrapped crickets into the ocean.

I did not grow up with the shipboard photograph of my grandmother's arrival in America. In fact, I can't remember hearing a single mention of Chinese immigration to the United States in all of my public school classes. I learned a catchall Ellis Island version in eighth-grade American Studies, when I worked with three other classmates to complete a group project on immigration. One winter afternoon we gathered with improvised costumes and props in tow. We each donned the personality of a member of our fictitious immigrant family, the Gianinis of Calabria, and posed for black-and-white photographs of our farewell and arrival scenes. A backyard deck served as the ship railing from which we waved goodbye as we watched our "beloved homeland" disappear into the distance.

I constructed a family album with an accompanying story written by the youngest Gianini, twelve-year-old Constantino. I combined our photographic reenactments with images copied from our textbook and pasted them together on the black construction-paper pages of a homemade cardboard book entitled "The Italian American Experience." In looping felt-tip cursive, I cobbled together a story that smacks of near encyclopedic plagiarism.

> We left because centuries of farming had exhausted the soil. America offered us a chance to improve our lives. Many people from our village had already gone, and they sent back letters filled with words praising the United States.
>
> We traveled from Cittanova, our hometown, to Siderno by train. Siderno was the port city where our voyage began. We boarded our ship, the *Princeton*, in March of 1903. Our fare for the trip was $13 per person, including food. To board the ship we had to have our passengers' contract ticket and exit papers. With us we took our feather pillows, extra clothing, a cooking pan, a bible, and my great-grandmother's gold cross.

Clutching a leather-bound Bible and a gold cross instead of a pair of singing crickets in a carved gourd cage is how I pictured my family's crossing. My friends and I, none of us Italian, passed as the Gianinis through the line inspection on Ellis Island. As four girls living in the gateway to the West on the banks of the Mississippi—one Anglo, two Jewish, and another Hapa—we arrived nonetheless in New York City in the year of 1903 and headed directly to the Society for Italian Immigrants.

Miss Grace ushered her charges into two yellow taxicabs. They caught their first glimpse of American streets through windows spotted with mist.

They ate in an automat cafeteria, and Amy delighted in the exotic amusement of self-serve sandwiches. Two days later, they boarded different eastbound trains. Grace accompanied one group of students, but Amy parted ways with her traveling companions in Seattle. Alone, she boarded a train headed on the northern line for Cleveland, where she would be the first Qinghua student to enroll in Western Reserve University. While crossing into Montana, she sat by a rain-streaked window and watched mountainous landscape pass by under ominous clouds. She suddenly remembered a story she had heard Hu Shi tell about his experience of riding a train across America. At dinnertime, he went to the dining car and ordered soup as a first course. While he was peacefully eating his soup, a white man sat down at the table next to him. After staring at the menu for some time, the man turned to Hu and asked, "Soupee goodee?" Hu's back straightened as he calculated his response, finally phrasing his reply in the expected laundryman pidgin, "No tickee, no shirtee." The startled diner grew red in the face and apologized.

Near Glacier Park, floodwaters swamped the tracks, and Amy's train was forced to stop until the water receded. The delay lasted three days, making her late for school. On one of these motionless days, Amy rented a horse and rode into the mountains. In a reprise of her Mount Tai story, in which dressed as a boy she accompanied her father up that mythical mountain in China, she described the beauty of the Montana peaks and her facility with horses. "I went to see the glaciers. When you have two feet and can ride horseback, you really can do everything. Everywhere you go, if they don't have automobiles, they have horses. Animals are just like people. They can feel you. If they don't like you, they throw you down. They kick like that, you know, and throw you down." She did not intend to let America throw her down.

For years I have listened to, recorded, and transcribed my grandmother Amy's stories, but when I told her directly that I wanted to write a book about her experiences, she told me the story of just one person wouldn't be very interesting. She suggested instead that we coauthor a book entitled *China New and Old* and proceeded to write down five themes to explore: "education revolution, idea of womanhood, idea of female in general, professions for women, and motherhood." Although Amy had dismissed the idea of a book about her life, my mother later found that she had filled the pages of a small yellow notepad with a recounting of her arrival in America. The three characters of her name in Chinese, Ling Shuhao, are written on the title page. In the next eighteen pages, she writes about her travels from Shanghai to Cleveland. The final page of this short narrative of immigration is signed, "By Amy

Ling Chen," and dated with the month and day in Chinese, followed by "1996 yr." in English.

More than two years after my mother copied those yellow pages with my grandmother's shaky handwriting for me, Amy announced one night at dinner that she had begun writing her autobiography. At ninety-four years old, she said, "I have experienced a lot. I might be old, but I'm not dumb; this story is interesting," as if she had to convince me. She had forgotten all the times I'd told her that I had also begun writing this book. When I asked her how much she had written, she equivocated. When I asked if I could read what she had written, she defensively told me she had to type it first. I offered to type the purported handwritten pages for her, and she put on a face of mock surprise, "*You* know how to type?" Then, intrigued, she considered my offer. Yes, she would like me to type for her, so I asked when we should begin. She waved me away with a dismissive hand, as she had so many times. "Next time, next time," she said while twisting her yarn-wrapped engagement ring around a bony, vein-roped finger.

And so our coauthored plot of dissimulation continued, unfolding in silent agreement; she didn't show me her version, and I didn't show her mine. When I wonder about this reciprocal obstinacy, I realize I'd learned some of her tricks, aimed directly at the heart of what I wanted. My questions about her life grew pointedly strategic, but she reveled in the attention and opportunity they provided for her to dangle pieces of incomplete information in front of me. She performed with finesse her dinner-table stories that trailed off ambiguously and that enigmatically marked what I could not know. I won't forget the time she told me that she and my grandfather had been sent on a trip to South America by the U.S. government. When I asked why, she pondered the question a long time, enjoying my expectant silence, before replying, "We're not supposed to tell." For a moment, she looked like she wanted to tell me anyway, but then she shook her head and said, "No, it's a secret." I pushed a little further, trying to figure out if there was any truth to a story that hinted of reckless exaggeration, if not pure fabulation. My aggressiveness got me nowhere, as she ended any discussion of the topic with a Chinese proverb, *bing cong kou ru, huo cong kou chu*, which she translated as "sickness enters through the mouth, and trouble exits from the mouth." She signaled the importance of strategic silence by placing her thin forefinger against mischievously smiling lips.

According to Amy's yellow-notepad autobiography, no one knew about her or her scholarship when she arrived. The registrar at Western Reserve University gave her a copy of the *Cleveland Plain Dealer* and told her to start by looking for a place to live. She wrote in English of how she rented a room from a German American family named Fritz near the university.

I get off the streetcar. The driver tells me to watch the streetlight, red is stop, watch for green to cross the street. I say to myself, this is a paradise. After I get off, I walk to a door and ring the bell. A white lady comes out and says little girl what can I do for you? Who are you, where do you come from? I tell her I come from China by boat to Seattle and I want to go to American medical school to study medicine to be a doctor. I need a place to sleep and get up early to go to school. She says little girl come in, I have a room upstairs facing the street. So I follow her upstairs. I say it is a beautiful room. She says I'll show you the bathroom. It has a white wall, white rack, white bath towels and white washrags.

The next day I get up early and wash my face. I go downstairs. I see her and her husband and their son. He is white face white hands and white and carries a white school bag. His mother made him a white sandwich.

My grandmother told me many times the story of her arrival in Cleveland: the clean page one of her version of an American named Amy. In one of these tellings, she slipped in a surprising detail, a clue to her written obsession with the color white. In this anomalous addition to her standard narrative, Amy mentioned some advice she received during her first days in town. After arriving at the train station, she made her way to the YWCA, where she stayed before finding Mrs. Fritz's address in the paper. An American woman who had done missionary work in China stopped by and invited her to tea. Several days later, Amy listened to her describe Cleveland's social geography. The former missionary warned her to stay away from the Chinese section of town. She explained that a police raid had recently swept through the area. The police had justified their action because of illegal tong wars among the Chinese that threatened the general public. Amy's host had her doubts about this official motive, since women and children had been arrested along with men. She cautioned her young guest about the danger of such harassment if she associated with other Chinese.

When I heard this brief hint of fighting between Cleveland tongs, I presumed Amy had dramatically embellished her story, adding elements to it from events she'd heard about in the Chinatowns of New York or San Francisco. She had always claimed to be one of the first Chinese in Cleveland. How could whole blocks of shops, restaurants, laundries, and residences have suddenly sprung from previously barren ground? Tongs, or Chinese secret societies, often controlled gambling, drug, and prostitution rackets but also regulated import-export trade and provided assistance to immigrant men in dealing with local oppression. Sensational descriptions of tong wars, which proliferated in the popular press throughout the 1920s and 1930s, bolstered a criminalized stereotype of Chinese Americans.[7] I thought Amy had been clever to add the detail about the missionary lady's counsel. It allowed her, I thought, to reveal a subtle awareness of the racially charged relationship between Chinese immigrants and white authorities. But then, just as the Western Reserve registrar had advised her, I got a copy of the *Cleveland Plain Dealer*.

If, before turning to the "Rent Rooms and Board" section, Amy had glanced at the front page of the Monday, September 21, 1925, issue, she would have seen that Washington defeated Chicago, 6-5, in a ten-inning contest, and that the Browns shut out the Yankees, 5-0. And below "For details, see sports pages," was this headline from New Albany, Mississippi: "Negro Burned at Stake by Mob of 1,000." And to the left was a local piece of news: "Flames Consume Bamboo Gardens." Firemen battled for six hours to subdue a conflagration that engulfed a Chinese-operated restaurant. Its supply room, wooden floor, and stage with orchestra instruments silently waiting for the next show had all gone up in flames. Called upon to comment, the secretary of the Cleveland branch of the On Leong Tong said he believed a cigarette not arson caused the fire, but the police hunt for a possible tong connection had begun.[8]

It was the era of prohibition and Al Capone, and since autumn of the previous year, a nationwide antagonism between the Hip Sing and On Leong Tongs over rival membership drives and trade rights had resulted in shooting deaths and injuries in Chinatowns across the country. In March 1925, leaders from Chinese communities in San Francisco, Chicago, Seattle, Portland, Philadelphia, Boston, and New York met for negotiations. By the end of the month, the two groups signed a peace treaty.[9] When the conflict flared up again, East Coast police raids began. In August, the *New York Times* reported that a Boston force of 132 police in thirty automobiles had conducted the "biggest and most spectacular raid ever made on the dens and dives of China-town." They made ninety-one arrests.[10] Two weeks later, at the very moment that representatives of the rival tongs signed a nationwide treaty in the New York office of the Chinese consulate, the city's police converged on the Bow-ery and Mott, Doyer, and Pell Streets.[11] The U.S. Attorney General announced, "I have put the United States Government in Chinatown, and I am going to keep it there whether a tong war is in progress or not."[12] In two days, police arrested over a thousand Chinese, and sent 191 to the Tombs or Ellis Island to await deportation.

One week later, on September 22, two days after the Bamboo Gardens burned, a man named Yee Chock was beheaded in Cleveland Chinatown. The *Plain Dealer* called it a hatchet murder, claiming that the execution-style killing pointed to tong involvement. On September 23, less than two weeks after Amy's train had pulled into a lakeside Cleveland station, the city manager ordered raids on Lower Ontario Street. He announced a plan to raze the entire Chinese settlement. After the arrest of 612 Chinese men, women, children, merchants, servants, and students, the city's safety director moved into deserted buildings to condemn them as fire and health hazards. Men in trench coats and felt fedoras broke down doors, overturned shop merchandise, rummaged through personal belongings, saw crowded bunks, smelled what they called squalor, and declared it criminal. The safety director defended his action by saying, "The Chinese are a clannish sort. It's no use questioning them because they can't talk English. But they know who did the killing and every Chinaman we can get our hands on is going to stay in jail until the slayers are turned up."[13]

What eventually became known as the Cleveland Incident aroused the indignation of local clergy, the Chinese government, and foreign expatriates in China. An article in a U.S. monthly called *The Chinese Christian Student* placed the use of force in international terms: "China is a weak nation. She will not and can not dispatch her navy and air force to the territory of America, as other powers, including the U.S.A., would if such a case should have happened in China."[14] An expatriate English-language newspaper in Shanghai declared the events harmful to the position of Americans abroad:

> It is peculiarly irritating, not to say humiliating that, at a time when the subject of extraterritoriality and its proposed abolition in China is very much to the fore in both native and foreign press, news should be received of what certainly appears to be a case of flagrant misjustice which has recently been perpetrated against Chinese nationals in the city of Cleveland, Ohio, U.S.A. . . . A Chinese with a sense of irony might be tempted to suggest that it would be well for China to demand extraterritorial privileges for her nationals in America![15]

I slowly put this background picture together in a sterile library basement, where I sat scrolling through a microfilm copy of the *Plain Dealer* delivered from Ohio by interlibrary loan. The front-page headlines from September 24, 1925, shouted in bold: "Orders Chinese Dens Be Razed." I turned the crank forward, anxious for the next day's news. I speeded through local features, sports pages, and stock quotes, past advertisements for Victor Records, Silk Canton Crepe, *Good Housekeeping Magazine*, and the paper's Sunday all-fiction magazine featuring "Another Chinese Murder Mystery." As the text moved across the screen in an accelerating blur, I saw a ghost face flicker by. I abruptly stopped and rewound to see my grandmother's passport photograph staring at me from page fifteen, accompanied by a two-column profile.

"Comes from Peking to Learn to Be a Doctor" © *[September 24, 1925]*
The Plain Dealer. *All rights reserved. Reprinted with permission.*

A little black-eyed maiden has left the land of almond trees and cherry blossoms and come to Cleveland to learn to be a doctor.

She is Miss Amy Ling, 21, who arrived eleven days ago in Seattle, Wash., from Peking, China, and immediately came to the Central Y. W. C. A. here. She is enrolled as a sophomore at Western Reserve University school of medicine.

Miss Ling will specialize in women's and children's diseases. And then she'll go back to a hospital in Peking.

"But that won't be for a long time," she said yesterday, "because after my three years here I want to go to Europe and study for two years."

"China needs more doctors. There aren't enough who have made special studies."

For three years Miss Ling was a student at Peking Union Medical College. There are four other girls and a boy in her home and, before China became a republic, the father was the financial governor of Peking and the province of Chil-Le [Zhili].

"One of my sisters is a very good artist," Amy explained. "She writes for the papers. And she writes beautiful stories and poems."

"I, too, like poetry," and her dark eyes glowed. "Lee Bei [Li Bai] is my favorite Chinese poet. His description is so beautiful. I don't read much English fiction, but I do like Silas Marner and Pride and Prejudice."

"I like your moving picture films better than ours," she added. "I loved 'Way Down East' and the 'Four Horsemen.'"

The president of her college advised her to go to Western Reserve as "the best medical school in America."

Cleveland's buildings are taller, but it isn't so different from Shanghai after all.

"In China, what do we do for amusement?" she said, in a soft voice and clear English. "Well, we don't dance very much. I don't dance at all," she admitted.[16]

If the reporter conducted his interview for this article eleven days after her arrival in Seattle, they would have met on September 13. It seems then that the newspaper editor chose not to run the article until more than a week later, on the same day that the headlines about the raids on Lower Ontario Street hit the front page. Was this a strategic bid to placate the Chinese community by showing that the city welcomed certain of their kind? Later, the safety director apologized to Chinese students arrested in the raids but to no one else.

Is it possible Amy was stopped, questioned, or arrested? My questions scatter in divergent directions. Is the advice of the benevolent missionary woman a cover story created to calm worried family members when they read about the Cleveland Incident in Chinese papers? Did she wait out the raids alone in her room at the YWCA or within the white walls of Mrs. Fritz's boarding house? Her words to the reporter, "I do like Silas Marner," now suggest how she learned to draw a line between herself and the "clannish sort," as she tightly pulled a blanket of white, white, white around herself.

Instead of any direct commentary on the police raids, Amy's memories of Cleveland lingered around the many small kindnesses she experienced while adjusting to a new life. Mrs. Fritz helped wash her laundry and packed lunches for her to take to school. The driver of the streetcar that stopped near the boarding house took a liking to her. He reminded her where to get off until she found her bearings. When Amy's mother sent her a care package from China, she saved a bag of peanuts and gave it to the streetcar driver.

Enrolling at Western Reserve University proved more difficult than finding lodging. None of her PUMC documents had arrived, so the registrar arranged for her to meet with the dean of the medical school. Amy showed him samples of her past work but failed to convince him that she was prepared to enter the second-year class. He wanted her to start in the freshman year, in spite of her two years of premedical and one year of medical school training in China. Amy explained why she protested his recommendation, which would require her to repeat anatomy: "Anatomy doesn't make sense to me. You just memorize, memorize. Where the nerve comes out, where the insertion is. How many bones are in the wrist, how many bones in the ankle, and all those things. I was tired of memorizing. Since I was a child I memorized Confucius's books, so I didn't want to repeat the first year medical." She agreed to take the final examination for first-year medical students. After she received a high score, the dean granted her admission as a sophomore.

On her first day of class, Amy felt her classmates silently assessing her. She learned to put up with how they teased her, always calling her "little girl," but for many weeks she could not understand why they stared so intently at her feet. Finally, she realized they thought she had bound feet, that underneath her plain black leather shoes, they imagined some exotic deformity. Laughing at their ignorance of how this practice had drastically declined in recent years, she explained, "They got this idea from some book. It's just like what Chinese think of women in the West, binding their waists so small." One day after class, she jumped up to sit on the lab table in front. While her classmates watched incredulously, she kicked off her shoes and pulled off her stockings. Sticking her feet out, she announced, "See, these are my feet. I don't have turned under toes. I don't have bound feet."

She soon discovered that the Chinese women's movement whose crest she had ridden across the Pacific began to seem at least as developed as its U.S. counterpart. She felt disillusioned by the gender disparity in Western Reserve's student body: "There were even fewer women in my class than there had been in China. And, I thought that America was advanced." As Amy attempted to assimilate into American life, the choices of what to transgress became more complicated than they had been in China, where she had grown up learning to reject the traditional female virtues of her mother's generation. To gain acceptance in a community with a small Chinese population during a time when the U.S. popular imagination ran rife with "yellow peril" stereotypes required compromise. The need to create a sense of security in a city so recently hostile to Chinese residents competed with her determination to overcome discrimination against women. Somewhere along the way, her dream of the clinic for women fell by the wayside.

A sense of loss comes through not in how she narrates her own life, but in the parallel story of Joan, Amy's white roommate during her second year at Western Reserve. In Amy's eyes, Joan possessed a unique passion that rubbed against convention. Ready with quick, witty answers in class, she also played the piano with fiery emotion. She was smart, Amy said, even brilliant. They became friends, studying together and sharing books to save on expenses. They even pooled their funds to buy a cheap, used car. One morning when they were low on gas money, Joan fashioned a double-sided hook from a wire clothes hanger and used it to link their front bumper to the streetcar. As the streetcar began to move forward, she jumped back into the driver's seat. They were slowly pulled along, the tires of their car rolling over the smooth metal tracks. Before the conductor realized what they'd done, they turned to each other and laughed triumphantly.

Joan's high spirits sometimes took a dark turn. When she and Amy worked as "ex-terns" at a local women's hospital, she constantly pushed the limits with their supervisor. Joan looked down upon her as only a nurse, and one of their conflicts turned into a violent yelling match. Amy couldn't remember what caused the dispute. She conjectured in wildly disparate directions that it had to do with food kept against the rules in the nurses' room or with a stillborn baby Joan wanted to use for dissection. That same year, Joan also fell for a fellow student and shocked Amy with her audacious pursuit of him. She wrote daily love letters and paid a neighbor's son to deliver them by hand. When the man discovered the identity of his admirer and refused her affections, she grew angry and brooding.

After they graduated, Amy heard that Joan married a Russian man and had a daughter. He expected her to stay at home, and this domestic life blotted out Joan's ambition of starting a private practice. Then the Russian walked out on Joan and their daughter. Strapped with increasing debt, Joan borrowed money from everyone she knew. Amy remembered sending her a check. One morning Joan took her daughter to her mother's house and returned home to a cold apartment. She went to the kitchen and opened the gas taps on the stove. Amy shivered and asked, "How did this talented woman do such a thing? Maybe she was too brilliant?" Amy repeatedly announced that sad things should get away from her, that she was the sister who hated depressing films, but tragic tales lurk at the edge of her memory. In this story, Amy ceded, for the first and only time, the position of daring and rebellion to someone else, a woman to whom she linked herself, like a car following behind. But Joan's headstrong ways led to tragedy rather than achievement. This change of hero and her fate marked a conservative shift in Amy's attitude. She followed in the shadow of a woman bolder than she could allow herself to be in the United States.

Her budding romance with K. K. Chen continued at a slow and cautious rate. KK had returned to Madison, Wisconsin, where he worked toward finishing his medical degree. Without a scholarship this time around, he worked as a lab and teaching assistant and waited tables at a Chinese restaurant on weekends. He wrote faithfully to his former student. On the days Amy came home from school to find an envelope with his familiar handwriting, she ran up the stairs to her room. Smoothing the creases of the folded page, she savored each word.

In 1926, Amy attended summer school at the University of Michigan in Ann Arbor. She needed to learn a third language, in addition to English and Chinese, to fulfill the requirements for her degree. She decided to study German, since it was one of the main international languages of scientific literature. She had also already learned a few words from Mrs. Fritz. Her German class met for four hours in the morning and two in the afternoon, but Amy remembered the summer as particularly pleasant because of the Chinese student community in Ann Arbor. For over thirty years, since the earliest Chinese women—Shi Meiyu, Kang Aide, and Amy's role model Dr. Ding—had studied at the University of Michigan, the campus had been a popular destination for Chinese students.

In the afternoons, Amy worked as a volunteer intern at a local hospital, where she completed tasks that she described as more janitorial than medical. For dinner, she usually met up with her new friends in the cafeteria. At least once a week, a group of them walked to one of the local Chinese restaurants. They would all pitch in some money and ask the cook to prepare the dishes from home that they missed the most. At the end of the summer, KK visited from Madison. As twilight cooled the air, they slowly circled the campus's groomed lawns. Sitting on a bench, their hands barely touching, they chatted about their plans for the future. When KK mentioned marriage to her, Amy laughed, "I can't cook, and I can't sew. What would you want with me for a wife?" He explained that he wanted a wife who could do more than cook and sew. Realizing the serious turn of their conversation, Amy replied that she couldn't consider the issue until she finished her degree. In a resolute tone, she reiterated to me, "I didn't come to America to get married. If I wanted to marry, I could have stayed in China for that. I didn't have to come to America to find a man."

After graduating from Western Reserve in June 1928, Amy moved to Pittsburgh to intern at the North Pennsylvania Hospital, a large teaching institution with six hundred beds. For several months she did rounds under a male surgeon. She found him arrogant and patronizing, and to the shock of the nurses and other interns, she repeatedly disagreed with his methods. With her hard-earned medical degree, she no longer tolerated being called the "little Chinese girl." She spoke her opinion, especially in her stance against using forceps in delivery. During their rounds in the obstetrics clinic, the attending physician often emphasized the need for forceps if the mother had the slightest trouble pushing the baby out. Amy was convinced that common sense should discourage this practice, since the hard metal could easily injure and even permanently deform an infant's soft head. One day as he launched into another lecture on the topic, she told him that she had never used forceps and never would. When he asked how she would deal with a difficult delivery, she replied that her hands were small enough that she could reach in and pull the baby out. When she completed her internship, the obstetrics staff presented her with a shiny new pair of forceps. Amy refused the expensive gift.

The same attending physician with whom she had clashed over forceps also insisted that female interns should not conduct rounds in the men's ward. He stated, "It's not right for female doctors to examine men's bodies." Amy asked, "What's the difference? We're all doctors." My grandmother angrily explained to me, "They just think you're a little girl. They're afraid I will examine men with genital disease. Do they stop men doctors from seeing women? They just want to exclude me." She received a transfer to a different rotation.

While Amy worked one morning at patient in-take, a harried nurse ushered her into a well-appointed hospital room she'd never seen before. In Amy's story, a silver-haired man sat in the middle of the room. Holding her clipboard in an authoritative manner, she began to ask the standard set of questions. He stopped her and said he was waiting for the doctor. She replied, "I am a doctor, and I need to take your medical history." He answered her questions while she took notes. When she reached the end, he asked her how a Chinese woman had become a doctor in Pittsburgh. As she began to explain, a senior doctor entered the room and abruptly asked what she was doing. He whispered loudly that her patient was Andrew Mellon, the famous financier, and motioned for her to leave. Mr. Mellon interrupted, "We're having a conversation here. Besides, this young doctor is the first in all of my visits to your hospital to think to take my medical history. I will call you when I need you." Amy described how Mellon listened with genuine attention to her story and then gave her some financial advice. She eagerly asked how he had gained such stature, and he attributed his success to individual perseverance, which lead to wealth and then social status.

He'd left her with some stock tips, and Amy credited his hospital-room lecture with sparking a lifelong interest in Wall Street. After that day she used her lunch breaks to go to the cool marble lobby of a nearby bank. She ate her sandwich while watching the ticker tape progress of rising and falling stock prices, which would come crashing down only a year later.

In Pittsburgh, Amy learned about the world of American wealth but also of its underlying poverty. In a story she often repeated, she'd reached the height of an independent professional career, the closest she would come to achieving her girlhood dream. Working in obstetrics, she occasionally made emergency house calls. One night, a young boy came running into the hospital. He stood in the doorway and yelled that his mother needed help. Amy picked up her black bag and followed him as he jogged through dark streets to a rundown building in the Italian section of town. From the base of the stairwell, where she stood to catch her breath, she heard a woman's screams echo down from the third floor. As she reached the top of the stairs, the boy pointed at a closed door. The cries had grown louder. Amy rapped on the door, but a loud male voice told her to go away. With slurred words, he shouted that his wife was just fine. The boy at Amy's side told her that his mother was having a baby. His father had started drinking and wouldn't let them call the doctor. "She's not having a baby," the drunken voice insisted. "We already have eight children, and I can't feed them. I told you, she's not having a baby." Neighbors had gathered in the hallway, and Amy sent one of them to call the police. The police finally arrived, broke down the door, and carted off the husband. The woman's children hovered in the kitchen, and Amy told them what she needed. Within an hour, she delivered a healthy baby. Several days later, the boy whose bobbing head she had followed through dimly lit, unknown streets delivered a cake from his mother to the hospital. Amy remembered how deliciously sweet the cream frosting tasted.

After a year at the University of Wisconsin, K. K. Chen had completed his third year of medical school and transferred to Johns Hopkins University in Baltimore, where he finished his fourth year of medical school and graduated in 1927. He remained at Johns Hopkins for two more years to lecture in pharmacology and continue his research on ephedrine and a toad venom, *chan su*, used in Chinese medicine. On visits to Pittsburgh from Baltimore, he tried to persuade Amy to marry him. Although she had finished her degree, she still brushed off his proposals. "Why marry me? There are eighteen Chinese girls in Pittsburgh alone. You should be able find one you like," she said, referring to the other female overseas students in town. Then, in a joking manner that revealed her underlying affections, she explained how to weigh various pros and cons for picking a wife and how she was unsuitable. In a melancholy moment several years after my grandfather's death, she mused out loud about how KK had responded to her half-mocking attempt at marital advice, "You are the funniest girl I've ever met."

· *Fifteen* ·

Adrift

*I*n Beijing, Shuhua had become her father's willow catkin and a modern girl who published twenty short stories in less than four years. She dined with poets, essayists, and playwrights at number 7, Pine Tree Lane, where she imbibed a new world of literature from writers who had spent years abroad. But northern warlords had grown suspicious of intellectuals and stopped supplying salaries to professors at national universities in Beijing. Fleeing like many others affected by the crisis, she and Chen Xiying saw the city of their brief romance fade from view, as a train bound for Tianjin transported them through a thunderstorm.

Many Crescent Moon Society members moved to Shanghai, where they established a bookstore and publishing house. Xu Zhimo and fellow poet Wen Yiduo would become coeditors of the new *Crescent Moon* monthly. Essays and stories by Chen Xiying and Ling Shuhua appeared regularly in the journal, linking them to this incarnation of the Crescent Moon Society even though they did not join their friends in Shanghai. They sailed instead from Tianjin to Japan on a travel scholarship arranged by Cai Yuanpei, former president of Beijing National University and current Guomindang minister of education.

The couple departed in October 1927 for a yearlong respite from the growing turmoil at home. They settled first in Kyoto, where they rented a simple house at the foot of the Higashiyama Mountain Range. Shuhua focused on improving her Japanese and read fiction and poetry by Japanese contemporaries. Xiying initially worked on editing *The Creation of Young Goethe*, his translation of André Maurois' 1926 *Meïpe, ou la Délivrance*. A year earlier Xiying had translated this account of Goethe's youthful unrequited love, reputed to be the basis for *The Sorrows of Young Werther*, and published it serially in *Contemporary Review*. He now found time to add a preface for its publication as a book, which came out at the end of 1927 under the imprint of the Crescent Moon Bookstore. Xiying claimed the book would satisfy the curiosity of the numerous Werther enthusiasts in China by providing insight into the relationship between fiction and life. Half a year later, the Crescent Moon Bookstore would also publish a collection of Chen Xiying's *Contemporary Review* essays in a volume titled *Causeries of Xiying*.

In a letter sent from Kyoto to Hu Shi in Shanghai, Xiying urged him to consider moving to Japan. He compared the ease of renting a house, the peaceful atmosphere, and the convenience of finding Chinese books with the difficult situation in Shanghai. He added, "The mountains and water are pure and beautiful and the ancient temples full of people. We live at the foot of the mountains, and as soon as you step outside, you enter wonderful scenery, so we don't feel lonely."[1] Worries about the future crept into his letter, as Xiying wrote that they hoped to move back to Beijing after the year in Japan. Recent news caused him to be pessimistic about this possibility. Eleven days earlier, the Beijing warlord government had executed their colleague Gao Ershan, a thirty-four-year-old professor in the education department of Beijing Normal University who had been arrested for alleged reactionary activity.[2] The charges against Gao implicated Hu Shi, and Xiying felt that even he and Shuhua would have to deal with police searches if they returned home.

Intellectuals in Shanghai grew polarized after the failure of the United Front between the Communists and the Guomindang. Some, outraged by the brutality of Chiang Kaishek's rule, aligned themselves with the Communists. Others supported the Guomindang, if not out of a belief in Chiang's nationalism, at least superficially in order to escape suspicion and continue writing. Historical accounts of this period often divide writers into these

Imprint of the Crescent Moon
Bookstore, Shanghai, 1927

opposing camps with little room for those who found the rhetoric of both sides bleak and militaristic. Xu Zhimo's choice of two epigraphs for the first edition of the *Crescent Moon* journal—"Let there be light" from the book of Genesis and "If Winter comes, can Spring be far behind?" from Shelley— might be interpreted as a plea for literature free from the political battles raging around them. However, Xu claimed in an accompanying manifesto that the Crescentists aimed to cleanse the intellectual and literary scene of thirteen bad habits: sentimentalism, decadence, aestheticism, utilitarianism, didacticism, negativism, extremism, preciosity, eroticism, fanaticism, venality, sloganism, and "ismism."[3] The Creation Society, a literary group that moved out of its romantic period with Guo Moruo's conversion from Goethe to Marx in 1924, now consisted of mainly Marxist writers who saw themselves as the target of Xu's attack. They responded in kind by interpreting the epigraphs Xu Zhimo chose to launch his journal as a sign of the group's elitist Anglo-American leanings. Antagonism between the two groups deepened in coming years and further politicized the literary scene.

This politicization also affected women writers especially when the relationship between women and literature surfaced as a topic of debate in literary magazines and several lengthy studies.[4] One side asserted that Chinese literature was essentially feminine in its "talented lady" tradition of lyricism and emotionality, an interpretation supported by the fact that male writers often adopted a female voice for poetic effect. One critic, attempting to reclaim this tradition for women writers, wrote that "graceful and restrained, warm and soft literature must be written by women to be really true."[5] Other critics agreed that Chinese literature exhibited feminine qualities but attacked tradition on exactly this point, disparaging its romanticism as bourgeois and lacking social commitment. They assailed women writers in particular because of this association of women with feminine ways of writing.

In Japan, Shuhua continued to write. She translated a Chekhov story, the Crescent Moon Bookstore brought out her first story collection, *Temple of Flowers*, and new stories appeared in the *Crescent Moon* journal. In interpreting her growing body of work, several critics branded her as a writer of the "New Boudoir Lady School," who merely spilled "pretty words" over "trivial family affairs."[6] This label stuck, and later studies of the Crescent Moon Society rarely mention her other than as Chen Xiying's wife.[7] Many leftist writers, who had once seen the oppressed woman as representative of the nation's need to overthrow its past, now focused on accounts of peasants and workers. By continuing to portray women trapped by the circumstances of gender hierarchy, family, and in her later stories, nationalism itself, Shuhua failed to fit within the developing political categories of the 1930s, in which literature was seen as either anti-Japanese, Communist, or Guomindang.

The example of Shuhua's contemporary Xiao Hong, the female author my Chinese teacher that summer in Beijing had dismissed, provides an illuminating comparison. Leftist critics would praise *The Field of Life and Death*, her 1935 novel about peasant life in Manchuria, for its anti-Japanese stance, but literary scholar Lydia Liu draws attention to its feminist aspects, long overlooked by critics focused on nationalism. Liu argues that Xiao Hong's female characters experience violence at the hands of both Chinese patriarchy and Japanese imperialism. The main protagonist disguises herself as an old woman to escape the sexual threat posed by Japanese soldiers, only later to be raped by a Chinese man. Liu concludes, "It is not that Xiao Hong did not wish to resist Japanese aggression or feel attracted to the national cause. Her dilemma was that she had to face two enemies, rather than one: imperialism and patriarchy. The latter tended to reinvent itself in multifarious forms, and national revolution was no exception."[8]

From the late 1920s on, Shuhua began to write stories about school-aged girls and children, a subtle shift that allowed her to explore the effect of patriarchy and nationalism on Chinese women. This shift echoes a similar pattern in the work of her literary exemplar Katherine Mansfield. In reaction to the mechanized destruction of World War I and her younger brother's death, Mansfield returned through writing to her childhood in New Zealand.

Shuhua's stories about children, many semiautobiographical, ostensibly depict a naive view of the world, but the perceptive child in them continually asks "why?" as she tries to comprehend the rules of adulthood. Rather than using the next generation to depict national progress, Shuhua's fiction uses children, particularly girls, to return to the past, often her own past in a traditional family compound or new school for female education. She gradually retreats into the world of childhood where gender conventions are not yet internalized. This strategy suggests an allegory of the available options at a political moment when gender critiques were viewed as a threat to national unity: a woman writer must become a girl if she wants to continue writing about female oppression.

Three months after the publication of *Temple of Flowers*, a new story by Shuhua appeared in the second issue of *Crescent Moon*. "A Poet Goes Mad," which traces an adult's regression into a childlike state, represents this turn toward child protagonists in her writing. The story opens with the poet Juesheng walking home down a mountain path to visit his wife, who has been ill since the death of her parents. The unfolding landscape moves him to quote poetry and remember paintings by ancient literati painters. At one point his hand drifts to his paint box, but overwhelmed by the panorama, he concludes that not even a camera would allow him to do it justice: "Even if our eyes can be as fast and accurate as a movie camera, our mental focus cannot be mechanically controlled. And how can a mechanical mind create an airy, unique masterpiece?"[9] Shuhua also rejects realist cinematic visualization, as her story unrolls like a scroll in long passages of painterly description.

When Juesheng arrives home, his mother describes his wife's illness, which causes her to sleep all day and roam about the garden at night. Juesheng observes Shuangcheng asleep in her room, which is strewn with garlands, flowers, and clothing. His modern books also lie scattered on the floor. Later that night, Shuangcheng walks into Juesheng's study looking much more alive than ever before. She pulls him into the garden and points out its delights before leading him over to her "little garden." In the moonlight, Juesheng sees a miniature landscape of undulating hills with sticks used to create trees, houses, and bridges. Shuangcheng pinches a piece of earth into a small figure, and placing it on a small platform, explains that it is Juesheng reading. Another clay figure represents her working in the garden. Juesheng finds himself pulled into the lyric beauty of her fantasy world. The story ends with an explanation that after this night Juesheng never left his wife's side. The two of them play together like children in the garden, so that everyone in the village gossips that Mrs. Zhang's son had gone crazy along with her daughter-in-law.

Shuangcheng draws the poet, previously able to view nature only through traditional painting and poetry, into a different world of aesthetic rapture, where her garden contrasts with his scholarly pursuits. In this sense, Shuhua's story dramatizes the male poet's retreat to the feminine world of emotion from which the lyrical tradition of Chinese painting and verse drew inspiration. Yet, Shuangcheng's long seclusion due to illness, her underlying sexual and social frustration, as well as her obvious state of mental disarray, hint at something more than a triumph of feminine subjectivity in artistic practices. Trapped within the inner chambers but given a glimpse at something broader through reading her husband's books, Shuangcheng has undergone a complete break in order to find beauty within the closed world available to her. In his seduction to her inner world of poetic sentiment, Juesheng also loses touch and becomes a childish figure, pitied by neighbors.

What does it mean that Shuangcheng, whose name is an anagram for "double" (*chengshuang*), has pulled Juesheng into her dream existence?[10] Shuhua's story suggests several interpretations without any clear resolution: Shuangcheng and Juesheng nostalgically yearn for an essentially Chinese understanding of the world before Western imperialism and the technological development of the movie camera; they reject the narrative of modern progress represented by Juesheng's books; or through regression to childish wonder, they create a utopia beyond gender roles and politics. Shuhua's painterly descriptions heighten the aesthetic effect of Juesheng's descent down the mountain and Shuangcheng's garden reverie, but the diagnosis of mental ill-ness indicated by the story's title and the villagers' pity leave the reader puz-zling over the final line: "What is to be done?" Is the dream of freedom from political battles to create art, a position Lu Xun vehemently criticized in his attacks on the Crescent Moon Society, dangerously escapist? Or did Shuhua represent an alternative to the one-dimensional rhetoric of emerging factions? With "A Poet Gone Mad," Shuhua presents the double bind of the woman writer: the national reform movement encouraged women to contribute to cultural production but presumed they were incapable of equal participation and therefore prone to psychological instability.

In July 1928, Xiying wrote to Hu Shi from an outlying area of Tokyo, where he and Shuhua spent the last few months of their year abroad in a rented room by the sea. He feared they would not be able to return to live in Beijing. Chiang Kaishek's troops continued to push Communist forces into the countryside, and a Guomindang general had just captured Beijing from the warlord who previously held the city. Friends and colleagues wrote that they did not feel safe in Beijing. Several had decided to join the faculty of the newly founded Wuhan National University and encouraged Xiying to do the same. Depressed by the thought of moving to an interior city like Wuhan, he told Hu Shi they wanted to find a way to go to Europe, where Shuhua could study painting in France and he could research French and German literature. Xiying admitted, however, that if this plan failed, teaching in Wuhan remained their only realistic option. He hoped only to settle down for a while, instead of seeing each place as a stepping-stone.[11]

In the same month that Xiying sent this letter, Shuhua wrote a travel essay about climbing Mount Fuji with the Tokyo Chinese Youth Association. The experience converted her to local reverence for the mountain, which she had previously belittled as a Japanese obsession resulting in lifeless drawings and tacky reproductions. Outfitted with a sturdy wooden walking stick, a white straw hat, split-toe socks, and straw sandals, she summited the moun-tain. From that vantage point, she finally comprehended the metaphor Japa-nese used to describe the ring of clouds around the mountain: "a white fan hovering over the sky of the Eastern Ocean."[12] This majestic vision of pan-Asian aesthetics served as a last moment of calm.

In late August, with no other feasible options, the couple returned to Beijing to pack their stored belongings. They then made their way south to Shanghai, where they boarded a river steamer for Wuhan, the commercial tricity region in Hubei province with Hankou and Hanyang on one side of the Yangzi River and Wuchang on the other. When their boat docked in Hankou, they disembarked beneath the clock tower of the British-built customs house in a trade center known as the "Nine-Headed Bird" because its confluence of rivers allowed for raw goods and products from nine different provinces to be collected for shipping downriver to Shanghai and then overseas. Wuhan ranked second only to Shanghai as a port, and in warehouses and packing facilities behind Hankou's main thoroughfare, workers prepared incoming oil, tea, tobacco, opium, medicinal herbs, leather, wool, cotton, fruit, and porcelain for shipment. Bearded Sikh policemen with white turbans patrolled the British concession, and the French employed Vietnamese gendarmes in their section of the riverfront. In addition to restaurants and shops catering to foreigners and wealthy Chinese, there were churches, a YMCA, a racetrack, and a red-light strip of cafés staffed by White Russians. Across the river in Wuchang, marked by the stately Yellow Crane Pagoda, lay Chinese residences, schools, and government offices.

The region had proven a political hotbed in the previous decades. In 1911, anti-Qing revolutionaries and mutinous troops took control of Wuchang in the first of linked uprisings that toppled the dynasty and ushered in the Republican era. This same period witnessed a growing labor movement in response to the harsh conditions and low pay for Chinese workers in foreign-owned factories. In 1927, aroused by calls for national independence, Chinese assaulted the British concession in Hankou, an event that led the British to relinquish control. The bloody breakup of the coalition between the Communists and Guomindang, set in motion by Chiang Kaishek's "Shanghai Spring," hit Wuhan in the spring of 1928. Public executions of captured Communists in Wuchang continued into the summer.

The executions had come to an end by September, when Xiying and Shuhua transferred their luggage from the Shanghai steamer to a Hankou ferryboat. During the half-hour crossing to Wuchang, they stared through the dirty coal smoke of river traffic toward the yellow bank on the other side. In the complex mix of political sentiments at the time, most Chinese had not yet aligned themselves with any camp. As control of the country's regions slid among warlords, left and right Guomindang, Communists, and foreign powers—especially encroaching Japanese troops—the best they could do was try to assess a murky situation and seek out as secure a life as possible.

Cai Yuanpei still held the position of Guomindang minister of education in Nanjing, Chiang Kaishek's new capital, and used it to secure funding for fifteen new national universities. In July 1928, Wuhan became the site for the first of these model schools, even as the violence of that spring and summer unfolded. Many of the new faculty came from Beijing, including several intellectuals once associated with either the *Contemporary Review* or Crescent Moon Society. All had studied abroad, mostly in England or France. A degree from a foreign institution became a prerequisite for all faculty members, disqualifying Ling Shuhua from an official appointment. Chen Xiying served as chairman of the foreign languages department and later as dean of arts. Shuhua taught a few basic English classes, but restricted from lecturing in literature or art, as she had in Beijing, she felt isolated from local intellectual circles.

When the couple first arrived, they stayed with Pi Zongshi, an economist who had studied at London University with Xiying. The two men had traveled together to Paris in 1919 to protest post–World War I denials of Chinese claims for national sovereignty and to prevent Chinese delegates from signing the Treaty of Versailles. After returning to China from England, they both taught at Beijing National University. Pi now lived in a large Western-style house near the Yellow Crane Pagoda. He showed Xiying and Shuhua to their room and left them to rest. When he sent his son to call them for dinner several hours later, the little boy spied on them through the keyhole. He saw Xiying in a chair holding Shuhua on his lap.

As a man in his seventies, Pi Gongliang giggled again as he recounted to me his glimpse of grown-up intimacy. This vivid image had stuck with him over all the years. His brief view into the life of this literary couple revealed to me the very reason I had contacted him, for can there be any better metaphor for the biographical impulse? Writers and readers of biography pore over other people's letters and peep through their keyholes, defending this transgression as an innocent act by a curious child. We think we can see how people actually lived in the midst of not-so-innocent times.

In October, classes began in the main building of the defunct Sun Yat-sen University, where months earlier administrators and professors had been arrested and students shot. While the newly assembled faculty scrambled to resume classes at this location, the search had already begun for a new campus site. By the end of fall, an agricultural area east of Wuchang had been chosen. Preparations to break ground began immediately, but it took several years to build what would become one of China's most impressive campuses. After moving into their own house, Shuhua found herself cooped up, longing for the vibrant life she had enjoyed in Beijing. Even Xiying despaired at the oppressive provincialism of Wuchang. In December 1929, he wrote from the damp cold of his study to Hu Shi:

> We sometimes rejoice to ourselves, because our life is very quiet, but sometimes a person visits from the outside, or occasionally a magazine comes, and the surface of this dead water pool is blown with a few ripples, making us feel sad again, like we are already lying inside a tomb. I manage to carry on, because I have some work and must go to school, where I still see a few people. This place for Shuhua though is really like being buried alive. She is suffocating to the point of tears, and I have no way to comfort her.[13]

Hoping to "stretch out his head to breathe in a few mouthfuls of fresh air," Xiying planned to start a new journal and asked Hu Shi to send some articles to help them make the best of a bad situation.

Earlier that year, Shuhua had published her short story "Little Liu." The denouement of this story, about the student who leads schoolgirl taunts against an older, pregnant classmate, jumps years into the future to depict the reunion of the narrator, named Lin, and Little Liu:

> It was twelve or thirteen years later, and I was living in Wuchang at the time. One day, after lunch, my husband rushed off to class as usual, leaving me with the endless boring routine of keeping house. Out of the blue came a knock on the door. It was a postman with a letter. It was from Big Wu—since we had attended the same college after graduating from high school, we had stayed more or less in touch.[14]

Wu's letter delivers the news that Little Liu also lives in Wuchang, in fact, only a street away from the narrator's home. As soon as Lin reads this news, she rushes out the door. She hopes her listless feelings will melt away upon hearing some of Little Liu's lively and vicious quips from the old days. The narrator's dissatisfaction with her life in Wuchang must have reflected Shuhua's own frustrations.

> I was really going crazy with boredom lately. The only time I ever got to escape the house was when I taught English, two hours a week; and that was so easy I could switch off my mind and still teach it perfectly. And the rest of the week? I just sat at home. Wuchang is not a very pleasant place, with high walls around the houses and shallow courtyards. Being new to the city, I found it really hard to take. . . . Nothing amused me in the town. I had no refined enthusiasm for sights like the Yellow Crane Pagoda, nor had a taste for window-shopping at the foreign stores across the river. And as for going into town—the streets there are so impossibly narrow that every time a car passes you have to fling yourself quickly into the nearest store, or be crushed.[15]

At Little Liu's front door, a servant lets Lin in and leads her to a parlor, where a little boy and girl fight over a dish of peanuts. As she waits for Little Liu, the room's disarray, the fighting children, and the cries of a baby from the other room grow increasingly disagreeable. When her old classmate finally enters, nothing of the girl she once knew remains in the sallow woman standing before her. Lin discovers that Little Liu married at seventeen and has already had five children and one miscarriage. She also learns that another classmate has died from complications during childbirth. Before long, Little Liu's son throws a tantrum, which escalates into eating all of the candy set out for the guest, bullying his younger sister, and knocking over a goldfish bowl. After the boy's father comes home and scrutinizes Lin with a humiliating "look men reserved only for women," she hurries home, clearly disillusioned by the fate of her once-rebellious classmate.

In 1930 the Shanghai Commercial Press published Shuhua's second book *Women*, which was reprinted twelve times over the next sixteen years. The eight stories in the collection, including "Little Liu," depict women who are frustrated or trapped by their circumstances. The stories focus mostly on elite or educated women except for one whose title character, Mother Yang, is a servant. According to Hu Shi's introduction to the story, Shuhua wrote it in response to a challenge he posed at a dinner party in Beijing that also included Chen Xiying, Ding Xilin, and Xu Zhimo. That night Hu recounted a moving story he'd heard about a servant employed in a friend's family and suggested they all try to write something based on it. He offered as a prize for the best piece the reproduction of Leonardo da Vinci's *Mona Lisa* hanging on his wall. Hu and Xu Zhimo proposed to write poems, Ding Xilin a play, and Ling Shuhua a short story. Four years later, Shuhua, the only one to complete a manuscript, sent Hu Shi her story from Wuhan.

In the story, Mother Yang works for the Gaos, a university professor and his wife. The servant fills her days with zealous industry and sews late into the night, so late that the Gaos worry about her health. When Mrs. Gao offers her a raise, thinking that she sews at night to earn extra money, Mother Yang explains that the clothes she is making are for her runaway son, whom she has heard joined the army. Mrs. Gao encourages her to use the extra money to buy clothes, so she can get more sleep, but the servant replies, "If I go to sleep early, my thoughts wander uncontrollably, until sometimes I arrive at despair and my heart aches so that I can't close my eyes the entire night."[16] One day, Mother Yang goes to search for her son. While she's out, her cousin stops by and eventually tells Mrs. Gao the tragic story of Mother Yang's life. Abused by her in-laws and destitute after her husband's death, she had to leave her only surviving child with his uncle while she went to work in the city. Her son grew up undisciplined, refused to study, and one day disappeared without a word. When Mr. Gao hears the story, he is so moved that he sends a notice about the missing boy to various military units. He learns that the boy's troop is engaged in dangerous fighting in Gansu province. Worried that Mother Yang's son had not survived, he and his wife decide not to pass on this information, but Mother Yang overhears their conversation and disappears that evening. When she does not return, the Gaos believe she is walking the hundreds of miles to Gansu by herself.

In "Mother Yang," Shuhua presents a microcosm of the stratified society in which she lived. Mrs. Gao's social world, which resembles the Wuhan

University enclave, is disrupted only by the story of her servant's suffering. While Mother Yang selflessly yearns to provide for her son, Mrs. Gao tries to dissuade her from fulfilling a traditional contract that defines motherhood as martyrdom. Intellectual debates about reform and the Gaos' sympathetic but ineffectual attempts at aid fail to alter Mother Yang's circumstances or determination to find her son, who has more than likely been killed. When Mother Yang departs on her perilous journey, she leaves behind a lonely Mrs. Gao, who lives vicariously through the stories of her servants.

After overseeing the publication of *Women*, Shuhua's production faltered. The dilemmas of motherhood in her recent stories may have reflected more than literary observation, as she was expecting her first child. When Shuhua gave birth to a daughter, she and Xiying named her Xiaoying. Xiaoying was probably born in 1931, but Shuhua later changed the year of her daughter's birth several times so that Xiaoying herself is not sure of her age. Presumably, Shuhua found herself caring for a young child when the Wuhan University campus was completed. In 1932, she published no new stories.

On the new campus, three white towers rose on one side of a quadrangle. They were topped with Chinese-style roofs of green glazed tile with peaked glass skylights for the lecture halls and laboratories. Opposite the main classroom building, the student dormitory, modeled after the Potala Palace, had been built into the side of a hill. On another hill behind the classroom complex, eighteen Western-style houses of gray stone with chimneys and pitched roofs housed the university's elite faculty in a private wooded area. Xiying, Shuhua, and Xiaoying settled into one of these two-story homes. Through the thick cover of trees, they could see green shading to gray in the expanse of East Lake at the bottom of Luojia Mountain. A car service that stopped once an hour at the nearby road delivered them down the hill to the campus buildings. It took a half hour by bus to get from campus to the old city of Wuchang, and another half hour by ferry from Wuchang to Hankou. Once the campus was fully occupied, the university enrolled approximately seven hundred students and employed nearly a hundred and fifty teachers. Registration was open to both male and female students, except in the school of technology, which accepted only men.[17]

I visited Wuhan in March 2002. Rain had fallen for two weeks, and I found myself wearing all of the clothes I had with me to fight off the damp chill of a city defined by rivers and lakes. In the Luojia Mountain Guesthouse, I huddled with a cup of tea in a faintly moldy armchair, waiting for Zha Quanxing. A seventy-seven-year-old retired chemistry professor from Wuhan University, Zha had offered to serve as my guide to the campus because he had lived next door to Chen Xiying and Ling Shuhua as a boy.

He fondly remembered that Xiaoying liked to eat at his house and tag along behind him and his two brothers, while they schemed to ditch the younger girl. After walking around the athletic field, past the outdoor amphitheater, and up to the rooftop of the dormitory building where he had once lived as a student, we headed back past the guesthouse and down a deserted road scattered with rain-slick leaves. As we picked our way through puddles, he explained that few people still wanted to live on the hill because they consider the houses old and inconveniently located. When it rains, he said, the road turns to mud, and the university no longer provides a car service. He turned to me in the pale, dappled light and said, "But back then, it was considered the best housing."

Pi Gongliang, the same age as Zha, had also grown up in one of the "eighteen houses" and regaled me with stories of the privileged life his family led then. Putting his father's monthly salary of four hundred yuan in context, he explained that they could buy a hundred eggs for one yuan. He and his boyhood friends watched Charlie Chaplin films at the Empire Theater in Hankou's French Concession. His mother had a cook and a maid to help at home and ordered Western cream pastries and ice cream delivered by refrigerated boat from Hankou to their door on Luojia Mountain.

As we rounded a curve, Zha indicated where the car service used to stop and then we could see the first houses among bare winter trees. There were two rows of old-fashioned houses. The path he led me down was strewn with discarded food wrappers. We passed the house where he used to live, and as he pointed out Ling Shuhua's house, a man overtook us. Zha called after the man and asked him if he knew that the writer Ling Shuhua and her husband had once lived there. The man fumbled in his pocket for keys and grunted, obviously uninterested in these details from the past. Honorably, Zha pressed on and inquired if it would be possible for us to see the inside of the house. Zha followed him up the porch steps as the door swung open, but catching one brief look inside, he seemed to give up. He headed back toward where I stood awkwardly with my camera, and motioned in disappointment that we should leave. He told me, "It's all been changed. The space has been split up between several families. It's not like it used to be."

Later in the afternoon, I wandered the campus by myself. I walked around the neglected hero-sized bust of poet and former dean of arts Wen Yiduo, past couples in the garden barely sheltered against a gray sky by cherry trees that had not yet begun to blossom, back to the abandoned muddy slope with its scattered eighteen old houses, and up to the top of the hill where a man in rolled-up shirtsleeves and dress shoes practiced some form of martial art. Moldering leaves filled the hollows of long-abandoned Red Guard bunkers, dug out during factional fighting in the Cultural Revolution. I had got-

Ling Shuhua and Chen Xiying's house on Luojia Mountain, Wuhan University, 2002. Photo by author.

ten turned around numerous times. The layout of the campus with its concrete walls giving way to hills and tree-lined paths confused me. I had come seventy years after the fact, looking for clues to an individual life and found it lodged within the layers of history that had accreted since 1931 to what was then a new site of national pride carved out of appropriated farmland and graveyards. The stillness of dusk on top of Luojia Mountain spooked me as I strained to catch a view of East Lake through the tangle of tree branches. I shoved my hands in my pockets and hurried back down the path to a solitary meal of hot soup noodles in the guesthouse dining room.

Upon accepting *Women*, the Shanghai Commercial Press also promised to publish Shuhua's next anthology, tentatively titled *Children*. The book, with the title changed to *Little Brothers*, would contain nine stories about children when it eventually came out in 1935. In the house on Luojia Mountain, she watched her husband leave in the morning for his office. She instructed the maid what to buy for dinner, observed her daughter growing into a willful tomboy, and tried to write. The stories from this period include "Moving House" and "A Happy Event," which drew upon her own childhood and eventually appeared, translated into English, in her memoir *Ancient Melodies*.

These stories are not written for young readers but serve as adult parables of disappointed childhood dreams. Shuhua had once imagined herself at the center of the Beijing art world—studying ancient paintings in her job at the Palace Museum, hosting literary salons, and writing to prove women's worth in all of these endeavors. Yet, as in one of her own stories, this dream was easily shattered. Trapped in the life of a faculty wife and mother, she turned to her fading youth, from *Women* to *Children*. The metaphor of youthful vitality figured large in the minds of May Fourth writers, who published in magazines like *New Youth* and defined themselves through opposition to the moribund tradition of their parents' generation. They envisioned New China as a nation that would grow like a child into a healthy, independent self. Taken up by the Communists, the figure of the powerless child represented the proletarian masses whom writers hoped to revolutionize through literature.[18] The child in Shuhua's stories, however, stares angrily from the past to criticize what the adult already sees, a present that falls short of what was once imagined. Her girl characters are disempowered rebels. They struggle with oppressive gender norms reinforced by *amahs*, siblings, parents, and institutions such as school, and their nascent rebellions ultimately fail.

On November 19, 1931, Xu Zhimo died at the age of thirty-five. A new enthusiast of air travel, he was flying from Nanjing to Beijing when the pilot of his small China Aviation Company plane flew off course in a thick fog and crashed into a mountainside. Shuhua reacted with plaintive disbelief in "Is Zhimo Really Not Coming Back?", an essay published in a special commemorative section of the Beijing *Morning Post*. When Xu Zhimo had heard of Katherine Mansfield's death at the age of thirty-five from tuberculosis, he wrote his hagiographic "Elegy for Mansfield." Now the Chinese writer he had likened to Mansfield performed a similar outpouring for him, also dead at thirty-five. As her grief-filled rhetorical questions build, she asks,

> Without you, how are we supposed to pass the days? Didn't you say to me: I think that though our strength is limited, before we leave this life, we must use all our power to add some beauty to an ugly world, to add some value to the cheapened standard of a fallen world? This world now grows uglier and cheaper by the day, how could you have the heart to steal away, before the rest of us?[19]

When Ling Shuhua returned to Beijing for Xu Zhimo's memorial, she provoked a battle over his "Eight Treasures Box," which contained the diaries, letters, and manuscripts he had left with her before departing for Europe in 1925. During Shuhua's travels to Japan and after her move to Wuhan, the box had remained in Beijing with her mother. Although the box changed hands in the intervening years, Shuhua had possession of the box when Zhimo died. Hu Shi planned to coordinate the publication of the poet's selected letters, so Shuhua gave the "Eight Treasures Box" to him, not knowing that he would pass it on to Xu Zhimo's former love Lin Huiyin to itemize the contents.[20] On learning this, Shuhua wrote a frantic letter to Hu Shi. She feared that Lin Huiyin might destroy the diaries of Xu Zhimo's widow Lu Xiaoman, now also in the box and full of curses for Lin. Shuhua defended her qualifications to serve as editor of Xu Zhimo's writing.[21] Once Lin Huiyin began her job of cataloging, she discovered that Shuhua had removed two of Xu Zhimo's diaries from the time at Cambridge when he met and fell in love with Lin. Hu Shi wrote to Shuhua, guessing that she wanted to write a biography based on the diaries, and criticized her for splitting up the poet's effects and creating bad feelings among friends.[22] Eventually Shuhua returned the diaries, but several pages remained missing. The melodrama of this scramble after a box of letters and diaries shows the extent to which this generation of authors saw themselves as actors in an era of momentous change. By incorporating their lives into their literature, they elevated personal details to the level of artistic and historical importance. The human casualties of Xu Zhimo's embrace of a romantic life still play themselves out in docudrama, as I discovered one evening in 2001 in Beijing. I turned on the television and saw an actress with short braids playing the bit part of Shuhua in a miniseries about Zhimo and his lovers.

Although denied a hand in the editing of the "Eight Treasures Box," Xu Zhimo's father remembered Shuhua. Months after his son's burial, he lay awake at night with the uneasy feeling that something was still missing. Hu Shi had written a simple calligraphic inscription for the tombstone reading, "The Tomb of Poet Xu Zhimo," but this marker lacked poetry in the old man's mind, so he asked a relative teaching at Wuhan University to contact Shuhua for him. He wanted her, as a fellow writer and friend of his son, to provide a line of poetry for a new stone. After deliberating for months, during which she wrote a fretful letter to Hu Shi asking for his opinion, she sent a simple five-character line to Xu's father. He had it carved on a smaller stone, which he placed next to the original burial marker.[23] Shuhua chose a line of poetry from the famous Qing dynasty novel *Dream of Red Mansions*: "A cold moon buries the soul of blossoms" 冷月葬花魂. By altering the third and fourth characters, she produced an elegant lament: "A cold moon illuminates the poet's soul" 冷月照诗魂.

By 1932, a combination of economic factors aggravated by devastating floods had led to a depression in the countryside around Wuhan. Hundreds of thousands of peasants sought refuge in shantytowns along the outskirts of the tricity region. In her letter to Hu Shi about Xu Zhimo's tombstone, Shuhua's attitude toward Wuhan had changed slightly. She closed the letter with a reflection on the recent past:

> These last years I've had even fewer achievements to believe in. Before, from early on, I thought of myself as the cricket in the corner: if it makes more or less noise, does it really matter? For this reason, it was easy to forgive myself. But for these two or three years, my feet haven't stopped, and my ears and eyes are no longer in the city, but in the country. I've come to meet more real Chinese people than our friends know. They are ordinary, destitute people.[24]

In the years since their return from Japan, tensions between China and Japan had continued to mount. At the end of 1931, the whole of Manchuria had fallen to the Japanese. Anti-Japanese boycotts and protests in Shanghai reached such a fever pitch in early 1932 that the city's municipal council deployed troops to protect the International Settlement. Japanese marines came ashore, and Guomindang soldiers in the impoverished workers' district of Zhabei fired on them. In response, the Japanese navy bombed Zhabei, killing thousands and turning hundreds of thousands into refugees. A Chinese resistance defended Shanghai from Japanese troops who attacked after the bombing, until both sides accepted an uneasy armistice to this "undeclared war." In the northwest, the Japanese persuaded the dethroned Qing emperor Puyi to serve as figurehead ruler and set up a puppet government in Manchuria, which they declared the independent state of Manchukuo despite international opposition. In March of 1934, Puyi donned the dragon robes of the last adult Qing emperor and ascended his new throne in the city of Changchun.

Shuhua's short story "Chiyoko," first published in the Beijing-based *Literary Quarterly* in 1934, makes reference to the skirmish in Shanghai from an unusual perspective, that of a twelve-year-old Japanese girl. Chiyoko, the only daughter of a fruit merchant and his wife, lives in an outlying district of Kyoto hard hit by economic depression. Since the Shanghai conflict, the neighborhood children have learned to mimic the anti-Chinese comments of the adults around them. After school, they shout them at the Chinese family that runs a local restaurant. Chiyoko overhears her father and a friend discussing China as a civilization in paralysis, whose men smoke opium and whose women have bound feet. Chiyoko repeats to her parents the lessons of a patriotic teacher, who regularly lectures on the backwardness of a nation where women have three-inch-long feet. When Chiyoko announces that she wants to see for herself what Chinese women's feet look like, her mother turns up her nose, proclaiming that they are dirty and stink.

As her mother cooks their meager dinner, Chiyoko smells the delicious aroma wafting over from their neighbors' kitchen. She remembers fondly when she and her parents still exchanged friendly words with their Chinese neighbors and ate at their restaurant. When she asks her father if they can move to Manchuria rather than starve in Japan, he looks up from his account book, removes his glasses, and explains that their troubles should be blamed on the Chinese boycott of Japanese goods.

The following morning, Chiyoko's mother surprises her with a few coins to go to the bathhouse with her friend Yuriko. Yuriko is a teacher's pet, who can perfectly parrot all the new patriotic slogans. As they walk down the road, she tells Chiyoko a secret discovery she made that morning. She saw the Chinese woman from their neighborhood carrying her baby to the bathhouse in the next district over, where she wouldn't be recognized. Yuriko convinces her younger friend to join her in following and publicly humiliating the woman. As they undress before entering the bath, Chiyoko catches a glimpse of herself in the mirror and sees an unnatural smile fixed on her face. She slips into the warm water of the pool and hears several women laughing in one corner. She swims over to see them playing with a chubby baby, and she too is caught up in their moment of joy. Watching from the side, Yuriko fumes that her friend has so quickly forgotten their pact against the Chinese woman. She mutters to herself, "Chiyoko is such a child!"[25]

By providing an account of everyday life as she imagined it might look on the other side, Shuhua reveals how national stereotypes are formed and how children are socialized to reproduce them. Stories like "Chiyoko" make it difficult to place Shuhua within the political camps of the 1930s. In a summary of the options available to writers at this moment, literary historian Wendy Larson maintains that they had to choose sides:

> In literature, authors on the right or without strong political affiliation had three choices: align themselves under the larger sign of the anti-Japanese, pro-Nationalist struggle; cooperate with the Japanese; or write works that were overtly socially and politically unengaged. . . . Leftist writers had to take a stance on the social and ideological debates of the late 1920s; they had to denounce their earlier works as naive and bourgeois, move on to write social realism (and stay away from emphasis on individual emotion and elite society), or stop writing fiction entirely.[26]

Shuhua's "Chiyoko," however, is not pro-Nationalist, pro-Japanese, or Communist, but neither is it politically unengaged; it refuses to takes sides, while simultaneously illustrating the use of women's bodies, in this case the bound foot, to symbolize a nation's predicament, not just by Chinese nationalists, but also by their aggressors.

In the same year as the publication of "Chiyoko," Chiang Kaishek launched the New Life Movement. Impressed by the organization of the nascent Nazi party in Germany, Chiang developed a plan that emphasized social order through a return to the tenets of Confucian moral conduct that the May Fourth generation had attacked so strongly. Guomindang leaders had discovered that sensationalized attacks on the sexual morality of the Communist Party, particularly of its female political organizers, was an effective propaganda method, and the New Life Movement promoted a return for women to the traditional realm of domesticity. Chiang's wife, director of the movement's women's department, praised the role of loving mother and devoted wife. At the New Life Movement schools she helped found, students were trained to improve their standards of housekeeping, supervise people's conduct in parks and theaters, and make home visits to advise housewives on cleaning methods.[27] This backlash against the gains achieved by May Fourth women provides the background for another of Shuhua's stories.

In 1935, ten years after Amy left for America, Shuhua wrote a short story titled "Wuliao," an adjective meaning "bored" or "listless." A year later, a translation appeared in the English-language *Tien Hsia Monthly* under the title "What's the Point of It?" Although published as fiction, with a main character named Ru Bi, this story provides clues to Shuhua's life. For example, three years earlier Shuhua, like Ru Bi in the story, had embarked upon a major translation project. Without telling anyone about her work, she began translating Jane Austen's *Pride and Prejudice*. Halfway through, she discovered that a better-known translator, a fellow member of the now-defunct Crescent Moon Society, intended to translate the novel; Shuhua never finished her version.[28]

Ru Bi wakes up to a rainy morning, disgusted with the damp and moldy air of her house. Her maid nags her for wasting money on trees and flowers planted to imitate the foreigners' gardens in the neighboring university compound, and Ru Bi escapes to her study. Just as she becomes absorbed in a passage of the book she is translating, the maid calls her downstairs to receive a visitor who talks endlessly about her children. After the visitor leaves, Ru Bi retreats again to her study, where she stares out the window.

> Looking at the neighbouring households she thought there was a great deal to be said for the scholar who had explained that the word for "home" (*jia*) is the same as that for "chains," and that the character is written as a pig under a roof.
>
> But why should a reasonable person be chained, and why should someone whole and sound have to be fed like a pig? The more she thought about it the more depressed she felt, and at last she left the window and sank heavily onto a chair.
>
> It was true, though, a pig's life was pointless, except for eating and sleeping and begetting, sleeping and eating and begetting again; what more could you expect? Pig, be calm and peaceful, stay in your pen! She repeated the words to herself with an ironical smile on her lips.[29]

In the afternoon, she goes into town to buy a birthday present for an uncle. Wandering through the shops, she feels oppressed by the sales pitches directed at her. One salesman tries to convince her to buy several yards of dowdy fabric advertised as "New Life Movement tweed." Ru Bi fails to buy the gift and gets in a rickshaw, but then decides to walk instead because she can think of no sensible reason to have a man use all of his energy to run her home.

Ru Bi's contemplation of the etymology of the word "home" reveals how confining its domestic space felt to a woman educated to consider the world beyond its walls. In contrast with Shuhua's earlier stories depicting the failures of women invested in traditional female roles, "What's the Point of It?" lodges its complaint against the post–May Fourth retreat from an agenda of gender equality. Ru Bi's fate parallels that of Shuhua's women who sacrificed themselves in "virtuous transactions" with patriarchal society. Her broken contract, however, is with May Fourth promises. Reformers had supported women's struggle for education because they saw it as part of the national goal of self-strengthening; they hoped, much as proponents of the New Life Movement did, to produce a healthy, informed corps of mothers to nurture China's future generations. As a result, women such as Ru Bi or Shuhua received an education, but one that subordinated the individual woman to a larger national order.

The maid's criticism of Ru Bi's attempt to cultivate a Western-style garden exposes the paradox of Chinese who resent but also emulate their foreign occupiers. Chiang Kaishek's New Life Movement attempted to counter Western cultural influence with a program of modernization regulated by neo-Confucian morality. In "What's the Point of It?" the foreign presence marked by alluring gardens and the Guomindang bid to supersede it with the New Life Movement represent dual forms of entrapment: the limitation of women's social mobility and of Chinese independence in a nation partially subjugated by foreign interests.

In spite of the ennui and frustration conveyed in her stories, Shuhua continued to write and publish, although at a slower rate than before. Shortly after the 1935 publication of *Little Brothers*, the woman writer Su Xuelin reviewed Shuhua's first two collections and emphasized the variety of female psychologies explored in her stories, including those of schoolgirls, young women, housewives, widows, single women, maids, and university wives. Through a comparison of two Mansfield stories with two of Shuhua's stories, she demonstrates how Ling Shuhua adapted her literary borrowings to illuminate uniquely Chinese situations. Su Xuelin draws particular attention to the gender-specific depression explored in "Ms. Li," the story of an aging teacher who refuses to marry out of a sense of duty to support her widowed mother. She concludes her review by comparing Ling Shuhua to the leftist writer Ding Ling and defends the overlooked strength of Shuhua's stories.

> Ding Ling's writing is boundless in its daring, but her strength is used on the exterior, where it's easily recognized. Ling Shuhua's writing is simple and serene, elegant and harmonious. It seems as if the word "strength" doesn't fit, but her writing does have strength, one contained deeply within and whose tone is calm. One could say that other people's strength is like a silver river rushing down with the violence of booming thunder and flashing lightning, while hers is a hot spring that moves stealthily underground. . . . Writing that deals mostly with the bourgeoisie and household trivialities does not conform to current trends and hence is ignored by readers; as a result, her reputation in today's literary world does not equal that of the tongue-clicking population of writers with no real learning who are simply good at shouting revolutionary slogans.[30]

In some respects, Su Xuelin lived the single life of a female teacher like that described in "Ms. Li." She had returned to China in 1925 from studies in France to enter a loveless marriage arranged by her ailing mother. She and her husband often did not live under the same roof and became increasingly estranged. In 1931, she became a professor of literature at Wuhan University and moved into one of the houses on Luojia Mountain. The author of a semi-autobiographical novel based on her four years as a student in France as well as a collection of short stories and travel essays, Su later threw herself into comparative research on classical Chinese, Greek, and Roman literature. At Wuhan University, she taught Chinese literary history and world literature and developed a course on modern Chinese literature.

Su Xuelin's arrival on Luojia Mountain marked the beginning of a literary circle of friendship that included herself, Ling Shuhua, and Yuan Changying, another woman writer who had been part of the Wuhan University faculty from its beginning in 1928. Yuan had studied at Edinburgh University from 1916 to 1921, earning a master's degree in English drama. In England, she met the close-knit group of Chinese students that included her future husband and Chen Xiying, who published her writing while he was editor of *Contemporary Review*. In Wuhan, she experimented with the new Chinese form of "spoken drama" (as opposed to opera) and wrote several plays, published in her 1930 collection *Southeast Flies the Peacock*. With her European credentials, she also held the position of professor. In addition to French, she taught modern drama, introducing playwrights such as Ibsen, Maeterlinck, Shaw, and Chekhov, and classical European drama, which gave students a foundation in the Greek tragedies of Aristophanes, Sophocles, and Euripides.

For Shuhua, life with Su Xuelin and Yuan Changying on Luojia Mountain provided a welcome camaraderie—casual visits to each other's homes, conversations about literature, and joint outings into the nearby countryside. An unusual gathering of several prominent women writers in a single location, they were identified as the "Three Female Talents of Luojia Mountain."[31] Yuan Changying wore large, round spectacles and paid careful attention to her dress and manners. Su Xuelin attributed her professional demeanor to years among the polite British and described her own appearance as wrinkled and sloppy in comparison, drawing the attention of improvement campaigns by Yuan Changying that included gifts of well-chosen fabric for new clothes. In the summer, they shed their stockings and ran bare-legged, their bobbed hair bouncing, down to the lake, with Su Xuelin hoping to offend Yuan Changying's propriety by joking that she'd never wear stockings again. Shuhua, the youngest of the group, was known as the beauty, but as the only one without a foreign education or university appointment, she struggled with the label of faculty wife.[32]

In 1935, students at the university performed Yuan's *Southeast Flies the Peacock*. This dramatic adaptation of a Han dynasty folk ballad retells a

Faculty at Wuhan University during visit by Hu Shi, 1932. Su Xuelin, Ling Shuhua, and Yuan Changying stand in the front row, with Hu Shi to the left of Su Xuelin. Chen Xiying stands on the left of the second to last row. Courtesy of Pi Gongliang.

famous love tragedy, but rather than emphasizing the plight of its doomed lovers, it focuses on the lovers' antagonist, Mother Jiao. Widowed at a young age, Mother Jiao pours all of her attention into the upbringing of her son Zhong. When Zhong marries and his young, talented wife Lan enters the family, Mother Jiao grows overwrought at the transfer of her son's affection to Lan. Jealous and tormented by the prospect of future loneliness, she drives Lan out of the house, an action that leads the lovers to commit suicide in a pact of romantic love.

Mother Jiao falls to the ground in anguish over her son's death. She struggles to get up, but then gathers a bundle of grass into a doll. She strokes its hair, unbuttons her robe, and holds the dried grass to her breast. "Here! Here! Drink some milk. Isn't a mother's milk good!" Suddenly, she throws the grass away from her, and turns to face the audience. "Whose son is this? This is rice straw! My son! My son is dead!" Yuan's stage directions read: "Covers her head and wails. At this point, a fierce gust of wind blows her disheveled hair like a tattered flag of a defeated army, surrendering to an invisible enemy. The mournful sound of the wind is like the wailing of defeated soldiers."[33]

These stage directions conflate the play's tragedy with the national emergency unfolding across the country. But the other political front, the one addressed by this drama's psychological exploration of a mother's struggle with traditional self-sacrificing gender roles, is now a distant battlefield, no longer deemed useful to the nation. According to Su Xuelin, leftist critics who reviewed *Southeast Flies the Peacock* attacked Yuan Changying for failing to address China's current struggle against Japan.[34] May Fourth women, like the "Three Talents of Luojia Mountain," who in their youth had burst onto the literary scene did not suddenly fall silent, as later accounts would suggest. Rather, the heavy velvet curtain of national exigency muffled their ongoing drama.

· Sixteen ·

Souvenirs

$\mathcal{A}$fter her internship year in Pittsburgh, Amy finally accepted KK's proposal. On July 15, 1929, they were wed in a Baltimore chapel. They took no pictures. Their marriage certificate, decorated with ringing bells, roses, and lilies of the valley, lists no witnesses other than Rev. C. M. Adams. Immediately after the ceremony, they hopped into KK's two-door Nash and spent four days on the road to Indianapolis. KK had received a job offer from Eli Lilly pharmaceuticals, whose father-and-son founders had closely followed his *mahuang* research. In 1926, they ordered tons of the herb from China and put ephedrine on the American market. When they recruited KK to become the first director of pharmacological research for their growing laboratories, he initially hesitated. The stock market crash made business uncertain, and working in industry would require him to resign from the American Society for Pharmacology and Experimental Therapeutics. He accepted the job when the Lillys promised him complete research freedom and access to Chinese herbs through the company's Shanghai branch.[1] According to Amy, he only agreed to sign a one-year contract, after which they believed they would return home. Amy still intended to open her own practice in China.

In Indianapolis, they checked into a noisy hotel with thin walls. KK dressed the next morning at dawn for their meeting with Eli Lilly. By the time Amy woke up, he sat in suit and tie, briefcase at his side, waiting for the appointed hour to arrive. After initial introductions, Eli Lilly walked KK and Amy, who would assist in the laboratory, through their facilities and asked when they could get to work. They expressed concern about the lack of several important pieces of equipment, and Lilly amazed them by telling them to make a list of everything they required. When Amy tactfully asked Lilly for his thoughts, he replied, "Every day I hear what people think I want. You just tell me what you need." Amy outlined basic improvements that should be made to the laboratory, including padded rubber floors, chemical-resistant countertops, and a hood for venting harmful fumes. Lilly noted their suggestions and offered them four weeks of paid vacation for a honeymoon while the equipment was ordered and installed.

Amy and KK continued the driving tour they had begun on their way to Indianapolis. KK donned a fedora, and Amy tied her hair back with a scarf. With the windows of the Nash rolled down, they traveled through fields of corn and over green summer hills humming with insect noise. They stayed in people's homes where a sign next to the mailbox on the road advertised "room for rent." When, in a rainstorm, their car slid off a narrow road into a ditch, a farmer towed them out with his tractor. My grandmother laughed, "He thought we were just two kids. He couldn't figure out what we doing there, stuck in a ditch." Their first morning back in Indianapolis, they started looking for an apartment and quickly recognized a pattern. As soon as they showed up, the landlord would say he was sorry but the apartment had just been rented. Amy explained, "In those days, they didn't want to take anyone Asian. They didn't want to take Blacks." They persisted until they found a second-floor apartment on Pennsylvania Street where the landlord was willing to rent to them.

As the new director of research, KK gradually won the esteem of the other scientists with his expertise. Amy described a key moment that took place at a meeting of Lilly scientists and salesmen. These meetings allowed salesmen to ask the company's scientists about any of the products. One eager young man stood up and asked for the chemical formula of a common local antiseptic. None of the chemists on stage could answer the question off the top of their heads. Eli Lilly turned to KK and asked, "Chen, do you know?" Only then did KK approach the blackboard. Without a pause, he sketched the crystalline structure for the mercury compound Lilly sold under the trademark Mercurachrome.

Respect did not always come so easily, as KK learned that year at an industrywide conference. Characteristically early for his panel, he waited outside a hotel conference room for his colleagues to arrive. As he glanced at his watch, he felt someone tap his shoulder. He turned to face a middle-aged man who instructed him to clean off the table in the room for the upcoming meeting. KK straightened the cuffs of his tailored suit, picked up a leather briefcase embossed in gold with Dr. K. K. Chen, and calmly walked into the room, where he assumed his position at the head of the table. The meeting began fifteen minutes later under his direction, and the man who had called him "boy" didn't look up once during the entire hour.

When KK traveled to conferences or on collecting trips for research materials, Amy replaced him as head of the lab. She described having to adopt a stern demeanor, reprimanding technicians if their work wasn't done carefully, to get them to take her seriously. Over time, her research skills also impressed them. She helped develop a procedure to test the effects of different drugs on a frog heart. The method, called perfusion, allowed them to keep the heart beating after it had been removed from the body. They mixed a solution containing the same chemical balance as the frog's blood and then fed it into the heart through a small tube inserted into a vein. The flow of solution, to which various drugs could be added, caused the heart to continue beating. A needle attached to the heart recorded the strength and speed of its beats on a rotating drum of paper. Amy boasted about the time she donned her white lab coat and demonstrated this procedure in the Lilly booth at a trade show in Atlantic City. She attracted the attention of an observer from one of their main competitors and overheard him say that they should consider hiring her. His colleague replied, "If you hire her, you'll have to hire her husband. Don't you know who she's married to? The other Dr. Chen."

When the Lillys extended KK's one-year contract, Amy gave up the idea of practicing medicine to assist him with his work on toad venom, which expanded to include sixteen toad species from around the world.[2] When I asked my grandmother why she didn't continue her career as a doctor, she brushed the question aside as if the answer were obvious. I turned to the only evidence I have for this period of her life. She and my grandfather lean toward each other in a photograph with a microscope captured in sharp focus on the table between them—a portrait of a modern, intellectual partnership in marriage. Staring at the still image, I also see the perdurance of the teacher-student origins of their relationship and Amy's suppressed impatience with how this picture constrains her ambition.

When I tried to imagine what she was thinking, I realized that in Indianapolis she had to contend not only with being a woman but also a Chinese woman, and one married to a researcher whose work had been recognized for years. Her dream of opening a clinic for women had been pushed aside by the more urgent concern of learning how to succeed in a country where it was difficult even to rent an apartment. The economic stability afforded by their association with Lilly gave her hope of regaining the social position her family had once held in China. She and KK moved into a rented house and considered building their own home, although the question of how long they would stay in the United States remained open. Not long after the photograph with the microscope was taken, Amy discovered she was pregnant. She insisted on working in the lab for the first seven months of her pregnancy, wearing an oversized lab coat to disguise the fact from coworkers she knew would disapprove.

I first learned the extent of my grandparents' research partnership in 1990 while taking a class on the anthropology of art and aesthetics. In a textbook, I read an article titled "Drug-induced optical sensations and their rela-

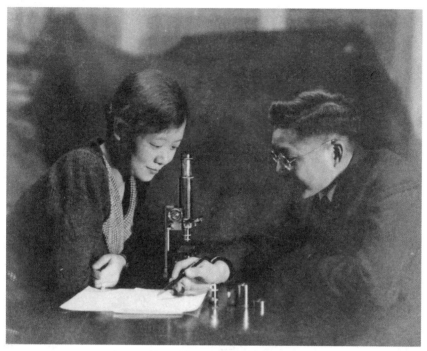

Amy and K. K. Chen, Indianapolis, ca. 1930s

tionship to applied art among some Colombian Indians." Buried in the
endnotes, the names of my grandparents jumped out at me from the tightly
packed text. In 1939, they coauthored an article in the *Quarterly Journal of
Pharmacy and Pharmacology* that documents their isolation of harmine from a
vine used by Colombian Indians to produce a hallucinogen for ritual and
medicinal purposes.[3] That I should find this husband-and-wife research team
listed among the references of an article on the aesthetic practices of the
Tukano Indians, as subjected to the scientific gaze of a fieldworker from the
Universidad de los Andes, Bogotá, provided one of the hallucinatory
moments of personal history that have fed my obsession with telling this
story. Evidence of my grandmother's alter ego sideswiped me once again
from a seemingly impossible source. I had always heard that after the birth of
her first child, my grandmother left her position in the lab to stay at home,
but her footnote appearance as A. L. Chen left me questioning my assumptions once again. Later, I would find, in the poisonous plant bibliography of
the U.S. Food and Drug Administration, six articles coauthored by A. L.
Chen, the last one published in 1942.

In the fall of 1933, during the final months of her pregnancy, she received a series of letters from home. Her mother described the details of her father's deteriorating health. He'd gone back to the south, where he could see his grove of lychee trees through the window by his bed. Amy wanted to return home to see him but was in no condition to undertake the long ocean journey. Shortly before the birth of Thomas Daoyuan Chen, she received another letter from home. Her father had died, and the family had buried him in Panyu.

When telling this story, my grandmother never disclosed her emotions. She would press her lips together for a moment and then abruptly begin to describe how they had returned to China once, several years later. Did she sit at her desk with a hand on top of the letter, as if this connection to home might also fly away if she didn't hold it down? I picture her staring out the window at their street, as the last leaves slowly fell from the trees, waiting for KK to come home. As she felt the baby move inside, perhaps she closed her eyes and pictured her father sending her off to a country he'd never seen. His body had grown thin with age, and he leaned his hands on the banquet table to slowly push himself to his feet. He stood with a small porcelain cup of wine raised in the air, holding it there for a long time, toasting her unknown future. Exactly how Amy felt realizing she would never see him again, I will never know. She kept her sorrow private, drawing strength from it, assuming I wouldn't be able to understand. She was right: I don't know how it feels to lose someone in a letter that has taken weeks to travel to one's hand from so far away.

Amy and KK wanted to see their mothers hold their American-born son, and finally in the summer of 1936, they filled their steamer trunks with clothing and gifts. The Chen family climbed aboard a westbound train early one June morning and traveled toward San Francisco, where they boarded an ocean liner to cross the Pacific. Her excitement still palpable, Amy told me, "I said we better go back to China to see our mothers. I had never met his mother. And he'd never met my mother. It was hard for us to buy three tickets then. Two tickets for ourselves and a half ticket for Tom. It was expensive and took seventeen days on the boat, but we did."

They arrived in Shanghai and visited first with KK's mother, who carried her grandson in her arms as much of the time as she could. Tom had begun walking months earlier, and Amy remembered coaxing her mother-in-law: "I said, 'Let him go walking. Two-year-olds like to walk.' She said, 'No, no, no.' She just held him so tight." After several weeks in Shanghai, they continued by train to Beijing, where Amy reunited with her family. Shuhua returned from Wuhan, bringing Xiaoying with her, for the months of July and August. During her visit to Beijing, meetings with writers, artists, and other friends occupied much of Shuhua's time, but for a few weeks the two youngest Ling sisters slept again under the same roof with their mother. Their older sister Shuzhi frequently came by the house to visit. She had arranged for an *amah* to take care of Tom, but Shuzhi and Ruolan hovered over Tom as much as the *amah*. Amy remembered how they spoiled him during their limited time together. They bought a child-size wooden train and pushed him around the garden in it. On temple days, they took him to the fair at the Fire God Temple. With each of them holding one of Tom's hands, they wove through the crowds to examine the stalls selling artificial flowers and cheap jewelry. They watched puppet shows and always stopped to buy Tom a treat. The candy man lowered his tall pole down from his shoulder for the boy to make a selection from the wooden rack of sugar lollipops blown into the shapes of different animals.

Amy and KK wandered among the familiar sights and smells of the city, caught unaware by forgotten details that brought intense memories of a previous life. The watchman at the front gate of PUMC recognized their faces and called out, "Teacher Chen, Little Ling, you're back; are you married or

Shuhua painting, Beijing, 1936. Photo by Amy Ling Chen.

not?" The persimmons growing on the tree in the Feng cousins' courtyard were still small and hard. The smell of hot oil and frying dough sputtered from the woks of street venders who squatted over low coal stoves. Together they bought overripe lychees. Words felt soft and comfortable in their mouths. The city walls, trees, and human voices all possessed real presence, more substantial than the memories they'd nurtured for over a decade.

They enjoyed leisurely meals with family and friends from PUMC. Their conversations meandered through the expanse of time that had gradually separated their lives. Between warm outbursts of stories and laughter, the dinner-table talk inevitably turned to the subject of Japanese aggression in the north, the antagonism between the Communists and the Guomindang, and the threat of war. Relatives urged Amy and KK to stay in the United States for the time being. Whether or not they still seriously thought about moving back to China, this advice from home dissuaded them from considering the option anytime soon.

As my grandmother remembered this trip nearly sixty years later, she knew what she didn't then, that it would be her last visit home. She expressed her sadness in the only way she allowed herself, in anger at what had been lost.

> We spent two months with my mother. She had two good rooms, one room for Tom and his *amah* and one room for us. I was really happy to have an *amah* take care of Tom. She spoke Cantonese, so my mother could talk to her. My mother could speak both Cantonese and Mandarin. Tom learned some, but he forgot after he came back to the United States. He forgot *both*. He could talk *both*. But when he came back to America, he forgot everything, just like you people. You people didn't learn, but he forgot it.

"You people," her preferred standard for the second person plural, often uttered with a dismissive wave of a hand, was her way of referring to the generations of us born and raised in America. "You people" was her way of drawing a line between her experience and ours.

Amy's story of the trip often ended with her description of shopping in Beijing for Chinese things to decorate the new American dream house she and KK had talked about building in Indianapolis. In a turn away from the people whom, aside from Shuhua, she never saw again, she lavished attention on the things that still reminded her of China as she pointed toward the paintings on her San Francisco walls and the curios that filled the glass cabinet in her living room. "Look at what I brought back, all these things." Shifting in her chair so she could look at the painted panels hanging over the sofa, she told me how she bought them from a Buddhist temple that had fallen into disrepair on the outskirts of Beijing. The canvas murals covering the walls of the temple had been retouched with vegetable dyes many times over the hundreds of years since they were originally painted, but the monks had fallen on hard times. They began to cut up the murals and sell them. Amy chose a series representing the shifting disguises of Buddha on earth and commissioned a craftsman to make thin wooden frames carved with bamboo, plum blossoms, peonies, and chrysanthemums for them. From her chair, she also pointed out several pieces of embroidery lying on various side tables. "My mother gave me all these in 1936. She gave me that red one for our wedding gift." These souvenirs that she collected for her home in America stood in for the relationships that were severed by immigration and war.

Amy would eventually lose touch with most of her extended family. What fate befell her father's other concubines and children remains a mystery to me. She maintained the closest contact, through an exchange of sporadic and sometimes tense letters, with Shuhua. One cause of that tension lies hidden in what Amy omitted from her recollections about her one return trip to China. Shuhua did not travel to Beijing in that summer of 1936 simply to reunite with her sister.

Seventeen

The Entangling Net

*S*huhua sat on the ferry from Wuchang to Hankou. A chill drizzle prickled the river's surface and muted the outline of the customs house that grew on the horizon as they approached Hankou. Coal smoke blew from the engine room. The deckhands called across the water and flung coils of rope to the workers waiting on the dock. After crossing the wooden gangplank, Shuhua hailed a rickshaw, giving the address of the *Wuhan Daily*. Knowing Shuhua felt depressed by her housewife existence at the university, Su Xuelin and Yuan Changying had suggested creating a weekly literary supplement for the Wuhan newspaper with Shuhua as editor.

Shuhua emerged from the covered rickshaw. Her black, strapped heels tapped down the corridor as she approached the editor's office to deliver the inaugural essay for the *Xiandai wenyi* (Contemporary literature and art) supplement. It appeared on February 15, 1935, not under a single author's name, but rather as the thoughts of an editorial collective. One Chinese literary scholar has argued that its authorship should be attributed to Ling Shuhua.[1]

The opening paragraph announced that the literature enthusiasts behind *Xiandai wenyi* had no high-sounding aims to profess but had discussed several concerns. They presented five guiding principles for the publication.[2]

First, at a time of internal strife and foreign invasion—when many claimed that only revolution could save China and that revolution required literature to be used as a propaganda tool—the editors defended the universalist impulse of literature and refused to circulate any particular "ism." They insisted that all stories written in a convincing way could make for good literature, no matter what the author's subject: the oppression of the proletariat, a tragedy of young love, a hero's failure on the historical battlefield, or the foibles of an ordinary person.

Second, they would avoid partisanship. With the rise of literary camps, many writers supported their own circle and attacked everything else regardless of literary quality. The influence of these camps had become excessive,

241

with some authors going so far as to use pseudonyms to write glowing reviews of their own work, thereby "passing off fish eyes as pearls."[3]

Third, they advocated building a robust Chinese literature, especially at a time of "strife, confusion, contradiction, obstinacy, frivolity, arrogance, and aggression."[4] They promoted a return to the May Fourth ideal of a humane literature, rather than the morbid, romantic (Goethe taken too closely to heart) literature that had replaced it. They opposed salacious work that corrupted young minds by relying upon sex, obscenity, violence, voyeuristic exposure of people's private lives, or attacks on their secret disgraces.

Fourth, they wanted to raise the quality of vernacular literature. They likened the new literature to a plant whose seeds must be carefully cultivated, because no modern Chinese literary works worthy of the "global forest" had yet been brought to maturity. *Baihua* writers had become sloppy, littering their writing with classical and European borrowings.

Fifth, now that political unrest had besieged Beijing, they hoped to foster Chinese literature elsewhere. They promoted Wuhan as particularly well suited to this goal: "Wuchang is an important post on the Yangzi River; Hankou is the Chicago of the East; Hanyang is the Chinese Pittsburgh. In terrain, commerce, and industry, this region serves as a center for the entire country. This desert should be turned into a magnificent park."[5]

This literary call to arms attempts to open a space between decadent romanticism and revolutionary utilitarianism and encourages a Chinese modernism whose growth could elevate Wuhan to global status. Just as Chen Xiying had helped shape the modern Chinese literary scene as editor of the *Contemporary Review* in Beijing, Shuhua now had a similar opportunity. She published numerous women, whose work made up nearly half of what eventually appeared in the supplement. The final sentences of the introductory essay called for a new beginning:

> Rise up, comrades, spring has arrived. The clear sun shines. The balmy east wind blows. Fine threads of rain cleanse. We must quickly pick up our hoes and reclaim this wasteland. Hasten to sprinkle the seeds of art and literature. Don't squander this time, waste this good soil, or be stingy with your sweat and energy. A bountiful harvest awaits us. Work hard! Comrades! Work hard![6]

Submissions flowed in, and Shuhua crossed weekly on the ferry with her selections.

In early issues, she published segments of Xu Zhimo's collected letters. She also included her own stories and essays, including an introduction to the novel *Seventeen* by Pulitzer Prize winner Booth Tarkington. Highlighting a writer famous for depicting his home state of Indiana suggests curiosity about

Amy's life, as well as Shuhua's increasing interest in representing children's psychologies. In *Seventeen*, the adolescent protagonist "Silly Billy" Baxter becomes disastrously infatuated with a flirtatious debutante. Shuhua had finally found a clear purpose in Wuhan. Until a wayward son from the Western world she knew only from books arrived on their doorstop and tempted her to jump the tracks.

Ten years earlier Xu Zhimo had collected a Roger Fry watercolor for Shuhua's scroll. Now Julian Bell, the son of Fry's onetime lover, British modernist painter Vanessa Bell, sailed toward China. Vanessa's oldest son, nephew of Virginia and Leonard Woolf, had grown up the golden child of Bloomsbury. Julian tried his hand at poetry but became restless amid an older generation of writers and painters. After graduating from King's College at Cambridge, he failed to win a desired fellowship and decided to break from his comfortable home at the heart of English letters. He applied for teaching jobs in the Far East and in July of 1935 received a post—recommended by Roger Fry's sister Margery after her travels to China—as professor of English at Wuhan University.

On board a Japanese ship, the *Fushimi Maru*, Julian strode across the deck in gray flannel trousers and a rumpled shirt with an air of assurance. In the middle of the Mediterranean Sea, on August 31, 1935, Julian wrote one of the scores of letters he would send to his mother over the next two years, and in which Shuhua would soon regularly appear. With the exuberance of a twenty-seven-year-old primed for adventure, he described his fellow travelers, including "an amiable Filipino youth travelling round the world . . . and a charming tea-planter from Assam, pure Somerset Maugham."[7] Julian wrote with unusual frankness to Vanessa, who adored her firstborn child and remained to the end his closest confidante. Several of his letters, for instance, reported on a lingering case of venereal disease. In his biography of Julian Bell, Peter Stansky remarks on his love of self-disclosure:

> The older generation of Bloomsbury, in rebellion against the taboos of their Victorian forebears, believed in clear, candid, truthful and rational personal relationships, and accordingly saw no reason to be reticent in matters of sex. But there is a quality in Julian's revelations that is very different from the candour of his elders, and suggests that he was involved not so much in a relationship as in a performance.[8]

Julian slid between poetic description of the landscape and of "ravishingly pretty girls." His allusion to future exploits—"I see I should lose my head fifty times over with half a chance"—evoked a colonial excitement for discovery.[9] Before his departure, Vanessa had photographed Julian, rifle in hand, wearing a new white tropical suit and pith helmet. In his third week

Julian Bell aboard the Fushimi Maru, September 1935. In a letter to Vanessa, Julian wrote, "I enclose photographs of a peculiar Japanese fancy-dress entertainment." Julian sits at the table in the foreground, second from the left, wearing his college gown and mortarboard. Courtesy of King's College Library, Cambridge. Charleston Papers 1/55/3/15.

aboard the *Fushimi Maru*, he exclaimed, "I saw my first wild animal to-day—a sea-snake."[10] Several paragraphs later, he described the "natives"; he wrote, "Then the port: I saw wild Chinese for the first time—coolies—and was fascinated."

By October 1, he was in China, where he made his way from Shanghai to Nanjing, continuing to Wuhan aboard a river steamer. On October 5, in his house on Luojia Mountain, he dashed off a letter to his mother: "I arrived safe and sound at last, on a Sunday morning; to-morrow I shall try and rush business, the day after I start lecturing. . . . Everyone here is being charming to me—I've spent the afternoon with the dean of my faculty and his wife and daughter—about 6—a fascinating child who fell for me. It's all very informal—a Mediterranean Cambridge."[11] The dean of foreign languages was Chen Xiying, and the wife and "fascinating child" were Ling Shuhua and Xiaoying.

A week later, Julian described for Vanessa his neighbors down the hill in glowing terms:

My dean, Prof. Cheng [sic] Yuan, and his wife, are my neighbors, and simply angelic . . . extremely cultured: he a critic and translator of Turgenev (also a friend of Goldie's), she a painter (Chinese style), writer of short stories and editor of a literary page in one of the big Hankow papers: I gather she's sometimes called the Chinese Katherine Mansfield, but I fancy there's more to her really, though she's very quiet and gentle.[12]

"Mrs. Chen" helped him order fabric with Han designs for curtains and chair covers. Attempting to recreate the domestic aesthetics he'd grown up with in Vanessa's Charleston home, Julian wrote to her, "Then I shall start to entertain . . . we all live in houses scattered about the hill-side, and there is a great deal of dropping in in a casual Cambridge fashion."[13] This mantra of comparison filled his early letters. Describing his neighbors, he wrote as if to assure himself, "They are very much a Chinese Bloomsbury."[14]

As the travels of Shuhua's scroll demonstrate, Julian Bell entered an established web of relationships when he accepted the Wuhan job. In the early twentieth century, as many May Fourth intellectuals saw the West as a model for reforming Chinese society, some British intellectuals used the East to critique the industrializing West's rapaciousness. Individuals from the two groups crossed and recrossed paths in London and Beijing.

The Bloomsbury elder most enamored with China was Goldsworthy (Goldie) Lowes Dickinson whose captivation began when Roger Fry suggested he adopt the persona of a Chinese official to critique Western capitalism, imperialism, and religious hypocrisy. Dickinson published his first four missives, written as open letters, in the *Saturday Review*. In 1901, a collection of eight "letters" appeared as *Letters from John Chinaman*. His Chinese official condemned the Western myth of progress, blind accumulation of wealth, and brutal crushing of the Boxer Rebellion, while waxing poetic about the aesthetic humanism of everyday life in China:

> A rose in a moonlit garden, the shadow of trees on the turf, almond bloom, scent of pines, the wine-cup and the guitar; these and the pathos of life and death, the long embrace, the hand stretched out in vain, the moment that glides for ever away, with its freight of music and light, into the shadow and hush of the haunted past, all that we have, all that eludes us, a bird on the wing, a perfume escaped on the gale—to all these things we are trained to respond, and the response is what we call literature.[15]

That nothing particularly Chinese characterizes Goldie's reverie reveals its very Britishness. It seeks redemption in the imaginary of an untainted, humanistic other culture—which in reality had been irrevocably changed by interactions with the West.

Goldie did not plan to deceive readers, but confusion arose over the volume when it appeared in the United States as *Letters from a Chinese Official*.

William Jennings Bryan—who later served as prosecutor in the Scopes Monkey Trial—read the *Letters* at face value and responded in 1906 with *Letters to a Chinese Official: Being a Western View of Eastern Civilization*. He accused his Chinese counterpart of ignorance about Christian civilization.[16]

Goldie did not travel to China until 1913, when he rhapsodized from Beijing to E. M. Forster, "China! So gay, friendly, beautiful, sane, hellenic, choice, human."[17] Others followed his path. Arthur Waley studied classics at King's College during Goldie's days and then took a job in the British Museum's Oriental subdepartment of prints and drawings, where he taught himself classical Chinese and Japanese. He never traveled to Asia but made his mark as a talented translator. Unlike Waley, Bertrand Russell and Dora Black jumped at the chance to go to China, which they toured in 1920 as invitees of the Chinese Society for Lectures on the New Learning. Painter and art critic Roger Fry drew British attention to Asian visual art in a 1910 essay titled "Oriental Art" and in 1934 gave a series of Cambridge lectures on Chinese art.

His sister Margery Fry went to China with Boxer Indemnity funds that supported educational exchange. She lectured at universities and made inspection tours of local prisons and factories. She met Ling Shuhua and Chen Xiying in 1933 and, before she left China, sent them a lithograph by her brother. On January 3, 1934, Shuhua wrote to thank her: "We shall hang this picture in our sitting room and we believe it will be greatly admired by our friends. . . . And will you please convey our hearty regards to Mr. Roger Fry who, ever since poor Hsu [Xu Zhimo] brought back his drawing on my scroll has seemed to be an old friend to us."[18] Margery Fry's connection led to Julian's job application at Wuhan University, where the cultural exchange represented by Shuhua's scroll soon came to life in a more personal way.

In China, Julian Bell continued to exhibit the contradictions that had driven him to leave Bloomsbury. Raised by pacifists who protested the First World War, he reveled as a boy in war games staged in the Charleston garden; a preoccupation with military strategy and a rustic love of hunting remained with him into adulthood. He criticized Chinese intellectuals to distinguish himself from earlier British romanticization of the East: "I can't really see why Goldie was so enthusiastic about them—except indeed for their niceness and charm. And perhaps he didn't mind sentimentality as much as his youngers do."[19] Of Julian's quest to avoid sentiment, biographer Peter Stansky observes, "He was in many ways . . . a romantic who did his best to conceal the fact from himself and others. . . . Julian thought he loathed violent emotions, but in everything, in politics and in love, he could not avoid them."[20] While he shouldered his gun and traipsed along the footpaths crisscrossing Luojia Mountain, Shuhua prepared the fabric for his curtains. He noted her appearance in his diary: "Mrs. Chen Yuan (spectacles, flattish face)."[21]

Julian began his modern literature course with the period 1890–1912, introducing Samuel Butler, Joseph Conrad, Oscar Wilde, and A. E. Housman. Shuhua, now "an intelligent and sensitive angel . . . a darling," sat in on this and his Shakespeare class. He confided to Vanessa that her presence had "the good effect of making me lecture my best," and compared her with the women he admired most: "How do you ever manage to both work and keep house? . . . Yet you, Virginia, Hsu Hwa . . . all of you are both housekeepers and active people."[22]

The Chens figured prominently in Julian's early correspondence. He reported on their distress about the Japanese. On a visit to their house, Shuhua unrolled her friendship scroll to show him the watercolor by Roger Fry. Julian saw the Fry lithograph in their living room and asked his mother to send a watercolor of her own for Shuhua. His appreciation for Chinese painting grew by looking at Shuhua's copies of Song and Ming masterpieces, and he sent an English essay Shuhua had written on Chinese landscape painting to his mother, asking her to help publish it in England. In early November, his new curtains hung, Julian hosted the Chens for his first dinner party. Of Shuhua, he wrote, "We go on, growing more and more intimate friends."[23]

By mid-November, in a letter to his mother's sister, Virginia Woolf, Mrs. Chen became Sue: "Are you pleased to hear that China's leading woman writer . . . is a passionate admirer of your work? . . . I'm still at the cordial acquaintance stage with everyone here but the young woman of p. 1—Hsu Hwa—Sue I've decided to call her. She tells me about the Chinese Bloomsbury in Peiping [Beijing], that's very like the London one indeed, so far as I can make out."[24]

He soon became bothered if he couldn't see Shuhua every day and started to jot notes to her during class. On November 22, drunk and alone, he confessed to his mother the intensity of his feelings:

> I've just realized how deeply I'm involved. Oh Nessa dear, you will have to meet her one of these days. She's the most charming creature I've ever met, and the only woman I know who would be a possible daughter-in-law to you (she isn't, being married with a charming child and 10 years too old) but she is really in our world and one of the most gifted, the nicest, most sensitive and intelligent people in it. I don't know what will happen. I think when I'm cured I shall probably get her involved: at present I'm not physically disturbed . . . but I know myself well enough to know that the parade follows the flag, etc.[25]

In early December, as he sat writing his weekly dispatch to Vanessa, Shuhua dropped by and saw her name in his letter. Scrutinizing the lines, she realized they described their intimacy. She demanded that Julian burn the letter while she watched, but he later recommitted it all to paper for his mother:

> I had started another letter to you yesterday but Sue came in and read it and took frantic offense at a passage about her, so that she now threatens to break off our affair—not, thank God, our friendship. We've been having an exhausting scene earlier this evening. But I think I can in the end bring her round— I'm by now very heavily involved, and shall be desperate if I can't. She's definitely the most serious, important, and adult person I have ever been in love with—also the most complicated and serious.[26]

This incident of epistolary betrayal—reminiscent of the quarrel over letters after Xu Zhimo's death—provides a reminder that almost everything in the archive about Ling Shuhua's relationship with Julian Bell comes from his perspective. I can speculate about what drew her regularly up the hill to his house or to Hankou with him for shopping expeditions. He needed a guide to Chinese culture. After years of playing protégé to her editor-husband, she reversed the roles and assumed the mantle of cultural authority. Julian offered knowledge of the West she'd never garnered through study abroad. She taught him Chinese painting and gave him Chinese lessons every morning. He asked his mother to send her a painting. She helped him buy a Chinese robe of dark blue silk lined with camel's hair.

I can speculate about why she risked the stability of her family life to flirt with a foreigner almost ten years her junior. Her husband, known for his serious demeanor and acerbic wit, worked long hours. She once likened his criticism of her writing to "cold water thrown on the fire."[27] Julian flowed with compliments and fed her ego with comparisons to Chekhov and other famous writers; Shuhua told him he reminded her of Xu Zhimo. She could become a mentor to him as Mansfield had been to Xu Zhimo while connecting with a wider artistic world. Shuhua and Julian shared both a romantic streak and a self-absorbed desire for literary fame. Yet the concrete details—of the flowers between their houses, of what she helped him purchase, of the paintings she unrolled for him—all come from Julian's pen. She would undoubtedly have revealed the details differently.

The Bloomsbury lives have been ruminated over in what can only be called literary voyeurism. In this aspect, a parallel exists between them and early Chinese modernist writers, whose personal lives excite similar curiosity. When I first discovered Shuhua's Bloomsbury connection I jumped into the fray. Perusing the published and archived letters of Virginia, Vanessa, and Julian, I eavesdropped on their intimate outpourings, until I had the uncanny sense that they wrote their letters to be read by just such hungry eyes. Janet Malcolm attributes the longevity of the Bloomsbury fascination to their abundant oeuvre of self-revelatory writing:

> Other early-modernist writers and artists, whose talents were at least equal to the Bloomsbury talents (except for Virginia's), recede from view, but the Bloomsbury writers and artists grow ever more biographically prominent. Were their lives so fascinating, or is it simply because they wrote so well and so incessantly about themselves and one another that we find them so? Well, the latter, of course.[28]

That Julian Bell loved gossip is evident in one of his Wuhan letters to a friend, which he closed with, "And write to me again, there's a darling. And put in *all* the scandal." But what about the peripheral actors caught up in this devotion to confessional writing? I hesitate to provide an incentive for Shuhua to be swept up in the Bloomsbury craze, a Chinese curiosity interesting only for her association with them. Several notices in the Virginia Woolf Society newsletter refer to Ling Shuhua as someone who entered the Bloomsbury fold through Julian Bell.[29] This fact remains important in an account of her life but fails to acknowledge that Julian likewise gained access to a Chinese intellectual circle that might otherwise have remained closed to him. Ling Shuhua did not first become famous in China for knowing Julian Bell; before his adventure in the Far East, she had already been canonized in the *Compendium of Modern Chinese Literature*.

Julian Bell's correspondence has enthralled and disgusted me; in it, I catch a refracted image of Shuhua, as well as a glimpse of his chauvinism and arrogance toward Chinese people and culture, reduced in his worst moments to "wild coolies" and "fiendish chinoiseries."[30] Despite all the indelicate details that unfold in these paper communiqués from another era, I realize how little I can ever know about the person whose life I've tried most carefully to trace, about who Shuhua was and why she did what she did.

Julian's indiscreet letters home meant the drama of his life became parlor conversation in London and Charleston, where Vanessa read his letters aloud at family gatherings. On December 17, Virginia wrote to him, making reference to the new object of his affections: "By the way give your lover, if she's my lover, my love. That's a Chinese box of a sentence for you!"[31] In a letter penned in Wuhan on that same day, Julian told Vanessa that their affair had grown in intensity and listed possible outcomes: "Be prepared for a cable saying 'all is discovered' . . . or news that I've married her and found some other job in the country. Or that she has committed suicide, as she fairly often threatens. But don't worry about it—the worst would be no more than annoying (I don't really believe in suicide, naturally) it's all a bit unreal."[32]

In a letter to his mother the following day, Julian described new developments. Chen Xiying had left town. When the Japanese seized the area south of Beijing, Shuhua turned to Julian with worries about her mother, who refused to leave the city in spite of rumors about rape and looting by occupying soldiers.

> Then she came and sat beside me on the sofa—said something emotional—of the kind we'd often said—I took her hand—and then felt her respond and in a few seconds she was in my arms . . . she's never been in love before, she says. . . . The whole atmosphere is like a Russian novel. . . . She's a desperately serious person, with great reserves of unhappiness: she says she's lost faith in everything, and is now working to find love, something to believe in. She's subtle, sensitive, very complicated—also torn between an introspective-analytic part and a very fragile easily-damaged sensibility. . . . She wouldn't let me make love to her to any extent at all last night. And she looks lovely—above all when I can get her to take off her spectacles—and is at once self-possessed, sure of her world, and devilish.[33]

Shuhua told him that she'd once been in love with Xu Zhimo, but couldn't admit it at the time, and married Xiying out of duty and a desire to get married. Julian wrote to his friend Eddie Playfair that it was his "oddest affair to date" and characterized Shuhua as "both jealous and not wanting to lose face."[34] He considered the problem of "the husband" in consummating the relationship but seemed oblivious of the possible effects on her family.

Julian had grown up with unconventional family arrangements. His mother Vanessa Stephen married the art critic Clive Bell. They had two sons, Julian and Quentin, but their marriage effectively ended several years later. After an affair with Roger Fry, Vanessa began a lifelong relationship with artist Duncan Grant. Grant, and sometimes his male lovers, lived with Vanessa and fathered her daughter, Angelica. Perhaps this background influenced Julian's heedlessness, although he also acknowledged—in a tense joke to his mother about the possibility of needing money for passage home—that, unlike Shuhua, he could eventually escape.

The household of Shuhua's upbringing had not followed a monogamous kinship pattern either. In *Ancient Melodies*, even the mothers allude in their fights to extramarital affairs, of one or the other having "a pale-faced young man" in her bed.[35] Free love had been a popular topic of conversation during Shuhua's youth; an emphasis on romantic choice and sexual drive had defined (and limited) the modern girl's freedom.[36] As the lives of Shuhua's literary contemporaries demonstrated, many experimented in amorous relationships that did not conform to previous standards. Whatever hesitations Shuhua had, they fell away as she and Julian plotted a winter rendezvous in Beijing.

They told others they would travel north to visit friends. In the end, Shuhua had a pressing reason to go. An old American friend was seriously ill. They'd met thirteen years earlier while escorting the painter Mary Augusta Mullikin around Beijing. She and her Tanté, as Shuhua affectionately called the older unmarried teacher, had often gone together to exhibits in the Forbidden City. Her Tanté had helped Shuhua practice English and encouraged her to continue writing and painting.

Shuhua left before Julian on the evening of January 3, 1936. As the train traveled northward, she observed the passing landscape and wrote to Julian. This letter, scrawled in pencil on paper now moth-eaten at the edges, survives as one of the few archived documents of the affair from Shuhua's perspective.

> I read [D. H.] Lawrence's short stories last night. . . . It is certainly the thing one like to read in a lonely trip with an absent mind. . . . The winter scenery is lovely. I am pleased to see again the wide plain scattering with white snow and filled with yellow grass. The shed of the distant mountains are lovely. I like its shape, standing out so clearly and "well cut." In the foot of the mountain there are always some forests with bare branches which match the rocky mountains. The river is frozen. I love to see the soft light of the ice again. Oh, how I love North China! What a world![37]

In a long postscript, her mood shifted. She had spent the afternoon reading a collection of short stories by Ernest Hemingway, recommended by Julian as similar to her stories. She disagreed, telling him, "I have not found great interest reading them." The woman in her compartment had disembarked, and she fell into gloomy reflection: "Scenery outside the window has lost its attraction, everything is dull in my mind. I fear it will be too late to see my sick Tanté tomorrow night. . . . It always happens that my fears prove to be true. . . . Well, I have to stop writing. It is not fair to tell one's sadness to some one who is going to his holiday."

Her fears came true. Just after she left Wuhan, her Tanté passed away. At the house on Ganmian Hutong, she sat by the stove feeling chilled. Her mother encouraged her to go out, but Shuhua thought that seeing the effects of recent military politics would depress her even more. On January 8, she wrote a eulogy, recalling her teacher's support of her as an aspiring young writer. She lamented everything lost since then. Her Tanté's courtyard, once filled with conversation, swaying bamboo, and a persimmon tree bedecked with pearls of orange, now stood locked and silent:

> Bamboo shadows flicker silently across the window, and camels pass by in the descending loneliness. . . . In the last few years, the deaths of relatives and

friends and the loss of national martyrs have added up in nearly equal ratio. My heart has already become a stalk of lightly frosted autumn grass; when the warm sun shines on the ground, I can live another day, but when yet another snowy wind blows by, I fear I can endure it no longer.[38]

The chill of Shuhua's first week in Beijing contrasted sharply with Julian's excitement at embarking on his holiday. To his friend Eddie he wrote, "Here I am in a dust storm, in the North Chinese plain, en route for Peking and a 20-days vac with my mistress."[39] Upon arriving, he checked into the German-run Hotel du Nord in the Foreign Legation quarter. Directly south of Ganmian Hutong, his hotel on Hatamen Street was a short rickshaw ride away. Shuhua finally let him make love to her in his room. In a letter to Vanessa dated January 18, written while Shuhua took a bath at a hot spring they'd gone to visit, Julian's ebullience overflowed:

> I'm enjoying life as I haven't done for years: Peking is one of the great capitals of the world—oddly like Paris, at times; could you imagine anything more perfect than coming to Paris with a mistress who really knows the town, is devoted to one, is perfectly charming, has an impeccable taste in food—it's the dream of a romantic-man-of-the-world. . . . Also, I am meeting Chinese intellectuals, and English, going to the theater, skating (badly on bad ice), and making love.[40]

His delight clashes with the despondency of Shuhua's essay written little over a week earlier. Had she gotten over her grief so quickly? Or had she thrown herself, devil may care, into an affair that would allow her to relive the Beijing of her youth? According to Julian's letters, she waved her hair, removed her spectacles, and dressed more extravagantly than usual. She guided him curio shopping, planned trips to sights outside of the city, and fed him sweet dried cabbage soup at her house one evening. He described the house as "a set of bungalows—no, let's say 'pavilions'—in a courtyard of flowering trees, now very bare and beautiful. The rooms are large, bare, uncarpeted, stove-heated, with big, one bow window[s]."[41]

Julian thrilled at going out on the town with Shuhua:

> You'll see that we are very happy and silly. . . . We eat together in restaurants, but alas in a Chinese restaurant you can't really flaunt a mistress, for you are all partitioned off in little rooms and cubicles. The chic Chinese restaurant of Peking has characters on the walls by a general and an ex-prime minister, and paintings by one of the most expensive living painters—on the walls of a room with a dusty stove, a stone floor, oil-papered windows. They really do treat the arts seriously.[42]

In Beijing, Julian looked up Harold Acton, a British writer and translator who taught at Beijing University. He hosted a dinner party for Julian, and his artistic taste impressed Shuhua. She took him and Julian to visit the painter Qi Baishi, famous for his spontaneous ink paintings. In an earlier letter to Vanessa, Julian had called him "the old man of Peiping who paints like Matisse."[43] Shuhua knew him from the parties she'd once helped her father host. Julian and Harold Acton inquired about purchasing paintings and were given a price by the foot. Julian chose a carp. Qi Baishi gave Shuhua two small paintings, which he had inscribed to her.

Late in January, the two lovers spent a day visiting temples in the Western Hills. A photograph of Shuhua shows her in a full-length fox fur coat and matching hat. She crouches between statues of cross-legged arhats, with an open smile on her face. But soon they had to consider returning to Wuhan. Julian answered concerns expressed by his mother, who worried about the risks he had taken. He raised the topic of marriage with Shuhua, but neither of them necessarily desired this outcome. They planned to covertly continue the relationship in Wuhan. To Eddie, Julian predicted that Shuhua would end up divorced if their affair became public knowledge. In what sounds like a rationalization to himself, he wrote that such a result would not endanger her, since she "is lucky enough . . . to both own a good deal of property, and to be easily able to earn her living by writing and painting."[44] To Vanessa, he defended her as "too proud to do anything like clinging" and announced she had a plan to go to America in a year to spend six months with her sister and then return by way of England.[45] He'd written earlier that she once wanted to study painting with Roger Fry but had been prevented from going abroad by her father.

On February 5, when Shuhua was in her midthirties, Julian turned twenty-eight. He complained to his mother, "I'm gloomy at being 28 and so little done. . . . Well, anyway I've got two years before I'm thirty . . . somehow or other I must get my incongruous box of tricks together. . . . The thing to do really, I believe, would be to write a biography, since that's what people like nowadays. Shall I . . . with Sue's help, invent a Chinese personage and invent a life of him?"[46]

China had become a stage upon which Julian could perform himself and become the sentimental hero of a biography. With Shuhua as his native "secretary-interpreter," he could produce a convincing account of how journeying abroad had led to his emotional development.[47] In England critics had reviewed his poetry with middling praise; perhaps by writing in a new genre, he might find a place in British literature. Back in Wuhan, a letter reflecting on their holiday revealed a sense of deflation: "I thought China would be an adventure, but I see it's going to be a period of self-inspection and meditation."[48]

If Julian seemed to care little about consequences, his mother and Eddie Playfair sent letter after letter urging him to be more circumspect. He'd written so openly of the affair that they feared gossip might travel back to Wuhan via England. Vanessa reprimanded him:

> You talk of Sue's getting a divorce—but what about the child? Then if it's true, as indeed I'm sure it must be, that you didn't want a *permanent* liaison with her, what would happen when it stopped on your side? Because if she's 10 years older than you it would, even if not tragic, surely be very difficult for her to find something else—I can see no end to it that isn't rather disastrous *if* you get too tied to each other either by scandal or by breaking bonds that are difficult to break without leaving her terribly in the lurch.[49]

In Wuhan, they disguised their affair as a work relationship. Before the trip to Beijing, Julian had begun helping translate Shuhua's stories into English. He'd also sent Vanessa an essay by Shuhua, on the difference between Western realism and Chinese ink painting and the Chinese practice of merging visual and textual expression. Vanessa tried, without success, to get the article published in England, but a reciprocal exchange of art and literature began. She sent one of her watercolors to Shuhua, who hung it in her living room opposite the Fry lithograph. Julian sent translations of Shuhua's stories to England, hoping to introduce her writing to a British audience.

Julian described for Eddie their translation process:

> I call it translating but it's a queer business really only possible given our very peculiar conditions. She turns her own Chinese into English—a quite comprehensible very grammatical language. Then I cross-examine her on the exact shade of meaning she wants, which usually includes some literal character translation. . . . Having got the exact idea of the meaning, I proceed to invent an English sentence and type it, putting in a good deal, particularly tenses, after expanding compressed words into images and supplying roughly parallel English idioms and conventions etc.[50]

Literary scholar Patricia Laurence argues that the way Julian unpacked Shuhua's compact language, especially her use of metaphorical proverbs, partially erased the elegant writing style she was known for in China.[51] By making her writing more accessible, Julian helped Shuhua cultivate a coveted literary connection with the West. He also admitted to Eddie that he hoped to make a name for himself: "I shall get my place in literary history, after all, as an important formative influence of the third period of her works."[52] The stories he helped translate were all written before they met, making this "third period of her works" the interpretation of them for a British audience. Translations of three stories, including "What's the Point of It?" and "A Poet Goes Mad," appeared in the *T'ien Hsia Monthly*, whose editors had published seven of Julian's poems the previous fall. In the spring of 1936, Julian sent the stories to writer David Garnett, who sent the typescripts on to Vanessa and suggested she try placing them in *The London Mercury*. She was again unsuccessful.

In his modern English literature course, which Shuhua continued to attend, Julian began introducing Bloomsbury writers. He wrote to his aunt Virginia, "I get a good deal of quiet fun, too, out of lecturing on all of you: Goldie, Maynard, Bertie I've done so far: Clive and Roger for next week."[53] But Julian's impression of Wuhan as a "Chinese Bloomsbury" soured. He derided his students and colleagues, claiming a primitive sentimental streak corrupted their critical faculties. In a letter to Virginia, his racism became clear: "I'm conducting an anti-sentiment and fine writing campaign, which they badly need. They seem to lap down the worst products of romanticism like negroes debauched with trade gin. That's what comes of living by sensibility alone."[54] Arguing Western superiority to Vanessa, he accused them of the quality he feared most in himself: "They're almost like savages sometimes in the way their intuitions can get debauched. . . . I feel that we're far better at understanding them than they us."[55] Julian conveniently overlooked the many Chinese, including most of the Wuhan University faculty, who had spent years in the West, learning to speak and write in English much better than he could in Chinese and becoming well tutored in Western culture.

The Bloomsbury modernists occasionally ventured beyond Europe, but travel served as a form of self-exploration, from which they could return assured of their cultural standing in the world. The voyages of their Chinese contemporaries arose out of Western imperial designs upon China and anxiety about the future of Chinese culture. As editor of the *Xiandai wenyi*, Shuhua called for modern Chinese literature worthy of the "global forest." Julian found his students' writing too imitative of certain branches of the "global forest" for inclusion. His correspondence reveals the persistence of a colonial mindset even among British liberals. In letters to Julian, Virginia Woolf compared China to blue-and-white porcelain, an example of how Chinese export ware designed to please a Western eye had come to represent the Chinese. She used this material sign of colonial circulation as an orientalizing metaphor: "Do you make friends with the Chinks—the students I mean? It all seems like a seraphic scene on a blue china plate to me. Here we never stop facing facts."[56] A few months later, she repeated the comparison: "I feel instinctively that China is a little like a blue pot; love a little flowery; learning a little scented."[57] She encouraged Julian to consider China as a way to enhance his personal development: "I expect in after years the reality will seem much more exciting than it does now. It will make a background. In fact I think you are much to be envied. I wish I had spent three years in China at your age."[58]

Julian saw Shuhua every morning when she came over to his house. He sent his servants away on errands, but they constantly feared discovery. Shuhua tried to prevent Julian from seeing other female friends or accepting invitations to gatherings she couldn't attend. Julian confided in Vanessa about her obsessive nature: "She's got the unreflecting egotism of most writers, so that she sees every situation in purely personal terms. . . . Rather like Virginia, perhaps; she makes pictures of people but doesn't ever get hold of an alien mood or tone—all Virginia's people live inside her own world."[59]

With the affair drained of its early excitement, Julian turned to his dream of becoming a man of action. Reality lay for him in Europe, even though this position required a willful blindness to local tensions. Japanese troops in northeast China threatened aggression, and the Guomindang continued to push for a centralized nation-state while the Communists organized at their Yan'an base. Unwilling to delve into the complexities of Chinese politics, Julian followed the rise of right-wing dictatorships in Europe through newspapers and letters, and felt drawn to pursue military experience there in the fight against fascism. When rumors of civil war circulated in Wuhan or when anti-Japanese student strikes caused the university president and deans to threaten resignation, Julian's main concern was that Shuhua would move away to the new wartime campus in Sichuan.

He shot ducks, had a sailboat built for excursions on nearby lakes, and searched for paintings and bronzes to add to his collection. In June, he left Wuhan for a trek with a student and an English geologist. They traveled upriver to Sichuan and on to Mount Emei. He sent a letter from Chongqing to Vanessa, enclosing a poem that referred to his relationship with Shuhua.

Post Coitum

Across, between, th' entangling net,
  Fragile Venus, bothered Mars,
The meshes of the trap are set,
  Red-rusted as the tidal stars.
Penetration Nature yet
  Admits; integument debars:
Sepia crustacea can beget
  As well amid their clicketing wars.

> Crab-limbed lock in ocean hold
>   Of saline mucus foundering deep;
> Escape, sea gale winged through the cold
>   Red sunsets, black bent trees, the steep
> English bird-voiced cliffs; till old,
>   Tangled across the bars, we sleep.[60]

This sonnet full of ocean metaphor charts an almost antagonistic sexual union, of entrapment rather than merging. He wrote it while separated from Shuhua, an escape from their "clicketing wars," and returned through verse to England, the comfort of home, and the deep emotions he felt for his mother, to whom he sent the poem instead of Shuhua.

To Shuhua, he wrote urging her to work on the autobiography he had suggested. His notion of her helping him invent a Chinese personage for a biography had switched to encouraging her to write about herself. He'd first written to his mother about the idea several months earlier. She would write about her childhood, and Julian would translate the book into English. He believed that Shuhua could make some money, enough for a cushion should her marriage fall apart, by selling the book in the United States and England. After Shuhua described for him a chapter on how her father's sixth concubine entered the family, he declared to Vanessa, "Absolutely fascinating—I imagine Virginia would adore having her passion for odd facts about other people really satiated for once."[61]

During his travels, Julian observed more of ordinary Chinese life but reacted with neither empathy nor political interest but rather with repulsion: "I have violent fluctuations of feeling about the country, which is often charming to look at, sometimes produces a beautiful human being and more often works of art, but is so squalid, diseased and populous it can give one the creeps, and one feels they are just a pullulation of bacteria."[62]

Toward the end of the summer, Julian flew from Chengdu to Beijing for a reunion with Shuhua. In May, he had described for Vanessa his itinerary, ending in the north where he would "join Sue and her sister, perhaps in a temple near Peking."[63] Shuhua had learned that Amy would be visiting from the United States and scheduled her summer travel accordingly. I don't know if Amy met Julian Bell that August in Beijing—perhaps while visiting the temple where she bought paintings for her Indianapolis home—but I assume that she guessed the truth of Shuhua's relationship with Julian and her half-formed plan to travel to England by way of the United States. Shuhua had even considered applying for a job at the University of Kansas. Amy would have been exasperated, warning Shuhua of the tragedy she courted by letting romantic tendencies guide her life. And Shuhua would have dismissed Amy as small-minded and incapable of emotional depth.

Julian stayed again at the Hotel du Nord, but this time Beijing offered few romantic pleasures. Chen Xiying and Xiaoying had come along, making private meetings difficult, and Shuhua spent several days in the hospital for a minor operation. Julian referred to the problem as "feminine troubles" but assured his friend Eddie it wasn't due to pregnancy. Still, Shuhua spent time in Beijing buying presents for his family, including a Manchu lady's court dress for his sister. Julian wrote letters and shopped, buying two small fresco pictures similar to the ones Amy purchased. In U.S. newspapers, he read about Spain and the July outbreak of civil war between the Second Spanish Republic and conservative Nationalists. Opposed to liberal British pacifism, he grew determined to volunteer for the Spanish Republican Army, but had at least one more year of a contract with Wuhan University to fulfill.

In early October, Julian wrote to Eddie from Wuhan that he thought many at the university already suspected the nature of his relationship with Shuhua. A few weeks later, Xiying confronted Shuhua about the amount of time she spent with Julian. A chilly silence between them ensued, with Xiying only able to communicate to her through a journal he left out for her to read. He told her she had to decide where her loyalties lay. Plagued by insomnia, Shuhua experimented with sleeping medicine and purchased a vile of rat poison. Her dramatic suicide threats replicated the method the mothers in her father's household had used to protest an untenable situation. The first stanza of an unfinished and undated poem in Julian's diary suggests her torment at this time.

> My love sleeps not in her cold bed
> The curtains flap like waves
> The phantoms chase through her head
> Where grace inhabits, beauty lives.[64]

Whether Chen Xiying showed up at Julian's house one late October day on purpose or by accident, he caught Julian and his wife in the act. He smashed the windows over the door and tried to force his way into the bedroom. Julian described the unraveling events to Vanessa on October 31, 1936:

Well, for the facts; we were caught—a ridiculous scene reflecting credit on no one; I thought it very comic at the time—so indeed it was—but don't feel like describing it now. Then, an éclaircissement, and a provisional agreement, finally decided this evening—or provisionally finally. Her husband behaved very reasonably considering what an idiotic position he was put in, and that he was pretty much bouleversé, not having got the full truth till the last moment. He offered the obvious alternatives of a divorce by consent—an easy and private affair—a separation without a divorce or returning to him and breaking completely with me. She has chosen the last. I am going to resign—to ease the tension—on perfectly indifferent grounds; I shall say my family want me to return for undisclosed reasons, presumably disgraceful, and shall tell my friends that I want to return for political reasons.[65]

Shuhua did not hold up her part of the bargain. She wrote secret letters to Julian and contrived meetings behind Chen Xiying's back. Although rattled by her desperation, Julian reciprocated and even bragged to Eddie that she planned to write a history of the affair. Julian wrote that it might be an important work and added, "I shall have a raison d'être in literature after all."[66] Shuhua entertained the possibility of escaping to America, where she could stay with Amy, but in the end simply bought a ticket on the Hankou-Beijing line.

In her absence, Julian spent time with two young women who had recently arrived at Wuhan University. Liao Hongying and Innes Jackson originally met as students under Margery Fry at Somerville College. Hongying had returned to China to lecture in the Wuhan University College of Agricultural Science, and Innes was a student of classical Chinese. Julian invited them over to his house for long dinners and tried to revive his Don Juan reputation by flirting with both.[67]

However, the volcano in Beijing, as Julian described Shuhua to Eddie, still threatened. She sent letters detailing her misery and plans to return to Wuhan. Fearing a confrontation with Chen Xiying that would lead to a public scandal, Julian advised her to stay put. He didn't realize that Shuhua had also written to her husband requesting another meeting with Julian, which Xiying rejected as too painful for him. Shuhua responded indignantly to Julian's attempt to counsel her, accusing him of treating her like a child. Julian wrote back in the form of a typed business letter, which he told Vanessa was a precautionary measure lest someone besides Shuhua open it.

> Dec 12 [1936]
>
> Dearest Sue
>
> You [sic] letter scolding me made me very cross, and tho' I'll try not to go on and scold you back, I can't say nothing about it. I don't in the least see what all the fuss is about, and why you should try to say unkind and wounding things as you do and tell me that I shall regret my behaviour when I am unhappy myself and so on. You could have prevented the whole trouble if you had simply taken the trouble to tell me the truth. . . . Considering everything that has happened, I think I was fully justified in supposing that you were going to do a very stupid thing, and in trying to prevent you. . . .
>
> And I think that you are simply silly about saying I treat you as a child and a person who has to be looked after. You know perfectly well that I have always

taken you extremely seriously, that I have often taken your judgment against my own, that I have accepted your advice about people and the university, and that I allowed you to run all the practical side of our affair. . . . Why should you think that means I don't treat you as a modern woman? Do you think it is disrespectful of me to think that I know more than you do about economics or strategy? And do you think you are superior to me when you show that you know far more about the arts than I do, and are a great writer, while I am not? . . .

Your Julian[68]

Soon after this string of letters, Shuhua returned to Wuhan, apparently against Xiying's wishes. She and Julian created a fantasy of future reunion in England, until Shuhua heard local gossip about Julian and Innes. Two days later, she left Wuhan again, slipping an unsigned letter under Julian's door.

I'm going away this evening. God knows when we could meet again. Within a few steps, we cannot see each other, it is so cruel! . . . I believe my going will do good for everyone here, at least I will not feel I am in somebody's way later on. The north west army is fighting fiercely with Japan and the bandits. The Peking-Hankow train may be cut off very soon. But instead of all this difficulties and my mother's and friends' advices, I still make up my mind to go to north, what a life I am carrying on! For whom I am doing this sort of torture? Nobody! Perhaps all my life will suffer the same thing.[69]

In the midst of this turmoil, the last issue of the *Xiandai wenyi* came out. A farewell essay on December 29, 1936, celebrated the success of ninety-five issues published over twenty-two months. The editorial board had initially feared a lack of submissions, but stories and essays streamed in from all parts of the country. The publication did not "die an illness" of literary cause but had met unexpected difficulties.[70] The essay does not indicate their nature, which could have been financial, political, or even Shuhua's personal troubles.

After a week or two in Beijing, Shuhua left for Shanghai. Julian wrote to her in both locations. Neither seemed capable of breaking things off. They planned for Julian to fly to Shanghai for a last meeting. When weather prevented Julian's departure, they switched their rendezvous to Hong Kong, where he would set sail for Europe in early February. In mid-January, Julian wrote, "Oh, and anyway, darling, we mustn't get 'last-timish' and end of the world about it: you'll come to England, we'll be happy and peaceful once again. . . . Only we must see each other again in China: I'll do anything to make certain of that."[71]

To conceal his plan to meet Shuhua, Julian pretended he would travel by river to Nanjing and then leave China from Shanghai. A friend in the Jardines shipping office printed a false departure notice in the newspaper. As dean, Chen Xiying was expected to officiate at Julian's farewell party. Julian had once described him in calculated terms: "A dry humour, a genuine taste—of a dry, narrow kind—for literature, and immense scholarship. Fond of his daughter. . . . Also was—and perhaps is—in love with his wife. . . . A proud—vain—stiff man: a frightening opponent—at least in intelligence and cunning."[72] Although some students accused him of firing their favorite foreign teacher, Dean Chen swallowed his pride and presented a professional face at the reception. In return, Julian secretly purchased a train ticket to Guangzhou.

Shuhua's trip south had a dual purpose. She had become embroiled in a family dispute. After her father's death, Shuhua's older half-sister, who had looked after Ling Fupeng's lychee garden in Guangzhou, laid claim to this now valuable piece of harbor frontage. Another sister with a large family in Mukden, most likely Shuzhi, took offense at the inequitable distribution of property, especially since First Sister had married into a wealthy Cantonese family, and enlisted Shuhua to fight for their shares. Julian, hoping victory would provide Shuhua with independent means, encouraged her involvement.

On January 29, 1937, a letter for a Mrs. Leo Chen arrived at the New Asia Hotel in Guangzhou. Workers at the university post office had opened several of Julian's letters in the past, and he resorted to this pseudonym for Shuhua. He addressed her as "Dearest Lucy" and brought up the issue of their future correspondence: "One thing you must consider is the address you will use when I am abroad. Could you have a post-office box here?"[73] The same day Shuhua read this letter, Chen Xiying sent Julian, on the eve of his departure, a handwritten note. Julian had made it known that he hoped to fight in Spain. Xiying intimated that he should not convey such news quickly to Wuhan, for fear that Shuhua would believe she had driven him to the dangers of battle. He also rejected a piece of advice Julian had given him—most likely that he separate from Shuhua.

> I still stand by my original decision. You could send any news about yourself to me or to both of us. It will not be suppressed.
>
> But if anything happened to you, I think it is much better to let silence be the token, or if it must be made known to us, let it be known in time. To communicate such news quickly does not do you any good and yet it will cause someone an eternal regret—that she would blame herself for what happened to you.
>
> I really don't think you know very much about me, for you had only the

version of me made up by someone to justify herself and I don't think you really know her. Of course you won't admit it. But it explains why your advice will not be acceptable to me.[74]

Reuniting in Guangzhou, Julian and Shuhua spent a few last days together in Hong Kong. They celebrated his birthday by strolling in the mountains and eating oranges straight from the tree; Shuhua talked of having exhibitions in China, America, and England. Innes Jackson had meanwhile arranged to travel back to England on the same ship as Julian, and he nervously prevented the two women from seeing each other at the dock. Julian continued to write to Shuhua during his weeks at sea and worried about her to Vanessa: "She's got no power at all of remembering a state of mind that she isn't experiencing, and when she's cheerful all's well, and when she's gloomy she's inconsolable."[75] Shuhua wrote to him two days after her return to Wuhan. Chen Xiying had learned from Liao Hongying of Julian's sailing from Hong Kong and accused her of seeing him.

When he saw me, he looked very sad and spoke little. I am afraid he hates me, but what can I do. I denied I had seen you. And I said I am not responsible if he wants to see me. I don't like to tell lies. But in such a situation, what can I say? I must stay in China till I can have enough money to go away for a certain time. I must work hard to get my share of my father's property. . . . I must work hard, I must write and paint. . . . It's still winter here, and my mind is winter too.[76]

Shuhua continued pretending Julian had pursued her to Guangzhou without her knowledge. On March 16, 1937, Chen Xiying sent a stinging reprimand to Julian in England.

I was very much pained, but still more surprised at your conduct. You definitely promised not try to write and still less to see S.H. unless she made you to. I thought that whatever might be your moral principles in some matters, an Englishman still had to keep his word and to consider his honour. I did not know that in throwing overboard some moral principles, such as loyalty to one's friends, you threw away all. No faith, no honour, no word to keep— nothing would prevent you to seek your selfish gratification. So you repeatedly wrote to her, followed her, pursued her and persecuted her, not only without her consent, but against her wish. A cad would be a cad, and I had only myself to thank for believing there might be still some good in him.[77]

Julian Bell once wrote Vanessa from China, "I like to imagine us all becoming very famous, and then, in some new Victorian age, our letters being published."[78] Little did he know how his intimacies would one day be displayed.

In early December of 2000, I purchased the *Beijing Youth News* at a subway kiosk. As I leafed through it, a headline caught my eye, "Hong Ying Recreates 1930s Legend," with a subtitle promising "revolution + love."[79] I soon realized that Hong Ying's novel centered on Ling Shuhua's affair with Julian Bell, material that I still struggled at the time to write about. The story contains elements of the Asian fetish story that audiences of U.S. personal ads and Hollywood movies seem too enamored of. I hesitated to deliver Shuhua up to their desiring eyes. Now, in a newspaper I casually picked up, the whole story appeared for public consumption.

K, the title of Hong Ying's book, revealed her sources and contravened accepted scholarly restraint from explicit mention of the affair. In the 1960s, the Bell family gave historian Peter Stansky access to Julian's unpublished letters for a biography. At the request of Ling Shuhua, the Bell family asked him not to reveal her identity when quoting from the letters. Stansky replaced Shuhua's name with the letter "K." Julian had a string of girlfriends in England before China, and Stansky also refers to them in ordinal fashion, "A," "B," and so forth. Anyone could put Stansky's *Journey to the Frontier* together with the published letters of Julian Bell and read between the lines, but Hong Ying's novel transgressed outrageously. While claiming her book was fictionalized, she capitalized on interest that could be piqued by disclosure of its historical basis. In *K*, she thinly disguised Ling Shuhua as Lin and Chen Xiying as Cheng; Julian remains Julian. The *Beijing Youth News* article I read revealed the "true identities" of her characters and made the titillating claim that Chinese readers could now learn about the real affair.

A month earlier Zhao Yiheng, a University of London lecturer in modern Chinese literature, had published an article titled "Julian and Ling Shuhua" in the Guangzhou *Southern Weekend*.[80] Zhao, not coincidentally Hong Ying's husband, described the novel as based on historical fact and gave an overview of the intimacies that linked Ling Shuhua to Julian Bell. The essay ran with period photographs of the two. His article was well timed to garner publicity for the book's upcoming release, and papers such as the *Beijing Youth News* and *Sichuan Youth Daily* picked up the story. The Chinese literary magazine *Writer* published a preview chapter, revealing the extent of Hong Ying's invention when it came to the novel's sex scenes, in which she endowed her protagonist with mystical Daoist erotic powers. Even Julian could only refer to those behind-closed-doors moments through the metaphor of "sepia crustacea."

Ling Shuhua's daughter Chen Xiaoying protested to the Chinese press from London, where Hong Ying also resides, claiming the book slanderously portrayed her mother as wanton and her father as impotent. In the spring of 2001, she filed proceedings in the Beijing Haidian District People's Court against Hong Ying for defaming her parents. In defense of her novel, Hong Ying declared she meant no harm. Of her fictionalized character, she told the press, "Lin is one of the very few women at that time to shake off the shackles of traditional ideas; she should be considered a heroine of feminism."[81] However, by focusing solely on the erotic details of Ling Shuhua's private life, she trivializes her as a writer. When the Julian of the novel presents Lin with a poem one night, it is a direct quotation of the sonnet "Post Coitum" that Julian Bell sent to Vanessa in 1936. In exchange for his literary offering, Lin gives him the most gratuitously imagined sex of the novel.

For all its fictional embellishments, the most shocking aspect of *K* is its lack of imagination when it comes to the psychological development of Lin's character. That Hong Ying tells the story from the perspective of Julian rather than her female protagonist is the result of lifting structure and innumerable details straight out of Julian Bell's published letters, while ignoring the archive of Ling Shuhua's writing. She squanders the imaginative possibility for which biographers so envy novelists.

The Beijing court overseeing the case brought by Chen Xiaoying against Hong Ying rejected the suit in July 2001 on the grounds that both parties were British citizens. Chen Xiaoying took her case to the Changchun People's Court, adding as codefendants the Changchun-based magazine *Writer* and the *Sichuan Youth Daily*. Both had published segments of *K*. The court delivered a final verdict in December of 2002, ruling in favor of the plaintiff. The judge ordered Hong Ying to pay a fine and publish a public apology. The court's decision was based on a provision on defamation in the General Principles of Civil Law. In 1988, a woman sued over a fictional story that included her late daughter, and the court established a landmark decision when it awarded her damages. A subsequent 1993 interpretation by the Supreme People's Court upheld this verdict and confirmed that cases could be brought by direct relatives for damages to the reputation of dead ancestors, within three generations of their death.[82] This precedent differs from Western legal codes, in which all defamation actions cease with the death of individuals involved. Chen Xiaoying told reporters, "It's in our cultural history, that when anyone should defame our ancestors or our parents or grandparents, it's like defaming ourselves."[83] She later told me that she would never have gone through the long and expensive legal ordeal if Hong Ying hadn't publicly connected *K* to her parents. She fought not to protect her mother's reputation but to redeem her father's endless, silent suffering.

Shuhua did not separate from Xiying despite Julian's appeals. She did not have the means or will to leave that Julian had presumed. She stayed with

Xiying to save face and her reputation in China. On Luojia Mountain, they waited for news from the north. A year earlier, Wuhan students had threatened a strike in support of Beijing faculty and students arrested as Communist sympathizers after a Guomindang raid on Qinghua University. Now, both parties issued propaganda for a second United Front, while the Japanese observed their maneuvers. During this period of wary calm, Shuhua tried to restore some semblance of domestic peace. In May, she published a short essay titled "Xiaoying" in a publication called *Youth World*. She recounted the relief of waking up to the sun one spring morning after weeks of rain. The trees glistened and sparrows chirped. Walking down a hill near home with Xiaoying, she listened to her daughter calculate the number of days until her father's birthday. After dinner, afraid that she would forget the date, the little girl went to their desk and wrote a few sentences on a piece of paper: "Next Sunday we will cross the river to eat out, watch a movie, and go shopping. Why? Because it's father's birthday."[84]

As an adult Xiaoying says she can't remember her mother ever holding her or expressing affection toward her. She has a scar on her back from where Shuhua pinned a diaper through her skin, failing to notice until she had to rush her infant daughter to the hospital. Shuhua claimed that as a fetus Xiaoying had pulled on her intestines and made them too long; she blamed her for the operation she had in Beijing in 1936. Xiaoying remembers it was her father who cuddled her as a child. He played with her and made her feel loved. That Shuhua often wrote from the perspective of a child does not mean she tried to understand her own daughter's emotional realm or the impact of her actions on it. Of Julian, Xiaoying recalls only that he once tossed her and a friend into the lake from his boat, not realizing they couldn't swim. The impression of almost drowning remains vivid. Xiaoying announced to her mother one day on Luojia Mountain that she was going to commit suicide in East Lake. She now surmises that she got this idea as a child by overhearing her mother's suicide threats during the affair. The affair did not, however, end with Shuhua's suicide, which is how Hong Ying brings her novel to a close.

No one in Wuhan knew it yet, but Julian had gone to Spain. As a compromise for Vanessa's sake, he arranged to work as a driver for the Spanish Medical Aid. In a Republican offensive to the west of Madrid, Julian evacuated wounded soldiers in a small Chevrolet ambulance. On July 18, 1937, as he drove down a road near Villanueva de la Cañada, a bomb hit. Shrapnel lodged in his chest. A friend at the hospital where he was taken claimed that Julian whispered, before dying, "Well, I always wanted a mistress and a chance to go to war, and now I've had both."[85]

· Eighteen ·

Rice Porridge

A little over a year after Amy and KK returned to Indianapolis, they held in their shaking hands more lightweight, airmail stationery bearing bad news. These letters left them cut off from home, stranded on the other side of the Pacific.

On July 7, 1937, the Japanese attacked the Marco Polo Bridge southwest of Beijing. Within weeks they took control of Beijing. Soldiers with rising-sun armbands marched down Chang'an Avenue. Tianjin and Baoding also fell, and Japanese troops advanced south along the Beijing-Wuhan and Tianjin-Nanjing train lines. By the end of August, fighting would engulf Shanghai. Amy described the situation as if she had experienced it herself: "The Japanese started war in China, that's what prevented us from going back home for good. Do you understand bombing? You feel nothing, you just feel like everything's gone. A bomb doesn't pick your house or their house. It comes down on one big place. Bomb."

Li Ruolan fled Beijing and moved to the family's vacant house in Tianjin's German Concession, thinking that this foreign-controlled area would be safer. Moved by the plight of refugees with nowhere to turn, she gave shelter to as many as she could. Some had infected wounds and suffered from untreated diseases. Amy believed her mother contracted pneumonia in the crowded conditions and died among strangers.

Amy linked the deaths of her siblings in Kobe's Nunobiki Falls with her mother's demise; her voice trembling with anger, she blamed the Japanese for all these losses. She told me that Shuhua buried their mother's ashes in the Western Hills. Shuhua planned to eventually move her remains to the Ling tomb in Panyu, but when she returned years later, she couldn't find the grave among the tall, dry grass. The university where I taught in the early 1990s is near the Western Hills. During my first fall in China, I often bicycled down the dusty road toward the university, gazing at the hills, their faint outline rising behind fuming factory smokestacks. As I pedaled past roadside grape and pear sellers calling out the price of their sweet, late-season fruit, I would think of my grandmother wondering where her mother lay.

KK's mother also passed away in 1938. For years he sent money every month to his brother in Shanghai to care for her, especially after her cancer returned. But according to Amy, this brother, a newspaper manager who aspired to high society, used it all for himself. He bought only a simple coffin for their mother and deserted the body at a local temple. When informed by relatives of his brother's disrespectful behavior, KK immediately wired money to an uncle for a proper funeral. Amy claimed the Communists later jailed this brother because of his involvement with a Guomindang paper. He disappeared and was never heard from again. When I asked my mother if this account sounded plausible, she had no answer. She explained her inability to comment by recalling a high school assignment she once received to draw a family tree. It wasn't until she approached her father one evening with this homework task that she even learned her father had a brother. She remembered the shock of registering the absence of this would-be uncle from her consciousness. With a ruler and pencil, she diligently drew a framework of lines, branching downward in spare vertical descent, and recorded her father's brief outline of a family, a geometry of relations of which she knew nothing more than their orderly unfolding on a blank piece of paper.

After her father's death decades later, my mother cleaned out his office. She discovered a plain white envelope in the middle drawer of his large metal desk. On the face of the envelope, he had scrawled "My Mother's Burial." She removed four black-and-white snapshots from their resting place. They show a group of men struggling to carry a large wooden coffin up a hill. The sun glares down on their creased fedoras, hat brims throwing their faces into shadow. Three thick ropes are wrapped around the width of the coffin and attached to wooden poles laid across the lid. The men bear the poles on their shoulders. A field of leafy crops fills the space they have crossed. The final photograph shows a mound of dry earth with a double-arched stone facade. The men in hats slide the coffin into an opened archway. A stone tablet between the two arches issues a fleeting piece of information to the generation left in ignorance. Two columns of chiseled characters, inked in black, reveal that KK's father was Chen Ruiqing and his mother's maiden name was Zhou.

Amy and KK gradually accepted Indianapolis as more than a temporary way station. They proceeded to buy their way into the American dream, detailing for a local architect a two-story, redbrick house. They ordered furniture and trees and rosebushes. Just months before the birth of their second child at the end of 1937, they moved in. Their house on Hampton Drive, across the street from Butler University, was a typical American colonial with a screened-in porch off the living room and a wooden swing in the backyard.

One evening, after Tom had been put to bed and KK closed the door to his study, Amy sat alone in the living room, gazing at the row of framed temple paintings she'd brought back from Beijing. In the creeping darkness of late autumn, she squinted at the fading colors of Buddha's transformations.

Mei-Fong Janet Chen was the child her parents knew would be American, with a permanent address in the country of her birth. Unlike her brother, who once uttered the words for "grandmother" and "auntie" in Cantonese and Mandarin, my mother did not travel to China until adulthood, soon after China reopened its doors to foreign tourists. I waited as a child at the airport, where she disembarked wearing hiking boots and carrying a large backpack full of film. What I know about the second half of my grandmother's life comes as much from her stories as from my mother's memories of their years on Hampton Drive.

Mei grew up an obedient child, trained not to talk back, never daring to ask about her parents' past until assigned to construct a family tree. She was a conscientious student, so she remembers clearly the obstacle that family caused in grade school when the teacher administered an intelligence aptitude test. My mother raced through the multiple-choice questions, until one stumped her: "What relation is your uncle's grandfather's son to you?" Having never known a grandfather or an uncle, she stared blankly at the question. She furtively glanced at the other students bent over their desks. Was this a test of who was American or not? Guessing, she circled "cousin" and moved on.

The theme of generational silence recurs throughout Asian American literature, as do stories of tearing down this wall of silence erected in the name of love and protection. Determined roots seekers, Asian American authors venture into the foreign territory of the past. They come to uneasy terms across vast differences in experience and restore some sense of continuity. As much as I want to reach this resolution, I cannot because I have witnessed my grandmother's cruelty as well as her strength. These are the pieces of Amy's character that I can only represent in irreconcilable contradiction.

I have watched my grandmother drive my mother to despair, relentlessly criticizing her every decision and concocting stories about unfilial behavior that exist only in the darkest corners of her imagination. Although Amy demanded freedom of choice for herself with a life that willfully diverged from that of her mother, she expected—with an immigrant's determination to be accepted—her daughter to conform to a rigid standard of American female success, including stylish dress, straight As, and self-sacrificing, attentive care of her husband, children, and parents.

Mei-Fong Chen, Indianapolis, ca. 1944. Photo by Amy Ling Chen.

Amy's version of the American nuclear family contained, however, remnants of her upbringing. Her relationship with her parents was more formal than one of active care; she and her siblings were nursed and mothered by *amahs*. When her children were young, Amy similarly hired a series of women to help care for them. A young German woman spent afternoons with Tom for two years. When Mei was five, Hazel Bell, a stately woman with freckled, light brown skin and waved curls, entered the household as a second mother. She provided Mei with an alternative model of female strength, as well as an education about U.S. social history that neither textbooks nor her parents taught. An African American woman employed as a housekeeper by a Chinese American family for over thirty years, Hazel instructed Mei in the ways of America's racial hierarchy and its malevolent undertow—lessons that Amy's attitude toward her "hired help" painfully reinforced.

There are times I find it extremely difficult to write about my grandmother for I feel shame as well as pride, not because she is too Chinese but because she too perfectly adopted the racist attitudes of middle-class white America. She played the assimilation trick of too many immigrants, who blend in and make their way up the ladder of success by adopting mainstream, white supremacist ideas. The difficult terrain of my mother's memories of certain childhood lessons makes a wholly redemptive narrative impossible.

Amy began to work less at the Lilly research lab. She filled her days instead with household chores and childcare, the concerns of a middle-class Indianapolis housewife. She did the grocery shopping, sometimes driving the 180 miles to Chicago's Chinatown to purchase bags of rice, canned goods, and tofu. She joined the PTA. She signed her children up for Sunday school because everyone else in the neighborhood did.

While Hazel prepared lunch in the kitchen and washed laundry in the basement, Amy typed lectures for the local ladies' club under a pool of light at her desk. Between the typewriter pecks of her careful English, in these moments of her privileged retreat, it is not difficult to imagine her repeating the question of her sister's story: "What's the point of it?" She responded to these attacks of boredom and despair by making herself up, dressing to the hilt, and going shopping.

Indianapolis in the 1940s did not have a Chinese community. One afternoon downtown, Amy met another Chinese family. Walking down the street with bags from L. S. Ayres department store, she saw the sign for a new restaurant called Bamboo Inn. Entering from the sunny sidewalk, her eyes adjusted slowly to see a plain room filled with round tables and red vinyl chairs. A woman her same age and height led her to a corner table. She handed her a menu and asked, in English, "Are you Chinese?"

Ann Jung worked as a hostess and her husband Harry as a cook. They had recently moved from Oakland, California, where they said it was too hard to make it in the restaurant business. Years later they bought their own restaurant on the north side, near the state fairgrounds. The Chens became regular customers at the Bamboo Inn and later at the Mandarin Restaurant, where the two families shared meals. My grandmother often narrated the friendship through a food that I also love:

> I gave the Jungs the name of their restaurant. They used to work in the Bamboo Inn but got very little per hour. I told them to start their own restaurant, up north on Thirty-Eighth Street and then gave the name for the sign, Mandarin Restaurant. Ann asked me the first time whether I am Cantonese or not. I said, "I was born in Canton. I can talk Cantonese if you want." So we began to talk in Cantonese. And then she asked whether I like *ham yu*. I said, "I haven't tasted that in so long." So she told me, "I'm going to fix some salty fish next time you come in." But we couldn't eat outside. We had to eat inside the kitchen, because that fish has a very strong smell. She and I just loved that dish.

Amy's American-born daughter turned out, much to her mother's dismay, to be not only a picky eater but also a queasy automobile passenger. Determined to cure Mei of her stationary sensibility, Amy lined the back seat of the family's Buick sedan with newspaper. She picked up her four-year-old and settled her on top of the papers. Then she climbed behind the steering wheel and began to drive, stopping and starting abruptly at intersections. As Mei whimpered, Amy cruised south on Meridian Street out of town and picked up speed, gliding between cornfields and over rolling wooded hills. When Mei leaned over and vomited repeatedly onto the newspapers, Amy kept driving. She drove for hours, until she was certain that her daughter was no longer nauseous with motion. Her friends told her she was cruel, but Amy was convinced that her method was the only surefire one for this second-generation brand of weakness.

My mother's first memory is of her parents huddled close to the wooden console radio in the living room. The Japanese had bombed Pearl Harbor on December 7, 1941, four days before her fourth birthday, and she grew up with the somber sound of war statistics broadcast into the living room each night. She remembers crouching in the dark, the lights turned off and the curtains pulled, with her brother under the kitchen table while air-raid sirens wailed in the background. The children of their neighbors, the Hudsons, the Rosses, and the Berkleys, also dove under the table during air-raid practices.

But there were other wartime worries, unique in the neighborhood to their family.

On December 22, 1941, *Life* magazine ran an article entitled "How to Tell Japs from the Chinese: Angry Citizens Victimize Allies with Emotional Outburst at Enemy." A few pages earlier in the same issue, "The Story of Christ in Chinese Art: Scholars at Peking University Make a Christmas Portfolio for *Life*" featured Chinese scroll paintings of the stages of Christ's life. Henry Luce's publication supported the American war effort by emphasizing the congeniality of the Chinese as allies, while demonizing the Japanese. The presumption that Chinese and Japanese Americans adhered to the politics of their "home" countries eventually led to the internment of Japanese American families, many who had considered themselves American for generations and sent husbands, brothers, and sons to the battlefront in U.S. uniform. In stereotyped phenotypic diagrams, which claim to be based on the "scientific objectivity" of physical anthropology, *Life*'s "how to" article identifies facial and bodily characteristics that distinguish Chinese from Japanese. The author implores readers to learn from these diagrams so as not to victimize those 75,000 U.S. Chinese "whose homeland is our staunch ally." In a caption beneath the photograph of a "Japanese Warrior," who is compared to a "Chinese Public Servant," readers are encouraged to see identifying clues: "Chinese wear rational calm of tolerant realists. Japs . . . show humorless intensity of ruthless mystics."[1]

Like the Chinese American journalist Joe Chiang, whose photograph is featured in the *Life* magazine article, KK often went to work with a button pinned to his lapel that read "I am Chinese, not Japanese." Strangers yelled "Jap" at them from their car windows. When Mei and Tom played in the front yard or pretended to drive in the Hudsons' army jeep, bouncing over rough imaginary roads in the vehicle parked in their neighbors' driveway, invisible and menacing voices sometimes yelled at them from the Butler University dormitory across the street. The transom of the front door to the Hampton Drive house held an arched glass window that looked onto the dining room. Before Sunday breakfasts, when the family ate large bowls of *xifan*, rice porridge with hard-boiled eggs, pickled cabbage, and cubes of tofu, Amy drew an improvised curtain tightly over the window so their neighbors would not see them eating with chopsticks.

They hid behind the facade of their solid redbrick American home, behind the maturing sweet gum tree in front, and behind the curtain over the front door window. The only intruders into this protected space were the nightly radio broadcasts and airmail envelopes bearing Shuhua's handwriting.

·Nineteen·

War Letters

𝒮huhua's wartime letters to Amy have disappeared, but another paper trail out of China remains from those years. A flurry of communication connected her to the other women in Julian's life. News of heavy casualties near Madrid reached Wuhan via Reuters on July 24, 1937, and listed Julian among the dead.[1] Shuhua may not have heard immediately because she and Chen Xiying were at a summit of intellectuals called by Chiang Kaishek at Mount Lu in Jiangxi province. Several months earlier, Guomindang troops had refused to continue fighting the Communists. Their dramatic kidnapping of Chiang Kaishek led to an agreement between the Generalissimo and Communist leaders to join forces in a second anti-Japanese United Front. Ten days after the Marco Polo Bridge attack, Chiang announced from Mount Lu the need to prepare for armed resistance.

Japanese planes began to appear over Wuhan that fall. In October, Shuhua joined a Wuhan University Women's Service League visit to soldiers wounded on the northern front. In a rare political commentary, she reported on their condition. "A Visit to the Hanyang Hospital for Wounded Soldiers" appeared in the November 1, 1937, issue of Tianjin's *National News*.

> Their wounds for the most part had already been operated on and they were in the stage of rest and medication. More than half of them were wounded by shells and bullets, or had been hit by shrapnel from a fragmenting bomb. The most painful were those hit in the bones of the arm, chest or leg, or the spine; there was danger that the bones were poisoned and would have to be removed. Some such patients had amputated limbs, while others lay in silent agony, their torsos in casts. No doubt they were worrying about their salvaged lives and how they would survive as cripples. Who says the Chinese are feeble? Here we saw two or three hundred soldiers, their painful wounds bandaged, but not once did we hear them moan or curse anyone.[2]

The following week, over two hundred Wuhan University faculty members and students attended a memorial for Julian, who had died of similar wounds. Shuhua had already shared her grief with Vanessa, and the two continued to exchange letters. On December 9, 1937, Vanessa wrote,

> I had a letter from you the other day, sending me some seeds. It seems so exciting that such lovely, tiny things should come all the way from China and will perhaps grow with red flowers. . . . I seem to be quite foolish about them, but I so liked your thought in sending them. . . . Anything you say to me is a help to me. Tell me too how you pass your time now—do you paint at all? And write? Or does the war upset life too much?[3]

The Japanese continued to advance southward. Chinese troops had already retreated from Shanghai. In nearby Wuxi, Chen Xiying's father died in a Japanese air raid. Xiying made the dangerous journey east for the funeral and to bring his mother and younger sister back to Wuhan. During his trip, the Japanese attacked Nanjing, which fell within days on December 13. The invading soldiers unleashed a frenzy of violence on the city that lasted for weeks. Foreign observers at the time estimated that twenty thousand women were raped, thirty thousand fugitive soldiers were killed, and twelve thousand civilians were murdered.[4] Although current estimates of the total number of Chinese casualties differ widely, none go below one hundred thousand. Refugees fled from the region, and the students and faculty members of northern Chinese universities began long treks toward the southwest. Deans served as commanders of their marching units. Engineering students set up radios along the way to listen for news broadcasts. Nankai, Qinghua, and Yanjing Universities joined to form a wartime campus in Kunming.[5]

Before the fall of Shanghai, workers had disassembled factory machinery and shipped the metal parts up the Yangzi River or overland on coolies' backs to be reassembled in Chongqing and Wuhan. Chiang Kaishek moved the capital from Nanjing to Wuhan, where he and Communist leader Zhou Enlai set up residence. Young recruits in quilted winter uniforms drilled in the streets. The Hankou film studio pumped out war pictures like *Fight to the Last*, using as props rifles and uniforms captured from the Japanese by the Communists' Eighth Route Army.[6] Japanese bombing targeted Hankou, the region's center of commerce and industry. Overcast skies provided the city with some protection, but when clearer spring weather arrived, air-raid sirens shrieked regularly. One Chinese general declared, "We will defend Wuhan as the Spanish did Madrid."[7]

Wuhan University remained outside the bombing perimeter, but nervous uncertainty pervaded the campus. The mood in their house on Luojia Mountain became tenser after Xiying's mother and sister moved in with them. Shuhua's sister-in-law had remained unmarried, devoting herself to Buddhism and to care for her aging mother. She ate a strictly vegetarian diet and spent several hours a day chanting sutras in Sanskrit.

Shuhua did not get along with them and fought with her husband. She found solace in reading and discovered, on a foray to the library, Virginia Woolf's *A Room of One's Own*. Reading the slim volume, she might have imagined herself a Newnham College student sipping wine with the author, discussing the difficulties of women who aspire to write fiction. She eventually wrote a letter describing the situation in Wuhan and asked Virginia what she would do in her place. Many weeks later a reply arrived, and then another.

52 Tavistock Square, W.C.1

5th April 1938

Dear Sue Ling,

I hope you have had the letter I wrote in answer to your first letter. I wrote only a few days after I had yours. Now Vanessa has just sent on your letter of March 3rd. I wish I could help you. I know that you have much more reason to be unhappy than we have even; and therefore how foolish any advice must be. But my only advice—and I have tried to take it myself—is to work. So let us think how you could fix your mind upon something worth doing in itself. I have not read any of your writing, but Julian often wrote to me about it, and meant to show me some of it. He said too that you had lived a most interesting life; indeed, we had discussed—I think in letters—the chance that you would try to write an account of your life in English. That is what I would suggest now. Your English is quite good enough to give the impression you wish to make; and I could change anything difficult to understand.

Will you make a beginning, and put down exactly anything you remember? As no one in England knows you, the book could be more free than usual. Then I would see if it could not be printed. But please think of this: not merely as a distraction, but as a work that would be of great value to other people too. I find autobiographies much better than novels. You ask what books I would advise you to read: I think the English in the 18th Century wrote in the best way for a foreigner to learn from. Do you like letters? There are Cowpers, [Horace] Walpoles; very clear and easy; Scotts novels; (Rob Roy); Jane Austen: then Mrs. Gaskells life of Charlotte Brontë: then among modern writers, George Moore's novels—they are simply written too. . . . I say nothing about politics. You know from what I said before how strongly the English are on your side but cannot do anything to help. We hear about China from friends here. But perhaps now there will be a change. The worst may be over.

At any rate please remember that I am always glad if you will write and tell me anything about yourself: or politics: and it would be a great pleasure to me to read some of your writing and criticise it: so think of writing your life, and if you only write a few pages at a time, I could read them and we could discuss it. I wish I could do more. We send you our best sympathy.

Yours

Virginia Woolf[8]

Around this time, friends of the Bloomsbury circle arrived in Wuhan. Novelist Christopher Isherwood and poet W. H. Auden were in China collecting material for a book about the Sino-Japanese War. On April 22, 1938, they visited Wuhan University and wrote about a tea party hosted for them: "Beneath their politely assumed gaiety the professors all seemed apprehensive and sad."[9] Shuhua presented them with fans she had painted that afternoon. Thick, accordion-folded paper opened into landscapes of East Lake, inscribed with the fragment of an old poem. "The mountain and the river in the mist not broken in pieces. / We should only drink and forget this immense sorrow." She had added two lines of her own, which she translated for them. "During this country's struggle / I paint in wonder to forget my sorrow."[10] She also pressed into Isherwood's hand a little box for him to take back to Virginia Woolf. A carved, ivory skull lay cushioned inside.

One week later, an air raid killed five hundred civilians in Hankou. In *Journey to a War*, the book Isherwood and Auden published in 1939, they describe the scene:

> Over by the other gate lie five civilian victims on stretchers, waiting for their coffins to arrive. They were terribly mutilated and very dirty, for the force of the explosion had tattooed their flesh with gravel and sand. Beside one corpse was a brand-new, undamaged straw hat. All the bodies looked very small, very poor and very dead, but, as we stood beside an old woman, whose brains were soaking obscenely through a little towel, I saw the blood-caked mouth open and shut, and the hand beneath the sack-covering clench and unclench.[11]

To block out the grim news, Shuhua decided to take Virginia Woolf's advice. She wrote to her that working on an autobiography would "make [her] recall all the happy hours with Julian when he was here."[12] She explained that due to the frequent bombing, she would leave soon for Sichuan.

Authorities had traveled that spring to inspect the site, a town almost one thousand miles west of Wuhan, where they would move the university. Chen Xiying moved his mother and sister temporarily to Chongqing, where they stayed with his younger brother. He then continued with the inspection team to Leshan, situated at the confluence of the Dadu, Min, and Qingyi Rivers in south-central Sichuan. The town's ancient name Jiading evoked a cultured past, evidenced by the Buddhist carvings that covered the stone cliffs of nearby Mount Emei. A female professor who had gone ahead wrote a letter to those awaiting evacuation about what to expect. Over a decade later, Shuhua wrote an essay in English remembering the woman's cautionary words.

> Kiating [Jiading] is a lovely little town. . . . The people are mostly pleasant and gentle looking, although they are very difficult to make friends with. This is

because some of them are natives of Szechuan, some come from Tibet, while others belong to the Mew-tze [Miao] tribes. . . . Yesterday I saw what appeared to be several black cats walking slowly across the street. When they came nearer I realized that they were rats! Enormous rats! When you come, bring as many tins as possible for storage, otherwise the rats will eat everything up. . . . I learned after I came that Kiating is a place which has suffered for centuries from a special kind of disease called Pa-ping that kills people in twenty-four hours. It is said to be caught if, while you are admiring the beautiful landscape, a puff of bitter and cold wind suddenly blows over you. . . . Do remember to bring your medicine boxes with you, when you come![13]

In June, a few days before their departure from Wuhan, two lily magnolias that Shuhua had planted on Luojia Mountain burst into white and purple flowers. In another later essay, she used a line of poetry by overthrown Tang emperor and poet Li Houzhu (936–978 CE) to describe the moment: "I shall never forget the hurried departure from the ancestral altar when the court musicians played a farewell song and my eyes, filled with tears, gazed at my maids."[14] On the appointed day, she and Xiaoying boarded a steamship at the Wuchang dock. As the boat packed with passengers and supplies moved through the Yangzi Gorges toward Chongqing, the stately outline of Yellow Crane Pagoda disappeared in the distance. Xiaoying's nose started bleeding and wouldn't stop for hours. A group of orphans dressed in identical clothing, sponsored by Sun Yatsen's widow Song Qingling, crowded the deck. Their chaperones led them in song to make them forget.

After a few days in Chongqing with Chen Xiying's brother, Shuhua and Xiaoying left on a small steamer and traveled further west, up the Min River. Their medicine kit included Lilly vitamins, sleeping pills, and antiseptic ointments sent by Amy. As they approached Leshan one August evening, a giant Buddha gazed down at them from narrow, heavy-lidded eyes. The massive carved figure, over two hundred feet tall, sat nestled in the side of the cliff, enormous hands on his knees. Leafy trees far above framed a contemplative face with long, drooping earlobes. Black whorls of sculpted hair covered his head. Moss crept over his tunic. Meeting the river's edge, his feet were larger than their boat. For more than a thousand years, this stone likeness of Maitreya, the future Buddha, had observed life in Leshan. Later Shuhua would reflect on this moment of beauty.

The surface of the river was pinkish orange. The river was full of sandy mud which flowed down from Mount Omei [Emei] and the Great Snow Mountains of Tibet, when the snow melted in the summer. This made the green mountains stand out against the evening sky. There were mountains on both sides of the river, all covered with green trees. . . . The whole side of a pinkish white cliff had been used to carve the Buddha.[15]

Shuhua's essays about Leshan written after the fact paint a pastoral scene, but in reality the Wuhan University evacuees struggled to adapt to their new environment. They lived at first in local teahouses and temples turned into makeshift housing. They cooked over wood fires and carried water uphill from the river. Chamber pots, diapers, vegetables, rice, and dishes were washed side by side on the pier. They purified drinking water with alum or a local herb and burned vegetable oil lanterns inside at night. When it rained, their leather city shoes caused them to slip and fall on the wet stones that paved the town's old streets. An essay Shuhua wrote during the first year at Leshan, "Scenes from Behind the Front Line," opens with a description of the chill night air penetrating their bamboo and mud walls and of the sicknesses that plagued them:

> The sound of coughing near and far fills the time when dreams should come. Their sounds, long and short, urgent and slow, are like the croaking of frogs in a pond on a summer night, only amplified by an anxious, labored mood. Which one is the breath of acute injury? Which one is influenza? Which one is whooping cough? Which one is the constant cough of tuberculosis?[16]

She reported that high school students in youth army caps paraded through town, waving flags on which they'd written patriotic slogans: "On the front bathe in blood to fight the war of resistance" and "Behind the front line diligently produce provisions." The cost of paper to make the flags had, like everything else, risen at an alarming rate. One student stood on top of a wooden teahouse stool and yelled, until beads of sweat ran down his face, about the need to seek revenge for slain compatriots. An old man remarked with ironic detachment that the burden of revenge had fallen on the shoulders of children.

After a month in Leshan, Shuhua wrote again to Virginia Woolf, sardonically commenting that a European might not understand her current attitude: "It's alright for us at present because I always think being a Chinese, one has to look for hardship, preparing the worst of luck, then by and by one may learn to amuse oneself with misery. . . . I have been very busy and unwell about some time, to look for a house or look after relatives all bore me to death, because I can't do my work as I want to."[17] Xiying, his mother, and his sister had joined them in Leshan. Shuhua searched the meager library holdings that had been transported to Leshan for models to guide her in writing an autobiography. She reread Marcel Proust's *Swann's Way* and *The Years*,

Watercolor of Leshan by Ling Shuhua, undated. Courtesy of Chen Xiaoying.

Virginia Woolf's recent novel chronicling the life of a British family. Shuhua wrote that these works inspired her, but she disliked *The Good Earth*, Pearl Buck's saga about a Chinese farming family, whose characters she found unconvincing.

When Virginia encouraged Shuhua by saying her work might be "of great value to people," she meant, of course, to Western readers. Shuhua's anxiousness to distinguish herself from Pearl Buck reveals some acknowledgment of the audience she had to satisfy, although her story would be autobiographical rather than fictional. She retreated into this realm of memory, of childhood composed through the forced simplicity of her English. She admitted that most of the book would be "about almost all thing I had seen, very little 'bout [what] I thought. Perhaps these will be more interesting for foreigners."[18] And she confided to Virginia, "If my book could give English readers some pictures of real Chinese lives, some impression about Chinese who are as ordinary as any English people, some truth of life and sex which your people never have a chance to see but is even seen by a child in the East, I shall be contented."[19] This hint of eroticism, repeated in other letters to Virginia, echoes Julian's advice that as a modern woman, she should write openly about sex. But rather than describing their affair, Shuhua delved into the relationships she had observed as a child. Eventually, the bawdier elements of the chapters she drafted in Sichuan—of Sixth Mother as a "wild cat" with several men at her beck and call; of Second Mother beating the night watchman's drum outside Li Ruolan's bedroom, where Father slept, to lure him to her bed instead; and of Father's friend being forced by his concubine to kneel for days before a pink handkerchief as punishment for philandering[20]—disappeared from the final manuscript of *Ancient Melodies*, its female characters tamed into jealous wives more overtly oppressed by patriarchy.

Obviously flattered by attention from an acknowledged modernist master whose work in translation had appeared frequently in *Crescent Moon*, Shuhua cultivated Virginia Woolf as a mentor as she once had Chen Xiying. She asked deferentially, "Will you allow me to call you my teacher or my tutor when I write to you?"[21] She wrote that she had just finished a chapter and would send it for criticism after copying it neatly.

Shuhua had already earned a name in China as a writer and editor. Why did she feel so compelled at this point to write a book in English? Julian had originally suggested an autobiography, and perhaps out of loyalty or guilt over his death, she committed to the project they once intended to work on together. This book would subtly recognize Julian's influence and help her foster connections with his family. At a bleak moment in China, she gambled on possible recognition in the West, knowing the value of a personal link to

Bloomsbury. Chinese literary politics at the time afforded little space for a writer like her, who remained invested in traditional Chinese aesthetics and the cosmopolitan dream of May Fourth modernism. Although she disdained the oppressive morality of Chiang Kaishek's New Life Movement and experienced occasional bursts of nationalist sentiment, she never sustained an active interest in politics or felt moved to write revolutionary literature as did some, like Ding Ling who'd fled to the Communists' base at Yan'an. The thesis of *A Room of One's Own*, that women must have money and privacy in order to write, provided a comforting return to May Fourth feminism. And writing an autobiography with Virginia Woolf as mentor kept her mind off the present "general disaster." She clung to this connection, a lifeline to a wider world of imagined ease and friendship with other talented women.

Virginia followed Julian's lead in pushing Shuhua toward an autobiography in English, thus revealing her own cultural biases. In her exhortation to work, Virginia never suggested that Shuhua continue to write fiction in Chinese or translate her short stories or those of other Chinese writers into English. Virginia presumed that Shuhua's most important audience was Western and could best learn about the East through an authentic account of her childhood in old China. At the end of July, Virginia wrote to thank Shuhua for the "lovely little box" that Christopher Isherwood had delivered.[22] In return, she sent two books, Mrs. Gaskell's life of Charlotte Brontë and essays by Charles Lamb: "I think Lamb wrote very good English prose—but do not bother to read it as an exercise; only for pleasure—The life of Charlotte Brontë will perhaps give you a feeling for the lives of women writers in England in the 19th century—their difficulties and how she overcame them."[23] In Virginia's description, the Brontë biography would provide Shuhua with a model of how to compose her life as a woman writer.

Days after Virginia mailed the books to China, Shuhua wrote again, enclosing the first part of her manuscript. She explained that translating her next chapters into English would take time. She also worried that the number of characters introduced might confuse readers and commented, "I think I will make a list of them and put in the front pages like Russian novels."[24] Virginia responded in October to Shuhua's initial chapters.

> Now I write to say that I like it very much. I think it has a great charm. It is also of course difficult for an English person, at first, there is some incoherence, and one does not understand the different wives; who they are, which is speaking. But this becomes clear after a time; and then I feel a charm in the very unlikeness. I find the similes strange and poetical. . . . Please go on; write freely; do not mind how directly you translate the Chinese into English. In fact I would advise you to come as close to the Chinese both in style and in

meaning as you can. Give as many natural details of the life, of the house, of the furniture as you like. And always do it as you would were you writing for the Chinese. Then if it were to some extent made easy grammatically by some-one English I think it might be possible to keep the Chinese flavour and make it both understandable yet strange for the English.[25]

Virginia's interest hinged on what struck her as strange and therefore charm-ing. Her suggestion to include "natural details" emphasized an ethnographic specificity that would not be necessary if "writing for the Chinese."[26] Although Shuhua would eventually take this advice by crafting her story for a Western eye, she did not receive Virginia's letter for many months. She waited anxiously for it to travel across battle lines.

Late in 1938, Wuhan fell to the Japanese. China's capital moved again, to Chongqing. In November, still not knowing if Virginia had received her chapters, Shuhua wrote from Leshan to describe the loss of Guangzhou and Hankou. As civilian casualties mounted, she dreamed of her house on Luojia Mountain in ruins. To Virginia she wrote, "I could not sleep in the night, if I fell to sleep I would dream the most unpleasant thing I had in my thought. I saw my house in the ruin and broken furnitures, outside of the house the laying corpse, the unburied corpses smelling badly."[27] As a diversion she was learning to type in order to prepare her manuscript.

With winter's approach, Shuhua's despair deepened. Japanese planes flew over Leshan three times a week. A student who had lost communication with her family after the occupation of Hankou committed suicide by jump-ing from a third-floor window. In mid-December, Shuhua observed that the war had already continued longer than anyone thought it would: "One can not help feeling it might be by God's will that He intends to put an end on the yellow race. . . . In my heart, I often feel I love Japanese ordinary people not less than I do to Chinese. But why do we have to fight?"[28] Refugees con-tinued to pour into their corner of Sichuan, where the local people had learned to fear modern airplanes. "Little children who never have the pleasure of ride in a train or a motor car, but they can tell you the difference between the enemy's plane or Chinese. Isn't this world ridiculous?"[29]

On the last day of 1938, Shuhua sat at her typewriter and wrote Virginia that she hadn't heard from her yet about the chapters sent almost six months earlier. She'd thought of Virginia while aimlessly wandering Leshan's streets. Fortune-tellers squatted on roadsides, and soldiers who would soon face tanks and machine guns asked for their futures to be told. Initial disdain for their superstition melted into sympathy: "When I came back to think of myself, especially about my work, I felt I am having the same fate as these soldiers. I know there is very little chance for me to write a good book in English for the tool I use to do my work is something which I can not handle well."[30] But declaring, "Among many women, I think I am a fighter," she enclosed another chapter.

In England, a month earlier, Julian Bell's collected essays, letters, and poems had been published. Anguished by the loss of her favorite child, Vanessa had steadied herself by going through his papers. She wrote to a friend that she worried how the book might affect Shuhua.

> Poor Sue—I heard from her only yesterday. . . . She sounds very miserable always. . . . I can't quite make out what she is doing. She writes fairly often and seems to be very charming and in an odd way I feel I know her quite well, but she must be terribly difficult to deal with. Julian tried to make her write her autobiography and I hope she may do it. . . . I'm rather nervous of the effect of the book on her with all the criticisms of the Chinese, but I've done my best to prepare her! She little knows what's been left out.[31]

By January 1939, it became clear that the books sent by Virginia were lost. Vanessa wrote to confirm that Virginia had received parts of Shuhua's manuscript and written a long response. Assuming this letter had also gone missing, Shuhua pleaded for her to send it again. "I think you will understand at once how important this lost letter is meant to me when you read this letter."[32] Conscripted soldiers filed into Leshan from nearby counties. Officers led them through the streets with their arms bound by rope and locked their barracks at night. Japanese air raids came closer; news from Chongqing reported high civilian losses as authorities scrambled to build underground shelters. Finally, at the end of February, Shuhua received Virginia's October letter and responded, "It is good to have something to work with since one can do nothing to save the misery nor to stop the disaster. Oh, I don't know how to say my thanks."[33]

Virginia assured her that she was keeping the chapters as they came. With more airplanes filling the skies over England, they also sensed war's approach. Virginia tried to provide comfort with a description of their garden, where Julian played as a boy. She compared this diminutive landscape to what she imagined of Leshan: "I often envy you, for being in a large wild place with a very old civilisation. I get hint of it in what you write."[34] Vanessa, like her sister, encouraged Shuhua to work as a form of detachment from the war: "All one can do is to concentrate on work and be thankful that one *has* work of such a nature to concentrate on. I really pity people who are not artists most of all, for they have no refuge from the world. I often wonder how life would be tolerable if one could not get detached from it, as even artists without much talent can, as long as they are sincere."[35]

In Virginia Woolf's last letter to Shuhua, written on July 16, 1939, she closed by saying she would dine with Vanessa that night. "And I wish you lived near and could come in. These little meetings are the best things we have at present. We talk about pictures not about war."[36]

After a year in Leshan, Shuhua took Xiaoying to Beijing. Li Ruolan had died, and Shuhua told her daughter that she had to take care of the funeral. Xiaoying never knew whether this was the main reason for their departure or an excuse to leave Leshan, where Chen Xiying remained with his mother and sister and managed to survive severe Japanese bombing of the city in mid-August of 1939.

When Shuhua and Xiaoying first arrived in Japanese-occupied Beijing, they stayed in the old Ling compound. Shuzhi, the oldest daughter of Li Ruolan, was living there with her fifteen children. In contrast to Amy's story about their mother dying alone in Tianjin, Xiaoying believes that Shuzhi had moved to Beijing to care for her at the end. Shuzhi had been married off as a teenager to a railway minister's son. Spoiled and uneducated, her husband had trouble holding a steady job, and their large family struggled to get by. Shuhua and Shuzhi now fought bitterly over the remaining piece of family property. Shuhua contrived to rent the courtyard to a Japanese family, effectively forcing her older sister out. Cowering under a table, Xiaoying watched as Shuzhi, enraged by this deception, chased Shuhua around the house with a kitchen cleaver brandished overhead.

Xiaoying suspects that her mother maintained Japanese connections from her past. After the renters moved in, Shuhua and Xiaoying left for rooms in the city's northwest, near Yanjing University, where Xiaoying would attend the affiliated grade school. As they departed the old family house, Xiaoying saw a tricycle gleaming in the courtyard. Two small flags, one for Japanese-occupied Manchuria and one for Japan, fluttered on its handlebars. Japanese visitors continued to stop by their new home for tea.

From Beijing, Shuhua resumed sending letters and gifts to England. In December, Vanessa wrote, "How sorry I am for all the difficulties you have had, which I hope are now over. But I am delighted that your Japanese friend has been so kind to you."[37] She commiserated with Shuhua on Julian's birthday, a day she struggled "not to be overcome by thoughts of him and longings for him."[38] And she exclaimed, "How much you give me!" Shuhua continually sent presents: Chinese New Year posters, a little bag, a piece of silk. Vanessa reciprocated with a lithograph she'd done, something Shuhua could hang in her room: "I'm so very glad that you seem to have got into a more peaceful and happy way of life where you can work and see friends."[39] She mailed seeds from flowers in the garden at Charleston for Shuhua's new home. She promised to send a copy of Virginia's recently published biography of Roger Fry.

As the two women entertained fantasies of future meetings, even of Vanessa traveling to China, bombs fell over Sussex and the war in China approached a tense stalemate. In early 1940, Shuhua wrote a long letter to Hu Shi, whom Chiang Kaishek had sent to the United States as ambassador. She and several friends wanted to smuggle a shipment of donated Chinese handicrafts to the United States to sell as a fundraising effort for children's welfare centers in China. Also, due to university politics in Leshan, Chen Xiying desperately wanted to leave. Praising her husband's sharp mind and recent writing on the international situation, Shuhua asked Hu Shi if he could help Xiying find a position overseas. She assured him that she and Xiaoying could manage on their own for a year or two.[40]

Hu Shi sent a letter recommending Chen Xiying to Kunming's Southwest Associated University, the joint wartime campus of Yanjing, Qinghua, and Nankai. They extended an offer. Torn, Chen Xiying wrote in August to Hu Shi.

> I've already completely lost hope in Wuhan University's future and don't have the slightest interest in staying here, so it's really difficult for me to give up this opportunity to leave. There is no place I'd rather go than Southwest Associated University. . . . But after a long period of reflection, I have no choice but to politely decline their offer. The reason is very simple. My mother is already seventy-five, and it was I who brought her to live in Leshan. This year she has suffered a succession of illnesses and has been unable to get out of bed for the last two to three months. Her children are scattered in different places, and travel at this time is difficult, as would be finding a new home because of air raids and her medical needs. If I go by foot, there's no way she could come with me, and there's no one here for her to rely upon. So no matter how much I loathe this place, I must temporarily just do my best to endure it.[41]

His mother died several months later. His devoutly Buddhist sister blamed herself for their mother's death and fell into perpetual mourning. Xiying remained in Leshan.

That spring Shuhua read disturbing news about Virginia Woolf. Shuhua's "teacher" had filled her pockets with stones and walked into the River Ouse. Less than a week later, Shuhua wrote to Vanessa to verify the news.

May 27, 1941

Dearest Sue,

Your letter of April 4th reached me very quickly—the first I have had for months. . . . The news you saw about Virginia was only too true. It has been very terrible. She had been getting ill for some time and felt that she was going out of her mind. I think it was true that she was very near it, but if only we could have kept her safe for a time she would have got better. It had happened so before and she had always recovered. This time I knew nothing and never suspected the danger. Poor Leonard he is alone after so many years of being completely devoted to her. I cannot write much about it, but you will understand what it means to us all. Life was sad enough without that and to me the loss of Julian is greater than ever for he would have helped. Well, one has to go on somehow. We are all well here and continue to lead very quiet lives, painting and gardening most of the time. . . . One is fortunate in being able to work. . . .

Dear Sue, I am glad you know that I think of you and love you.

Your Nessa[42]

It's not clear if Shuhua ever won her share of the contested property in Guangzhou. The rent she received from the Japanese family must have helped her get by in Beijing. She no longer sent chapters to England. After "Scenes from Behind the Front Line" in 1939, she did not publish another essay until 1943. That essay, a remembrance of the painting party she once helped her father host, may have been inspired by her return to Beijing. Literary scholar Chen Xueyong argues that Shuhua also wrote a novella based on her two years in occupied Beijing.[43]

The Guilin-based *Literary Creation* magazine published *China's Sons and Daughters* serially over 1942 and 1943 under the name Su Hua. The novella tells the story of a single mother and her son and daughter during a period when at least one thousand Beijing residents involved in underground anti-Japanese activity were arrested in a brutal roundup. The older child, high school student Jianguo, boycotts his school's observance of a Japanese Imperial Army parade and sneaks away with a classmate in search of the resistance movement. On the outskirts of Beijing, they witness local villagers punishing captured Japanese policemen and Chinese collaborators. After Jianguo disappears, his mother goes in search of him, only to be arrested herself. Jianguo's younger sister Wanying makes multiple appeals for help and finally locates her mother, who is released but only after being tortured. Following her mother's return, Wanying slips out, leaving behind a letter with which the story ends.

Dearest Mama:

When you read this letter, please don't become frantic and send someone to search for me. I'm determined to find Older Brother. Please don't worry. . . . You know that no one would have the heart to mistreat or murder a child like me. After you disappeared, I learned a lot about the ways of the world . . .

and am no longer a little girl. Dear Mama, please don't worry, Brother and I will definitely return to your arms within a few days. Please, please don't send anyone after me! Please take care of your health. Goodbye, Mama.[44]

The evidence that Shuhua published this work under the penname Su Hua is compelling. In the afterword of a later anthology of her stories, she claims to have published during the war in a Guilin magazine, and in a resumé sent to Hu Shi in 1944, she listed *Literary Creation* as one of the magazines where her work had appeared. Much of the story is also narrated from the perspective of the young girl Wanying. If Shuhua is indeed the author of *China's Sons and Daughters*, she may have written it to make money, as a cover for her ongoing, potentially traitorous connections with Japanese in occupied Beijing, as an experiment in revolutionary, national sentiment, or all of these.

Shuhua and Xiaoying left Beijing to return to Leshan late in the fall of 1941, a timely decision. The Japanese, frustrated by months of stalemate and growing resistance in occupied areas, stepped up a policy of "burn all, kill all, destroy all." Shuhua and Xiaoying traveled by ship, first to Shanghai and then to Hong Kong. They crossed from Hong Kong in early December to Guang-zhouwan, a small French-held port on the south coast of China. While wait-ing for friends coming from Hong Kong on the next boat, Shuhua took Xiaoying to a cinema showing the new Disney cartoon *Pinocchio*. When they emerged from the darkened theater, people were swarming through the streets, frantically buying up food and supplies. It was December 8, 1941, and the Japanese had just bombed Hong Kong, less than eight hours after Pearl Harbor. Their friends never made it out of Hong Kong, which fell on December 25.

They then made their way back to Leshan via Guilin, Guiyang, and Chongqing. They walked along rivers; they rode boats, buses, and donkeys; they were carried in sedan chairs, pushed in wheelbarrows, and propelled by railroad handcar. Shuhua hid her money in the bib pocket of Xiaoying's cov-eralls. At one point, Xiaoying scrambled up a hill to an outhouse with a beau-tiful view of the surrounding countryside. When she pulled up her coveralls, the money fell out of her unfastened pocket into the deep pit below. Shuhua exploded in a rage when she discovered what had happened. Xiaoying says her mother never forgave her for this accident. On a mountain road treacher-ous with hairpin turns, the fan belt of their bus broke. After the passengers lodged rocks behind the wheels, the driver demanded that the women hand over their hair elastics. He fashioned them into a band sturdy enough to use as a temporary replacement. Finally, in February 1942, they arrived in Leshan and reunited with Chen Xiying for a year. His sister, who had retreated completely into Buddhist meditation and then fallen ill, died in 1943. Shortly afterward, Xiying left for the United States, where he'd been invited to join a speaking tour promoting the joint Sino-American war effort.

The main record of the years Shuhua spent in Sichuan between 1942 and 1946 comes from essays she wrote in the 1950s for British *Country Life* magazine. In "Happy Days in Kiating [Jiading]," she describes how, after her husband's departure, she decided to have a small house with a second-story studio built on a hill with a view of the giant Buddha.[45] The walls were made of bamboo and wood, and black tiles covered the roof. To a tree trunk that served as one corner of the structure, the carpenter attached a stairway leading to her studio. Upstairs, where Shuhua spent her days painting and reading, windows on three sides framed views of the mountains and rivers. She and friends hiked to nearby caves, in spite of stories told by locals about snakes, ghosts, and madwomen. They stood in cool, dark caverns, and ancient carvings emerged in vivid relief from the damp, moss-covered walls: elegantly curving animal and flowers motifs and human figures of kings and court women, some almost life size.[46]

This depiction of carefree country life contrasts dramatically with a letter Shuhua wrote to Hu Shi in 1944. She attached a short resumé and asked him to help her find a teaching position in the United States. She and others in Leshan suffered from a thyroid condition, which no local doctors had been able to treat. Several people had died, and she had very little energy. She felt that if she could find a way out, she would be able to recover her health and help with the war effort.

Xiaoying's memory of these years also differs significantly. She remembers the "tree house" as cold and drafty. On occasion, her mother went to Chongqing or Chengdu to arrange painting exhibits and left her for several weeks with Yuan Changying's teenage daughter as company. The older girl slept in the bedroom downstairs, and Xiaoying slept upstairs on a wood plank balanced across two sawhorses, which sometimes shifted in the night, dumping her onto the floor. Her mother had locked all of the trunks before leaving, and when the weather suddenly turned, they shivered at night without blankets. She also remembers executions of Guomindang officers accused of internal crimes taking place further up the hill behind their house. A college student came around their school. He showed her a picture of Chiang Kai-shek and asked if he didn't resemble Hitler. Stories about corruption circulated. The value of their money rapidly declined.

Xiaoying developed her own daily routine. Every morning, she would climb a high hill and loudly sing a revolutionary song before starting the two-and-a-half-kilometer walk to school through fields of wild azalea and rhododendron. She and two other girls, Guo Yuying and Yang Yanzhi, became inseparable. After school they discussed recent developments in the war and gave each other nicknames based on characters from classic martial tales.

In 1944, the government called on students to join the Youth Volunteer Army, and the three declared they would fight as "sworn blood brothers." Xiaoying wrote out, in careful calligraphy on a white silk handkerchief, an oath to give her life to the country. She cut open her finger and signed her new name, Tieyun or Iron Cloud. She also sent a letter to her father, who had recently moved to London to head the Sino-British Cultural Association. Shocked but also moved by her fierce patriotism, he showed the letter to the editor of a Chinese newspaper in London, who published it on January 18, 1945.

> Dearest Father:
>
>   I haven't had letters from you or mother these last few days. You can imagine how anxious and worried I am.
>
>   On the first of this month, Yuying, Yanzhi, and I signed up to join the army. I imagine that you will scold me, but we have many reasons for finally deciding to enroll. For one thing, the enemy has already attacked Liuzhai [Guangxi province]. Yesterday we heard they'd advanced to Dushan [Guizhou province]. Our army has retreated step by step and no longer has the strength to resist. Our nation is in the midst of imminent danger. I believe the time has come when the only thing left is its people who with their blood and passion

Yang Yanzhi, Guo Yuying, and Chen Xiaoying, Leshan, 1944.
Courtesy of Chen Xiaoying.

can no longer endure this situation and must put everything at stake. This country gave me life and nurtured me until today, so I want to return my life to the country, to contribute my flesh and blood as an offering on the altar, my life as the price to fight for national survival.[47]

The girls, only fourteen years old, were too young to officially enlist. As Shuhua and Xiaoying bided their time in Leshan, the tree overhead grew taller, casting thick shade over a house less romantic than it would become in later years.

A photograph of Chen Xiying from this time shows him in an empty office on New Cavendish Street. He stands in a suit and tie next to the fireplace, his elbow propped on the mantle and a pipe in his hand. The only thing hanging on the wall is a bold charcoal sketch, drawn by a friend, of a young Chinese woman wearing a military cap.

· *Twenty* ·

An American Home

*A*my packaged up more vitamins to send to a distant corner of Sichuan and, during summer evenings on the screened-in porch, told her children stories of an earlier war. She described the White Russian soldiers she'd seen as a girl. They fled from the Soviets with jewelry sewn into the linings of their disheveled uniforms and sold these family heirlooms in Beijing, proffering rubies and gold from torn seams. Amy hid money in the attic of the house on Hampton Drive. She hid her jewelry in biscuit tins in the back of her wardrobe. Meanwhile, jerky newsreel images of Pearl Harbor played in the local cinema. Japanese Americans boarded trains for camps in the desert, their homes looted or yanked by bulldozers from their foundations and hauled away.

Amy drew no connection between these everyday invasions of home and the wartime fears nesting in her attic. For her, to be mistaken as Japanese was the ultimate insult. But their American house, which they learned to call home, intimately embodied the losses exacted for citizenship in the American dream, as well as the disparity of access to its promises. If Amy and Shuhua's mutating memories of the house their father built in Tianjin reproduced the mixed, unequal conditions of semicolonial China, the brick colonial on Hampton Drive housed the racial hierarchies that haunt U.S. history.

On Sundays, KK cleared the table after their breakfast of *xifan* and set out materials for his weekly Chinese lesson: a stack of homemade flashcards, two slim exercise books, and a row of ten pennies. He would pull a card from the top of the deck. If either Tom or Mei could remember the character written on it, he slid one penny with his index finger over the Formica tabletop toward them. They repeated basic words out loud after their father and slowly copied the characters in the red squares of their exercise books. But as soon as they stepped outside their house, they never dared use these words, and by Monday they slid back into English. Eventually, KK's Chinese lessons gave way to mechanical drawing lessons, and they learned to use compasses to trace circles and measure arcs instead.

293

Most afternoons, Amy placed a folding screen in front of her bedroom window before taking a short nap. Sometimes she let Mei lie next to her on top of the smooth coverlet. As she gently pulled at the edge of her daughter's ears to scrape out wax with a tiny metal spoon, she would ask, "Did I tell you about the time my older sister got married out?" Or she would teach Mei to count from one to ten in Cantonese, instead of the Mandarin KK taught on Sundays. Or she played their one Chinese record, a 78 mm of Guomindang political songs, featuring a speech by Chiang Kaishek at the beginning. She and Mei sang softly together, "Qi lai, qi lai!"—an oddly private version of a nationalist call to arms across the ocean, where her sister's daughter had cut open her finger to sign a blood oath.

In 1942, Madame Chiang Kaishek toured the United States and addressed a joint session of Congress on the war in Asia. She sought out key congressmen and told them that repealing the Chinese exclusion laws would strengthen Sino-American relations and the joint war effort. Chinese American lobbyists increased pressure for a repeal bill that would overturn the Chinese Exclusion Act. The American Federation of Labor launched an opposition campaign that fanned the fear of Chinese laborers displacing white workers. Only after the Japanese began broadcasting propaganda about the United States as anti-Chinese was Roosevelt able to turn the congressional vote in favor of a repeal, which passed in 1944. Still, at only 105, the new annual quota for Chinese immigrants remained tiny.[1]

The bill also extended the right of naturalized citizenship to Chinese immigrants if they could present documentation of legal entry and pass competency exams in English, U.S. history, and the Constitution. These strict qualifying factors meant that only 1,428 Chinese successfully applied for citizenship in the eight years between 1944 and 1952. Amy and KK were among them. Twenty-nine years after his first arrival in the United States, KK became an American citizen. Several months later, Amy followed his lead. According to her naturalization certificate, Amy Shu-Hao Ling Chen raised her hand to pledge allegiance on "June thirteenth, in the year of our Lord nineteen hundred and forty-seven, and of our Independence the one hundred and seventy-first, in the Southern District of Indiana."

In second grade, registration cards were passed out to my mother's class. The teacher instructed them to have their parents help fill out the cards. Mei sat at the breakfast table and carefully printed her parents' names and their address. Then she came to a blank box with the word "color" above it. She stared at the white card and at the skin of her hand. After a few more minutes, she slowly walked to her father's study. Handing him the card, she asked, "What color am I?" He carefully considered the blank box and finally told her to just put down "white."

Although she followed her father's advice, Mei feared discovery, of what she wasn't quite sure. She only knew that her friends' families did not request special items at the Mandarin Restaurant, that their parents did not switch into a foreign language when they fought, and that their mothers did not recede into impenetrable silence as they read letters from another country.

Small packages arrived for Mei from the auntie in China she had never met. The gift she prized most was a pair of carved wooden dogs connected by a thin chain. Mei kneeled in her bed and walked the dogs in tandem through the moonlight on her windowsill. One afternoon, she took them outside to show to her friends, and the dogs disappeared. Mei combed through the grass frantically until called in for dinner. Tears spilled down her cheeks. Her mother said, "Eat your dinner." Her father said, "The children in this family do not cry at the dinner table." Mei lowered her eyes but couldn't control her sobs. Her father slowly placed his napkin on the table and stood up. "Follow me," he said and marched her into the basement, where he locked her in the storeroom.

Mei gripped the seat of a folding chair her parents used for bridge parties. Her tears slowly dried, and a chill rose up her legs from the damp concrete floor. She studied the sagging plywood shelves loaded with jars of pickled radish with dusty Chinese labels, slumped canvas bags of rice, cardboard boxes with peeling masking-tape labels, and a round cardboard box of Hazel's snuff, which Mei had covertly investigated on a previous occasion.

Suddenly, Hazel swung the door open and Mei followed her up the creaking stairs to the kitchen where a dinner plate had been set aside for her. As Mei sat down alone at the table, Hazel winked at her. She hung up her flowered apron, picked up her shiny, black purse by its stiff handle, and stepped into the evening dusk, where her husband sat waiting in his car to pick her up. Later, Mei learned from her brother that Hazel had lobbied with their father to let her out sooner than he intended. She'd made a show of untying her apron and getting ready to leave early. When KK asked her where she was going, she replied, "Doc Chen, I just can't stand to see that child locked up down there. I'm leaving."

It was also Hazel who bribed Mei with chewing gum to finish the milk American doctors insisted she drink but that she couldn't digest. She made spaghetti or hamburgers for Mei's lunch when Amy and KK weren't home, and Mei trailed her in and out of the back door, and up and down the basement stairs. In the kitchen, while Hazel rolled out circles of pie dough on the counter, Mei played with scraps of the soft dough beside her. In the square backyard patch of grass, Mei handed wooden, knob-headed clothespins one by one to Hazel as she hung laundry, wet sheets flapping before them in the breeze.

The basement, unfinished, cold, and easily flooded during heavy thunderstorms, was a separate region of the house, where Hazel had a bathroom and cabinet for her things. This underground space offered Mei a secret life beyond her parents' supervision. Usually quiet and reticent, she strapped on roller skates and zoomed back and forth across the sloping floor, between the metal pickling tub, the ironing board, and the wardrobe-like contraption where wet clothes hung over glowing gas pipes to dry.

Hazel cranked a batch of wet clothes through the wringer on top of the washing machine and waited for the next load to finish. She sat in a folding chair, massaged cream into her knuckles, and watched Mei do figure eights through the slanted light of the high, narrow windows near the ceiling. And Mei sat on the wooden work bench, with her skates dangling, and talked to Hazel about whatever came to mind.

In spite of KK's dedication to their Sunday morning Chinese lessons, Mei didn't understand the name her parents used for Hazel when they spoke in Chinese. She only knew that when she heard them referring to *hei gui*, they were talking about her. One day, she asked what these words meant. When they translated them as "black ghost," she felt a slap of anger and shame. Her parents were guilty of the same meanness unleashed upon her by the college students in the dormitory across the street who yelled, "Hey Jap, go home!" when she played alone in the front yard. It was only between the shadowy corners and the blue flames flickering beneath the hanging clothes dryer in the basement that my mother heard fragments of Hazel's story and learned how much deeper than names violence could cut.

In a previous life, in western Tennessee, in the town of Dickson west of Nashville, Hazel had started working at age nine, washing diapers for the woman her mother worked for and then for all of that woman's friends. Eventually, she cleaned homes and took in sewing. In the evenings, she rested while waiting for her teenage son to return from work. After a series of odd jobs, he'd landed a position as a short-order cook. Hal had gotten the job over several other applicants, including a white boy. When leaving the restaurant through the kitchen door, Hal sometimes saw this boy and his friends staring menacingly at him from the corner.

One summer afternoon, he arrived home with the news that his boss had given him two tickets to a big-band concert at the county fairground. He offered to take Hazel, but she told him he would have more fun if he went with a friend. She was too tired anyway. Before he left, mother and son sat together to eat the dinner she had cooked.

Later, much later that night, after being roused from sleep by the milkman's wild knocking on her door, Hazel heard the details of what happened at the fairground that night.

Hal and one of his friends found seats in front of the band shell. On their way up the bleachers, they passed the milkman's familiar face and exchanged nods. The boys were tapping their feet to the music when a group of white teenagers crept down a few rows and sat, unnoticed, behind them. The audience broke into applause. Hal raised his hands to clap when someone thrust a knife into his neck. The milkman heard a scream and turned to see several figures jumping off the side of the bleachers.

He and the friend carried Hal, as blood soaked his shirt, through the crowd to his delivery truck. He sped through the night to the German doctor's house. Hazel had worked for years at parties thrown by Doc Muller and his wife, and the doctor had served as their family physician since Hal's birth. The doctor opened his door to find him nearly unconscious, covered in blood, supported between the arms of two men.

When Hazel arrived at the doctor's house, Hal appeared to be resting. The doctor quietly explained that he had sewn up the wound. He thought he had saved her son, but then his heart stopped. A clot of blood must have broken loose and blocked his heart. He struggled to meet her horrified gaze as he said, "I'm sorry."

Even though everyone in town knew who was responsible, the Dickson police claimed they'd found no suspects. The white sheriff warned the murderer's friends to get him out of town as quickly and quietly as possible, giving the authorities an excuse to look the other way. Under this unofficial Southern code of law, whites blamed blacks for stealing the few available jobs, and lynchings were on the rise again. The brutality and injustice of America's color line had stolen, while Hazel slept, into the heart of her home, leaving in its wake the nightmares and rage that led to her flight to the North. When in her early thirties, she climbed onto a bus to visit a friend who'd moved to Indianapolis, she left behind the only life she'd known: the sound of wood thrush in the yellow poplar tree, Sunday picnics at her church, smoking on the back step while the moon rose. With a worn leather Bible in her hand, she sought refuge from the memory of a coffin lid closing on her son's face.

Hazel related a basic outline of this loss to the child she ended up mothering with her wooden spoon of cake batter and comfort. When I asked my mother about her childhood, she passed on to me the story of how the woman partly responsible for raising her had arrived in Indianapolis. I pushed for more information, but my mother could only tell me the spare version she had pieced together as a child. When I went with her to visit Hazel in 2000, I tried to learn more about this half-spoken past, but my questions—asking a ninety-three-year-old woman to relive what she had spent so many intervening decades trying to lay to rest—felt like another violation.

Hazel added a few details to the story my mother had told me, like those of Doc Muller and his late-night ministrations. The main difference was that her story did not end simply with the escape of her son's murderer. She followed it with an epilogue of biblical dimension that helped me partly understand how she had survived. "They got him out of town all right, but later that boy went blind. He lost a hand and then both legs, one and then the other, just like that." She explained he had diabetes that went untreated. The disease's ill effects were divine retribution for the violent theft of her only child.

Amy told me she met Hazel in an Indianapolis laundry she had been sent to inspect. Knowing her association with Lilly, the municipal minister of health asked her to check that the city's laundry shops were in compliance with new sanitation regulations. During one of her inspection trips she interviewed Hazel, who complained of inadequate drainage of overflow water. Workers often had to stand with wet feet all day. After recording this violation, Amy asked Hazel if she would like to work for a private family instead.

In Hazel's story, she first met the Chens because the friend she went to visit in Indianapolis worked for them. They were having a party. Her friend was several months pregnant, and she went along to help serve. While Hazel was cleaning up the kitchen, Amy asked her if she might want her friend's job after she left to have her baby. Hazel told me she replied, "Well, Miss Chen, I'm just visiting from Tennessee, but if I move up here I'll surely consider it." A month later, she stopped by to ask if the offer still stood. By Amy's assessment, in a statement that revealed what she knew of Hazel's past, she was happy to work for a Chinese family: "See, she could never work for white people. She was afraid if she turned around, they'd stab her in the back."

In Indianapolis Hazel met and married Leverett Bell, a tall, solid man whom everyone called Bell. He worked as a doorman in a downtown hotel. They didn't have children and lived in the steady comfort of each other's presence. Over the years, they saved to buy a modest home in the suburbs, where they moved when Bell retired. My mother remembers driving out by herself to this house on visits back to Indianapolis from college. On the front porch, over card games with Hazel, she heard how their white neighbors snubbed them and made them feel unwanted. In the 1960s, when Amy and KK challenged the whites-only community charter of another suburb to move into the bigger home with the acre of green lawn that they wanted, Hazel and Bell moved back to an apartment in a neighborhood north of downtown that had become predominantly black.

Until shortly before her death on her ninety-fourth birthday in 2001, Hazel still lived in this rectangular block building, around the corner from the Catholic hospital where Mei was born. It was the newest structure on the street in the 1960s, but it had aged more quickly than the older row houses that surrounded it. The flat, tarred roof gathered water and leaked during thunderstorms. Since Bell's death, Hazel had lived alone, "still kicking," in her words, "just not very high." She complained about the increase of dope sellers, the murders she read about in the paper, and the three deadbolts that cluttered her front door, but her neighbors and "Bell's people" dropped by regularly to visit. The last time I saw her, she grinned and said, "I won't move unless that leak in the ceiling gets so bad I'm washed away. And then, I'll be sure to let you know where I've got washed away to."

My mother began visiting Hazel almost every year after Bell's passing. She would arrive bearing photographs of her family, gospel tapes as gifts, and take-out boxes of Chinese food. They'd sit together in the apartment, eat at Hazel's kitchen table, and talk about the old days. My mother told me Hazel loved the take-out dishes she brought and would always add, "But nobody makes chop suey like Mrs. Chen." And then Hazel would lift the lid from her famous lemon cake to cut it for dessert.

In 2000, I drove from Chicago through a raging yellow-gray thunderstorm to meet my mother's plane from St. Louis at the Indianapolis airport. Together, we drove up Capitol Avenue to where Hazel stood, waiting for us behind the glass front door of her building. We followed her slowly up the stairs. My mother's bag contained bottles of oyster sauce, and I carried three five-pound red boxes of dried Chinese noodles for the winter. At the top of the stairs, Hazel introduced my mother to a neighbor as Mei-Fong, "the child I helped raise." My mother turned to me, glowing like a child who'd been praised, and said, "Nobody calls me that anymore." It was true. Not even her mother did. Only Hazel, who had worked so hard alongside time to blunt the pain of the past, recalled Mei-Fong—the child of hopeful immigrant parents whose name still bore the traces of their origins.

Hazel Bell was almost the same age as my grandmother, having also survived the death of her husband and lived into her nineties. She was my mother's second mother, who after my birth taught her how to wash me and nourished her with tastes from the home she had fled—baked ham, fried chicken, and homemade sweet rolls. My grandmother was an obstetrician, but Hazel taught Mei the skills of mothering. It was Hazel who was there when my umbilical cord fell off. In her Indianapolis apartment, I was proud to see grade school photographs of my sister and myself displayed, alongside her kin, on the television console—and the grainy black-and-white photograph taken by my mother of Hazel gazing down at me on her lap during my second day of life. My grandmother always insisted that she was the first to hold me in her arms, but my mother confirms that Hazel arrived days before Amy, even though my grandmother had traveled by plane rather than bus.

Hazel Bell's almost century-long life, braved with strength and resilient optimism, told me what my grandmother's stories refused to acknowledge about the America where she won a compromised success at assimilating. Their intersecting lives tell of the different movements, voluntary and involuntary, that make up a country where the foundations of home are far from stable.

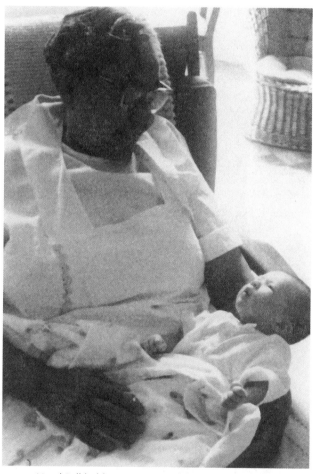

Hazel Bell holding me as a newborn, Chicago, 1969.
Photo by Mei Chen Welland.

· Twenty-One ·

Wandering

$\int$huhua told Xiaoying that everything she wanted to take with her would have to be sewn into the lining of her coat. When they climbed into the truck in Leshan headed for Chongqing, the coat hung heavy on her shoulders. Letters, paintings, photographs, and the white silk handkerchief signed in blood padded her teenaged body. She stared out the window as they slowly pulled away from the giant Buddha's steady gaze. When the American GIs smiled and offered her snacks, Xiaoying turned away. The way they held peanuts out in their open palms made her feel like a monkey.

In early August of 1945 the United States had dropped atomic bombs on Hiroshima and Nagasaki. Japanese troops in China officially surrendered on September 9, leaving China on the brink of civil war between the Guomindang and the Communists. Shuhua and Xiaoying spent several months in Chongqing with Xiying's younger brother, waiting. Chen Xiying's position in the Guomindang government enabled him to arrange a departure for his wife and daughter. At the Chongqing landing strip, they climbed metal stairs to a U.S. military plane, which took them to Shanghai. Early in 1946, they flew from Shanghai to Beijing, and then made their way to Tianjin, where they boarded a ship to cross the Pacific. In San Francisco, they connected to an eastbound train to New York, with a stopover in Indianapolis.

Xiaoying remembers hating Indianapolis. In Leshan, she had roamed hills green with wild vegetation, with a view of snaking rivers that flashed silver in the sun. Although cold and damp in winter, their house of wood and bamboo had always been filled with fresh air, the windows thrown open to the outside. The house on Hampton Drive, tightly sealed against the October chill, felt close and suffocating. Amy and KK took them to church on Sunday. She and her mother wore dress hats borrowed from Amy's closet. When the minister introduced them as refugees from China, Xiaoying's blood rose to her cheeks in humiliation. When Amy gave her a suitcase of her old clothes, she fell silent. While the clothes were perfectly good, so fancy that future

301

schoolmates in England would admire them, she cringed at the thought of wearing Amy's middle-aged castoffs and wished her aunt had thought to buy just one new outfit appropriate for a girl her age.

From New York, Shuhua and Xiaoying traveled to England on an ocean liner converted into a troop ship. Toward the end of 1946, they joined Chen Xiying in London, where he had settled in St. John's Wood, near the Chinese Embassy and Regents Park. Around the same time, he was appointed as Chinese representative to the newly formed United Nations Educational, Scientific, and Cultural Organization (UNESCO), headquartered in France. He soon began to divide his time between London and Paris.

From San Francisco, Shuhua had mailed a letter to Vanessa Bell, resuming a correspondence silenced by the war's last years. The two women again exchanged letters, now over the one hundred kilometers between Charleston and London. Vanessa worried about stirring up bad feelings between Shuhua and her husband by serving as a reminder of the affair with Julian, but Shuhua persisted. Finally, in January 1947, Vanessa visited her in London. Four days later, Vanessa wrote,

> You must not blame yourself for breaking down with me—I understood so well. It has been very strange after knowing you intimately for so many years by letter to see you at last, and I seemed to be in an unreal world where I could hardly tell what I felt. I have had for so long now to make up my mind to life without Julian and to try all the same to get something from it—and I think that at first your presence made me feel again how much I wanted him.[1]

Driven by sentiment and necessity, Shuhua pursued her connection to Bloomsbury in an effort to make a life for herself in England. Margery Fry counseled her on finding a boarding school for Xiaoying; neither seemed to consider what an alienating environment it would be for a recently uprooted teenager with unpracticed English. Focused on her own predicament of adapting to a strange city, Shuhua wrote letters to Vanessa describing lonely evenings. Vanessa, always slightly distant but sympathetic, particularly when moved by memories of Julian, did what she could. She arranged for Shuhua to study English with Marjorie Strachey, writer and sister of Bloomsbury biographer and essayist Lytton Strachey. She provided Shuhua with an introduction to Arthur Waley, the well-known translator of Chinese and Japanese poetry. And after a severely cold winter made more difficult by fuel shortages, Vanessa invited her to Charleston as spring finally bloomed. Shuhua arrived by train, bringing her friendship scroll. She unrolled it, and the landscape in monochrome ink wash that Xu Zhimo had collected over twenty years earlier from Roger Fry caused Vanessa to gasp. Shuhua produced a new fan-shaped album and asked Vanessa and Duncan Grant to contribute paintings. Julian's younger brother Quentin had become a ceramicist, and Shuhua painted some of his pots in a Chinese style.[2]

In September of 1947, Vanessa wrote to her daughter Angelica about these efforts to help Shuhua.

> I have been unlucky in the people I have introduced her to. Waley evidently didn't take to her, pretended he was just going abroad and has never seen her again, and Old Gumbo [Marjorie Strachey] is horrified by her emotionalism and only accepts her as a pupil because she gets some rice out of her. Luckily Clive [Bell] liked her and so does Duncan and so in fact do I—but of course it's difficult to provide a circle of friends, which is what she really wants, and one can't have her here constantly. However we shall see what happens. I hope it will be fine and she can sit and draw the willow as she did before.[3]

This hint of Vanessa's pity and patience worn thin colors my understanding of the latter half of Shuhua's life, for one way of tracing it is through the archive of Bloomsbury letters. This record of her interactions with its members reveals an edge of desperation as she strove in her late forties to remake herself as a writer and artist in England. Forced to work outside her native language and environment, she also saw her reputation in China fading as literary politics shifted. During her first years in London, she appealed to Vanessa for advice on many things: attending classes at Newnham College, where to buy canvas and stretchers, how to study lithography, and galleries for exhibiting her paintings. In return, she sent a flow of gifts—silk scarves, jewelry, paintings, cheese, and chocolates—even though Vanessa rebuked her every time. Vanessa, ensconced in her Charleston farmhouse, couldn't have understood Shuhua's cultural dislocation, but she shared a feeling of being surpassed by a younger generation of artists. She wrote consolingly, "I know it is desperately difficult for anyone now to sell or get recognition, unless they are quite young and in the fashion."[4]

In December of 1949, shortly after Mao Zedong stood on a Tiananmen reviewing stand to declare the founding of the People's Republic of China, Shuhua held her first overseas exhibit at the Adams Gallery on New Bond Street. The show contained still-life and landscape paintings, ink on silk and paper, hung in a spare, elegant manner against white walls. With Xiying posted part of the time in Paris, she had traveled to France and Switzerland, as well as around England, and her European scenes painted in a Chinese style garnered the greatest attention. After Vanessa went with Duncan to the exhibit she wrote, "It is most interesting of course to see European landscape through Chinese eyes."[5] Quentin Bell wrote an unsigned review in *The New Statesman and Nation* and commented, "This particular exhibition gains peculiar interest from the rare opportunity which is given us to see our Western world through the eyes of an accomplished artist working in an alien tradition."[6] Praised for her paintings that provided viewers with an estranged picture of familiar surroundings, Shuhua continued for years to produce similar works. This aesthetic emblematized her struggle to survive in England while longing for a homeland that grew stylized and precious as it receded into poetic mists. As early as 1950, she began considering when, whether, and how to return to China—a tormenting game of anticipation and remorse played out over the remaining decades of her life. She awaited news from friends about the political climate, weighed the ramifications of her husband's Guomindang affiliation, and plotted ways to recover family belongings left in Beijing.

As Shuhua's English improved under Marjorie Strachey's tutelage, she considered the possibility of writing for local publications. In her perusal of various newspapers and magazines, she became a regular reader of Vita Sackville-West's weekly "In Your Garden" column in the *Observer*. Her interest piqued by an article on Chinese herbs, Shuhua sent a letter via the paper and asked if she might visit Sackville-West's famous garden at Sissinghurst Castle in Kent. Shuhua soon found herself sipping tea in the study of another Bloomsbury member.[7] In addition to being an avid gardener, Vita was a poet and novelist, and the evocative language of Shuhua's letter had intrigued her. She asked Shuhua if she wrote much in English. When Shuhua mentioned the chapters of an attempted autobiography sent years earlier to Virginia Woolf, Vita's eyes widened. She and Virginia had once been lovers and then close friends—Woolf had modeled the title character of her novel *Orlando* after Sackville-West—and she remembered Virginia talking about stories sent to her from China. Vita encouraged Shuhua to resume the project. Over the following years, she actively supported Shuhua's writing career in England and influenced her presentation of China as a distant dreamscape. In one of her gardening columns, Vita describes falling asleep on a winter evening and being suddenly surrounded by blooming plants from all corners of the world. Moments before waking up, she sees the walls of the room melt away, "giving place to a garden such as the Emperors of China once enjoyed, vast in extent, varied in landscape, a garden in which everything throve and the treasures of the earth were collected in beauty and brotherhood."[8] She displaced a slowly disintegrating British imperial dream onto China's lost empire, and Shuhua returned many times to Sissinghurst, where she painted in the gardens, copying them as the character Ru Bi in her story "What's the Point of It?" had once imitated the gardens of her foreign neighbors in China.

In 1950 two of Shuhua's stories appeared in *The Spectator*, a publication with which Vita and her husband Harold Nicolson had close connections.

"Red Coat Man" depicted how as a child she witnessed a prisoner's execution, and "Childhood in China" gave an account of her father presiding over the court case of a beautiful woman who had killed her mother-in-law.[9] Merged together, these two pieces would become the opening chapter of her autobiography. She wrote, as in much of her short fiction, from the perspective of a child. However, within an autobiographical mode, this voice produced a distancing effect such that Vita would characterize her stories as "delightful sketches of a vanished way of life on the other side of the world."[10] Vanessa wrote of Shuhua's first publication effort, "You have managed to make something lovely out of a strange and rather horrible experience and you somehow make me feel it from the child's point of view which is very rare."[11] In 1951 two more reminiscences, "Our Old Gardener" and "Visit to a Royal Gardener," accompanied by her paintings, appeared in *Country Life*.[12]

Shuhua still talked about returning to China, but this initial publication success led her to believe she might find a place in England. Vita had put her in touch with Leonard Woolf. He searched through Virginia's letters and found the original chapter drafts Shuhua had sent from Sichuan. Determined to finally complete the autobiography, Shuhua edited her early chapters, wrote several new ones, and composed simple line drawings as illustrations. On May 29, 1952, she sent a preliminary manuscript to Leonard Woolf and explained her emotional impulse.

> My plan to write this book started at the time I first wrote to Virginia. She was the *first* and *only* person [who] encouraged me to go on writing it at that time. When I heard she died, I could not continue writing this book. As you know the Second World War spreaded over China, I had to face all the difficulties and to take up all the duties of a Chinese, I had to put off writing until the war ended.[13]

They lunched together at the Asiatic Restaurant in Leicester Square to discuss details. After Leonard confirmed that the Hogarth Press would publish the book, Shuhua corresponded frequently with him. Aware from the beginning of her audience, she wrote him, "There are many books about China in the West, most of them were written to satisfy the curiosity of the West. The authors sometimes tried to make stories about Chinese people from their imagination only. Their attitude towards their readers is not honest. Chinese people then appear to be a sort of half ghost and half man beings in the West."[14] She felt sure she could keep her "Chinese style," as Virginia had advised. Leonard, restrained and patient, kept her on track to finish and invited her several times to Monk's House, the Sussex home he had shared with Virginia. Overwhelmed by the experience of sitting in Virginia's study,

Shuhua heaped gratitude upon this new mentor; she sent bean sprouts and ginger cuttings for his greenhouse and a bottle of fruit gin made with longan fruit, noting how much Julian Bell had enjoyed it.

While she pulled the book together for Marjorie Strachey to edit, Chen Xiying was temporarily recalled to Taiwan, the Guomindang base after their flight from mainland China. Loyal to the government he had supported during the war, he prepared to depart, much to the dismay of Shuhua who tried to persuade him not to go. She wrote to Leonard Woolf, "I know by experience when the Communist government finds out his visit to Formosa [Taiwan], our property, most of it belongs to my family will be taken by the Communist 'state.' We shall be penniless when we go back. I am afraid I shall have to lose all family treasures such as books and paintings I inherited from my father."[15] This consideration only of what she personally had to lose led her daughter to eventually judge her a profoundly apolitical person. Xiaoying elucidated this point for me by quoting the opening line of an early essay by her father in which he critiqued the self-interested nature of the Chinese character: "Chinese people have only a sense of loss and gain, not one of right and wrong."[16]

In November of 1953, the Hogarth Press published Shuhua's autobiography *Ancient Melodies*. At the suggestion of Vita Sackville-West, she drew her title from a Tang dynasty poem translated by Arthur Waley. Bai Juyi's "The Old Lute" opens with the line "Of cord and cassia-wood is the lute compounded; Within it lie ancient melodies."[17] Shuhua dedicated the book to Virginia Woolf and Vita Sackville-West. Vita provided an introduction, in which she wrote, "Su Hua is blessed, or cursed, according to the way you look at it, with the soul and eye of an artist and a poet, and seems, living in London now, to bring with her the flavour of a forgotten world in which the desire for the good life of peaceable contemplation and exquisite thoughts were axiomatic."[18]

This sentiment glossed over Shuhua's descriptions of female entrapment in the old-style household, which had been the main point of her stories in their original May Fourth context, a telling oversight since *Ancient Melodies* ends with her schoolgirl experience of the anti-imperial, antitradition student movement. The reviewer for *Time and Tide* identified a similar fairy-tale aspect in the book: "What distinguished the book is an intense curiosity and zest for life, and a childlike purity of vision."[19] The *Spectator* review concluded with a comment on Shuhua's illustrations: "A few of her drawings are included in this book; delightful sketches which show a stiff, doll-like, little creature busy flying kites with her foster mother, buying flowers with the gardener, learning poetry with Tutor Ben: an enchanting record!"[20] A longer review in the *Times Literary Supplement* picked up more of the ironic detachment in her narrative voice:

> Each chapter has a special pungency of its own, beginning with the first—what a contrast with European nurseries and kindergartens of the same period!—when the tiny author was taken by a good-natured servant to watch a typical old-fashioned execution. . . . A western writer might dwell on its macabre aspects, or attribute to this early shock a life-long Angst. Not Mrs. Su Hua. . . . The whole incident is sketched boldly, as with a Chinese brush: just the right proportion of sentiment, but no sentimentality, no canting gush.[21]

Shuhua claimed that fifteen years later she learned that Harold Acton, whom she'd taken with Julian Bell to visit the painter Qi Baishi in Beijing, had written this unsigned review.[22]

Even before *Ancient Melodies* came out, she began discussing with Leonard Woolf her next project. On June 3, 1953, she wrote,

> I was thinking to write a better book next time. That was why I told you sometime ago that I wanted to go to China or somewhere near China to refresh my memories. I have had this in mind for several years to write a book—a novel something like Tolstoy's War and Peace. . . . I think I have enough experiences and enough materials which can make a book interesting but all I need is the time and the fresh mind for such a book. I have stayed in England too long—five whole years.[23]

The idea of traveling to Asia as inspiration for the great novel she hadn't written yet increasingly preoccupied her. After returning her proofs for *Ancient Melodies*, she wrote Leonard about wanting to go to Korea to translate for Chinese soldiers wounded in the war.

> I can speak nearly all the dialects in China which would be very useful to them because most of these soldiers come from the country. They don't speak Mandarin. I was greatly touched when I saw the Chinese POW in the film (the news) during their repatriation. They looked pathetic. They seemed to hate everyone and everything in the world. This sight haunted me very often.[24]

She apparently wrote to several organizations offering to serve as an interpreter. She met with Nora Waln, a travel writer and foreign correspondent for the *Saturday Evening Post* and *Atlantic Monthly* during the Korean War, about accompanying her on her next trip to Asia. She continued to publish magazine articles and exhibit paintings but saw these endeavors as fundraising efforts for future travel. An ambitious plan developed in her mind:

Next spring I am planning to be able to go to the United States—perhaps I shall have a show in New York or San Francisco to get some money to prepare my journey to go to the Far East. . . . Then I shall return to England to write a good book as I have always wished to. . . . After I made a good study of the present situation in the Far East, I should be quite willing to remain abroad to write and paint or to go back China to join the great movement over there.[25]

In the spring of 1954, the Musée Cernuschi in Paris, a museum devoted to Asian art, exhibited her paintings—bamboo, orchids, magnolia, and landscapes—for a three-month run. French writer André Maurois, who had read *Ancient Melodies*, wrote a short introduction for the show.[26] Shuhua communicated with Amy about the possibility of exhibiting her paintings in the United States. Shuhua and Leonard Woolf had also discussed a U.S. release of *Ancient Melodies*, but it becomes clear from their correspondence that Amy had seen the book and objected to its depiction of their family. In June of 1954, Shuhua wrote to Leonard, "There are really many problems which will rise if I publish my book in America. I have to think it carefully and see how far I can manage to leave out some parts yet without any bad effect to the book."[27] An American edition of the book did not appear until 1988. Perhaps knowing that her opposition to the U.S. release could affect her sister's finances, Amy helped her arrange an exhibit in Indianapolis. I suspect it is at this moment that Amy began describing her sister as an artist, not a writer.

On October 16, 1954, an exhibit of sixty-nine paintings on silk and paper by Ling Shuhua opened at the John Herron Art Museum. A reviewer for the *Indianapolis News* focused on her European scenes, "There's a charming other-worldliness, a Shangri-la quality in landscapes oddly enough titled 'Lock Katrine,' 'Kirkcudbright Harbour,' 'A Bridge on the River Dee,' 'Hampstead Heath,' 'Winter in Hyde Park' and the like. . . . I do believe Ling Shu-hua could portray trailer-trucks in a traffic jam with delicacy and charm."[28] Shuhua arrived in Indianapolis at the end of the month and gave a museum talk on "How to Look at a Chinese Picture." Amy hosted a luncheon for her at the Propylaeum, a local women's club, and the society reporter for the *Indianapolis Times* seemed most interested in Shuhua's "authentic native costume of light green satin with a woven bamboo leaf design" and her husband's current visit to Uruguay for UNESCO meetings.[29] Before her departure for the United States, Shuhua had spoken somewhat disdainfully about the provincial museum showing her work, but eight of her pieces sold in Indianapolis for a total of almost $2,600. From there, she continued to New York, taking her paintings to the China Institute for a ten-day exhibit, and then to a gallery in Boston. During these travels, she spent most of the money earned in Indianapolis and had to return to England rather than continuing on to Asia.

Over a year later, she continued to save for her planned trip and complained to Leonard Woolf about the predicament of working as a Chinese artist in London.

> People in this country, most of them are unwilling to accept new ideas and new kind of arts unless they are something like their own. Most Chinese pictures sold here are a mixture of the East and West. The subjects or pictures must suit the taste of the Westerners. If an artist neglects this point, his picture would be no market. I hate to think of this unavoidable failure but what can I do?[30]

Shortly after, Leonard bought one of her paintings of young bamboo for Monk's House.

Finally, an opportunity came Shuhua's way: an invitation to teach Chinese literature at the newly founded Nanyang University in Singapore. She arrived in May of 1956 and moved into a three-room cottage provided by the university. Singapore struck her as a "semi-Chinese country."[31] She found it hard to understand local politics, and aside from her light teaching load and helping the library build a modern Chinese literature collection, she led a self-described "hermit life" in a sparsely populated neighborhood atop a hill covered with profuse plant life. She burned incense in the evenings to keep away insects, and its fragrant smoke sent her into dreams of traveling to Hong Kong, Taiwan, and Japan to get "some fresh thoughts which I want to use in my second book."[32]

In the hilltop cottage in Singapore, she tried to start her novel and, toward the end of 1956, mentioned sending preliminary scenes to Leonard Woolf. Having introduced many characters at the outset, she dramatically declared that she'd reached a difficult juncture and required advice. But in the next sentence of her letter, her confidence suddenly crumbled in the face of her own delusions of grandeur: "[Julian] said I had a Russian-like style, sometimes French atmosphere. He said if I could use it in a right way, I might write a remarkable book. I tried to follow his advice but I haven't done very successfully. Every day life now is a bore. Talent has been dried by time I suppose."[33]

For four years, she traveled back and forth between England and Singapore. During this time she managed to visit Japan and Hong Kong and wrote several impressionistic accounts of her travels. She assembled these essays, together with recent articles on art and literature, for a 1960 volume titled *Dreams from a Mountain-Lover's Studio*. She also compiled an anthology of her collected short stories for publication in Singapore. Conscious that she had reached the point of trying to preserve a literary legacy, she closed her afterword on a humble note: "I have chosen the stories for this book simply for those young friends in Singapore and Malaysia keen about modern literature and offer this bunch of flowers and grass picked from the old country. While fine if appreciated, there's no harm done if it doesn't attract attention, for at least I've given my heart."[34]

Toward the end of her tenure at Nanyang University, Shuhua returned for the first time to China, visiting Beijing, Guangzhou, and Wuhan. She sent postcards of Wuhan University to an ailing Vanessa, who died shortly after in 1961. She confessed to Leonard the covert nature of her travels. "I have been advised by Chinese friends that I better not to tell people about my China trip."[35] She continued throughout her life to take secret trips back to China, often not even telling her husband or daughter about them. When on one such occasion, Xiaoying inadvertently discovered her plans, she was shocked not only by her mother's clandestine schemes but also by the jeopardy in which she knowingly put her father. If his wife's trips to the mainland had become known, he might have been judged a spy or traitor by the Taiwanese government that employed him.

Back in London, five years after Shuhua started work on her novel, she sent a first chapter to Leonard and wrote, "The story is about the last war which has broken the dreams of some promising youths and also some happy families' future. And the war between China and Japan was tragic. Both of them did not quite understand why they went to war, but they had to fight and pretended that they were fighting for a noble aim!"[36] Leonard politely responded that the chapter was too short to get a sense of her overall direction. For many years, she continued to sporadically mention the book, often giving excuses for her lack of production, such as Marjorie Strachey's declining health and inability to help with editing. Eventually, she stopped raising the topic and focused her energy on short essays and painting exhibitions. For several years, she wrote radio scripts about overseas Chinese for BBC's Asia broadcast. In the winter of 1962, another exhibit at the Museé Cernuschi in Paris featured paintings, calligraphy, and stone rubbings from the portion of her father's collection she'd managed to bring from China when she first left. Several years later, the Arts Council of Great Britain presented the same exhibit in London under the title "A Chinese Painter's Choice."

In 1966, Chen Xiying began at the age of seventy to suffer from high blood pressure and requested permission to retire as soon as a replacement could be found. Shuhua traveled several times to Paris to help prepare for his return to London, worrying all the while about how they would live on the reduced income of his pension. At this time, she signed a two-year contract with the University of Toronto to teach as a visiting professor in East Asian Studies. She departed for Canada just as her husband moved back to London.

During the one year she eventually stayed in Toronto, where she felt isolated and still unable to write, she taught Chinese literature and calligraphy. Most of her students came from Hong Kong or Malaysia, and their limited knowledge of China dismayed her. News about the Cultural Revolution in the mainland began to circulate, and she grew even more depressed upon hearing about fellow writers and artists who had committed suicide. Her hope of writing another book died when Leonard Woolf did in 1969.

Chen Xiying's health continued to weaken. Xiaoying remembers that shortly after his return to England, she gave him a newly released book, *Journey to the Frontier*, for his birthday. This biography of two young British men who died in the Spanish Civil War covered the life of Julian Bell, a name she recognized as familiar from her childhood in Wuhan. Months later, sick with influenza, she asked her father if she could borrow the book to read in bed. Turning the pages, she slowly put the pieces together. A half-submerged history that had haunted much of her life was suddenly revealed. The sorrow that flooded her was only heightened by the marginal comments her father had penciled throughout the book. Scholar always, he'd made annotations correcting the chapter "Julian Bell in China" from his perspective. Shortly before her father's death in 1970, Xiaoying sat by his side on a park bench and tried to ask why he had married her mother and why they had stayed together after everything that had happened. He said only, "Your mother is a very talented woman," before slowly rising to walk back to the car.

Shuhua continued to take semisecret trips to China, always plotting her final return. When Vita Sackville-West's son, editor of Virginia Woolf's collected letters, contacted Shuhua in 1979 regarding Virginia's letters to her, she still strove to promote herself in the way she'd learned best in England. She sent him an article about her recent trip to the Dunhuang Buddhist caves and asked if he could help find a publisher.

What perhaps best captures Shuhua's later years is a poem she translated and enclosed in her final letter to Vanessa on October 7, 1960. "Last night I dreamed I returned to my native country" was written by Song dynasty poet Su Dongpo, who traveled throughout his life from place to place, including Leshan, and spent many years in political exile.

> She was sitting, as she used to, at the toilet table
> Near the window of her room.
> We faced each other silently
> And tears fell as suddenly as summer rain.
>
> For years I have longed to go where I could weep—
> To that hill covered with young trees on a moon lit night.[37]

Who is the woman at the table by the window? She might be the sister who died in the Nunobiki Falls. She could be Virginia, who similarly disappeared from Vanessa's life the day she stepped into a cold river. Perhaps "she" is China. In the end, I believe she is most of all a younger incarnation of Shuhua herself.

· *Twenty-Two* ·

The Chinese House

*M*y mother described to me over the phone a photograph she'd received in the mail. At her fortieth high school reunion, she ran into an old classmate whose parents had worked at Lilly. Both his parents had died recently, and while going through their belongings, he found a photograph of her parents. She told me the faded color photograph showed her parents with Lilly colleagues at a lakeside summer cottage in Michigan. Everyone was dressed casually except for Amy, who wore a silk brocade dress. My mother said incredulously over the phone, "Can you imagine, a brocade dress in the middle of a Michigan summer? Well, that's my mother."

With her Propylaeum Club membership and tailored clothes, Amy sought acceptance in an American social world she'd first glimpsed at PUMC. She became director of the PTA at her children's elementary school and organized a fair in the gymnasium. With proceeds earned from baked goods, cotton candy, and game ticket sales, she purchased red velvet curtains for the auditorium stage. After fighting for membership in the whites-only Riviera Club, Amy took Mei and Tom to the pool in the summer and watched them swim while she sat wearing a wide-brimmed sun hat to protect her light skin.

The role she could play in these circles depended in part, however, on a brocade dress with a high Mandarin collar. Like her sister in London, who organized exhibits of her own but eventually ended up as conservator of her father's collection, Amy became a goodwill ambassador. Chinese students, scholars, diplomats, and merchants had been exempt from exclusion laws and generally received better treatment than working-class Asian immigrants. This acceptance came more readily when they worked to bridge the gap between East and West. They performed their pleas for tolerance, according to Asian American literature scholar Elaine Kim, "by making usually highly euphemistic observations about the West on the one hand while explaining Asia in idealized terms on the other."[1]

313

Amy grew adept at this role. She gave lectures with titles like "Philosophy of Confucius," "History of Chinese Medicine," "Chinese Women," and "Chinese Customs and Festivals" to local women's clubs. In my grandmother's box of newspaper clippings, I found a yellowed piece of newsprint from 1957 with a photograph of her, perfectly coiffed. She sits beaming in the corner of her living room and points for the photographer at a porcelain "heirloom fruit bowl." In the accompanying article, "Oriental Beauty Fills Chen Home," the women's editor of the *Indianapolis News* writes, "Like slowly turning the pages of a mystic book, whose beginnings are in the fairy tale past across the seas and whose ending is in the modern-day America, is the feeling one has after a visit in the Dr. K. K. Chen home, 519 W. Hampton."[2] She concludes by listing the various skills Amy has channeled into cultivating an enviable domestic life. "Both Dr. and Mrs. Chen enjoy a fast game of tennis. She has her own photography darkroom where she develops and prints her films of landscapes and portraits of people. Equally at home in kitchen or garden, she has developed the culinary arts to a high plane by applying her chemistry background to the superb techniques of Chinese cookery." When Amy applied in 1958 for membership to the Indianapolis Branch of the National League of American Pen Women, she included a set of thirty-five reprints of pharmacological publications she had authored or coauthored. However, when I spoke on the phone in 1991 with the woman who still served as branch president, she described Amy as their "most wonderfully exotic member" and remembered vividly a luncheon lecture on jade during which Amy had passed around different jade pieces.

In his notes for an autobiography, Eli Lilly attributed his interest in Chinese art to "our friends, Dr. and Mrs. K. K. Chen (both doctors)."[3] He also wrote that *The Meeting of East and West*, a book by Yale philosopher Filmore S. C. Northrop, had given him a motive for collecting. Northrop proposed that contemporary conflicts between Asia and the West might be partly resolved by greater mutual understanding of the other civilization's aesthetic view of life. In 1947, Eli Lilly stated that he admired Chinese culture because of its "abiding serenity of spirit and gentle sympathy," a difficult statement to make as civil war raged in China and his company sent medicines to aid Chiang Kaishek's troops.[4]

Eli Lilly purchased the first pieces of his art collection, now in the Indianapolis Museum of Art, through a New York dealer recommended by Amy and KK. His enthusiasm went so far that he renovated an old two-story frame house on a wooded bluff over the White River into a "Chinese house." He enlisted Amy and KK as decor consultants. With their input, a painter adorned ceiling beams in the living and dining rooms with Chinese designs. The walls were painted celadon green, and yellow shantung draped the windows. Lilly furnished the first-floor rooms with Chinese antiques and several tables he'd made himself. He even crafted a four-panel screen in black and white, using powdered graphite for the decorative work. The Chens presented Eli Lilly and his wife Ruth with several scroll paintings and portraits of six Song dynasty emperors. Finally, KK translated a name chosen by the Lillys, "The House of Sylvan Harmonies," and wrote out the Chinese characters for a tablet to be placed over the main door.[5] Mei remembers being fitted as a teenager into a high-collared silk *qipao* with long slits up the sides and serving tea at parties hosted by the Lillys at the house. During this period, my grandparents also added artifacts of a homeland left behind to their house, turning it into the showcase that seemed to me as a child like a stage set.

Toward the end of his career, my grandfather wrote Eli Lilly to thank him for supporting his research: "It must be providence that made me and Amy enjoy the American way of life through your initial arrangements—free from the contamination of Chinese communism!"[6] For his contributions, KK had been offered stock options many years earlier, and he'd purchased shares for himself and Tom. When Amy discovered this arrangement, her seeming satisfaction at the transition from doctor and researcher to housewife dis-

"House of Sylvan Harmonies," Conner Prairie Farm, Indiana, ca. 1950.
Courtesy of Eli Lilly and Company Archives.

solved into fury. The next day, in a story I heard many times, after her husband left for work and Mei and Tom set off for school, she donned her best suit and drove to the Lilly headquarters. She marched to the president's office and asked his secretary for an appointment that day. The secretary looked her up and down, checked the calendar, and said she would try to fit her in. Amy sat and waited, hands carefully folded over the leather briefcase in her lap.

After shaking her hand, Mr. Lilly motioned for her to sit. Across the wide expanse of his desk he said, "Mrs. Chen, what a pleasant surprise. What can I do for you?" Amy nodded and asked to be told how many shares of stock her husband had purchased. "I would like to purchase the exact same number for myself and my daughter." As he prepared to respond, she added firmly, "I have my own bank account. I can write a check right now."

Amy's interest in the stock market, kindled during her days as an intern, grew from this point on. Shortly before the annual meeting of Lilly stockholders, she invited Ruth Lilly to lunch and talked her into attending. On the morning of the meeting, she drove to pick up her reluctant companion, convinced that without the ride Mrs. Lilly might fail to join her as the only other woman at the gathering. Her obsession with the stock market continued well into her nineties, when she still spent hours every day poring over *Wall Street Journal* numbers with a magnifying glass. At dinner, she explained her economic theories to me, insistent in spite of what I considered my obvious disinterest (I had other questions to ask), and preached the virtue of financial independence.

If this preoccupation might be explained as a form of displaced feminism, a substitute for the women's clinic in China never opened, Amy's advice to her daughter was strangely mixed. While she emphasized female financial independence, she and KK assumed that their son but not their daughter would become a doctor. While they pushed Tom toward medical school, they instructed Mei to settle for a master's degree in pharmacology. My mother still occasionally wonders aloud about what kind of doctor she would have been if her parents had held similar expectations for both their children. Instead she found herself subjected to her parents' introductions to whatever young Chinese men they could find between Indianapolis and Lafayette, where she attended Purdue University, or in San Francisco, where the family sometimes spent summers close to the Chinatown herb shops that KK scoured for new samples.

In 1965, after my mother graduated from college, she wanted to learn more about Chinese painting. She arranged to visit her aunt in London for painting lessons, and then to see her uncle in Paris. Many months after she returned from the trip, Shuhua wrote Mei a long, emotional letter. Xiaoying found a typescript copy after her mother's death, but Mei doesn't remember receiving it. Nonetheless, it reveals a recurrent irresolvable contradiction between Shuhua and Amy, and how Shuhua tried to use her niece as a pawn in the fight.

Yesterday I was on the point to write to you, your mother's letter arrived. For the past nine months, I wrote her at least five or six letters, but never had I got an answer. Now she wrote in a both angry and rude tone. I was terribly upset of course, but after I calmed down myself, I decide to write to you. Perhaps I'd better tell you how your mother wrote and I hope you will kindly let me know what was really the cause of her being so angry and rude. I believe you understand us very well and I do sympathise with your situation. I will not tell your mother what you said about her. I am worrying about her health, if she is healthy, she would not bear to hurt my feeling as much as this.

The following I copied from her letter, "As far as writing letters, I have lost all interest to write to you on account of what you said to Mei about our mother and our great grandmother and me. I never can imagine that, especially mother is dead and cannot defend herself in person. Our great grandmother was not a Spanish woman. Where did you get the idea? Mother and I were very close, anything said about her is also against me. As you are as good that you don't have to belittle your relatives in order to get ahead. Mei-fong got so confused after her trip to London that I really wish that I never advise her to learn painting from you."

I don't remember that I had mentioned about my mother to you because you never met her. Nor did I talk about our great grandmother, all I know is from my parents' talk that we had had a great grandma who had yellow curly hair, so our relatives called her the yellow hair lady. No one said she was foreigner besides if she were a Spanish, she should have black hair. We all know many good American citizens have European grandparents; they never feel ashamed of themselves. So, I really don't see what the fuss your mother are making on me. As about my mother, I never feel ashamed of to say that she is not the first wife of my father. In the East, a man can have several wives, this is a different social system, properly recognised for several thousand years. A concubine in China is a member of the family, in the old days if a concubine's son passed the imperial court examination, she was able to ask the Emperor's favour to wear the special honourable robe and enjoy all the privileges that the first wife had. . . .

I could not believe what I read when I had your mother's letter. She looks at me and my long time love for her like dirt. I cannot believe she could be so heartless. I never lied to her all my life, nor did I take advantage from her. I always sent her unusual and expensive gifts every Xmas, not only because I wanted her to be happy to be able to get some gift from a nearest relative, but also because I have loved from our childhood. Now I rather feel ashamed of being so silly for years, specially the last nine months, I wrote to her and sending gifts, not having an answer. Instead, a rude and heartless accusation letter was for me.

The sisters continued in old age to communicate—even when only bickering held them together—but they never overcame their difference over how to represent the past. Each fiercely protected her version, although both versions had internal inconsistencies, for these continual reinventions of themselves and their past had become, in a sense, the story of their lives. As they approached the final chapter, they obsessively renarrated youthful achievement in a distant homeland. In my grandmother's favorite stories, she prided herself on being in control—of the horse she rode up Mount Tai, her education, her marriage, and her finances. I often find myself pondering the compromises she made for assimilation in a country that turned out not to be as advanced as she'd imagined, as well as the vagaries of historical influence on Chinese women of her generation.

It's impossible to know the turns her life might have taken if she had returned to open her women's clinic. The Yanjing University roommate with whom she once shared her dreams of attending PUMC provides one alternative scenario. Li Dequan, who married the "Christian General" Feng Yuxiang, became a middle school biology teacher after graduation. During the Sino-Japanese War, she emerged as a leading figure in Chongqing-based women's organizations. After the war and the death of her husband, who toward the end had denounced Chiang Kaishek, she became vice president of the All-China Federation of Democratic Women and, in 1949, minister of health for the People's Republic of China. She established policies that increased the availability of socialized medicine and pushed women's health initiatives. Under her direction, prostitutes received medical treatment and training in farm or factory trades, the rate of venereal disease decreased, a network of nurseries provided childcare for working mothers, and women's medical cooperatives trained midwives.[7] These advances in Chinese women's health care were exactly what Amy had once hoped to promote. Would she have joined her former roommate's efforts if she'd gone back?

In 2002, I met two retired PUMC pharmacologists, a couple whose troubled story provides another glimpse at what might have been: my grandparents' lives seen through the looking glass. The husband once worked in a PUMC lab assisting my grandfather and admired his research. Like my grandparents, they both eventually studied in the United States. When the civil war in China ended, they were working in San Francisco at the University of California. In 1950, they received a letter from Premier Zhou Enlai asking them to return to the mainland to help build the new nation. My grandparents probably received a similar invitation. Unlike them, this couple was stirred by Zhou's entreaty and soon moved into one of the American-style houses on the PUMC campus built for the original faculty. Throughout the 1950s, a period they remember as filled with promise, their research thrived. But when the Cultural Revolution swept Beijing, they suffered for their U.S. connections in ways they didn't want to talk about. They had managed to preserve a black-and-white studio photograph of my grandfather at the height of his Lilly career. They pulled the old image out to show me and explained how proud they were to receive it in the mid-1950s with a letter of encouragement from their former mentor.

I only once heard my grandmother tell a story admitting to fate's hand in the unfolding of her life. In 1972, my grandfather was elected honorary president of the International Union of Pharmacology. The annual meetings were held that year in San Francisco, and KK and Amy invited the delegates to a banquet at the Empress of China, overlooking Portsmouth Square in Chinatown. Amy stood at the entrance as guests arrived. Suddenly someone shouted, "Ling Shuhao," a name she seldom heard anymore. She turned toward the voice, and her eyes came to rest on a smiling face she couldn't immediately place. She squinted at the tag pinned to his shirt and recognized the name of a neighbor on Ganmian Hutong, her tennis partner from over sixty years earlier. He explained he'd come from Taiwan for the conference and then blurted out, "But Shuhao, how did *you* get here?" She shrugged and laughed at me over the dinner table, as she recounted her response, "I'm here . . . I'm here for no good reason whatsoever."

Epilogue: Return

$\mathcal{I}$n the last chapter of *Ancient Melodies*, Amy and Shuhua's Feng cousins visit them in Tianjin. Both men have studied abroad, one in Europe, the other in Japan. They praise the sisters' participation in the student movement and say to Li Ruolan, "You see, Aunt, nowadays you must have some activities besides learning if you want to be superior to others. Men and women are alike, the competition is much more serious than in our day."[1] During the course of their stay, they also convince Ling Fupeng to move back to Beijing, where his youngest daughters will be able to continue their education. Delighted, Shuhua and Amy run into the garden. A light dusting of snow covers the ornamental rocks, and Shuhua rhapsodizes about the city where she was born.

> A beautiful carpet began to be woven in my mind. Its background was gold and silver. There were magnificent palaces, gardens decorated with flowers, peacocks, storks, and hawks. Golden fishes of various kinds swam in the lotus ponds; tree peonies which were taller than human beings grew everywhere and gave their gay touch of splendor. Kind and intimate faces were to be seen in the theatres, tea-houses, temples, and fairs of all kinds. . . . How fortunate I was to be able to go back to Peking![2]

Sixty-eight years later, at the age of eighty-nine, Shuhua discovered that her cancer had returned. Her left breast had been removed ten years earlier, but her doctors believed she wouldn't be able to survive another operation. Shuhua flew from London back to Beijing. At the airport, her son-in-law pushed her in a wheelchair to a waiting car. The driver sped through the city to Shijingshan Hospital, where she was admitted on December 1, 1989. Only six months earlier, student protests in Tiananmen Square had ended violently. As Shuhua lay dying, she enabled nurses and doctors to symbolically pay obeisance to a cohort of intellectuals denounced as bourgeois by the government that had recently opened fire on a new generation of students. At the side of her bed, they mourned one of their own, a young doctor caught by a bullet and numbered among the dead on June 4th. Shuhua received reporters who asked why she had returned home after all these years. She asked to eat snacks from every season of her childhood, and they brought pea flour cakes, mountain haw jelly, sesame seed pastries, scallion pancakes, and *you tiao* dipped in sweet, hot soy milk.

She wanted to see Ganmian Hutong, and they carried her to the old Ling property, which had become a kindergarten. She lay on a stretcher in the garden, where she once helped Lao Zhou ladle horse-hoof soup into the pots of orchids, and watched white clouds travel across a lapis blue sky. The faces of small children gathered around her; they touched her hands softly and held out tiny branches of crumpled cloth flowers. Her daughter had her carried through Beihai Park. The ponds had melted, and closed lotus blossoms had started pushing toward the water's surface. Soon their green leaves and strong pink flowers would cover the ponds, blossoms as big as boats!

She sat propped up in bed in a hospital room with green and white walls, filled with flowers, stuffed animals, and bottles of pain relievers, and looked at her daughter, son-in-law, granddaughter, and grandson. They'd flown from Scotland and the United States, waiting while her body slowly betrayed the wandering poet still trapped inside. The last sentence she spoke was, "I won't die."

Her official obituary read:

Professor Ling Shuhua (female, 1900–1990) original name Ling Ruitang, pen names Shuhua, Suxin, etceteras. Native place Guangdong Panyu, born in Beijing. In 1922 enrolled in the foreign literature department at Yanjing University, and in 1925 became famous after the publication of her short story "Intoxicated." The majority of her stories were first published in *Contemporary Review*, *Crescent Moon*, and *Morning Post*; anthologies of her work include *The Temple of Flowers*, *Women*, and *Little Brothers*. Stories such as "Embroidered Pillows" depict the dejection of women secluded in old-fashioned households, in a psychologically acute and fluid style of writing, exposing the injurious harm caused by the Confucian code of ethics. She was also skilled at portraying the sensibilities of children. At the end of 1989, filled with the yearning of "fallen leaves return to their roots," left England to return to Beijing. Seriously ill, carried on a stretcher to visit the places longed after for so many years, Beihai Park and her old house on Ganmian Hutong. On May 22, 1990, at 6:45 p.m., passed away in her hometown of Beijing at the age of 90.[3]

My grandmother would never return to Beijing. Although looking through old letters from the time of her sister's hospital stay in Beijing, I remembered how seriously she once considered it—or how seriously I had considered her to be. In the spring of 1990, at her urging, I wrote to Xiao-ying, explaining that my grandmother wanted to see her sister one last time. I offered to accompany her on the trip to Beijing. I received a reply, dated ten days before Shuhua's death, from her son-in-law. He wrote that, in light of my grandmother's frailty, he did not think it wise for her to undertake the journey to China. The doctors did not give Shuhua more than two weeks; it was unlikely we could arrive in time. Thinking back on the moment, I realized my grandmother never really intended to go. Her inquiry, made through me, had been a gesture of respect and an expression of earnest longing.

My grandmother would return to Beijing through me. I'd once unwittingly offered to be her escort back. Only later would I understand how successful she was at tempting me into this role. On my first trip to China, I arranged to see Bing Xin, my grandmother's friend who had played the traditional bride to her groom on the Yanjing University stage. Bing Xin lived in the faculty apartments of the institute where her husband taught for years. My taxi slowly navigated the work unit's narrow streets lined with winter piles of coal. Bing Xin's daughter opened the apartment door and ushered me in. A professor of American literature with extremely good English, she introduced me to her mother, who sat at a large wooden desk. I awkwardly handed her a letter from my grandmother, in which she had enclosed a recent photograph. Looking at the picture, Bing Xin smiled. Her daughter interpreted for me: "Your grandmother likes to put on makeup and things." I glanced at the picture and saw my grandmother in a San Francisco Chinatown restaurant. She wore a purple silk jacket and a string of pearls. She had been to the beauty shop to have her hair dyed black and curled. By contrast, Bing Xin wore a simple blue coat. Her gray hair was combed back and cut straight across above her collar. My grandmother had signed her name Amy Ling Chen. Bing Xin giggled, amused by how my grandmother used her husband's name, the unenlightened habit of overseas Chinese.

Bing Xin asked why I was visiting China, and I tried to explain my project as best I could at the time. When I told her that I was interested in Chinese women writers of her generation, she shook her head. "You shouldn't read that old stuff. You should read what the women here are writing now."

Soon I will do this, but it has taken me all of my twenties and most of my thirties to piece together the lives of two women who preceded the current generation of women who refuse to stay silent. I have dwelt at length, as they also did, upon the sisters' youth and have sped through their later years. Perhaps it's not such a coincidence that I have spent my youth writing about the years of their youth. This book is also an account of my education in twentieth-century history, one that I couldn't have gotten otherwise.

"How fortunate I was to be able to go back to Peking!" wrote Shuhua at the end of her autobiography. During one of our early tape-recording sessions, Amy provided an impromptu conclusion for her life's story.

> My life was very lucky. I was born in a good home. I'm very thankful for that. And I had very good parents. Then I always met good people. Even my landlady, the one in Cleveland. The first time I rang the doorbell, she opened the door, and I wanted that room right away because I liked her. Every examination I had, I passed. That's another lucky. I don't like to see tragic things. Anything tragic, let me alone. I just want to see good things in my life. I don't know if you should feel that way, but I saw too many tragic things in life.

This version, however, was not her last attempt to close the book. Ten years later, she would tell me another story. I had just returned from a research trip to China in the fall of 1999. While I was away, my grandmother celebrated her ninety-fourth birthday, although in the middle of dinner she declared that she was, in fact, ninety-five. I felt guilty to have missed the occasion, so I spent an afternoon in Beijing searching for a gift. I wandered the cluttered antique stalls on Liulichang Street, which display tourist trinkets, old curios, and new ones made to look old. A Chinese friend came along to help me pick something suitable and bargain the price down. I finally found a bamboo *bitong*, or brush pot, carved with cranes for longevity, in a vendor's jumbled case at the back of a long labyrinth of stalls. It was a weekday afternoon, and there were no other customers. The unshaven, middle-aged man behind the counter set his jar of tea on the floor and pulled the *bitong* out for me to examine. He took his time explaining the age and quality of the piece. When I expressed disbelief of his claim that it dated from the Qing dynasty, he shrugged his shoulders. After my friend bargained the price down, it was cheap, so cheap that it couldn't be from the Qing dynasty, so cheap that I felt slightly ashamed buying it for an event as significant as someone's ninety-fourth birthday. The vendor polished it with a dirty strip of towel and wrapped it in a sheet of newspaper tied with pink nylon twine.

My grandmother was very excited before my trip because she had read in the newspaper about improvements to the Beijing Capital Airport. She told me new runways would make it possible for seven airplanes to take off simultaneously. Could I believe how modern Beijing had become? She charged me with investigating the newspaper report, so she could confirm how far China had progressed since she last saw the city in 1936. I only remembered her request late one night during my trip as I caught the end of a television report about the new airport terminal. A smiling China Central TV reporter described how a high-tech computer system would efficiently check in passengers. She said nothing about runways.

In a taxi headed back to the airport, I chatted with the driver. He didn't know anything about the runway situation and grumbled about what a waste of money the whole project was—one more example of the government pouring resources into a showy display as proof of the Chinese Communist Party's advancements, just in time for their fiftieth anniversary celebration. "Why don't they really do something for the people?" he asked. In the end, I returned home with no more information and only a cheap piece of carved bamboo wrapped in newspaper as a gift.

I imagined that she would reproach me about the inadequacy of my airport report, so on the way to her apartment I listed in my mind all the other city development projects I knew about. As it turned out, she came nowhere close to asking me about modern details of the city.

Family members later told me she'd been sick the previous week. She'd probably had a minor stroke that left her mentally disoriented. What I know is that she spoke that night with the force of someone with an urgent message and wove a story that contained every story she had ever told me. Her eyes grew wide. She accentuated important points by crashing her fists together. Her voice never faltered.

My mother didn't have enough milk to nurse me. I was born before SMA formula was invented. In those days, there was no milk powder. When Tom and Mei were born, I didn't have milk. Not everybody's born a jersey. The doctors all recommended SMA formula. But when I was born, they hired a milk *amah*. My mother had nothing, all girl babies and not enough milk.

Before that, at the beginning, the moon collided with the sun, and mother's milk rained down to earth. Wheat, rice, all kinds of crops grew. People rose from the mud and started to walk.

Then, the Manchus invaded China. They rode on horseback down from the north, and blood ran into the earth. The Qing dynasty was established.

My father's life was threatened because he wanted to widen the streets and make the city modern. People in teahouses whispered about assassinating him. In order to widen the streets, he had to dig up the family tombs in front of those people's houses. But, he did it, he really did. He widened the street into Chang'an Avenue, all paved with cement.

The moon crashed into the sun. Mother's milk rained down to earth. The Manchus invaded. And then I was born. My mother didn't have enough milk. I was born a girl, but I could ride horseback because I dressed in boy's clothing.

Milk rained down to the earth. Wheat and rice grew from the mud. I was born. Then your mother. Then you.

After I passed the examination, I had no time to buy Western clothes. I arrived in Cleveland wearing Chinese clothes. They called me "little girl." Listen, young lady, I don't mean to lecture, but this is important. They just think you're a little girl. But I can ride a horse. I talk back. I state my opinion.

As she thumped her fist on the table for punctuating effect, I took advantage of the pause to try to redirect a monologue that I found mesmerizing but also disquieting in its attempt to make sense of a life near its end.

I set her birthday present on the table. Her hearing was bad that night, even with the hearing aid, so I wrote a message on her pad of paper, explaining that this was my birthday present to her. I had brought it back from China. I was sorry to have missed the party. She picked up the package and deftly unknotted the twine. She turned the *bitong* in her hands, tracing the carved cranes with her fingers.

"This is very old," she declared. "It belonged to my father. His calligraphy was very good. He put brushes in this. When I left China, my father gave it to me. I packed it in my steamer trunk when I came to the United States on the SS *President Jackson*."

She fixed her gaze on me as if I were an intruder. "You, how did you get this?" she demanded. "I thought it was lost. My father gave it to me before I left China."

I wrote note after frantic note on her small pad, trying to correct her story. She picked up my notes and then put them back down, like playing cards. She sat with her hands folded in her lap and stared at me, as if she did in fact have something on me. I started to believe in my own guilt. If I had not stolen the *bitong*, she knew I would steal her story the moment she turned her back. She'd left it sitting on the table to tempt me.

A week later, I went back to see her. The possessed storyteller of my previous visit had disappeared. I leaned to kiss her cheek, which smelled of dusting powder, and she held my hand in hers. "Oh, you're so tall. You look good. How are you? I haven't seen you for so long." Midway through dinner, I asked her if she liked the birthday present I had brought from Beijing. She stared at me blankly, so I pointed to the bamboo *bitong*, where it sat on the table next to the salt and pepper shakers, the bottles of vitamins, and the squat crystal toothpick holder. "Oh yes," she said, "I saw that this morning for the first time." I explained to her that I had brought it back for her birthday. She picked it up and said, "I was wondering where it came from. It's beautiful." She placed it back on the table and stuck a pen in it. "Now," she said, "tell me about Beijing. Did you see the airport?" Her eyes lit up. "They say it's very modern."

At the close of the sisters' long twentieth century, Amy's obsession with the Beijing airport, with travel and modernity, reminded me of just how far she and Shuhua had traveled since their birth at the century's beginning. For

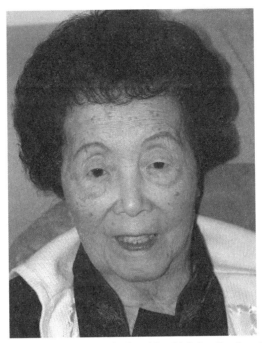

Amy Ling Chen on her hundred-and-first birthday, San Francisco, September 10, 2005. Photo by Grant V. Welland.

all of their dreams, broken and realized, these two modern girls never stopped yearning for more. A souvenir of their shared ambition lies pressed in my grandmother's PUMC yearbook. Shuhua's graceful calligraphy runs down a slim bookmark of faded yellow silk inscribed with fragments of classical poems, including the last line of Wang Zhihuan's "Climbing White Stork Tower": "Trying to see for a thousand miles, I climb one more story." Shuhua's final line is "I record these scattered sentences for my younger sister Shuhao to use between the pages of her book."

Sources

Sources cited by abbreviation:

AM   Ling Shuhua. *Ancient Melodies*. London: Hogarth Press, 1969.

BERG   The Henry W. and Albert A. Berg Collection of English and American Literature. New York: New York Public Library.

JB   Bell, Quentin, ed. *Julian Bell: Essays, Poems and Letters*. London: Hogarth Press, 1938.

KCC   Modern Archives. Cambridge, UK: King's College, Cambridge University.

LSHWC   Ling Shuhua. *Ling Shuhua wencun* [Collected writings of Ling Shuhua], ed. Chen Xueyong. Chengdu, China: Sichuan wenyi chubanshe, 1998.

SUSSEX Special Collections. Brighton, UK: University of Sussex.

TATE   Archive. London: Tate Gallery.

A comprehensive bibliography of Chinese and English language materials by and about Ling Shuhua and other further reading suggestions are available on the Rowman & Littlefield webpage for *A Thousand Miles of Dreams*, at www.rowman.com/isbn/0742553132.

References

PROLOGUE: DEPARTURE

1. Chow Tse-tsung, *The May Fourth Movement: Intellectual Revolution in Modern China* (Cambridge: Harvard University Press, 1960), 1–15; Roxane Witke, "Transformation of Attitudes toward Women during the May Fourth Era of Modern China" (Ph.D. diss., University of California at Berkeley, 1970).

2. Nie Hualing, *Ren, zai ershi shiji* [People in the twentieth century] (Teaneck, N.J.: Bafang wenhua qiye gongsi, 1990), 87.

3. Perry Link, *Evening Chats in Beijing* (New York: W. W. Norton, 1992), 3–10.

4. Susan Mann, *Precious Records: Women in China's Long Eighteenth Century* (Stanford, Calif.: Stanford University Press, 1997), 13–15, 35–44.

5. Virginia Woolf, *A Room of One's Own* (New York: Harcourt Brace Jovanovich, 1929), 45–46.

6. Dorothy Ko, *Teachers of the Inner Chambers: Women and Culture in Seventeenth-Century China* (Stanford, Calif.: Stanford University Press, 1994), 59–65; Mann, *Precious Records*, 10.

7. Wang Wei, "Preface to *Yueguan shi*," in *Women Writers of Traditional China: An Anthology of Poetry and Criticism*, ed. Kang-i Sun Chang and Haun Saussy, trans. Dorothy Ko (Stanford, Calif.: Stanford University Press, 1999), 689.

PART I: MOVING HOUSE

Chapter One: Origins

1. AM, 10.

2. Burton Watson, *Ssu-Ma Ch'ien: Grand Historian of China* (New York: Columbia University Press, 1958), 40–69; Pei-yi Wu, *The Confucian's Progress: Autobiographical Writings in Traditional China* (Princeton, N.J.: Princeton University Press, 1990), 3–14.

3. Hu Shi, *Sishi zishu* [Autobiography of a man at forty] (Shanghai, China: Yadong tushuguan, 1933), 3.

4. AM, 8–9.
5. AM, 81–82.

Chapter Two: Ambition

1. Anne Farrer and Mary Tregear, *Ling Suhua: A Chinese Painter and Her Friends* (Oxford: Ashmolean Museum, 1983), 14.

2. AM, 116–19; *Zhongguo fangzhi congshu* [Chinese regional gazateer collection], vol. 49 (Taibei, Taiwan: Chengwen chubanshe, 1970), 348–49.

3. AM, 140; *Zhongguo fangzhi congshu*, 294.

4. T. C. Lai, *A Scholar in Imperial China* (Hong Kong: Kelly & Walsh, 1970); Ichisada Miyazaki, *China's Examination Hell: The Civil Service Examinations of Imperial China* (New Haven, Conn.: Yale University Press, 1981).

5. Jung-Pang Lo, ed. and trans., *K'ang Yu-Wei: A Biography and Symposium* (Tuscon: University of Arizona Press, 1967), 29.

6. Jonathan D. Spence, *The Gate of Heavenly Peace: The Chinese and Their Revolution* (New York: Penguin Books, 1981), 35–44.

7. Lo, *K'ang Yu-Wei*, 67.

8. AM, 97.

9. Kenneth Rexroth and Ling Chung, eds. and trans., *Women Poets of China* (New York: New Directions Publishing, 1972), 19.

10. Susan Mann, *Precious Records: Women in China's Long Eighteenth Century* (Stanford, Calif.: Stanford University Press, 1997), 76–120.

11. Dorothy Ko, *Teachers of the Inner Chambers: Women and Culture in Seventeenth-Century China* (Stanford, Calif.: Stanford University Press, 1994), 232–42; Dorothy Ko, "Lady-Scholars at the Door: The Practices of Gender Relations in Eighteenth-Century Suzhou," in *Boundaries in China*, ed. John Hay (London: Reaktion Books, 1994), 198–216.

12. Liu Xiang, "Biographies of Heroic Women," in *Chinese Civilization: A Sourcebook*, ed. Patricia Buckley Ebrey, trans. Nancy Gibbs (New York: Free Press, 1993), 73.

Chapter Three: Disappointment

1. AM, 29.

2. AM, 34–35.

3. Zheng Liyuan, "Ru meng ru ge" [Like a dream, like a song], in LSHWC, 959.

4. Chen Xueyong, *Cainü de shijie* [World of talented women] (Beijing: Kunlun chubanshe, 2001), 98.

5. Susan Mann, *Precious Records: Women in China's Long Eighteenth Century* (Stanford, Calif.: Stanford University Press, 1997), 121–42.

6. Rey Chow, "Virtuous Transactions: A Reading of Three Stories by Ling Shuhu," *Modern Chinese Literature* 4, no. 1/2 (Spring/Fall 1988): 71–86.

Chapter Four: Courtyards

1. AM, 68.
2. Paul A. Cohen, *History in Three Keys: The Boxers as Event, Experience, and Myth* (New York: Columbia University Press, 1997), 14–56.
3. AM, 69.
4. Fu Wenshe, ed., *Zuijin guanshen lüli huibian* [Assembled biographies of recent officials and gentry] (Taibei, Taiwan: Wenhai chubanshe, 1970).
5. Zheng Liyuan, "Ru meng ru ge" [Like a dream, like a song], in LSHWC, 958.
6. Stephen R. MacKinnon, *Power and Politics in Late Imperial China: Yuan Shi-kai in Beijing and Tianjin, 1901–1908* (Berkeley: University of California Press, 1980), 137–79.
7. MacKinnon, *Power and Politics in Late Imperial China*, 154; Frank Dikötter, *Crime, Punishment and the Prison in Modern China* (New York: Columbia University Press, 2002), 53–58; Douglas R. Reynolds, *China 1898–1912: The Xinzheng Revolution and Japan* (Cambridge, Mass.: Harvard University Press, 1993), 172–74.
8. Dikötter, *Crime, Punishment and the Prison in Modern China*, 46.
9. AM, 11.
10. Qian Xingcun, "Guanyu Ling Shuhua chuangzuo de kaocha" [Observations regarding Ling Shuhua's creative work], *Haifeng zhoubao* [Ocean wind weekly], December 8, 1928, reprinted in *Dangdai Zhongguo nüzuojia lun* [A discussion of contemporary Chinese women writers], ed. Huang Renying (Shanghai, China: Guanghua shuju, 1933), 260.
11. Ling Shuhua, "The Lucky One," in *Chinese Women Writers: A Collection of Short Stories by Chinese Women Writers of the 1920s and 30s*, trans. J. Anderson and T. Munford (Hong Kong: Joint Publishing Co., 1985), 65.
12. Shuhua, "The Lucky One," 73.
13. AM, 19.
14. AM, 18.
15. AM, 57.
16. AM, 60.
17. AM, 62.
18. AM, 89.
19. AM, 89.
20. AM, 90.
21. AM, 98.
22. AM, 92.
23. AM, 114.
24. AM, 67.
25. AM, 201.

Chapter Five: Mountains and Walls

1. Clara Yü Cuadrado, "Portraits of a Lady: The Fictional World of Ling Shuhua," in *Women Writers of 20th-Century China*, ed. A. Jung Palandri (Eugene: Asian Studies Program, University of Oregon, 1982), 46–52.

2. AM, 79.

3. AM, 82.

4. AM, 85.

5. Chen Xueyong, *Cainü de shijie* [World of talented women] (Beijing: Kunlun chubanshe, 2001), 98.

6. AM, 86.

7. Ling Shuhua, undated typescript of autobiography, VII: 3, BERG.

8. AM, 107.

9. Yi-tsi Feuerwerker, "Women as Writers in the 1920s and 1930s," in *Women in Chinese Society*, ed. M. Wolf and R. Witke (Stanford, Calif.: Stanford University Press, 1975), 158.

10. AM, 87.

PART II: CASTING OFF

Chapter Six: Lessons

1. AM, 121–22.

2. Charlotte Beahan, "Feminism and Nationalism in the Chinese Women's Press, 1902–1911," *Modern China* 1, no. 4 (October 1975): 380–81.

3. Susan Mann, "Western Missionary Views of Educated Chinese Women at the Turn of the Twentieth Century," in *Tradition and Metamorphosis in Modern Chinese History*, ed. Hao Yanping and Wei Xiumei (Taibei, Taiwan: Academia Sinica Institute of Modern History, 1998), 2:1039–66.

4. Liang Qichao, "Lun nüxue" [On women's education], in *Yinbing shi heji: Wenji* [Writings from the ice-drinker's studio: Collected essays] (Shanghai, China: Zhonghua shuju, 1936), 1:39.

5. Hu Ying, "Naming the First Woman," *Nan Nü: Men, Women, and Gender in Early and Imperial China* 3, no. 2 (2001): 199–205.

6. Yu-Shih Chen, "The Historical Template of Pan Chao's *Nü Chieh*," *Transactions of the International Conference of Orientalists in Japan* 82, no. 4/5 (1996): 229–57.

7. AM, 151.

8. Charlotte Beahan, "The Women's Movement and Nationalism in Late Ch'ing China" (PhD diss., Columbia University, 1976), 37–38; see also Jane Hunter, *The Gospel of Gentility: American Women Missionaries in Turn-of-the-Century China* (New Haven, Conn.: Yale University Press, 1984), 1–26.

9. Beahan, "The Women's Movement," 40–41.

10. Beahan, "The Women's Movement," 37–38, 49–50.

11. Hu, "Naming the First Woman," 205–16; Weili Ye, "Nü Liuxuesheng: The Story of American-Educated Chinese Women, 1880s–1920s," *Modern China* 20, no. 3 (July 1994): 318–24.

12. Dorothy Ko, "The Body as Attire: The Shifting Meanings of Footbinding in Seventeenth-Century China," *Journal of Women's History* 8, no. 4 (Winter 1997): 8–27.

13. Beahan, "The Women's Movement," 51; Alison R. Drucker, "The Influence of Western Women on the Anti-Footbinding Movement, 1840–1911," in *Women in China: Current Directions in Historical Scholarship*, ed. R. W. Guisso and S. Johannesen (Youngstown, N.Y.: Philo Press, 1981), 179–99.

14. Jonathan D. Spence, *The Gate of Heavenly Peace: The Chinese and Their Revolution* (New York: Penguin Books, 1981), 72–73.

15. Liang Qichao, "Chang she nü xuetang qi" [A suggestion to establish girls' schools], in *Yinbing shi heji: Wenji* [Writings from the ice-drinker's studio: Collected essays] (Shanghai, China: Zhonghua shuju, 1936), 2:20.

16. Beahan, "Feminism and Nationalism," 413.

17. Ono Kazuko, *Chinese Women in a Century of Revolution, 1850–1950*, ed. J. A. Fogel, trans. K. Bernhardt et al. (Stanford, Calif.: Stanford University Press, 1989), 89.

18. John K. Fairbank and Edwin O. Reischauer, *China: Tradition and Transformation* (Boston: Allen & Unwin, 1989), 399.

19. Ono, *Chinese Women in a Century of Revolution*, 73–80.

20. Ono, *Chinese Women in a Century of Revolution*, 80–84.

21. AM, 81.

22. AM, 182.

23. AM, 182–83.

24. Chen Xueyong, *Cainü de shijie* [World of talented women] (Beijing: Kunlun chubanshe, 2001), 99.

Chapter Seven: Mist

1. "Shimai yonin takitsubo ni oboru" [Four siblings drown in waterfall basin], *Kobe Shimbun*, August 11, 1913.

2. Rebecca E. Karl, "Creating Asia: China in the World at the Beginning of the Twentieth Century," *American Historical Review* 103, no. 4 (October 1998): 1109–13.

3. Charlotte Beahan, "Feminism and Nationalism in the Chinese Women's Press, 1902–1911," *Modern China* 1, no. 4 (October 1975): 410.

4. Mary Backus Rankin, "The Emergence of Women at the End of the Ch'ing: The Case of Ch'iu Chin," in *Women in Chinese Society*, ed. M. Wolf and R. Witke (Stanford, Calif.: Stanford University Press, 1975), 39–66.

5. Douglas R. Reynolds, *China 1898–1912: The Xinzheng Revolution and Japan* (Cambridge, Mass.: Harvard University Press, 1993), 141–48.

6. Reynolds, *China 1898–1912*, 80.

7. "Shimai yonin."

8. AM, 209.

9. AM, 216.

10. AM, 217.

11. "Shimai yonin."

12. AM, 231.

Chapter Eight: Amid Ghosts

1. Gail Hershatter, *The Workers of Tianjin, 1900–1949* (Stanford, Calif.: Stanford University Press, 1986), 9–24.

2. Li Xin and Sun Sibai, *Minguo renwu zhuan* [Biographies of Republican-era figures] (Beijing: Zhonghua shuju, 1980), 2:181–87; see also Howard L. Boorman, ed., *Biographical Dictionary of Republican China* (New York: Columbia University Press, 1968), 3:195, 4:85–86.

3. Li and Sun, *Minguo renwu zhuan*, 186.

4. Ernest P. Young, *The Presidency of Yuan Shih-k'ai: Liberalism and Dictatorship in Early Republican China* (Ann Arbor: University of Michigan Press, 1977), 201–5.

5. AM, 152.

6. AM, 158.

7. AM, 218.

8. Yen-chu Sun, "Chinese National Higher Education for Women in the Context of Social Reform, 1919–1929" (PhD diss., New York University, 1985), 65–67.

9. Ling Shuhua, "Little Liu," trans. V. Ling Hsu and J. Fitzgerald, in *Born of the Same Roots: Stories of Modern Chinese Women*, ed. V. Ling Hsu (Bloomington: Indiana University Press, 1981), 65.

10. James Reeve Pusey, *Lu Xun and Evolution* (Albany: State University of New York Press, 1998), xiii.

11. Lung-Kee Sun, "The Presence of the Fin-de Siècle in the May Fourth Era," in *Remapping China: Fissures in Historical Terrain*, ed. G. Hershatter, E. Honig, J. N. Lipman, and R. Stross (Stanford, Calif.: Stanford University Press, 1996), 194–209.

12. Lu Xun, "Women xianzai zenyang zuo fuqin" [How do we behave as fathers now?], in *Lu Xun quanji* (Beijing: Renmin wenxue chubanshe, 1982), 1:132.

13. Charlotte Beahan, "Feminism and Nationalism in the Chinese Women's Press, 1902–1911," *Modern China* 1, no. 4 (October 1975):390; see also Wendy Larson, *Women and Writing in Modern China* (Stanford, Calif.: Stanford University Press, 1998), 110–22.

Chapter Nine: In the Streets

1. Chow Tse-tsung, *The May Fourth Movement: Intellectual Revolution in Modern China* (Cambridge, Mass.: Harvard University Press, 1960), 20–22.

2. Leo Ou-fan Lee, *The Romantic Generation of Modern Chinese Writers* (Cambridge, Mass.: Harvard University Press, 1973), 5.

3. E. Perry Link Jr., *Mandarin Ducks and Butterflies: Popular Fiction in Early Twentieth-Century Chinese Cities* (Berkeley: University of California Press, 1981), 1–23.

4. Hershatter, *The Workers of Tianjin, 1900–1949* (Stanford, Calif.: Stanford University Press, 1986), 11; Lin Xi, *Lao Tianjin* [Old Tianjin] (Nanjing, China: Jiangsu meishu chubanshe, 1998), 153–63.

5. Chow Tse-tsung, *The May Fourth Movement*, 59.

6. Henrik Ibsen, *Four Major Plays*, trans. J. McFarlane and J. Arup (Oxford, UK: Oxford University Press, 1981), 82.

7. Chow Tse-tsung, *The May Fourth Movement*, 91.

8. John Dewey and Alice Chipman Dewey, *Letters from China and Japan*, ed. E. Dewey (New York: E. P. Dutton & Co., 1920), 247.

9. Chow Tse-tsung, *The May Fourth Movement*, 108.

10. Chow Tse-tsung, *The May Fourth Movement*, 99–116.

11. AM, 233.

12. Chow Tse-tsung, *The May Fourth Movement*, 129–30; Chae-Jin Lee, *Zhou Enlai: The Early Years* (Stanford, Calif.: Stanford University Press, 1994), 124.

13. This event bears striking resemblance to a factory death in Shanghai that precipitated that May Thirtieth Incident in 1925, but in *Ancient Melodies*, Shuhua dates her involvement in an anti-Japanese protest to 1920.

14. AM, 234.

15. Chow Tse-tsung, *The May Fourth Movement*, 148–51.

16. Chae-Jin Lee, *Zhou Enlai*, 36–74.

17. AM, 236.

18. AM, 237.

19. AM, 239.

20. Burton Watson, trans., *Chuang Tzu: Basic Writings* (New York: Columbia University Press, 1964), 140.

21. AM, 253.

22. Ling Shuhua, "Xinjiapo ban *Ling Shuhua xuanji* houji" [Afterword to the Singapore edition of the selected writings of Ling Shuhua], in *Ling Shuhua xiaoshuo ji* [Collected stories of Ling Shuhua] (Taibei, Taiwan: Hongfan shudian, 1984), 469.

23. Jonathan D. Spence, *The Gate of Heavenly Peace: The Chinese and Their Revolution* (New York: Penguin Books, 1981), 254–55.

24. Wendy Larson, *Women and Writing in Modern China* (Stanford, Calif.: Stanford University Press, 1998), 91.

25. AM, 255.

26. AM, 255–56.

Chapter Ten: Romance

1. Zheng Liyuan, "Ru meng ru ge" [Like a dream, like a song], in LSHWC, 967.

2. Philip West, *Yenching University and Sino-Western Relations, 1916–1952* (Cambridge, Mass.: Harvard University Press, 1976), 34–35.

3. Yen-to, "Shida chaoliu zhong de yige nüzi" [A girl in the trend of time], *Xin nüxing* [New woman] 1, no. 7 (July 1926): 485; quoted in Leo Ou-fan Lee, *The Romantic Generation of Modern Chinese Writers* (Cambridge, Mass.: Harvard University Press, 1973), 33–34.

4. Miriam Silverberg, "The Modern Girl as Militant," in *Recreating Japanese Women, 1600–1945*, ed. G. L. Bernstein (Berkeley: University of California Press, 1991), 239–66; Barbara Hamill Sato, "The *Mogo* Sensation: Perceptions of the *Modan Garu* in Japanese

Intellectual Circles During the 1920s," *Gender & History* 5, no. 3 (Autumn 1993): 363–81.

5. Roxane Witke, "Transformation of Attitudes toward Women during the May Fourth Era of Modern China" (PhD diss., University of California at Berkeley, 1970), 168–75; Bertrand Russell, *The Autobiography of Bertrand Russell* (Boston: Little, Brown and Co., 1967), 183.

6. Lau Shaw, "Hollywood Films in China," *The Screen Writer* 2, no. 6 (November 1946): 2.

7. D. W. Griffith, *Way Down East* (D. W. Griffith Productions, 1920).

8. Tze-lan Deborah Sang, "The Emerging Lesbian: Female Same-Sex Desire in Modern Chinese Literature and Culture" (PhD diss., University of California, Berkeley, 1996), 143–89.

9. Ling Shuhua, "Once Upon a Time," in *Writing Women in Modern China: An Anthology of Women's Literature from the Early Twentieth Century*, ed. A. M. Dooling and K. M. Torgeson (New York: Columbia University Press, 1998), 186.

10. Bing Xin, "Autobiographical Notes," trans. J. Cayley, *Renditions* 32 (Autumn 1989): 84–87.

Chapter Eleven: Gatherings

1. Bing Xin, "How I Wrote *A Maze of Stars* and *Spring Water*," trans. J. Cayley, *Renditions* 32 (Autumn 1989): 88–91; Zhou Zuoren, quoted in Leo Ou-fan Lee, *The Romantic Generation of Modern Chinese Writers* (Cambridge, Mass.: Harvard University Press, 1973), 20.

2. Zhou Zuoren, quoted in Shu-mei Shih, *The Lure of the Modern: Writing Modernism in Semicolonial China, 1917–1937* (Berkeley: University of California Press, 2001), 178.

3. Leo Ou-fan Lee, *The Romantic Generation*, 12.

4. Bing Xin, "How I Wrote," 88.

5. Ling Shuhua, quoted in Zhang Yanlin, "Ling Shuhua, Zhou Zuoren, 'Nü'er shenshi tai qiliang" [Ling Shuhua, Zhou Zuoren, and "A daughter's lot is too miserable"], *Xin wenxue ziliao* [New literature historical materials] 1 (2001): 127–28.

6. Ling Shuhua, "Ling Shuhua, Zhou Zuoren," 128.

7. Ling Shuhua, "Nü'er shenshi tai qiliang" [A daughter's lot is too miserable], in LSHWC, 4.

8. Ling Shuhua, "Nü'er shenshi," 12–13.

9. LSHWC, 893.

10. See, for example, C. T. Hsia, Joseph S. M. Lau, and Leo Ou-fan Lee, eds., *Modern Chinese Stories and Novellas, 1919–1949* (New York: Columbia University Press, 1981), 195–96.

11. AM, 167–68; Zheng Liyuan, "Ru meng ru ge" [Like a dream, like a song], in LSHWC, 958–59.

12. LSHWC, 894–925.

13. Ling Shuhua, "Huiyi yige huahui ji jige lao huajia" [Remembering a painting party and several old painters], in LSHWC, 677–84; Ling Shuhua, "The Wen-jen-hua

School," in *A Chinese Painter's Choice: Some Paintings from the 14th to the 20th Century from the Collection of Ling Shuhua* (London: Arts Council of Great Britain, 1967), 5–6.

14. Mary Augusta Mullikin, "An Artists' Party in China," *Studio International* 110, no. 512 (November 1935): 288.

15. Mullikin, "An Artists' Party in China," 284.

16. Ling, "Huiyi yige huahui," 683.

17. Leo Ou-fan Lee, *The Romantic Generation*, 8.

18. Pang-Mei Natasha Chang, *Bound Feet and Western Dress* (New York: Doubleday, 1996), 109–27.

19. Chen Xiying, "Liu Shuhe," in *Xiying xianhua* [The causeries of Xiying] (Beijing: Dongfang chubanshe, 1995), 148–57.

20. Shifen Gong, *A Fine Pen: The Chinese View of Katherine Mansfield* (Dundedin, New Zealand: University of Otago Press, 2001), 11–21.

21. Gong, *A Fine Pen*, 119.

22. Chen Xiying to Cai Yuanpei, January 23, 1922, in *Hu Shi yuangao ji micang shuxin* [Original manuscripts and personal letters of Hu Shi], ed. Geng Yunzhi (Hefei, China: Huangshan shushe, 1994), 35:53.

23. Rabindranath Tagore, quoted in Leo Ou-fan Lee, *The Romantic Generation*, 145.

24. Leo Ou-fan Lee, *The Romantic Generation*, 17–19; Liang Shiqiu, "Yi xinyue" [Recalling crescent moon], in *Wenxue yinyuan* [Notes in literature] (Taibei, Taiwan: Wenxing shudian, 1964), 291–303; Xu Zhimo, poem quoted in Jonathan D. Spence, *The Gate of Heavenly Peace: The Chinese and Their Revolution* (New York: Penguin Books, 1981), 200.

25. Jiang Fucong and Liang Shiqiu, eds., *Xu Zhimo quanji* [Collected works of Xu Zhimo] (Taibei, Taiwan: Zhuanji wenxue chubanshe, 1980), 6:595.

26. Guo Moruo, quoted in Spence, *The Gate of Heavenly Peace*, 215.

27. Ling Shuhua, "Wo de lixiang ji shixian de Taige'er xiansheng" [My idealized and realized Mr. Tagore], in LSHWC, 603.

28. Ling, "Wo de lixiang ji shixian," 602.

29. Zheng, "Ru meng ru ge," 960–62.

30. Gong, *A Fine Pen*, 14–15; Zheng, "Ru meng ru ge," 960.

31. Ling Shuhua, "Jiemen suiji" [Jottings to kill time], in LSHWC, 605.

Chapter Twelve: Modern Medicine

1. Mary E. Ferguson, *China Medical Board and Peking Union Medical College: A Chronicle of Fruitful Collaboration, 1914–1951* (New York: China Medical Board, 1970), 27–55.

2. Ferguson, *China Medical Board*, 13–26; John Z. Bowers, *Western Medicine in a Chinese Palace: Peking Union Medical College, 1917–1951* (Philadelphia: Josiah Macy Jr. Foundation, 1972), 29–62.

3. Bowers, *Western Medicine*, 54.

4. Mary Bullock Brown, *An American Transplant: The Rockefeller Foundation and Peking Union Medical College* (Berkeley: University of California Press, 1980), 38–40.

5. Brown, *An American Transplant*, 27–30.

6. Brown, *An American Transplant*, 7.

7. Brown, *An American Transplant*, 22.

8. Brown, *An American Transplant*, 21.

9. Bertrand Russell, *The Problem of China* (New York: Century, 1922), 233–34.

10. Brown, *An American Transplant*, 81.

11. Ling Shuhao, "Gan zao che" [Catching the early train], in *The Unison* (Peking, China: Peking Union Medical College, 1924), 1:182–83.

12. "The Class of 1928," in *The Unison* (Peking, China: Peking Union Medical College, 1924), 85.

13. Lorin Webster, "PUMC Forever," in *The Unison* (Peking, China: Peking Union Medical College, 1924), 144.

14. Bowers, *Western Medicine*, 26.

15. Y. C. Wang, *Chinese Intellectuals and the West, 1872–1949* (Chapel Hill: University of North Carolina Press, 1966), 71–72, 111–16.

16. E. J. Kahn Jr., *All in a Century: The First 100 Years of Eli Lilly and Company* (Indianapolis: Eli Lilly & Co., 1976), 104–5.

17. K. K. Chen, "Two Pharmacological Traditions: Notes from Experience," *Annual Review of Pharmacology and Toxicology* 21 (1981): 1–6; Kahn, *All in a Century*, 105.

18. Bowers, *Western Medicine*, 104; Kahn, *All in a Century*, 105.

19. Bowers, *Western Medicine*, 104.

20. Marie-Claire Bergère, *Sun Yat-sen*, trans. Janet Lloyd (Stanford, Calif.: Stanford University Press, 1998), 396–408.

21. Tsing Hua Alumni Association, *The Tsing Hua Alumni Yearbook, 1925–1926* (1926).

22. Ling Shuhua to Hu Shi, July 1925, in LSHWC, 900.

Chapter Thirteen: Crescent Moon

1. Ling Shuhua, "Intoxicated," in *Writing Women in Modern China: An Anthology of Women's Literature from the Early Twentieth Century*, ed. A. M. Dooling and K. M. Torgeson (New York: Columbia University Press, 1998), 179.

2. Ling, "Intoxicated," 182.

3. Lu Xun, "*Zhongguo xin wenxue daxi* xiaoshuo erji xu" [Introduction to the second volume of fiction in the compendium of modern Chinese literature], in *Lu Xun quanji* [Complete works of Lu Xun] (Beijing: Renmin wexue chubanshe, 1996), 6:250.

4. Ling Shuhua to Hu Shi, [1924], in LSHWC, 901–4.

5. Ling to Hu, 902–3.

6. Ling Shuhua, "Embroidered Pillows," trans. Jane Parish Yang, in *Modern Chinese Stories and Novellas, 1919–1949*, ed. C. T. Hsia, J. S. M. Lau, and Leo Ou-fan Lee (New York: Columbia University Press, 1981), 199.

7. Ling, "Embroidered Pillows," 199.

8. Chen Xiaoying, letter to author, June 18, 2003.

9. Chen Xiaoying, letter to author, August 6, 2003.

10. Chen Xueyong, *Cainü de shijie* [World of talented women] (Beijing: Kunlun chubanshe, 2001), 101.

11. Chen Xueyong, *Cainü de shijie*, 101.

12. Liu Hong and Xia Xiaofei, eds., *Ling Shuhua Chen Xiying sanwen* [Essays of Ling Shuhua and Chen Xiying] (Beijing: Zhongguo guangbo dianshi chubanshe, 1995), 2, 8.

13. Yen-Chu Sun, "Chinese National Higher Education for Women in the Context of Social Reform, 1919–1929" (PhD diss., New York University, 1985), 200–208.

14. Lu Xun, "Sudden Notions (2)," in *Lu Xun: Selected Works*, trans. Yang Xianyi and Gladys Yang (Beijing: Foreign Language Press, 1980), 2:162; "After 'Knocking Against the Wall,'" *Lu Xun*, 2:176.

15. Zheng Liyuan, "Ru meng ru ge" [Like a dream, like a song], in LSHWC, 961.

16. Lu Xun, "Sudden Notions (9)," 2:168.

17. Lu Xun, "Not Idle Chat (3)," in *Lu Xun: Selected Works*, trans. Yang Xianyi and Gladys Yang (Beijing: Foreign Language Press, 1980), 2:209; "On Deferring 'Fair Play,'" *Lu Xun*, 2:28.

18. Lu Xun, "Not Idle Chat (3)," 2:210.

19. Lu Xun, "Guafuism," in *Lu Xun: Selected Works*, trans. Yang Xianyi and Gladys Yang (Beijing: Foreign Language Press, 1980), 2:212–18.

20. Michael Sullivan, "A Small Token of Friendship," *Oriental Art* 35, no. 2 (Summer 1989): 76–85.

21. G. E. Moore, *Principia Ethica* (Cambridge, UK: Cambridge University Press, 1903), vii.

22. Leo Ou-fan Lee, *The Romantic Generation of Modern Chinese Writers* (Cambridge, Mass.: Harvard University Press, 1973), 18.

23. Chen Xueyong, *Cainü de shijie*, 102; Jiang Fucong and Liang Shiqiu, eds., *Xu Zhimo quanji* [Collected works of Xu Zhimo] (Taibei, Taiwan: Zhuanji wenxue chubanshe, 1980), 1:63.

24. Rey Chow, "Virtuous Transactions: A Reading of Three Stories by Ling Shuhu," *Modern Chinese Literature* 4, no. 1/2 (Spring/Fall 1988): 84.

25. Shu-mei Shih, *The Lure of the Modern: Writing Modernism in Semicolonial China, 1917–1937* (Berkeley: University of California Press, 2001), 228.

26. Rey Chow, "Virtuous Transactions," 74.

27. LSHWC, 602.

28. Don Holoch, "Everyday Feudalism: The Subversive Stories of Ling Shuhua," in *Woman and Literature in China*, ed. A. Gerstlacher, R. Keen, W. Kubin, M. Miosga, and J. Schon (Bochum, Germany: Studienverlag Brockmeyer, 1985), 379–93.

29. Shu-mei Shih, *The Lure of the Modern*, 159–75.

30. Shu-mei Shih, *The Lure of the Modern*, 224.

31. Ling Shuhua to Hu Shi, [1925], in LSHWC, 895.

32. Chen Xueyong, *Cainü de shijie*, 102.

33. Chen Xiying, "Piaoqie yu chao xi" [On plagiarism], in *Xiying xianhua* [The causeries of Xiying] (Beijing: Dongfang chubanshe, 1995), 192–99.

34. Liu Fu, "Ma xia le yan de wenxue shijia" [Literary historians who curse blindly], *Yusi* [Thread of talk] 63 (January 25, 1926): 1–2.

35. Lu Xun, "Bu shi xin" [Not a letter], *Yusi* [Thread of talk] 65 (February 8, 1926): 1–6.

36. Hu Shi to Lu Xun, Zhou Zuoren, Chen Yuan, May 24, 1926, in *Hu Shi laiwang shuxin xuan* [Selected letters of Hu Shi] (Hong Kong: Zhonghua shuju, 1983), 1:379–82.

37. Ling Shuhua to Hu Shi, April 31, 1926, in LSHWC, 906.

38. Zheng, "Ru meng ru ge," 960.

39. Agnes Smedley, *Chinese Destinies* (New York: Vanguard Press, 1933), 85.

40. Helen Foster Snow, *Women in Modern China* (Paris: Mouton, 1967), 241–42.

41. AM, 242.

PART III: SEEKING A MOORING

Chapter Fourteen: Arrival

1. Tsing Hua Alumni Association, *The Tsing Hua Alumni Yearbook, 1925–1926* (1926).

2. John Fitzgerald, *Awakening China: Politics, Culture, and Class in the Nationalist Revolution* (Stanford, Calif.: Stanford University Press, 1996), 180–85.

3. Ronald Takaki, *Strangers from a Different Shore: A History of Asian Americans* (New York: Penguin Books, 1989), 111.

4. Jonathan D. Spence, *The Search for Modern China* (New York: W.W. Norton, 1990), 237–38.

5. Victor G. Nee and Brett de Bary Nee, *Longtime Californ': A Documentary Study of an American Chinatown* (Stanford, Calif.: Stanford University Press, 1986), 24–25.

6. Takaki, *Strangers from a Different Shore*, 235.

7. Elaine H. Kim, *Asian American Literature: An Introduction to the Writings and Their Social Context* (Philadelphia: Temple University Press, 1982), 298–89; Nee and Nee, *Longtime Californ'*, 68–69; Takaki, *Strangers from a Different Shore*, 118–19.

8. "Flames Consume Bamboo Garden," *Cleveland Plain Dealer*, September 21, 1925, sec. 1, 4.

9. "Rival Tong Chiefs Agree on a Truce," *New York Times*, August 29, 1925, sec. 12, 5.

10. "Arrest 91 in Raids on Boston Chinese," *New York Times*, August 31, 1925, sec. 3, 3.

11. "450 Chinese Seized; Tong Peace Signed," *New York Times*, September 15, 1925, sec. 1, 2.

12. "Chinatown Cowers as Raids Continue," *New York Times*, September 16, 1925, sec. 27, 3.

13. "Orders Chinese Dens be Razed," *Cleveland Plain Dealer*, September 24, 1925, sec. 1, 7; "Barry Puts Boot through Chinese Mystery Curtain," *Cleveland Plain Dealer*, September 24, 1925, sec. 1, 7; see also "Sze Moves to Aid Cleveland Chinese," *New York Times*, September 26, 1925, sec. 8, 3.

14. "Cleveland Incident," *Chinese Christian Student* 1, no. 1 (November 1925): 2.

15. "Cleveland Chinese and American Justice," *China Weekly Review*, January 2, 1926, 122–23.

16. "Comes from Peking to Learn to Be a Doctor," *Cleveland Plain Dealer*, September 24, 1925, sec. 15, 5.

Chapter Fifteen: Adrift

1. Chen Xiying to Hu Shi, January 28, 1928, in *Hu Shi laiwang shuxin xuan* [Selected letters of Hu Shi] (Hong Kong: Zhonghua shuju, 1983), 1:461–62.

2. *Minguo renwu dacidian* [Dictionary of Republican-era figures] (Shijiazhuang, China: Hebei renmin chubanshe, 1991), 737.

3. Leo Ou-fan Lee, *The Romantic Generation of Modern Chinese Writers* (Cambridge, Mass.: Harvard University Press, 1973), 148.

4. Wendy Larson, *Women and Writing in Modern China* (Stanford, Calif.: Stanford University Press, 1998), 173.

5. Hu Yunyi, "Zhongguo funü yu wenxue" [Chinese women and literature], quoted in Larson, *Women and Writing*, 174.

6. Yi Zhen, "Jiwei dangdai Zhongguo nüxiaoshuojia" [A few contemporary Chinese women fiction writers], in *Dangdai Zhongguo nüzuojia lun* [A discussion of contemporary Chinese women writers], ed. Huang Renying (Shanghai, China: Guanghua shuju, 1933), 1–36 (first used the term "New Boudoir Lady School" to describe Ling's work); He Yubo, *Zhongguo xiandai nüzuojia* [Modern Chinese women writers] (Shanghai: Fuxing shuju, 1935), 49–88 (reinforced this view of Ling's work as lightweight and trivial); Larson, *Women and Writing*, 183–86.

7. See, for example, Shifen Gong, *A Fine Pen: The Chinese View of Katherine Mansfield* (Dundedin, New Zealand: University of Otago Press, 2001), 18; and Leo Ou-fan Lee, *The Romantic Generation*, 17. Constantine Tung, *The Crescent Moon Society: The Minority's Challenge in the Literary Movement of Modern China* (Buffalo: Special Studies Council on International Studies, State University of New York, 1972) does not even mention Ling Shuhua.

8. Lydia H. Liu, *Translingual Practice: Literature, National Culture, and Translated Modernity—China, 1900–1937* (Stanford, Calif.: Stanford University Press, 1995), 211.

9. Quoted in Clara Yü Cuadrado, "Portraits of a Lady: The Fictional World of Ling Shuhua," in *Women Writers of 20th-Century China*, ed. A. Jung Palandri (Eugene: Asian Studies Program, University of Oregon, 1982), 54; see also Ling Shuhua, "A Poet Goes Mad," trans. Ling Shuhua with Julian Bell, *Tien Hsia Monthly* 4, no. 4 (April 1937): 401–21.

10. Shu-mei Shih, *The Lure of the Modern: Writing Modernism in Semicolonial China, 1917–1937* (Berkeley: University of California Press, 2001), 228.

11. Chen Xiying to Hu Shi, July 30, 1928, in *Hu Shi laiwang shuxin xuan* [Selected letters of Hu Shi] (Hong Kong: Zhonghua shuju, 1983), 1:490–92.

12. Ling Shuhua, "Deng Fushi shan" [Climbing Mount Fuji], in LSHWC, 609–10.

13. Chen Xiying to Hu Shi, December 26, 1929, in *Hu Shi laiwang shuxin xuan* [Selected letters of Hu Shi] (Hong Kong: Zhonghua shuju, 1983), 1:555–56.

14. Ling Shuhua, "Little Liu," trans. V. Ling Hsu and J. Fitzgerald, in *Born of the Same Roots: Stories of Modern Chinese Women*, ed. V. Ling Hsu (Bloomington: Indiana University Press, 1981), 72.

15. Ling Shuhua, "Little Liu," 73.

16. Ling Shuhua, "Yang Ma" [Mother Yang], in LSHWC, 173.

17. Chi Li, *Lao Wuhan* [Old Wuhan] (Nanjing, China: Jiangsu meishu chubanshe, 1999), 163–72; Stephen R. MacKinnon, "Wuhan's Search for Identity in the Republican Period," in *Remaking the Chinese City: Modernity and National Identity, 1900–1950*, ed. J. W. Esherick (Honolulu: University of Hawaii Press, 1999), 166–67; Peter Stansky and William Abrahams, *Journey to the Frontier: Two Roads to the Spanish Civil War* (Boston: Little, Brown and Company, 1966), 252–54.

18. Rey Chow, *Primitive Passions: Visuality, Sexuality, Ethnography, and Contemporary Chinese Cinema* (New York: Columbia University Press, 1995), 113–16.

19. Ling Shuhua, "Zhimo zhende bu huilai le ma" [Is Zhimo really not coming back], in LSHWC, 620.

20. Gao Wen, *Xu Zhimo yu ta shengming zhong de nüxing* [Xu Zhimo and the women in his life] (Tianjin, China: Tianjin renmin chubanshe, 2000), 225–44.

21. Ling Shuhua to Hu Shi, December 10, 1931, in LSHWC, 913–15.

22. Hu Shi to Ling Shuhua, December 28, 1931, *Hu Shi laiwang shuxin xuan* [Selected letters of Hu Shi] (Hong Kong: Zhonghua shuju, 1983), 2:98–99.

23. Bao Tong, "'Leng yue zhao shi hun'—ji wo de biaojiufu Xu Zhimo mu shang de shi bei" ["A cold moon illuminates the poet's soul"—remembering the poetic inscription on the tombstomb of my great-uncle Xu Zhimo], *Mingbao yuekan* [Mingpao monthly] 37, no. 1 (January 2002).

24. Ling Shuhua to Hu Shi, January 31, 1933, in LSHWC, 918–19.

25. Ling Shuhua, "Qiandaizi" [Chiyoko], in LSHWC, 310.

26. Larson, *Women and Writing*, 170.

27. Elizabeth Croll, *Feminism and Socialism in China* (Boston: Routledge & Kegan Paul, 1978), 158–60; Norma Diamond, "Women under Kuomintang Rule: Variations on the Feminine Mystique," *Modern China* 1, no. 1 (January 1975), 3–45.

28. Ling Shuhua to Hu Shi, 1932, in LSHWC, 916.

29. Ling Shuhua, "What's the Point of It?" trans. Ling Shuhua with Julian Bell, *T'ien Hsia Monthly* 3, no. 1 (August 1936): 58.

30. Su Xuelin, "Ling Shuhua de *Hua zhi si* yu *Nüren*" [Ling Shuhua's *Temple of flowers* and *Women*], *Xin bei chen* [New north morning] 2, no. 5 (May 1936).

31. Pi Gongliang, "Luojia san nü jie" [The three female talents of Luojia], *Wuhan chun qiu* [Wuhan spring and autumn] 24 (June 1996): 14–17.

32. Su Xuelin, "Ji Yuan Changying nüshi" [Remembering Yuan Changying], in *Feihui de kongque: Yuan Changying* [Peacock in flight: Yuan Chuangying], ed. Yang Jingyuan (Beijing: Renmin wenxue chubanshe, 2002), 1–5.

33. Yuan Changying, *Southwest Flies the Peacock*, in *Writing Women in Modern China: An Anthology of Women's Literature from the Early Twentieth Century*, ed. A. M. Dooling and K. M. Torgeson (New York: Columbia University Press, 1998), 252.

34. Dooling and Torgeson, *Writing Women in Modern China*, 210.

Chapter Sixteen: Souvenirs

1. K. K. Chen, "Two Pharmacological Traditions: Notes from Experience," *Annual Review of Pharmacology and Toxicology* 21 (1981): 3.
2. Chen, "Two Pharmacological Traditions," 4; E. J. Kahn Jr., *All in a Century: The First 100 Years of Eli Lilly and Company* (Indianapolis: Eli Lilly & Co., 1976), 106.
3. A. L. Chen and K. K. Chen, "Harmine, the Alkaloid of Caapi," *Quarterly Journal of Pharmacology* 12 (1939): 30–38.

Chapter Seventeen: The Entangling Net

1. LSHWC, 809n1.
2. "*Wuhan ribao* fukan *Xiandai wenyi* fakan ci" [Inaugural words on the *Wuhan daily* publication of *Contemporary literature and art*], in LSHWC, 809–14.
3. "*Wuhan ribao* fukan *Xiandai wenyi* fakan ci," 811.
4. "*Wuhan ribao* fukan *Xiandai wenyi* fakan ci," 811.
5. "*Wuhan ribao* fukan *Xiandai wenyi* fakan ci," 813.
6. "*Wuhan ribao* fukan *Xiandai wenyi* fakan ci," 813–14.
7. JB, 29.
8. Peter Stansky and William Abrahams, *Journey to the Frontier: Two Roads to the Spanish Civil War* (Boston: Little, Brown and Company, 1966), 263.
9. JB, 34.
10. JB, 33.
11. JB, 41.
12. JB, 42.
13. JB, 43.
14. JB, 47.
15. Goldsworthy Lowes Dickinson, *Letters from a Chinese Official: Being an Eastern View of Western Civilization* (New York: McClure, Phillips & Co., 1903), 38–39.
16. Jonathan Spence, *Chinese Roundabout: Essays in History and Culture* (New York: W. W. Norton, 1992), 74–75.
17. E. M. Forster, *Goldsworthy Lowes Dickinson and Related Writings* (London: Edward Arnold, 1973), 122.
18. Ling Shuhua to Margery Fry, January 3, 1934, REF/14/3, KCC.
19. JB, 123.
20. Stansky and Abrahams, *Journey to the Frontier*, 99–100.
21. Julian Bell's China diary, JHB/3/2, KCC.
22. JB, 49–50.
23. JB, 56.
24. JB, 58–59.
25. Julian Bell to Vanessa Bell, November 22, 1935, CHA/1/55/3/15, KCC.
26. Julian Bell to Vanessa Bell, December 6, 1935, CHA/1/55/3/15, KCC.
27. Zheng Liyuan, "Ru meng ru ge" [Like a dream, like a song], in LSHWC, 960.

28. Janet Malcolm, "A House of One's Own," *New Yorker* 71, no. 15 (June 5, 1995): 64.

29. Selma Meyerowitz, "Virginia and Ling Su Hua: Literary and Artistic Correspondences," *Virginia Woolf Miscellany* 18 (Spring 1982): 2–3; Patricia Laurence, "The 'Chinese Katherine Mansfield': Ling Shu-hua and Virginia Woolf," *Virginia Woolf Miscellany* 39 (Fall 1992): 7.

30. JB, 83.

31. Virginia Woolf, *The Sickle Side of the Moon: The Letters of Virginia Woolf*, ed. N. Nicolson (London: Hogarth Press, 1979), 452.

32. Julian Bell to Vanessa Bell, December 17, 1935, CHA/1/55/3/15, KCC.

33. Julian Bell to Vanessa Bell, December 18, 1935, CHA/1/55/3/15, KCC.

34. Julian Bell to Edward Playfair, December 27, 1935, MISC/82/9, KCC.

35. AM, 90–91.

36. Tani E. Barlow, *The Question of Women in Chinese Feminism* (Durham, N.C.: Duke University Press, 2004), 49–55.

37. Ling Shuhua to Julian Bell, January 4, 1936, CHA/1/55/3/16, KCC.

38. Ling Shuhua, "Dao Ke'enci nüshi" [Mourning Ms. Kuntz[?]], in LSHWC, 664.

39. JB, 73; Stansky and Abrahams, *Journey to the Frontier*, 267.

40. JB, 75.

41. JB, 76.

42. JB, 78.

43. JB, 56.

44. Julian Bell to Edward Playfair, February 3, 1936, MISC/82/9, KCC.

45. Julian Bell to Vanessa Bell, January 26, 1936, CHA/1/55/3/16, KCC.

46. JB, 82.

47. Patricia Laurence, *Lily Briscoe's Chinese Eyes: Bloomsbury, Modernism, and China* (Columbia: University of South Carolina Press, 2003), 69.

48. Stansky and Abrahams, *Journey to the Frontier*, 270.

49. Vanessa Bell to Julian Bell, January 25, 1936, TGA 9311.24, TATE.

50. Julian Bell to Edward Playfair, March 17, 1936, MISC/82/9, KCC.

51. Laurence, *Lily Briscoe's Chinese Eyes*, 93–94.

52. Julian Bell to Edward Playfair, March 1, 1936, MISC/82/9, KCC.

53. JB, 102.

54. JB, 122.

55. JB, 103–4.

56. Virginia Woolf, *Leave the Letters till We're Dead: The Letters of Virginia Woolf*, ed. N. Nicolson (London: Hogarth Press, 1980), 21.

57. Woolf, *Leave the Letters till We're Dead*, 32.

58. Laurence, *Lily Briscoe's Chinese Eyes*, 59.

59. Julian Bell to Vanessa Bell, May 9, 1936, CHA/1/55/3/16, KCC.

60. JB, 141.

61. Julian Bell to Vanessa Bell, June 16, 1936, JHB/2/6, KCC.

62. JB, 143.

63. JB, 113.

64. Julian Bell, China diary, JHB/3/2, KCC.

65. Stansky and Abrahams, *Journey to the Frontier*, 290–91.

66. Julian Bell to Edward Playfair, November 27, 1936, MISC/82/9, KCC.

67. Innes Herdan, *Liao Hongying: Fragments of a Life* (Dereham, England: Larks Press, 1996), 81.

68. Julian Bell to Ling Shuhua, December 12, 1936, CHA/1/123, KCC.

69. Ling Shuhua to Julian Bell, December 20, 1935, CHA/1/123, KCC.

70. "*Wuhan ribao* fukan *Xiandai wenyi* tingzhi ci" [Final words on the *Wuhan daily* publication of *Contemporary literature and art*], in LSHWC, 815.

71. Julian Bell to Ling Shuhua, [January 1937], BERG.

72. Julian Bell to Edward Playfair, February 22, 1936, MISC/82/9, KCC.

73. Julian Bell to Mrs. Leo Chen (Ling Shuhua), [January 1937], BERG.

74. Chen Xiying to Julian Bell, January 29, 1937, CHA/1/124, KCC.

75. Julian Bell to Vanessa Bell, March 1937, CHA/1/55/3/18, KCC.

76. Ling Shuhua to Julian Bell, March 2, 1937, CHA/1/123, KCC.

77. Chen Xiying to Julian Bell, March 16, 1937, CHA/1/124, KCC.

78. Stansky and Abrahams, *Journey to the Frontier*, 98.

79. Shang Xiaogang, "Hong Ying zaizao sanshi niandai chuanqi" [Hong Ying recreates 1930s legend], *Beijing qingnian bao* [Beijing youth news], December 4, 2000, 12.

80. Zhao Yiheng, "Juli'an yu Ling Shuhua" [Julian and Ling Shuhua], *Nanfang zhoumo* [Southern weekend], November 2, 2000.

81. Zhu Yuan, "Novelist Loses Out in Libel Case," *China Daily*, December 9, 2002, 10.

82. Ge Yunsong, "Sizhe shengqian renge liyi de minfa baohu" [Civil law protection of the moral interests of the deceased], *Bijiao fa yanjiu* [Comparative legal studies] 4 (2002): 22–34.

83. Hamish McDonald, "Erotic Fiction? Pornographic Fact, Court Rules," *The Age*, January 27, 2003.

84. Ling Shuhua, "Xiaoying," in LSHWC, 667.

85. Stansky and Abrahams, *Journey to the Frontier*, 412.

Chapter Eighteen: Rice Porridge

1. "How to Tell Japs from the Chinese," *Life* 11, no. 25 (December 22, 1941): 81–82.

Chapter Nineteen: War Letters

1. Liao Hongying to Vanessa Bell, July 25, 1937, CHA/1/364, KCC.

2. Quoted in Charles A. Laughlin, *Chinese Reportage: The Aesthetics of Historical Experience* (Durham, N.C.: Duke University Press, 2002), 181–82.

3. Vanessa Bell to Ling Shuhua, December 9, 1937, BERG.

4. Jonathan Spence, *The Search of Modern China* (New York: W. W. Norton, 1990), 448.

5. Theodore H. White and Annalee Jacoby, *Thunder out of China* (New York: William Sloane, 1946), 58–59.

6. W. H. Auden and Christopher Isherwood, *Journey to a War* (New York: Random House, 1939), 166–67.

7. Dick Wilson, *When Tigers Fight: The Story of the Sino-Japanese War, 1937–1945* (New York: Penguin Books, 1982), 123.

8. Virginia Woolf, *Leave the Letters till We're Dead: The Letters of Virginia Woolf*, ed. N. Nicolson (London: Hogarth Press, 1980), 221–22.

9. Auden and Isherwood, *Journey to a War*, 160.

10. Auden and Isherwood, *Journey to a War*, 161.

11. Auden and Isherwood, *Journey to a War*, 174–75.

12. Ling Shuhua to Virginia Woolf, May 25, 1938, BERG.

13. Su Hua Ling Chen, "Happy Days in Kiating," *Country Life* 110, no. 2857 (October 19, 1951): 1304.

14. Ling Shuhua, "Ai shan lu meng ying" [Dreams from a mountain lover's studio], in LSHWC, 690.

15. Su Hua Ling Chen, "Happy Days," 1304.

16. Ling Shuhua, "Houfang xiaojing" [Scenes from behind the front line], in LSHWC, 673.

17. Ling Shuhua to Virginia Woolf, July 24, 1938, BERG.

18. Ling Shuhua to Virginia Woolf, August 4, 1938, MHP Letters III, SUSSEX.

19. Ling Shuhua to Virginia Woolf, July 24, 1938, BERG.

20. Ling Shuhua, undated manuscript of autobiography, BERG.

21. Ling Shuhua to Virginia Woolf, July 24, 1938, BERG.

22. Woolf, *Leave the Letters*, 259.

23. Woolf, *Leave the Letters*, 259.

24. Ling Shuhua to Virginia Woolf, August 4, 1938, MHP Letters III, SUSSEX.

25. Woolf, *Leave the Letters*, 289–90.

26. Shu-mei Shih, *The Lure of the Modern: Writing Modernism in Semicolonial China, 1917–1937* (Berkeley: University of California Press, 2001), 217–18.

27. Ling Shuhua to Virginia Woolf, November 16, 1938, BERG.

28. Ling Shuhua to Virginia Woolf, December 12, 1938, BERG.

29. Ling Shuhua to Virginia Woolf, December 12, 1938, BERG.

30. Ling Shuhua to Virginia Woolf, December 31, 1938, BERG.

31. Vanessa Bell, *Selected Letters of Vanessa Bell*, ed. R. Marler (New York: Pantheon Books, 1993), 452.

32. Ling Shuhua to Virginia Woolf, January 11, 1939, BERG.

33. Ling Shuhua to Virginia Woolf, February 28, 1939, BERG.

34. Woolf, *Leave the Letters*, 328.

35. Bell, *Selected Letters*, 456.

36. Woolf, *Leave the Letters*, 347.

37. Vanessa Bell to Ling Shuhua, December 5, 1939, BERG.

38. Vanessa Bell to Ling Shuhua, February 4, 1940, BERG.

39. Vanessa Bell to Ling Shuhua, February 4, 1940, BERG.

40. Ling Shuhua to Hu Shi, February 1, 1940, in LSHWC, 920–22.

41. Chen Xiying to Hu Shi, August 14, 1940, in *Hu Shi laiwang shuxin xuan* [Selected letters of Hu Shi] (Hong Kong: Zhonghua shuju, 1983), 2:481–82.

42. Vanessa Bell to Ling Shuhua, May 27, 1941, BERG.

43. Chen Xueyong, *Cainü de shijie* [World of talented women] (Beijing: Kunlun chubanshe, 2001), 19–20.

44. Ling Shuhua, *Zhongguo ernü* [China's sons and daughters], in Chen Xueyong, *Cainü de shijie* [World of talented women] (Beijing: Kunlun chubanshe, 2001), 85.

45. Su Hua Ling Chen, "Happy Days," 1307.

46. Su Hua Ling Chen, "Rock Carvings 1,800 Years Old," *Country Life* 113, no. 2936 (April 23, 1953): 1236–38.

47. Chen Xiaoying, "Yi feng shisi sui nühai de xin" [The letter of a fourteen-year-old girl], *Zhonghua zhoubao* [China weekly] 31 (January 18, 1945): 6.

Chapter Twenty: An American Home

1. Ronald Takaki, *Strangers from a Different Shore: A History of Asian Americans* (New York: Penguin Books, 1989), 376–78.

Chapter Twenty-One: Wandering

1. Frances Spaulding, *Vanessa Bell* (New York: Ticknor & Fields, 1983), 339.

2. Spaulding, *Vanessa Bell*, 339.

3. Vanessa Bell, *Selected Letters of Vanessa Bell*, ed. R. Marler (New York: Pantheon Books, 1993), 512–13.

4. Vanessa Bell to Ling Shuhua, February 15, [n.y.], BERG.

5. Vanessa Bell to Ling Shuhua, December 13, 1949, BERG.

6. "Ling Su Hua, at the Adams Gallery," *New Statesman and Nation* 38, no. 982 (December 31, 1949): 780.

7. Ling Shuhua, undated manuscript of memoir of Virginia Woolf, BERG.

8. Vita Sackville-West, *In Your Garden* (London: Frances Lincoln, 2004), 30.

9. Su-Hua Ling Chen, "The Red Coat Man," *Spectator*, no. 6387 (November 24, 1950): 540; Su-Hua Ling Chen, "Childhood in China," *Spectator*, no. 6391 (December 22, 1950): 540.

10. AM, 8–9.

11. Vanessa Bell to Ling Shuhua, December 7, 1950, BERG.

12. Su Hua Ling Chen, "Our Old Gardener," *Country Life* 59, no. 2882 (February 16, 1951): 466–67; Su Hua Ling Chen, "Visit to a Royal Garderner," *Country Life* 59, no. 2884 (April 25, 1952): 1242–43.

13. Ling Shuhua to Leonard Woolf, May 29, 1952, LWP III, SUSSEX.

14. Ling Shuhua to Leonard Woolf, July 6, 1952, LWP III, SUSSEX.

15. Ling Shuhua to Leonard Woolf, August 20, 1952, LWP III, SUSSEX.

16. Chen Xiying, *Xiying xianhua* [The causeries of Xiying] (Beijing: Dongfang chubanshe, 1995), 140.

17. Arthur Waley, *Chinese Poems* (London: George Allen & Unwin, 1983), 116.

18. AM, 9.

19. Hugh Gordon Porteus, "Chinese Childhood," *Time and Tide* 35, no. 3 (January 16, 1954): 87.

20. "Other Recent Books," *Spectator*, no. 6556 (February 19, 1954): 218.

21. "Childhood in Peking," *Times Literary Supplement*, no. 2717 (January 22, 1954): 55.

22. Ling Shuhua, undated manuscript of memoir of Virginia Woolf, BERG.

23. Ling Shuhua to Leonard Woolf, June 3, 1953, LWP III, SUSSEX.

24. Ling Shuhua to Leonard Woolf, September 29, 1953, LWP III, SUSSEX.

25. Ling Shuhua to Leonard Woolf, November 24, 1953, LWP III, SUSSEX.

26. André Maurois, *10 Reproductions en Couleurs de Shu-Hua Ling Chen* (Paris: Editions Euros).

27. Ling Shuhua to Leonard Woolf, June 4, 1954, LWP III, SUSSEX.

28. Filomena Gould, "Artist Makes Visit Do Double Duty," *Indianapolis News*, 27 October 1954, 36.

29. "Mrs. Chen Fetes Sister," *Indianapolis Times*, 31 October 1954.

30. Ling Shuhua to Leonard Woolf, February 9, 1956, LWP III, SUSSEX.

31. Ling Shuhua to Leonard Woolf, [1956], LWP III, SUSSEX.

32. Ling Shuhua to Leonard Woolf, June 3, 1956, LWP III, SUSSEX.

33. Ling Shuhua to Leonard Woolf, November 28, 1954, LWP III, SUSSEX.

34. Ling Shuhua, "Xinjiapo ban *Ling Shuhua xuanji* houji" [Afterword to the Singapore edition of the selected writings of Ling Shuhua], in *Ling Shuhua xiaoshuo ji* [Collected stories of Ling Shuhua] (Taibei, Taiwan: Hongfan shudian, 1984), 470.

35. Ling Shuhua to Leonard Woolf, April 23, 1960, LWP III, SUSSEX.

36. Ling Shuhua to Leonard Woolf, October 23, 1961, LWP III, SUSSEX.

37. Ling Shuhua to Vanessa Bell, October 7, 1960, BERG.

Chapter Twenty-Two: The Chinese House

1. Elaine Kim, *Asian American Literature: An Introduction to the Writings and Their Social Context* (Philadelphia: Temple University Press, 1982), 24.

2. Thelma Machael, "Oriental Beauty Fills Chen Home," *Indianapolis News*, July 20, 1957, 3.

3. Eli Lilly, "Reminiscences," April 1, 1968, Lilly Archive, Indianapolis.

4. Unpublished history of Eli Lilly and Company, Lilly Archive, Indianapolis, 168.

5. Yutaka Mino and James Robinson, *Beauty and Tranquility: The Eli Lilly Collection of Chinese Art* (Indianapolis: Indianapolis Museum of Art, 1983), 9–12.

6. K. K. Chen to Eli Lilly, May 21, 1965, Lilly Archive, Indianapolis.

7. Howard L. Boorman, ed., *Biographical Dictionary of Republican China* (New York:

Columbia University Press, 1968), 3:335–36; Helen Foster Snow, *Women in Modern China* (Paris: Mouton, 1967), 85–87.

EPILOGUE: RETURN

1. AM, 247.
2. AM, 256.
3. Taken from official notice distributed at funeral.

Permissions

Index

Note: Page reference in *italics* indicate a figure or photograph.

355

About the Author

Sasha Su-Ling Welland grew up in St. Louis, Missouri. She received a PhD in anthropology from the University of California, Santa Cruz, for her research on contemporary art worlds in Beijing. She is currently assistant professor of anthropology and women studies at the University of Washington, Seattle. The Artist Trust, Blue Mountain Center, Bread Loaf Writers' Conference, Hedgebrook Retreat for Women Writers, and Millay Colony for the Arts have supported her writing. This is her first book.